Beginning PL/SQL

From Novice to Professional

Donald J. Bales

Apress®

Beginning PL/SQL: From Novice to Professional

Copyright © 2007 by Donald J. Bales

ISBN-13 (pbk): 978-1-59059-882-5

ISBN-10 (pbk): 1-59059-882-2

Printed and bound in the United States of America 9 8 7 6 5 4 3 2 1

Lead Editor: Jonathan Gennick
Technical Reviewer: Connor McDonald
Editorial Board: Steve Anglin, Ewan Buckingham, Gary Cornell, Jonathan Gennick, Jason Gilmore, Jonathan Hassell, Chris Mills, Matthew Moodie, Jeffrey Pepper, Ben Renow-Clarke, Dominic Shakeshaft, Matt Wade, Tom Welsh
Project Manager: Denise Santoro Lincoln
Copy Edit Manager: Nicole Flores
Copy Editor: Marilyn Smith
Assistant Production Director: Kari Brooks-Copony
Senior Production Editor: Laura Cheu
Compositor: Susan Glinert Stevens
Proofreader: Lori Bring
Indexer: Toma Mulligan
Artist: April Milne
Cover Designer: Kurt Krames
Manufacturing Director: Tom Debolski

Distributed to the book trade worldwide by Springer-Verlag New York, Inc., 233 Spring Street, 6th Floor, New York, NY 10013. Phone 1-800-SPRINGER, fax 201-348-4505, e-mail orders-ny@springer-sbm.com, or visit http://www.springeronline.com.

For information on translations, please contact Apress directly at 2855 Telegraph Avenue, Suite 600, Berkeley, CA 94705. Phone 510-549-5930, fax 510-549-5939, e-mail info@apress.com, or visit http://www.apress.com.

The source code for this book is available to readers at http://www.apress.com in the Source Code/Download section.

To my wife Diane,
With you all things are possible.

To my daughter Kristyn,
Even astronauts should know how to program.

To Donald E. Lancaster,
"The best technical writer ever!"
I try hard to live up to your standard of writing.

Contents

Foreword

What good is a foreword? I think it's good if it answers the question, "If I use this book, what will be the outcome for me?" I think the answer should be from someone who is already at the outcome end, and who didn't write the book.

If you're a programmer who hasn't yet worked in Oracle's realization of the relational database implementation, and wants to (or must) take full advantage of Oracle's procedural programming language, PL/SQL, this is probably the best book to use. If you are inclined (or compelled) to write substantial and rock-solid applications, this is probably the *only* book to use. A bold statement like that could use a dash of elucidation and a little amplification. So here goes.

First, a little about me. I've been developing computer applications for more than 40 years. I graduated from college as a mechanical engineer with as much computer education as I could get. I started out in the aircraft business, then moved to the missile business, then into computer analysis and testing, and then into flight simulation with actual pieces of the missile in the simulation. After 20 years, I jumped off the aerospace bus and climbed onto the business application bus. I started working with relational databases, the past 12 years exclusively with Oracle. What I do most and probably do best is applications with complex mathematical or technical requirements. I've had fun.

When Don Bales asked me to write the foreword for this book, he took a chance. Don and I have never coded a line of PL/SQL or SQL together. Furthermore, my background in coding is procedural, while Don's background is object-oriented. I got to know him over five years ago when I had some questions about his first book, *Java Programming with Oracle JDBC*. Imagine my surprise when I read this book and found that I agree with Don in every major way. Like Don, I've learned these things through a lot of trial and error.

In *Beginning PL/SQL: From Novice to Professional*, Don starts out laying the groundwork by concisely covering PL/SQL code writing, a review of SQL, and also "fingers-on," do-it-yourself exercises. Don combines all these elements to instill a way of thinking about Oracle application development. Then he moves into a larger scope by addressing how an application should be built relating to the real world. Now starts the juicy part: how to construct an application that can be easily debugged and sensibly tested. Then even more juice: letting other people (and perhaps yourself, later on) in on what's happening. Finally, he wraps up his introduction to PL/SQL in application development with some advice about design and where to go next. It's that juicy part that I spoke of that leads to substantial, rock-solid applications.

Don's background has helped him approach things with a strong bent toward the practical. For example, Don talks about database query performance and introduces "physics"—contrasting the difference between logical and physical attributes—showing how the more abstract logical attributes can lead to unintended consequences. I can identify with Don's practical approach to software development. In the aerospace business, a test pilot's only interest is answering the question, "Does it work?" If something in a test aircraft doesn't work, you can have all the elegant theories in the world about the plane's design, and no pilot will care. Likewise, in Don's and my line of work, getting things done is what counts.

But don't think for a moment that Don ignores theory when it matters. Object-oriented design principles, for example, are very important in software development today. Yet other books on PL/SQL largely ignore object-oriented techniques. I am no Java expert, as Don is, but I find that understanding object-oriented design principles has definitely improved my work. Don approaches PL/SQL very well when it comes to practical application of object-oriented design principles. If you've been thinking of PL/SQL as just a "procedural" language, Don will definitely open your eyes to another, and more productive, point of view.

Don's book doesn't cover everything you *might* need to know about developing applications using Oracle, but I say it covers everything you *should* know. And that's a good beginning.

Larry Johnson
Principal Consultant
KeepItSimpleEngineering, Inc.

About the Author

 DONALD J. BALES is a business analyst and computer applications consultant specializing in the analysis, design, and programming of client-server and web-based distributed applications, internationalization of existing applications, systems integration, and data warehousing. Don has more than 20 years of experience with Oracle, as both a developer and a database administrator, and over ten years of experience with Java. He is currently working on the infrastructure of a spatial database for a major geographic information system (GIS) vendor. When he is not developing applications, Don can often be found working with horses, playing the piano, or playing the bagpipes. Don has had several careers, at various times serving as a mechanic, a general contractor, Mr. Mom, a developer, a chief technical officer, and currently, a consultant. He has a Bachelor of Science degree in Business from Elmhurst College in Elmhurst, Illinois. Don currently resides in Downers Grove, Illinois, with his wife Diane and his daughter Kristyn. He can be contacted by email at don@donaldbales.com.

Acknowledgments

Everything in the universe is constantly trying to change the behavior of everything else in the universe, all the time. Some behavioral modifications promote order; others promote chaos.

So nothing we do—any of us—is actually a totally independent action. Whether we realize it or not, others as well as ourselves are taking part in both our successes and failures.

With that in mind, you should be able to understand why I say this book is the result of collaboration. Every person I've known, along with every situation I've experienced, has helped shape the text of this tutorial.

Since I have a seeming limited amount of memory, let me at least thank those who are directly responsible for bringing it to you. To that end, thank you:

Yelena Bumar, Nick Granata, Natalyia Lopatina, Mariana Takacs, and Svetlana Vladimirova, peers, for being my PL/SQL tutorial guinea pigs

Jonathan Gennick, Lead Editor, for enduring my strange sense of humor

Connor McDonald, Technical Reviewer, for being open-minded despite a 180-degree point of view

Denise Santoro Lincoln, Project Manager, for keeping things on track

Marilyn Smith, Copy Editor, for making me look like a good writer

Laura Cheu, Production Editor, for making the book look good

Susan Glinert Stevens, for putting all the pieces together

Lori Bring, for proving that someone can read it

Toma Mulligan, for making it easy to dip into the book

April Milne, for making my artwork look good

Kurt Krames, Cover Designer, you know all about first impressions

Tom Debolski, Manufacturing Director, for taking the last step in this book's production

Introduction (The Big Picture)

This is a book about writing stored procedures for an Oracle database. A *stored procedure* in this context is a generic term for a program written in the Procedure Language extension for SQL (PL/SQL) that is stored inside the database when it is compiled. This means that you can then execute the program from inside the database. Why would you want to do that? Because your program will run faster inside the database.

Let's slow down for a minute, so I can explain what a stored procedure is and why you would want to use one.

What's a Stored Procedure?

In order for me to answer the question, "What's a stored procedure?" I need to cover a little material on databases and networks first. By now, you've probably already seen three of the four diagrams I'm about to show you a few hundred times, but bear with me if you will, so I can make sure everyone is on the same page as we start out.

I'm going to assume, since you're ready to start writing programs against an Oracle database, that you already know what a relational database management system (RDBMS) is. For our purposes, an RDBMS, or database as I'll refer to it from here forward, is a hardware/software machine (server) that allows us to store, retrieve, and manipulate data in a predictable and organized manner using Structured Query Language (SQL).

SQL acts as the interface to the database. A client program, whether it exists on the same computer or on another, makes a connection to the database, sends a request in the form of SQL to the server, and in return gets back structured data, as in Figure 1.

Figure 1. *Client-server architecture on the same host*

A client program that utilizes Oracle on the same host computer, as in Figure 1, is a client-server program, because it accesses a server program to perform some of the client program's work. The communication between the two processes, client and server, takes place through an interprocess communication (IPC) system provided by the host operating system. This is typically done through memory. Suffice it to say that some communication overhead takes place when communicating between the client and the server in this fashion. This overhead takes time and operating system resources. Regardless, it's pretty fast.

But not everyone can run the program on the same computer, so some applications resort to the use of client-server architecture over a network. This is what is referred to when most people use the term *client-server*. Figure 2 is a diagram that shows the communication between the client and server in a networked client-server architecture, specifically, a client-server diagram with one network connection in between the client (program) and server (database).

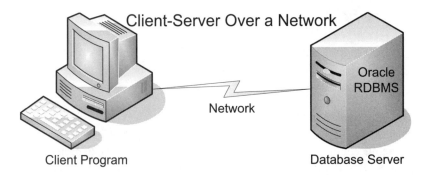

Figure 2. *Client-server architecture over a network*

The communication between the two processes, client and server, in Figure 2, is much slower than the architecture shown in Figure 1, where IPC is used. Even with the best network hardware available, this connection is usually 20 times slower than IPC, or worse. Plus, a second software protocol stack, to allow the network communication, must be added to the use of resources. What's the net result? The connection between the two processes becomes the slowest, most time-consuming part of any application.

Nowadays, not every application can be run on a computer attached to a high-speed network. Nor can any one machine handle all the end-user requests, so architecture has effectively stretched the bus of the good old mainframe on to the network, and created what is commonly called *n-tier architecture*. In n-tier architecture, client programs communicate with an application server, which in turn communicates with one or more servers. You might call this *Client-Server Gone Wild*, but don't hold your breath waiting for the video. Figure 3 is a diagram that shows an example of n-tier architecture where a notebook computer, a personal information manager (PIM), and a cell phone communicate with an application server in order to use the same application through different devices.

Now there are three different kinds of clients, with three different kinds of networks, using networked client-server architecture to communicate with an application server, which in turn uses networked client-server architecture to communicate with a database. Is this complex? Yes, but it's still just networked client-server architecture. Of course, this means that all the various networks involved conspire to slow down the response time of the application!

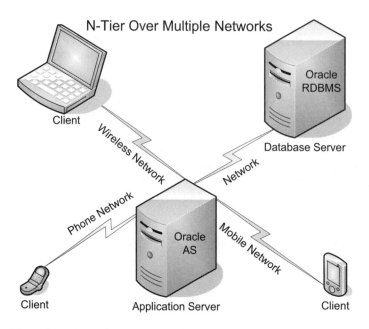

Figure 3. *N-tier architecture over a network*

With the network being a bottleneck for any networked application, if we can perform some of our application's computer processing without using the network at all, that portion will simply run faster. With that in mind, examine Figure 4. It's a diagram that shows how a stored procedure exists inside the database. Therefore, any computer processing that take place will occur inside the database before data is even sent to a client program, regardless of what type of client-server communication is used. In turn, that portion of the application will simply be more efficient and run faster.

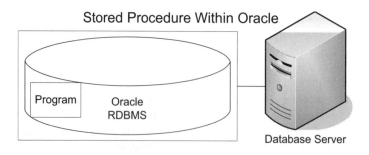

Figure 4. *A stored procedure resides inside an Oracle database.*

So what's a stored procedure? In Figure 4, it's the box labeled "Program" that exists inside the database. So a stored procedure is a program that resides inside an Oracle database that manipulates data in the database before the data is used outside the database.

Why Use Stored Procedures?

Why use stored procedures? Well, I've already touched on that, haven't I? Here's my favorite list of reasons to use stored procedures:

- They eliminate the network.

- They allow you to more accurately model the real world in your database.

- They provide you with access to functionality that is not available through the standard database interface: SQL.

First, as I already stated in the previous section, using stored procedures allows you to eliminate the network from your data processing work. I can't emphasize this fact enough. If you write a Java Database Connectivity (JDBC) program that retrieves one million rows from the database, then queries the database for three related pieces of information, and then conditionally updates the retrieved rows, it can take days in Java; it will take only minutes inside Oracle using PL/SQL. That's a huge difference in performance. I often like to say, "The difference between any fast and slow application is that the fast application uses stored procedures."

Second, we basically use computers to automate what we do in the real world. Most people use databases to store only the characteristics of the real world, completely ignoring the behavior. Instead, behavior is temporarily kept in the code base for an application. If a change in the code is required, past behavior is lost forever. Yet no one would think of throwing away the data! What's going on here? Is the history of behavior unimportant or are we ignorant of the problem? I argue it's the latter. If you want to save both real-world characteristics and behavior, stored procedures allow you to do just that in either a pseudo-object-oriented or a truly object-oriented manner.

Finally, the standard database interface, SQL, is great, but its use is limited to four operations: insert, update, delete, and select. With stored procedures, you have unlimited possibilities. You are free to create as many new operations as needed to satisfy requirements. The important point here is to perform work where it is done most efficiently. Presentation code should reside in the presentation layer, application code should reside in the application layer (the application server), and persistence code, like entity behavior, should reside in the persistence layer (the database).

Using PL/SQL, you can write stored procedures for the following:

- Data processing

- Data migration

- Data warehousing

- Entity behavior, including so-called business rules

- Interfaces

- Reports

- Service-oriented-architecture routines

Now that you know the what and the why of stored procedures, are you still interested in learning PL/SQL? If so, then please read the next section, where I will tell you what the book is about, how I'm going to teach you PL/SQL, and why.

What's This Book About?

This book is not a reference. It's an immersion-based tutorial that teaches you how to program in PL/SQL by making you mimic successful PL/SQL programming.

Do you know that you have free access to outstanding reference materials directly from Oracle? If you download and install the database on your computer, these reference manuals will be accessible from the installation. Or you can download just the manuals to your computer. Oracle has always had superior technical documentation. I believe that has played a huge part in Oracle's success as a company and a product. Free access to Oracle's documentation and software for trial purposes has removed any barriers from anyone learning how to use Oracle.

How I'm Going to Teach You and Why

What do I mean by "an immersion-based tutorial?" I'm going to require you to read each and every program listing as part of the learning process. I'm going to start showing you program listings right away. Most listings will be complete contexts. By that, I mean there will be a lot of code in them that I have not yet discussed. I do this because I want you to get used to looking at the code and where things belong in the code from the get-go. Concentrate on the subject of the section and ignore the rest.

Whenever possible, I'm going to ask you to do an exercise that will make you think about and apply what I've just covered in the section. You should almost always be able to mimic (or copy and change) code that I've shown you before the exercise. I'm going to ask you to program all along. And the next section will often be dependent on completing a prior exercise, so there's no skipping an exercise.

Why am I making you look at code, then read code, then try to understand my code, and then prove you understand my code by having you write code? For several reasons:

- You didn't learn how to speak by having those around you discuss the merits and drawbacks of various languages you might want to speak. You learned by mimicking those who spoke.

- You didn't learn how to read by talking about reading. You learned by reading.

- You don't learn a new language by reading about it. You need to speak it and then write it.

- You don't learn a new concept by reading about it. You must do your homework, where you actually use it.

So, how can you read a reference and be ready to solve business problems using a programming language? You can't. In the beginning, you must learn by mimicking someone else's work (hopefully, good examples)—something that someone has done before you. Then later, using your own creativity, you expand upon your basic knowledge with a reference.

But there's more to learning PL/SQL than just coding. I'm going to teach you good programming habits, such as these:

- Document as you go.

- Leave bread crumbs.

- Keep it simple for the next person's sake.

- Make it obvious by using prefixes or suffixes when it helps.

- Make it obvious by using a coding style and sticking to it; consistency is important.

- Make it obvious by adding comments to your code when it's not obvious.

- Prepare for disaster ahead of time.

- Prepare for testing ahead of time.

And finally, here are my assumptions:

- You've programmed in another programming language, so you already know the difference between a function and a procedure.

- You already know SQL.

I'm going to get you started down the right path, not tell you everything about PL/SQL. Your time is precious, so I'm not going to tell you anything that you don't need to know to get started (except for an occasional joke, or perhaps, my poor attempt at one). You may find my style terse. To me, that's a compliment.

This is not *Oracle PL/SQL for Dummies*. Remember that the examples are shown in a full-blown context. Pay attention to the subject; ignore the rest. You can do it!

What PL/SQL Am I Going to Teach You?

What am I going to teach you? Succinctly, how to get you, a programmer, from a novice to professional PL/SQL programmer in ten chapters. I've spent 20 years hiring programmers and then teaching them how to code properly, the past 10 years focusing on how to code in PL/SQL. In this book, I will apply the 80/20 rule in order to teach you the fundamentals of PL/SQL programming without bogging you down in the ever-so-increasing details.

As a scientist, I gather data about what I do all the time, so I have statistics about all the stored procedures that I and others have written since Oracle 7 became a production product. From these statistics, I've learned what's used often and not at all. In this book, I intend to touch on anything that is used 25% or more of the time when writing stored procedures.

Here, I'd like to share some interesting fun facts derived from more than 30,000 stored procedures.

PL/SQL Pie, Anyone?

Figure 5 shows that on average, only 31% of a stored procedure is actually logic. The rest is declaration, built-ins, and SQL. SQL makes up a whopping 26%. So if you don't know SQL, you're already behind the eight ball when you start to learn how to write stored procedures using PL/SQL.

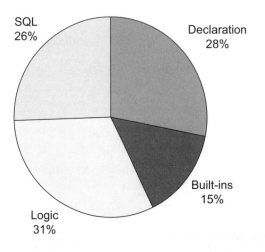

Figure 5. *What is a PL/SQL stored procedure composed of?*

SQL, SQL, SQL!

The pretty little histogram in Figure 6 shows the SQL keywords that are used in 25% or more of all stored procedures. So I need to start out with a SQL refresher for those of you who say you know SQL, but don't actually have much SQL experience. After all, I want you to buy this book and then go back and buy the Apress book on SQL, right?

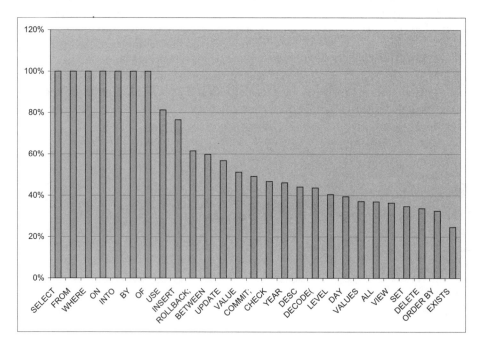

Figure 6. *SQL keywords used in 25% or more of all stored procedures*

What About Those Declarations?

Figure 7 shows the PL/SQL declaration keywords that are used in 25% or more of all stored procedures. Why teach any more than these to a beginner?

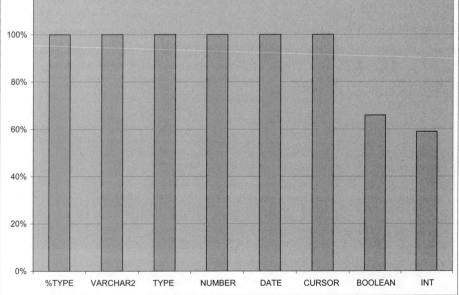

Figure 7. *PL/SQL declaration keywords that are used in 25% or more of all stored procedures*

And How About Those Built-Ins?

Figure 8 shows the PL/SQL built-ins (functions and procedures that are part of the language) that are used in 25% or more of all stored procedures. Why teach any more than these to a beginner?

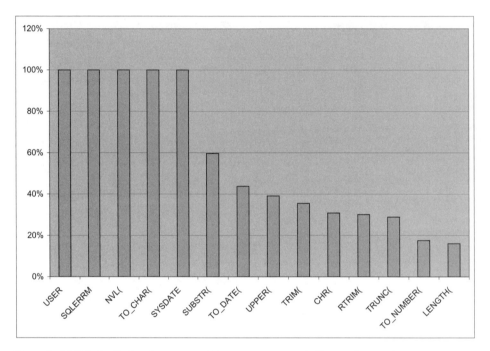

Figure 8. *PL/SQL built-ins that are used in 25% or more of all stored procedures*

What Exactly Am I Supposed to Be Doing?

And last, but certainly not least, the histogram in Figure 9 shows the PL/SQL keywords that are used in 25% or more of all stored procedures. The list isn't that large, so introducing these as we go will ease you right into coding logic.

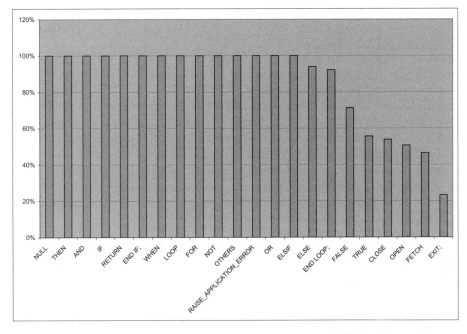

Figure 9. *PL/SQL logic keywords that are used in 25% or more of all stored procedures*

In What Order Am I Going to Teach You PL/SQL?

First, I'm going to help you review your knowledge of SQL. If you don't understand something in Chapter 1, go buy the Apress book on SQL (*Mastering Oracle SQL and SQL*Plus* by Lex de Haan), as I mentioned earlier, then continue.

Next, I'm going to teach you the basic structure of every PL/SQL program unit type. I'll show you each program unit type. Concentrate on understanding PL/SQL block structure, and you'll be OK. Try to understand all the stuff I show you and don't discuss, and you'll be totally lost. Remember to focus on the subject being discussed. If you were mining for gold, you wouldn't stop and examine every grain of dirt, rock, and sand you encountered along the way; you would concentrate on the gold. So concentrate on the gold!

Assuming you understand block structure, the next chapter discusses the use of memory. Basically, it covers data types and variable declarations. You're a programmer, so there should be nothing really mind-boggling and new for you in this chapter, except maybe NULL.

The next topic is the singleton SQL statement. Whether it's a select, an insert, an update, or a delete, a singleton should always return one result. So what happens when it doesn't? Read Chapter 4 to find out!

From singleton's to multitons? Something isn't right here. Anyway, Chapter 5 will cover the use of cursors. Cursors allow you to retrieve multiple rows from a database, one row at a time. At this point, you'll have coded a couple stored procedures. Wow. Then I want to rock your world.

In Chapter 6, you're going to learn to model an entity just as it exists in the real world. You'll be introduced to object-relational technology. And then you can decide which way to go: relational or object-relational. Or maybe you'll swing both ways?

Chapter 7 is about troubleshooting. It's always nice to know how to find an insect in your program. I'll also show you how to prevent insects in the first place. Oh yeah, did I tell you that I like to call defects *defects*, not *bugs*?

Professional programmers create programs with few defects. How do they do that? By testing. Chapter 8 is about automating the testing of your PL/SQL program units. Low error rates mean higher paychecks, too. So don't skip Chapter 8.

Concerning object-oriented development, it allows you to build reusable components, but reusable components are valuable only if you provide others with documentation, the subject of Chapter 9, so they know the components exist and how they can use them. Professional programmers document as they go!

And finally, in Chapter 10, I'll tell you some fairy tales. Sit back, relax, and enjoy these captivating bedtime stories about the heroic journeys that PL/SQL programmers have taken in the past. These are fairy tales, not war stories (my editor wanted to use that term instead). No one ever wins at war, but fairy tales always have a lesson and sometimes a happy ending. I'll show you examples of what works.

OK, I was lying about that "finally." The book's appendix explains how to acquire and install Oracle RDBMS, and how to use SQL*Plus for PL/SQL programming, in case you really don't have any experience with SQL before you start with PL/SQL (I knew it).

If you have access to an Oracle database where you can create objects like tables, indexes, types, and stored procedures, then you're ready to dive right in to Chapter 1. Otherwise, you may want to flip to the appendix, which tells you how to download and install a trial version of Oracle.

Good skill! Luck is for losers!

CHAPTER 1

■ ■ ■

Genesis

The question is, "Where do I start?" In the beginning, Codd created the paper "A Relational Model of Data for Large Shared Data Banks." Now the relational database was formless and empty, darkness was over the surface of the media, and the spirit of Codd was hovering over the requirements. Codd said, "Let there be Alpha," but as usual, the development team said, "Let there be something else," so SEQUEL (SQL) was created. Codd saw that SQL wasn't what he had in mind, but it was too late, for the Ellison separated the darkness from the SQL and called it Oracle. OK, that's enough of that silliness. But that's the short of it.

Did you know that about 25% of the average stored procedures written in the Procedural Language for SQL (PL/SQL) is, in fact, just SQL? Well, I'm a metrics junkie. I've kept statistics on every program I've ever written, and that's the statistic. After writing more than 30,000 stored procedures, 26% of my PL/SQL is nothing but SQL. So it's really important for you to know SQL!

OK, maybe you don't know SQL that well after all. If not, just continue reading this light-speed refresher on relational SQL. If you're a genius, just move on to the exercises in the last section of the chapter ("Our Working Example").

This chapter covers Data Definition Language (DDL) and Data Manipulation Language (DML), from table creation to queries. Please keep in mind that this chapter is not a tutorial on SQL. It's simply a review. SQL is a large topic that can be covered fully only with several books. What I'm trying to accomplish here is to help you determine how familiar you are with SQL, so you'll be able to decide whether you need to spend some additional time learning SQL after or while you learn PL/SQL.

Tables

The core idea behind a relational database and SQL is so simple it's elusive. Take a look at Table 1-1 and Table 1-2.

Table 1-1. *Relational Database Geniuses*

ID	Name	Born	Gender
100	Edgar F Codd	1923	Male
200	Chris J Date	Unknown	Male
300	Hugh Darwen	Unknown	Male

Table 1-2. *Relational Genius's Publications*

ID	Title	Written
100	A Relational Model of Data for Large Shared Data Banks	1970
100	The Relational Model for Database Management	1990
200	An Introduction to Database Systems	2003
200	The Third Manifesto	2000
200	Temporal Data and the Relational Model	2002
200	Database in Depth: Relational Theory for Practitioners	2005
300	The Third Manifesto	2000
300	Temporal Data and the Relational Model	2002

We can find which publications were written by each genius simply by using the common datum in both of these tables: the ID. If we look at Codd's data in Table 1-1, we see he has ID 100. Next, if we look at ID 100's (Codd's) data in Table 1-2, we see he has written two titles:

- A Relational Model of Data for Large Shared Data Banks (1970)

- The Relational Model for Database Management (1990)

These two tables have a relationship, because they share an ID column with the same values. They don't have many entries, so figuring out what was written by each author is pretty easy. But what would you do if there were, say, one million authors with about three publications each? Oh yeah, baby, it's time for a computer and a database—*a relational database.*

A relational database allows you to store multiple tables, like Tables 1-1 and 1-2, in a database management system (DBMS). By doing so, you can manipulate the data in the tables using a query language on a computer, instead of a pencil on a sheet of paper. The current query language of choice is Structured Query Language (SQL). SQL is a set of nonprocedural commands, or language if you will, which you can use to manipulate the data in tables in a relational database management system (RDBMS).

A table in a relational database is a logical definition for how data is to be organized when it is stored. For example, in Table 1-3, I decided to order the columns of the database genius data just as it appeared horizontally in Table 1-1.

Table 1-3. *A Table Definition for Table 1-1*

Column Number	Column Name	Data Type
1	ID	Number
2	Name	Character
3	Birth Date	Date
4	Gender	Character

Perhaps I could give the relational table defined in Table 1-3 the name genius? In practice, a name like that tends to be too specific. It's better to find a more general name, like author or person. So how do we document our database design decisions?

An Entity Relationship Diagram

Just as home builders have an architectural diagram or blueprint, which enables them to communicate clearly and objectively about what they are going to build, so do relational database builders. In our case, the architectural diagram is called an entity-relationship diagram (ERD).

Figure 1-1 is an ERD for the tables shown in Tables 1-1 and 1-2, now named author and publication. It shows that one author may have zero or more publications. Additionally, it shows that an author's ID is his primary key (PK), or unique way to identify him, and an author's primary key is also used to identify his publications.

Figure 1-1. *An entity-relationship diagram for the author and publication tables*

ERDs, like blueprints, may have varying levels of detail, depending on your audience. For example, to simplify the ERD in Figure 1-1, I've left out the data types.

In an ERD, the tables are called *entities*. The lines that connect the tables—I mean entities—are called *relations*. So given an ERD, or even a narrative documentation as in Table 1-3, you can write a script to create a table.

Data Definition Language (DDL)

To create the author table, as defined in Table 1-3, in Oracle, you'll need to create a SQL script (for SQL*Plus) that in SQL jargon is called Data Definition Language (DDL). That is, it's SQL for defining the relational database. Listing 1-1 shows our author table's DDL.

Listing 1-1. *DDL for Creating the Author Table, author.tab*

```
1  CREATE TABLE author (
2  id                          number,
3  name                        varchar2(100),
4  birth_date                  date,
5  gender                      varchar2(30) );
```

The syntax for the CREATE TABLE statement used in Listing 1-1 is as follows:

```
CREATE TABLE <table_name> (
<column_name_1>    <data_type_1>,
<column_name_2>    <data_type_2>,
<column_name_N>    <data_type_N> );
```

where `<table_name>` is the name of the table, `<column_name>` is the name of a column, and `<data_type>` is one of the Oracle data types.

The following are the Oracle data types you'll use most often:

VARCHAR2: Allows you to store up to 4000 characters (data like *ABCD*) in a column. You must define the maximum number of characters (or constrain the number of characters) by specifying the desired number in parentheses after the keyword VARCHAR2. For example, in Listing 1-1, line 3, specifies varchar2(100), which means a name can be up to 100 characters in length.

NUMBER: Allows you to store a decimal number with 38 digits of precision. You do not need to constrain the size of a number, but you can. You can specify the maximum number of digits (1, 2, 3, 4 . . .) to the left of a decimal point, followed by a comma (,), and optionally the maximum number of decimal digits to the right of the decimal point, by specifying the desired constraint in parentheses after the keyword NUMBER. For example, if you want to . . . oh, I can never find a good reason to constrain a number—every time I do, there's a better reason not to constrain it. How about this: you want to make sure that the id column in Listing 1-1, line 2, is an integer. You could specify number(38). (Again, personally, I would never constrain a number.)

DATE: Allows you to store a date and time value. The great thing about Oracle DATE types is that they allow you to easily perform time calculations between dates. For example, if you want to store the date and time of birth for someone born on January 1, 1980, at 8 a.m., you could use the Oracle to_date() function to convert a VARCHAR2 value in a proper format into a DATE data type as follows: to_date('19800101080000', 'YYYYMMDDHH24MISS').

Of course, there are other Oracle data types, but you'll end up using VARCHAR2, NUMBER, and DATE most of the time. The rest are specialized versions of these three, or they are designed for specialized uses.

It's Your Turn to Create a Table

OK, it's time to stop reading and start doing. This section gives you chance to put into practice some of what you've learned so far. I'll be asking you to perform exercises like this as we go along in order for you to verify that you understood what you just read well enough to put it into practice.

■**Tip** First, if you don't have access to Oracle, see this book's appendix. Second, create a directory for the book's source code listings. Next, download the source code listings from the Source Code/Download section of the Apress web site (www.apress.com), and work within the book's source code listing directory structure for each chapter. Add your source code listings to the book's directory structure as you work. Last, create a shortcut, an icon, or whatever you want to call it, to start SQL*Plus from your working source code listing directory. Then you won't need to specify the entire path when trying to execute your scripts in SQL*Plus.

To create the `publication` table, follow these steps:

1. Start your Oracle database if it's not already running.

2. Start SQL*Plus.

3. Open your favorite text editor.

4. Write a DDL script to create a table for publications, as in Table 1-2.

5. Save the DDL script with the same filename as your table name, but with a .tab extension.

6. Execute your script in SQL*Plus by typing an at sign (@) followed by the filename at the SQL> prompt.

If you didn't have any errors in your script, the table will now exist in the database, just waiting for you to populate it with data. If it didn't work, try to make some sense out of the error message(s) you got, correct your script, and then try again.

Listing 1-2 is my try.

Listing 1-2. *DDL for Creating the Publication Table, publication.tab*

```
1  CREATE TABLE publication (
2  id                      number,
3  title                   varchar2(100),
4  written_date            date );
```

Now you know how to create a table, but what if you put a lot of data in those two tables? Then accessing them will be very slow, because none of the columns in the tables are indexed.

Indexes

Imagine, if you will, that a new phone book shows up on your doorstep. You put it in the drawer and throw out the old one. (OK, I know, most of us would keep both, or maybe all of them—all the way back to when we first moved in.) You pull the phone book out on Saturday evening so you can order some pizza, but when you open it, you get confused. Why? Well, when they printed the last set of phone books, including yours, they forgot to sort it by last name, first name, and street address. Instead, it's not sorted at all! The numbers show up the way they were put into the directory over the years—a complete mess.

You want that pizza! So you start at the beginning of the phone book, reading every last name, first name, and address until you finally find your local pizza place. Too bad it was closed by the time you found the phone number! If only that phone book had been sorted, or properly indexed.

Without an index to search on, you had to read through the entire phone book to make sure you got the right pizza place phone number. Aaahhh! Well, the same holds true for the tables you create in a relational database.

You need to carefully analyze how data will be queried from each table, and then create an appropriate set of indexes. You don't want to index everything, because that would unnecessarily slow down the process of inserting, updating, and deleting data. That's why I said "carefully."

DDL Again

You should (*must*, in my opinion) create a unique index on each table's primary key column(s)—you know, the one that uniquely identifies entries in the table. In our author table, that column is id. However, we will create a unique index on the id column when we talk about constraints in the next section. (It's a kind of the chicken vs. the egg story here—which comes first?) Instead, let's create a unique index on the name, birth_date, and gender columns of the author table. Listing 1-3 shows our example.

Listing 1-3. *DDL for Creating an Index on the Author Table, author_uk1.ndx.*

```
1  CREATE UNIQUE INDEX author_uk1
2  on                  author (
3  name,
4  birth_date,
5  gender );
```

The syntax for the CREATE INDEX statement is as follows:

```
CREATE [UNIQUE] INDEX <index_name>
on                  <table_name> (
<column_name_1>,
<column_name_2>,
<column_name_N> );
```

where <index_name> is the name of the index, <table_name> is the name of the table, and <column_name> is the name of a column. The keyword UNIQUE is optional, as denoted by the brackets ([ ]) around it. It just means that the database must check to make sure that the column's combination of the values is unique within the table. Unique indexes are old-fashioned; now it's more common to see a unique constraint, which I'll discuss shortly. But unique indexes are still useful.

It's Your Turn to Create an Index

OK, it's time to stop listening to me blab on about indexes, and time for you to start creating one. Here's the drill:

1. Write a DDL script to create a non-unique index on the publication table.

2. Save the DDL script with the same filename as your index name, but with an .ndx extension.

3. Execute your script in SQL*Plus by typing an at sign (@) followed by the filename at the SQL> prompt.

You should now have a non-unique index in the database, just waiting for you to query against it. If not, try to make some sense out of the error message(s) you got, correct your script, and then try again.

My shot at this is shown in Listing 1-4.

Listing 1-4. *DDL for Creating an Index on the Title Column in the Publication Table, publication_k1.ndx*

```
1  CREATE INDEX publication_k1
2  on          publication (
3  title );
```

Now you know how to create a table and an index or two to make accessing it efficient, but what prevents someone from entering bad data Well, that's what constrains are for.

Constraints

Constraints are rules for a table and its columns that constrain how and what data can be inserted, updated, or deleted. Constraints are available for both columns and tables.

Column Constraints

Columns may have rules that define what list of values or what kind of values may be entered into them. Although there are several types of column constraints, the one you will undoubtedly use most often is NOT NULL. The NOT NULL constraint simply means that a column must have a value. It can't be unknown, or blank, or in SQL jargon, NULL. Listing 1-5 shows the author table script updated with NOT NULL constraints on the id and name columns.

Listing 1-5. *DDL for Creating the Author Table with NOT NULL Column Constraints, author.tab*

```
1  CREATE TABLE author (
2  id                      number                    not null,
3  name                    varchar2(100)             not null,
4  birth_date              date,
5  gender                  varchar2(30) );
```

Now if you try to insert data into the author table, but don't supply values for the id or name column, the database will yell at you. (OK, really it will just respond with an error message, but it would be a lot more fun if it yelled.)

Table Constraints

Tables may have rules that enforce uniqueness of column values and the validity of relationships to other rows in other tables. Once again, although there are many forms of table constraints, I'll discuss only three here: unique key, primary key, and foreign key.

Unique Key Constraint

A unique key constraint (UKC) is a rule against one or more columns of a table that requires their combination of values to be unique for a row within the table. Columns in a unique index may be NULL.

Just as an example, if I were going to create a unique key constraint against the author table columns name, birth_date, and gender, the DDL to do that would look something like Listing 1-6.

Listing 1-6. *DDL for Creating a Unique Constraint Against the Author Table, author_uk1.ukc*

```
1  ALTER TABLE author ADD
2  CONSTRAINT  author_uk1
3  UNIQUE (
4  name,
5  birth_date,
6  gender );
```

Primary Key Constraint

A primary key constraint (PKC) is a rule against one or more columns of a table that requires their combination of values to be unique for a row within the table. Hey, that's just like a unique key! One big difference is that the unique key called the primary key is acknowledged to be the primary key, or primary index, of the table. Semantics, right? No, not really, as you'll see when I talk about foreign keys in the next section.

You should have a primary key constraint defined for every table in your database. I say "should," because it isn't mandatory, but it's a really good idea. Listing 1-7 shows the DDL to create a primary key constraint against the author table.

Listing 1-7. *DDL to Create a Primary Key Constraint Against the Author Table, author_pk.pkc*

```
1  ALTER TABLE author ADD
2  CONSTRAINT  author_pk
3  primary key (
4  id );
```

The syntax used in Listing 1-7 for creating a primary key constraint is as follows:

```
ALTER TABLE <table_name> ADD
CONSTRAINT  <constraint_name>
PRIMARY KEY (
<column_name_1>,
<column_name_2>,...
<column_name_N> );
```

where <table_name> is the name of the table, <constraint_name> is the name of the primary key constraint, and <column_name> is a column to use in the constraint.

Now that you have a primary key defined on the author table, you can point to it from the publication table.

Foreign Key Constraint

A foreign key is one or more columns from another table that point to, or are connected to, the primary key of the first table. Since primary keys are defined using primary key constraints, it follows that foreign keys are defined with foreign key constraints (FKC). However, a foreign key constraint is defined against a dependent, or child, table.

So what's a dependent or child table? Well, in our example, we know that the publication table is dependent on, or points to, the author table. So we'll need to define a foreign key constraint against the publication table, not the author table. The foreign key constraint is represented by the relation (line with crow's feet) in the ERD in Figure 1-1.

Listing 1-8 shows the DDL to create a foreign key constraint against the `publication` table that defines its relationship with the `author` table in the database.

Listing 1-8. *DDL for Creating a Foreign Key Constraint Against the Publication Table, publication_fk1.fkc*

```
1  ALTER TABLE publication ADD
2  CONSTRAINT  publication_fk1
3  FOREIGN KEY        (id)
4  REFERENCES  author (id);
```

The syntax used in Listing 1-8 for creating a foreign key constraint is as follows:

```
ALTER TABLE <table_name> ADD
CONSTRAINT  <constraint_name>
FOREIGN KEY (
<column_name_1>,
<column_name_2>,…
<column_name_N> )
REFERENCES <referenced_table_name> (
<column_name_1>,
<column_name_2>,…
<column_name_N> );
```

where `<table_name>` is the name of the table to be constrained, `<constraint_name>` is the name of the foreign key constraint, `<referenced_table_name>` is the name of the table to be referenced (or pointed to), and `<column_name>` is a column that is both part of the referenced table's key and corresponds to a column with the same value in the child or dependent table.

As my mother-in-law would say, "But what do you get for that?" Now that you have a foreign key defined on the `publication` table, you can no longer delete a referenced row in the `author` table. Or, put another way, you can't have any parentless children in the `publication` table. That's why the primary and foreign key constraints in SQL jargon are called *referential integrity constraints*. They ensure the integrity of the relational references between rows in related tables. Many developers ask me: "Ooooh, do I really have to use foreign keys?" My answer is always, "Yes—it's a relational database, isn't it?"

It's Your Turn to Create a Constraint

Too much talking and not enough walking! Guess what? It's time to put you to work on creating a primary key constraint against the `publication` table.

1. Write a DDL script to create a primary key constraint against the `publication` table. (Hint: there are two columns in this primary key: `id` and `title`.)

2. Save the DDL script with the same filename as your constraint name, but with a `.pkc` extension.

3. Execute your script in SQL*Plus by typing an at sign (@) followed by the filename at the `SQL>` prompt.

The primary key constraint should now exist against the `publication` table in the database, just waiting for you to slip up and try putting in a duplicate row (or as Clint Eastwood would say, "Go ahead punk, make my day."). Otherwise, try to make some sense out of the error message(s) you got, correct your script, and then try again.

My version of a DDL script to create a primary key constraint against the `publication` table is shown in Listing 1-9.

Listing 1-9. *DDL for Creating a Primary Key Constraint Against the Publication Table, publication_pk.pkc*

```
1  ALTER TABLE publication ADD
2  CONSTRAINT  publication_pk
3  PRIMARY KEY (
4  id,
5  title);
```

Now you know how to create a table along with any required indexes and constraints, what do you do if you need a really complex constraint? Or, how about if you need other actions to be triggered when a row or column in a table is inserted, updated, or deleted? Well, that's the purpose of triggers.

Triggers

Triggers are PL/SQL programs that are set up to execute in response to a particular event on a table in the database. The events in question can take place FOR EACH ROW or for a SQL statement, so I call them row-level or statement-level triggers.

The actual events associated with triggers can take place BEFORE, AFTER, or INSTEAD OF an INSERT, an UPDATE, or a DELETE SQL statement. Accordingly, you can create triggers for any of the events in Table 1-4.

Table 1-4. *Possible Trigger Events Against a Table*

Event	SQL	Level
BEFORE	DELETE	FOR EACH ROW
BEFORE	DELETE	
BEFORE	INSERT	FOR EACH ROW
BEFORE	INSERT	
BEFORE	UPDATE	FOR EACH ROW
BEFORE	UPDATE	
AFTER	DELETE	FOR EACH ROW
AFTER	DELETE	
AFTER	INSERT	FOR EACH ROW
AFTER	INSERT	

Table 1-4. *Possible Trigger Events Against a Table*

Event	SQL	Level
AFTER	UPDATE	FOR EACH ROW
AFTER	UPDATE	
INSTEAD OF	DELETE	FOR EACH ROW
INSTEAD OF	DELETE	
INSTEAD OF	INSERT	FOR EACH ROW
INSTEAD OF	INSERT	
INSTEAD OF	UPDATE	FOR EACH ROW
INSTEAD OF	UPDATE	

So let's say we want to play a practical joke. Are you with me here? We don't want anyone to ever be able to add the name Jonathan Gennick (my editor, who is actually a genius in his own right, but it's fun to mess with him) to our list of database geniuses. Listing 1-10 shows a trigger created to prevent such an erroneous thing from happening.

Listing 1-10. *A Trigger Against the Author Table, author_bir.trg*

```
01  CREATE OR REPLACE TRIGGER author_bir
02  BEFORE INSERT ON         author
03  FOR EACH ROW
04
05  BEGIN
06    if upper(:new.name) = 'JONATHAN GENNICK' then
07      raise_application_error(20000, 'Sorry, that genius is not allowed.');
08    end if;
09  END;
10  /
```

The syntax used in Listing 1-10 is as follows:

```
CREATE [OR REPLACE] TRIGGER <trigger_name>
BEFORE INSERT ON         <table_name>
FOR EACH ROW
BEGIN
  <pl/sql>
END;
```

where <trigger_name> is the name of the trigger, <table_name> is the name of the table for which you're creating the trigger, and <pl/sql> is the PL/SQL program you've written to be executed BEFORE someone INSERTs EACH ROW. The brackets ([ ]) around the OR REPLACE keyword denote that it is optional. The OR REPLACE clause will allow you to re-create your trigger if it already exists.

Views

A view represents the definition of a SQL query (SELECT statement) as though it were just another table in the database. Hence, you can INSERT into and UPDATE, DELETE, and SELECT from a view just as you can any table. (There are some restrictions on updating a view, but they can be resolved by the use of INSTEAD OF triggers.)

Here are just a few of the uses of views:

- Transform the data from multiple tables into what appears to be one table.

- Nest multiple outer joins against different tables, which is not possible in a single SELECT statement.

- Implement a seamless layer of user-defined security against tables and columns.

Let's say we want to create a view that combines the author and publication tables so it's easier for a novice SQL*Plus user to write a report about the publications written by each author. Listing 1-11 shows the DDL to create a view that contains the required SQL SELECT statement.

Listing 1-11. *DDL to Create an Author_Publication View, author_publication.vw*

```
1   CREATE OR REPLACE VIEW author_publication as
2   SELECT author.id,
3          author.name,
4          publication.title,
5          publication.written_date
6   FROM   author,
7          publication
8   WHERE  author.id = publication.id;
```

The syntax for the CREATE VIEW statement used in Listing 1-11 is as follows:

```
CREATE [OR REPLACE] VIEW <view_name> AS
<sql_select_statement>;
```

where <view_name> is the name of the view (the name that will be used in other SQL statements as though it's a table name), and <sql_select_statement> is a SQL SELECT statement against one or more tables in the database. Once again, the brackets around the OR REPLACE clause denote that it is optional. Using OR REPLACE also preserves any privileges (grants) that exist on a view.

That does it for our DML review. Now let's move on to the SQL for manipulating data—SQL keywords like INSERT, UPDATE, DELETE, and SELECT.

Insert

At this point in your journey, you should have two tables—author and publication—created in your Oracle database. Now it's time to put some data in them. You do that by using the SQL keyword INSERT.

INSERT is one of the SQL keywords that are part of SQL's Data Manipulation Language (DML). As the term implies, DML allows you to manipulate data in your relational database. Let's start with the first form of an INSERT statement, INSERT...VALUES.

Insert . . .Values

First, let's add Codd's entry to the author table. Listing 1-12 is a DML INSERT statement that uses a VALUES clause to do just that.

Listing 1-12. *DML to Insert Codd's Entry into the Author Table, author_100.ins*

```
01  INSERT INTO author (
02          id,
03          name,
04          birth_date,
05          gender )
06  VALUES (
07          100,
08          'Edgar F Codd',
09          to_date('19230823', 'YYYYMMDD'),
10          'MALE' );
11  COMMIT;
```

The syntax for the INSERT VALUES statement used in Listing 1-12 is as follows:

```
INSERT INTO <table_name> (
        <column_name_1>,
        <column_name_2>, …
        <column_name_N> )
VALUES (
        <column_value_1>,
        <column_value_2>,…
        <column_value_N> );
```

where <table_name> is the name of the table you wish to INSERT VALUES INTO, <column_name> is one of the columns from the table into which you wish to insert a value, and <column_value> is the value to place into the corresponding column. The COMMIT statement that follows the INSERT VALUES statement in Listing 1-12 simply commits your inserted values in the database.

So let's break down Listing 1-12 and look at what it does:

Line 1 specifies the table to insert values into: author.

Lines 2 through 5 list the columns in which to insert data.

Line 6 specifies the VALUES syntax.

Lines 7 through 10 supply values to insert into corresponding columns in the list on lines 2 through 5.

Line 11 commits the INSERT statement.

It's Your Turn to Insert with Values

Stop looking and start cooking. Insert the entries for Codd's publications into the publication table. Here are the steps to follow:

1. If you haven't actually executed the scripts for the author table yet, you'll need to do so now. The files are: author.tab, author_uk1.ndx, author_pk.pkc, and author_100.ins. Execute them in that order.

2. Write a DML script to insert Codd's two publications from Table 1-2. (Hint: use January 1 for the month and day of the written date, since we don't know those values.)

3. Save the DML script with the same filename as your table name, but with a _100 suffix and an .ins extension.

4. Execute your script in SQL*Plus by typing an at sign (@) followed by the filename at the SQL> prompt.

The publication table should now have two rows in it—congratulations! If it didn't work, try to make some sense out of the error message(s) you got, correct your script, and then try again. Listing 1-13 shows how I would insert the publications into the table.

Listing 1-13. *DML for Inserting Codd's Publications, publication_100.ins*

```
01  INSERT INTO publication (
02          id,
03          title,
04          written_date )
05  VALUES (
06          100,
07          'A Relational Model of Data for Large Shared Data Banks',
08          to_date('19700101', 'YYYYMMDD') );
09
10  INSERT INTO publication (
11          id,
12          title,
13          written_date )
14  VALUES (
15          100,
16          'The Relational Model for Database Management',
17          to_date('19900101', 'YYYYMMDD') );
18
19  COMMIT;
```

There's a second form of the INSERT statement that can be quite useful. Let's look at it next.

Insert . . . Select

The second form of an INSERT statement uses a SELECT statement instead of a list of column values. Although we haven't covered the SELECT statement yet, I think you're intuitive enough to follow along. Listing 1-14 inserts Chris Date's entry using the INSERT ... SELECT syntax.

Listing 1-14. *DML to Insert Date's Entry into the Author Table, author_200.ins*

```
01  INSERT INTO author (
02          id,
03          name,
04          birth_date,
05          gender )
06  SELECT 200,
07          'Chris J Date',
08          NULL,
09          'MALE'
10  FROM    dual;
11
12  COMMIT;
```

The syntax for the INSERT SELECT statement used in Listing 1-14 is as follows:

```
INSERT INTO <table_name> (
        <column_name_1>,
        <column_name_2>, …
        <column_name_N> )
SELECT <column_value_1>,
        <column_value_2>,…
        <column_value_N>
FROM    <from_table_name> ...;
```

where <table_name> is the name of the table you wish to INSERT INTO, <column_name> is one of the columns from the table into which you wish to insert a value, <column_value> is the value to place into the corresponding column, and <from_table_name> is the table or tables from which to select the values. The COMMIT statement that follows the INSERT SELECT statement in Listing 1-14 simply commits your inserted values in the database.

Let's break down Listing 1-14:

Line 1 specifies the table to insert values into: author.

Lines 2 through 5 list the columns in which to insert values.

Line 6 specifies the SELECT syntax.

Lines 6 through 9 supply values to insert into corresponding columns in the list on lines 2 through 5.

Line 10 specifies the table or tables from which to select the values.

Line 12 commits the INSERT statement.

So what's the big deal about this second INSERT syntax? First, it allows you to insert values into a table from other tables. Also, the SQL query to retrieve those values can be as complex as it needs to be. But its most handy use is to create conditional INSERT statements like the one in Listing 1-15.

Listing 1-15. *Conditional INSERT ... SELECT Statement, author_300.ins*

```
01  INSERT INTO author (
02          id,
03          name,
04          birth_date,
05          gender )
06  SELECT 300,
07          'Hugh Darwen',
08          NULL,
09          'MALE'
10  FROM    dual d
11  WHERE not exists (
12    SELECT 1
13    FROM    author x
14    WHERE  x.id = 300 );
15
16  COMMIT;
```

The subquery in Listing 1-15's SQL SELECT statement, on lines 11 through 14, first checks to see if the desired entry already exists in the database. If it does, Oracle does not attempt the INSERT; otherwise, it adds the row. You'll see in time, as your experience grows, that being able to do a conditional insert is very useful!

JUST WHO IS THIS DUAL GUY ANYWAY?

Have you noticed that I'm using a table by the name of dual in the conditional INSERT . . . SELECT statement? dual is a table owned by the Oracle database (owner SYS) that has one column and one row. It is very handy, because anytime you select against this table, you get one, and only one, row back.

So if you want to evaluate the addition of 1 + 1, you can simply execute the SQL SELECT statement:

```
SELECT 1 + 1 FROM dual;
```

Oracle will tell you the answer is 2. Not so handy? Say you want to quickly figure out how Oracle will evaluate your use of the built-in function length()? Perhaps you might try this:

```
SELECT length(NULL) FROM dual;
```

Oh! It returns NULL. You need a number, so you try again. This time, you try wrapping length() in the SQL function nvl() so you can substitute a zero for a NULL value:

```
SELECT nvl(length(NULL), 0) FROM DUAL;
```

Now it returns zero, even if you pass a NULL string to it. That's how you want it to work!

See how using dual to test how a SQL function might work can be handy? It allows you to hack away without any huge commitment in code.

It's Your Turn to Insert with Select

It's time to practice inserting data once again. This time, insert the publications for Date and Darwen, but use the conditional INSERT SELECT syntax with detection for Darwen's publications.

1. Add Darwen's entry to the author table by executing the script author_200.ins.

2. Write the DML scripts to insert the publications by Date and Darwen from Table 1-2.

3. Save each DML script with the same filename as your table name, but with a _200 suffix for Date and a _300 suffix for Darwen, and add an .ins extension to both files.

4. Execute your scripts in SQL*Plus by typing an at sign (@) followed by the filename at the SQL> prompt.

The publication table should now have eight rows. And, if you run the Darwen script again, you won't get any duplicate-value errors, because the SQL detects whether Darwen's entries already exist in the database.

Listings 1-16 and 1-17 show my solutions.

Listing 1-16. *DML for Inserting Date's Publications, publication_200.ins*

```
01  INSERT INTO publication (
02         id,
03         title,
04         written_date )
05  VALUES (
06         200,
07         'An introduction to Database Systems',
08         to_date('20030101', 'YYYYMMDD') );
09
10  INSERT INTO publication (
11         id,
12         title,
13         written_date )
14  VALUES (
15         200,
16         'The Third Manifesto',
17         to_date('20000101', 'YYYYMMDD') );
18
19  INSERT INTO publication (
20         id,
21         title,
22         written_date )
23  VALUES (
24         200,
25         'Temporal Data and the Relational Model',
26         to_date('20020101', 'YYYYMMDD') );
27
```

```
28  INSERT INTO publication (
29        id,
30        title,
31        written_date )
32  VALUES (
33        200,
34        'Database in Depth: Relational Theory for Practitioners',
35        to_date('20050101', 'YYYYMMDD') );
36
37  COMMIT;
```

Listing 1-17. *DML for Inserting Darwen's Publications, publication_300.ins*

```
01  INSERT INTO publication (
02        id,
03        title,
04        written_date )
05  SELECT 300,
06        'The Third Manifesto',
07        to_date('20000101', 'YYYYMMDD')
08  FROM   dual
09  WHERE not exists (
10    SELECT 1
11    FROM   publication x
12    WHERE  x.id    = '300'
13    AND    x.title = 'The Third Manifesto' );
14
15  INSERT INTO publication (
16        id,
17        title,
18        written_date )
19  SELECT 300,
20        'Temporal Data and the Relational Model',
21        to_date('20020101', 'YYYYMMDD')
22  FROM   dual
23  WHERE not exists (
24    SELECT 1
25    FROM   publication x
26    WHERE  x.id    = '300'
27    AND    x.title = 'Temporal Data and the Relational Model' );
```

You're a genius! Oh, it didn't work? Well then try, try again until it does—or cheat and look at the examples in the appropriate source code listing directory for the book.

Hey, you know what? We were supposed to put the data in the database in uppercase so we could perform efficient case-insensitive queries. Well, we should fix that. I guess we'll need to use the UPDATE statement.

Update

An UPDATE statement allows you to selectively update one or more column values for one or more rows in a specified table. In order to selectively update, you need to specify a WHERE clause in your UPDATE statement. Let's first take a look at an UPDATE statement without a WHERE clause.

Fix a Mistake with Update

As I alluded to earlier, I forgot to make the text values in our cute little database all in uppercase (I was distracted making yet another pot of coffee). Listing 1-18 is my solution to this problem for the author table.

Listing 1-18. *A DML Statement for Updating the Author Table, author.upd*

```
1  UPDATE author
2  SET    name = upper(name);
3
4  COMMIT;
```

The syntax used by Listing 1-18 is as follows:

```
UPDATE <table_name>
SET    <column_name_1> = <column_value_1>,
       <column_name_2> = <column_value_2>,...
       <column_name_N> = <column_value_N>;
```

where <table_name> is the name of the table to update, <column_name> is the name of a column to update, and <column_value> is the value to which to update the column in question.

In this case, an UPDATE statement without a WHERE clause is just what we needed. However, in practice, that's rarely the case. And, if you find yourself coding such an SQL statement, think twice.

An unconstrained UPDATE statement can be one of the most destructive SQL statements you'll ever execute by mistake. You can turn a lot of good data into garbage in seconds. So it's always a good idea to specify which rows to update with an additional WHERE clause. For example, I could have added the following line:

```
WHERE  name <> upper(name)
```

That would have limited the UPDATE to only those rows that are not already in uppercase.

It's Your Turn to Update

I've fixed my uppercase mistake in the author table. Now you can do the same for the publication table. So please update the publication titles to uppercase.

1. Write the DML script.

2. Save the DML script with the same filename as your table name, but add a .upd extension.

3. Execute your script in SQL*Plus.

The titles in the `publication` table should be in uppercase—good job. Listing 1-19 shows how I fixed this mistake.

Listing 1-19. *DML for Updating Titles in the Publication Table, publication.ups*

```
1  UPDATE publication
2  SET    title = upper(title)
3  WHERE  title <> upper(title);
4
5  COMMIT;
```

`UPDATE` statements can be quite complex. They can pull data values from other tables, for each column, or for multiple columns using subqueries. Let's look at the use of subqueries.

Update and Subqueries

One of the biggest mistakes PL/SQL programmers make is to write a PL/SQL program to update selected values in one table with selected values from another table. Why is this a big mistake? Because you don't need PL/SQL to do it. And, in fact, if you use PL/SQL, it will be slower than just doing it in SQL!

We haven't yet had an opportunity to work with any complex data, nor have we talked much about the SQL `SELECT` statement, so I won't show you an example yet. But look at the possible syntax:

```
UPDATE <table_name> U
SET    U.<column_name_N> = (
  SELECT S.<subquery_column_name_N>
  FROM   <subquery_table_name> S
  WHERE  S.<column_name_N> = U.<column_name_N>
  AND    ...)
WHERE u.<column_name_N> = <some_value>...;
```

This syntax allows you to update the value of a column in table `<table_name>`, aliased with the name U, with values in table `<subquery_table_name>`, aliased with the name S, based on the current value in the current row in table U. If that isn't powerful enough, look at this:

```
UPDATE <table_name> U
SET   (U.<column_name_1>,
       U.<column_name_2>, ...
       U.<column_name_N> ) = (
  SELECT S.<subquery_column_name_1>,
         S.<subquery_column_name_2>, ...
         S.<subquery_column_name_N>
  FROM   <subquery_table_name> S
  WHERE  S.<column_name_N> = U.<column_name_N>
  AND    ...)
WHERE u.<column_name_N> = <some_value>...;
```

Wow! It's like SQL heaven, SQL nirvana! You can update multiple columns at the same time simply by grouping them with parentheses. Hang on a second! I've got to go splash some cold water on my face.

OK, I'm back. The moral of the story is don't use PL/SQL to do something you can already do with SQL. I'll be harping on this soapbox throughout the book, so if you didn't get my point, relax, you'll hear it again and again in the coming chapters.

Delete

In practice, data is rarely deleted from a relational database when compared to how much is input, updated, and queried. Regardless, you should know how to delete data. With DELETE however, you need to do things backwards.

A Change in Order

So you don't think Hugh Darwen is a genius? Well I do, but for the sake of our tutorial, let's say we want to delete his entries from the database.

Since we created an integrity constraint on the publication table (a foreign key), we need to delete Darwen's publications before we delete him from the author table. Listing 1-20 is the DML to delete Darwen's entries from the publication table.

Listing 1-20. *DML to Delete Darwen's Publications, publication_300.del*

```
1  DELETE FROM publication
2  WHERE  id = 300;
```

The syntax for the DELETE statement used in Listing 1-20 is as follows:

```
DELETE FROM <table_name>
WHERE  <column_name_N> = <column_value_N>...;
```

where <table_name> is the name of the table to DELETE FROM, and <column_name> is one or more columns for which you specify some criteria.

Did you happen to notice that I didn't include a COMMIT statement? We will wait until you're finished with your part first.

It's Your Turn to Delete

Now that I've deleted the publications, it's time for you to delete the author.

1. Write the DML script without a COMMIT statement.

2. Save the DML script with the same filename as your table name, suffix it with _300, and then add a .del extension.

3. Execute your script in SQL*Plus.

Darwen should no longer be in the database. Listing 1-21 shows how I got rid of him.

Listing 1-21. *DML for Deleting Darwen from the Author Table, author_300.del*

```
1  DELETE FROM author
2  WHERE  id = 300;
```

Oooooh, no more Darwen. Let's fix that quickly!

Type ROLLBACK; at your SQL*Plus prompt and then press the Enter key. The transaction—everything you did from the last time you executed a COMMIT or ROLLBACK statement—has been rolled back. So it's as though we never deleted Darwen's entries. You didn't *really* think I was going to let you delete Darwen, did you?

Now we are ready to reach the summit of the mountain SQL, the ultimate, heavy-duty query statement: SELECT.

Select

In the end, all the power of a relational database comes down to its ability to manipulate data. At the heart of that ability lies the SQL SELECT statement. I could write an entire book about it, but I've got only a couple of pages to spare, so pay attention.

Listing 1-22 is a query for selecting all the author names from the author table. There's no WHERE clause to constrain which rows we will see.

Listing 1-22. *DML to Query the Author Table, author_names.sql*

```
1  SELECT name
2  FROM    author
3  ORDER BY name;
```

```
NAME
-------------------
CHRIS J DATE
EDGAR F CODD
HUGH DARWEN
```

Listing 1-22 actually shows the query (SELECT statement) executed in SQL*Plus, along with the database's response.

The syntax of the SELECT statement in Listing 1-22 is as follows:

```
SELECT <column_name_1>,
       <column_name_2>,
       <column_name_N>
FROM   <table_name>
[ORDER BY <order_by_column_name_N>]
```

where <column_name> is one of the columns in the table listed, <table_name> is the table to query, and <order_by_column_name> is one or more columns by which to sort the results.

In Listing 1-23, I add a WHERE clause to constrain the output to only those authors born before the year 1940.

Listing 1-23. *DML to Show Only Authors Born Before 1940, author_name_before_1940.sql*

```
1  SELECT name
2  FROM    author
3  WHERE   birth_date < to_date('19400101', 'YYYYMMDD')
4  ORDER BY name;
```

```
NAME
----------------------------------------------------------
EDGAR F CODD
```

So while this is all very nice, we've only started to scratch the surface of the SELECT statement's capabilities. Next, let's look at querying more than one table at a time.

Joins

Do you remember that way back in the beginning of this chapter we went through the mental exercise of matching the value of the id column in the author table against the same column in the publication table in order to find out which publications were written by each author? What we were doing back then was *joining* the two tables on the id column.

Also recall that to demonstrate views, I created an author_publication view? In that view, I joined the two tables, author and publication, by their related column, id. That too was an example of joining two tables on the id column.

Joins in a Where Clause

Listing 1-24 shows the SQL SELECT statement from that view created in Listing 1-11 with an added ORDER BY clause. In this example, I am joining the two tables using the WHERE clause (sometimes called *traditional join syntax*).

Listing 1-24. *DML to Join the Author and Publication Tables, author_publication_where_join.sql*

```
SQL> SELECT a.id,
  2          a.name,
  3          p.title,
  4          p.written_date
  5  FROM    author a,
  6          publication p
  7  WHERE   a.id = p.id
  8  ORDER BY a.name,
  9          p.written_date,
 10          p.title;
```

```
   ID NAME                TITLE
----- ------------------  --------------------------------------------------
  200 CHRIS J DATE        THE THIRD MANIFESTO
  200 CHRIS J DATE        TEMPORAL DATA AND THE RELATIONAL MODEL
  200 CHRIS J DATE        AN INTRODUCTION TO DATABASE SYSTEMS
  200 CHRIS J DATE        DATABASE IN DEPTH: RELATIONAL THEORY FOR PRACTITION
  100 EDGAR F CODD        A RELATION MODEL OF DATA FOR LARGE SHARED DATA BANK
  100 EDGAR F CODD        THE RELATIONAL MODEL FOR DATABASE MANAGEMENT
  300 HUGH DARWEN         THE THIRD MANIFESTO
  300 HUGH DARWEN         TEMPORAL DATA AND THE RELATIONAL MODEL

8 rows selected.
```

Line 7 in Listing 1-24 has this code:

```
WHERE   a.id = p.id.
```

Line 7 joins the author table a with the publication table p on the column id.

However, there's a second, newer, form of join syntax that uses the FROM clause in a SQL SELECT statement instead of the WHERE clause.

Joins in a From Clause

Listing 1-25 shows the newer join syntax. The join takes place on lines 5 through 6, in the FROM...ON clause.

Listing 1-25. *DML to Join the Author and Publication Tables, author_publication_from_join.sql*

```
SQL> SELECT a.id,
  2          a.name,
  3          p.title,
  4          p.written_date
  5  FROM    author a JOIN
  6          publication p
  7  ON      a.id = p.id
  8  ORDER BY a.name,
  9          p.written_date,
 10          p.title;
```

Both forms of the join syntax give the same results. I suggest you use the syntax that is consistent with the previous use of join syntax in the application you're currently working on, or follow the conventions of your development team.

Query Your Heart Out

It's time to put your query hat on. Show me all the authors who have coauthored a book.

1. Write the DML script.

2. Save the DML script with the filename `coauthor.sql`.

3. Execute your script in SQL*Plus.

You should get results something like this:

```
NAME
------------------
CHRIS J DATE
HUGH DARWEN
```

Next, show me all the publications that have been coauthored along with the author's name. Save the script with the filename `coauthor_publication.sql`. You should get results like this:

```
TITLE                                               NAME
--------------------------------------------------  ------------------
TEMPORAL DATA AND THE RELATIONAL MODEL              CHRIS J DATE
TEMPORAL DATA AND THE RELATIONAL MODEL              HUGH DARWEN
THE THIRD MANIFESTO                                 CHRIS J DATE
THE THIRD MANIFESTO                                 HUGH DARWEN
```

You can find my solutions to these two exercises in the source code listings you down-loaded for the book. If you had difficulty writing the queries for these two exercises, then you need more experience with SQL queries before you can be proficient with PL/SQL. You'll be able to learn and use PL/SQL, but you'll be handicapped by your SQL skills.

In fact, everything we just covered should have been a review for you. If any of it was new, I recommend that you follow up learning PL/SQL with some additional training in SQL. As I said when we started on this journey together, you need to know SQL really well, because it makes up about 25% of every PL/SQL stored procedure.

Now that we reviewed the SQL basics, I need to introduce you to a fictional example that we will use in the rest of the book. So go take a nap, then consume your favorite form of caffeine, and we will get started.

Our Working Example

I know it's a lot of work, but you really need to buy into the following fictional example in order to have something realistic to work with as you proceed through this book. I would love to take on one of your real business problems, but I don't work at the same company you do, so that would be very difficult. So let me start by telling you a short story.

Our Example Narrative

You're going to do some software development for a company called Very Dirty Manufacturing, Inc. (VDMI). VDMI prides itself with being able to take on the most environmentally damaging manufacturing jobs (dirty) in the most environmentally responsible way possible (clean).

Of course, VDMI gets paid big bucks for taking on such legally risky work, but the firm is also dedicated to preventing any of its employees from injury due to the work. The managers are so dedicated to the health and well-being of their workforce that they plan on having their industrial hygiene (IH), occupational health (OH), and safety records available on the Internet for public viewing (more on what IH and OH are about in just a moment).

Your job is the development of the worker demographics subsystem for maintaining the IH, OH, and safety records for VDMI. Internally, management will need to review worker data by the following:

- Organization a person works in

- Location the employee works at

- Job and tasks the employee performs while working

For IH, environmental samples will be taken in the areas where people work to make sure they are not being exposed to hazardous chemicals or noise without the right protections in place. For OH, workers who do work in dirty areas will be under regular medical surveillance to make sure that they are not being harmed while doing their work. And last, any accidents involving workers will also be documented so that no similar accidents take place, and to ensure that the workers are properly compensated for their injuries.

Externally, the sensitivity of the information will prevent the company from identifying for whom the data presented exists, but the information will still be presented by the high-level organization, location, and job. Therefore, the same demographic data and its relationship to workers in the firm need to be in place.

Our Example ERD

Now that you have an overview of the situation, let's take a look at an architectural representation of the demographic subsystem. Figure 1-2 shows the ERD for the demographic subsystem.

In order for you to get a better understanding of the ERD, think of each table in the diagram as one of the following:

- Content

- Codes

- Intersections

What do these terms mean? Read on to find out.

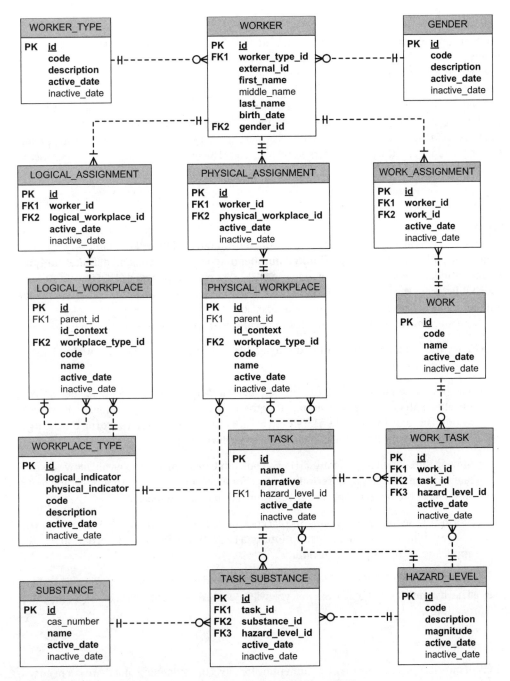

Figure 1-2. *VMDI's IH, OH, and safety demographic subsystem ERD*

Content

Think of content as anything your users may actually need to type into the system that varies greatly. For example, information like a worker's name and birth date changes a lot from one worker to the next. Since that data is kept in the WORKER table, think of the WORKER table as a content table.

Data in the WORKER table is the kind of information that you're unlikely to translate into another language should you present the information in a report. I would also classify as content tables the LOGICAL_WORKPLACE, PHYSICAL_WORKPLACE, and WORK tables, which describe the organization, location, and the job of a worker, respectively. However, we might also think of them as codes.

Codes

In order to make the categorization, classification, or typing of data specified in a content table consistent across all entries—for example, workers entered into the WORKER table—I've added some code tables. There are only a limited number of types of workers, and definitely only a limited number of genders, so I've added a WORKER_TYPE code table and a GENDER code table. Code tables act as the definitive source of categories, classes, types, and so on when specifying codified information in a content table like WORKER.

Here are some of the reasons that it's important to use code tables:

- They constrain the values entered into a table to an authoritative list of entries. This improves quality.

- The primary key of a code table is typically an identifier (ID) that is a sequence-generated number with no inherent meaning other than it is the primary key's value. An ID value is a compact value that can then be stored in the content table to reference the much larger code and description values. This improves performance.

- Storing the sequence-generated ID of a code table in a content table will allow you to later change the code or description values for a particular code without needing to do so in the content table. This improves application maintenance.

- Storing the sequence-generated ID of a code table in a content table will also allow you to later change the code or description for a code on the fly for an internationalized application. This improves flexibility.

Think of the WORKER_TYPE, GENDER, WORKPLACE_TYPE, and HAZARD_LEVEL tables as code tables. They all have a similar set of behaviors that you will later make accessible with PL/SQL functions and procedures.

Intersections

Think of intersections as a means of documenting history. Understanding that there is a history of information is the single-most portion missing in the analyses of business problems. Most often, a many-to-many relationship table (an intersection) will be created that captures only the "current" relationship between content entities, but there's always a history, and the history is almost always what's actually needed to solve the business problem in question.

In our refresher earlier in this chapter, we worked with two tables (or entities) that did not require us to keep a history. However, in our example here, we definitely need to maintain a history of who workers reported to, where they actually did there work, and what they did. Intersections document timelines, as shown in Figure 1-3.

Figure 1-3. *An employment timeline*

Examining Figure 1-3, you can see that the employee in question has the following history:

- Worked in the Chemicals department from 1994 through 1999, and then in the Biologicals department since (logical assignment)

- Worked at the Newark, New Jersey location from 1994 through 1996, in Gary, Indiana through 2002, and then in sunny San Diego since (physical assignment)

- Worked as a chemist from 1994 through 1996, and then as a chemical engineer since (work assignment)

An intersection table has a beginning and end date for every assignment period. Think of the LOGICAL_ASSIGNMENT, PHYSICAL_ASSIGNMENT, and WORK_ASSIGNMENT tables as history tables that hold an intersection in time between the WORKER table and the LOGICAL_WORKPLACE, PHYSICAL_WORKPLACE, and WORK tables, respectively.

Now that you're familiar with the ERD, you can start creating the tables.

Create a Code Table

Let's create some code tables. I'll write the script for the first code table, and then you do the other three. Listing 1-26 is a script to create the WORKER_TYPE code table.

Listing 1-26. *DDL for Creating the WORKER_TYPE_T Code Table, worker_type_t.tab*

```
01  rem worker_type_t.tab
02  rem by Donald J. Bales on 12/15/2006
03  rem
04
05  --drop   table WORKER_TYPE_T;
06  create table WORKER_TYPE_T (
07  id                          number              not null,
08  code                        varchar2(30)        not null,
```

```
09   description                    varchar2(80)                    not null,
10   active_date                    date          default SYSDATE   not null,
11   inactive_date                  date )
12   tablespace USERS pctfree 20
13   storage (initial 10K next 10K pctincrease 0);
14
15   --drop   sequence WORKER_TYPE_ID_SEQ;
16   create sequence WORKER_TYPE_ID_SEQ
17   start with 1;
18
19   alter  table WORKER_TYPE_T add
20   constraint   WORKER_TYPE_T_PK
21   primary key ( id )
22   using index
23   tablespace USERS pctfree 20
24   storage (initial 10K next 10K pctincrease 0);
25
26   alter  table WORKER_TYPE_T add
27   constraint   WORKER_TYPE_UK
28   unique ( code )
29   using index
30   tablespace USERS pctfree 20
31   storage (initial 10K next 10K pctincrease 0);
```

This listing is more complex than the previous ones in this chapter. Here's the breakdown:

Lines 1 through 3 document the name of the script, the author, and the date it was written. This is typical—everyone wants to know who to blame.

Lines 5 through 15 have DROP statements that I've commented out. Those were really handy when I was in the iterative development cycle, where I had to edit my script to refine it and then recompile.

Lines 6 through 13 contain the DDL to create the table WORKER_TYPE_T.

Lines 16 and 17 contain the DDL to create a sequence, WORKER_TYPE_ID_SEQ, for the table's primary key column, id.

Lines 19 through 24 contain the DDL to alter the table in order to add a primary key constraint.

Lines 26 through 31 contain the DDL to alter the table in order to add a unique key constraint. This constraint will allow only unique code values in the code table.

Since it's a code table, I can seed it with some initial values. I've written a second script for that, as shown in Listing 1-27.

Listing 1-27. *DML Script to Populate the WORKER_TYPE_T Code Table, worker_type_t.ins*

```
01  rem worker_type_t.ins
02  rem by Donald J. Bales on 12/15/2006
03  rem
04
05  insert into WORKER_TYPE_T (
06          id,
07          code,
08          description )
09  values (
10          WORKER_TYPE_ID_SEQ.nextval,
11          'C',
12          'Contractor' );
13
14  insert into WORKER_TYPE_T (
15          id,
16          code,
17          description )
18  values (
19          WORKER_TYPE_ID_SEQ.nextval,
20          'E',
21          'Employee' );
22
23  insert into WORKER_TYPE_T (
24          id,
25          code,
26          description )
27  values (
28          WORKER_TYPE_ID_SEQ.nextval,
29          'U',
30          'Unknown' );
31
32  commit;
```

Here's what's happening in Listing 1-27:

On lines 1 through 3, I've added "who to blame."

On lines 5 through 12, 14 through 21, and 23 through 30, I've added three DML INSERT VALUES statements in order to add three worker types to the WORKER_TYPE_T table.

On lines 10, 19, and 28, I'm allocating a new sequence value from the primary key's sequence using the pseudo-column .nextval.

On line 32, I commit the inserts so they are permanently accessible to everyone on the database.

After I execute these two scripts, I can query WORKER_TYPE_T and get results like this:

```
SQL> column code format a4;
SQL> column description format a11;
SQL> select *
  2  from   WORKER_TYPE_T
  3  order by code;


ID CODE DESCRIPTION ACTIVE_DATE      INACTIVE_DATE
-- ---- ----------- ---------------- ----------------
 1 C    Contractor  20070111 181451
 2 E    Employee    20070111 181451
 3 U    Unknown     20070111 181451
```

HEY! WHAT'S WITH THIS _T SUFFIX ON THE TABLE NAME?

The _T suffix has to do with coding conventions (or standards), which all professional programmers follow religiously (really—I'm not kidding here). Here's the deal: I'm not only going to teach you how to code PL/SQL for relational data, but also object-relational data. So while I normally *would not* suffix a table name with _T, I am doing that here in order to allow both the relational and object-relational examples to exist in the database at the same time. I'll use the suffix _T for relational tables and the suffix _OT for object-relational tables.

As long as I have your attention and we're focusing on SQL in this chapter, let me take a moment to talk about my SQL coding conventions.

SQL Coding Conventions

In the refresher part of this chapter, I capitalized the SQL keywords so it would be easy for you to notice them in the syntax statement that followed their use. In practice, I don't do that. When I code SQL, I follow these simple rules:

- I type table names in all caps, literals in uppercase/lowercase/mixed case as required, and everything else in lowercase. Why? First, since SQL is table-centric, I want table names to stick out like a sore thumb. Second, lowercase is actually easier to read. And finally, lowercase is easier to type, and after 30 years of typing, you'll know why that's important.

- I format my code so column names, table names, and parameters in WHERE clauses all line up in nice left-justified columns. That way, the text is easy to scan.

- I name scripts with the same name as the object they are creating, dropping, inserting, updating, and so on, and an appropriate filename extension in order to make the names of the scripts as obvious as possible.

SQL Filename Extension Conventions

The following are the filename extensions I use:

- `.tab`: Create table

- `.alt`: Alter table (to add, modify, or drop a column)

- `.ndx`: Create index

- `.pkc`: Alter table/add constraint/primary key (usually included in the create table script)

- `.fkc`: Alter table/add constraint/foreign key (usually included in the create table script)

- `.ukc`: Alter table/add constraint/unique (usually included in the create table script)

- `.drp`: Drop table

- `.ins`: Insert into

- `.upd`: Update

- `.del`: Delete from

- `.sql`: Select from

It's Your Turn to Create Code Tables

Now that you've seen me do it, you should be able to code the scripts to do the same for the GENDER, HAZARD_LEVEL, and WORKPLACE_TYPE code tables (pssst, don't forget to suffix them with _T). Code the scripts, saving them with the filenames gender_t.tab, hazard_level_t.tab, and workplace_type_t.tab, respectively. Then execute each script. You can see my solutions to these scripts in the book's source code directory for Chapter 2. Now let's move on to creating content tables.

Create a Content Table

This time, let's create some content tables. I'll write the first two scripts, and then you do the rest. Listing 1-28 is a script to create the WORKER table.

Listing 1-28. *DDL to Create the WORKER Table, worker.tab*

```
01  rem worker_t.tab
02  rem by Donald J. Bales on 12/15/2006
03  rem
04
05  --drop   table WORKER_T;
06  create table WORKER_T (
07  id                          number                    not null,
08  worker_type_id              number                    not null,
```

```
09   external_id                  varchar2(30)           not null,
10   first_name                   varchar2(30)           not null,
11   middle_name                  varchar2(30),
12   last_name                    varchar2(30)           not null,
13   name                         varchar2(100)          not null,
14   birth_date                   date                   not null,
15   gender_id                    number                 not null )
16   tablespace USERS pctfree 20
17   storage (initial 10K next 10K pctincrease 0);
18
19   --drop   sequence WORKER_ID_SEQ;
20   create sequence WORKER_ID_SEQ
21   start with 1;
22
23   --drop   sequence EXTERNAL_ID_SEQ;
24   create sequence EXTERNAL_ID_SEQ
25   start with 100000000 order;
26
27   alter  table WORKER_T add
28   constraint   WORKER_T_PK
29   primary key ( id )
30   using index
31   tablespace USERS pctfree 20
32   storage (initial 10K next 10K pctincrease 0);
33
34   alter  table WORKER_T add
35   constraint   WORKER_T_UK1
36   unique ( external_id )
37   using index
38   tablespace USERS pctfree 20
39   storage (initial 10K next 10K pctincrease 0);
40
41   alter  table WORKER_T add
42   constraint   WORKER_T_UK2
43   unique (
44   name,
45   birth_date,
46   gender_id )
47   using index
48   tablespace USERS pctfree 20
49   storage (initial 10K next 10K pctincrease 0);
50
51   alter  table WORKER_T add
52   constraint   WORKER_T_FK1
53   foreign key                 ( worker_type_id )
54   references   WORKER_TYPE_T ( id );
55
```

```
56  alter  table WORKER_T add
57  constraint    WORKER_T_FK2
58  foreign key              ( gender_id )
59  references    GENDER_T    ( id );
```

Looks familiar, doesn't it? It looks a lot like the code table scripts you created earlier. The exceptions are lines 51 through 54 and 56 through 59, where I've added DDL to create two foreign key (FK) constraints. The first foreign key creates an integrity constraint between the code table WORKER_TYPE_T, while the second does the same for code table GENDER_T. These constraints will prevent anyone from deleting a code that is in use by the WORKER_T table.

Listing 1-29 shows the code to create the LOGICAL_WORKPLACE table. I'm showing you this listing because this table has some interesting new columns: parent_id and id_context.

Listing 1-29. *DDL to Create the LOGICAL_WORKPLACE Table, logical_workplace_t.tab*

```
01  rem logical_workplace_t.tab
02  rem by Donald J. Bales on 12/15/2006
03  rem
04
05  --drop    table LOGICAL_WORKPLACE_T;
06  create table LOGICAL_WORKPLACE_T (
07  id                        number                        not null,
08  parent_id                 number,
09  id_context                varchar2(100)                 not null,
10  workplace_type_id         number                        not null,
11  code                      varchar2(30)                  not null,
12  name                      varchar2(80)                  not null,
13  active_date               date          default SYSDATE not null,
14  inactive_date             date )
15  tablespace USERS pctfree 20
16  storage (initial 10K next 10K pctincrease 0);
17
18  --drop    sequence LOGICAL_WORKPLACE_ID_SEQ;
19  create sequence LOGICAL_WORKPLACE_ID_SEQ
20  start with 1;
21
22  alter  table LOGICAL_WORKPLACE_T add
23  constraint    LOGICAL_WORKPLACE_T_PK
24  primary key (
25  id )
26  using index
27  tablespace USERS pctfree 20
28  storage (initial 10K next 10K pctincrease 0);
29
30  alter  table LOGICAL_WORKPLACE_T add
31  constraint    LOGICAL_WORKPLACE_T_UK1
32  unique (
33  id_context )
```

```
34  using index
35  tablespace USERS pctfree 20
36  storage (initial 10K next 10K pctincrease 0);
37
38  alter  table LOGICAL_WORKPLACE_T add
39  constraint   LOGICAL_WORKPLACE_T_UK2
40  unique (
41  code,
42  name,
43  active_date )
44  using index
45  tablespace USERS pctfree 20
46  storage (initial 10K next 10K pctincrease 0);
47
48  alter  table LOGICAL_WORKPLACE_T add
49  constraint   LOGICAL_WORKPLACE_T_FK1
50  foreign key                     ( parent_id )
51  references   LOGICAL_WORKPLACE_T ( id );
52
53  alter  table LOGICAL_WORKPLACE_T add
54  constraint   LOGICAL_WORKPLACE_T_FK2
55  foreign key                     ( workplace_type_id )
56  references   WORKPLACE_TYPE_T ( id );
```

A logical workplace like a department may belong to a business unit, while its business unit may belong to a company. The parent_id column allows you to store the id of a department's parent business unit with the department, so you can document the organization hierarchy. With this information, you can present an organization chart, find everyone in a business unit, and so on.

The id_context column is a convenience or performance column for the mechanics of querying the database. You are going to write a PL/SQL function that will create an ID context string for this column. The ID context string will list all of the parent IDs, plus the logical workplace ID of the current row, separated by a known character, such as a period (.)—for example, 1.13.14. This will greatly improve the performance of any LIKE queries against the hierarchy of the organizations in the table.

It's Your Turn to Create Content Tables

Now that you've seen me do it, you should be able to code the scripts to do the same for the WORK and PHYSICAL_WORKPLACE tables (again, don't forget to suffix them with _T). So code the scripts, saving them with the filenames work_t.tab and physical_workplace_t.tab, respectively. Then execute each script. You can view my solutions to these scripts in the book's source code directory for Chapter 2.

Now let's move on to creating intersection tables.

Create an Intersection Table

It's time to create some intersection tables. I'll write the first script, and then you write the rest. Listing 1-30 is a script to create the LOGICAL_ASSIGNMENT table.

Listing 1-30. *DDL to Create the LOGICAL_ASSIGNMENT Table, logical assignment_t.tab*

```
01  rem logical_assignment_t.tab
02  rem by Donald J. Bales on 12/15/2006
03  rem
04
05  --drop   table LOGICAL_ASSIGNMENT_T;
06  create table LOGICAL_ASSIGNMENT_T (
07  id                          number                      not null,
08  worker_id                   number                      not null,
09  logical_workplace_id        number                      not null,
10  active_date                 date         default SYSDATE not null,
11  inactive_date               date )
12  tablespace USERS pctfree 20
13  storage (initial 10K next 10K pctincrease 0);
14
15  --drop   sequence LOGICAL_ASSIGNMENT_ID_SEQ;
16  create sequence LOGICAL_ASSIGNMENT_ID_SEQ
17  start with 1;
18
19  alter  table LOGICAL_ASSIGNMENT_T add
20  constraint   LOGICAL_ASSIGNMENT_T_PK
21  primary key ( id )
22  using index
23  tablespace USERS pctfree 20
24  storage (initial 10K next 10K pctincrease 0);
25
26  alter  table LOGICAL_ASSIGNMENT_T add
27  constraint   LOGICAL_ASSIGNMENT_T_UK
28  unique (
29  worker_id,
30  active_date )
31  using index
32  tablespace USERS pctfree 20
33  storage (initial 10K next 10K pctincrease 0);
34
35  alter  table LOGICAL_ASSIGNMENT_T add
36  constraint   LOGICAL_ASSIGNMENT_T_FK1
37  foreign key         ( worker_id )
38  references   WORKER_T ( id );
39
```

```
40  alter  table LOGICAL_ASSIGNMENT_T add
41  constraint   LOGICAL_ASSIGNMENT_T_FK2
42  foreign key                         ( logical_workplace_id )
43  references   LOGICAL_WORKPLACE_T ( id );
```

I know, you don't even need me to explain it anymore. I just wanted to make sure you have a nice pattern to mimic.

It's Your Turn to Create Intersection Tables

Just do it!

Summary

By now, you should have a fairly complete set of sample tables that you can work with when programming in PL/SQL. We've reviewed the basics of relational SQL, and then put that to work to create our working example. If you had any trouble with the SQL we used so far, I sincerely encourage you to get some supplemental materials and/or training in order to improve your SQL skills. You've heard the old adage, "A chain is only as strong as its weakest link," haven't you?

So you think your SQL is up to the task of programming in PL/SQL? Well, then let's get started!

CHAPTER 2

■■■

PL/SQL Is Square, Man!

Don't know any 60's speak? Back in the 1960s, calling an authority figure square was meant to be an insult. It meant "the man" was always playing by and enforcing the rules. That could be a real drag, a downer, something that could blow your scene. However, when it comes to a programming language, it's good to be square.

The Procedure Language extension for SQL (PL/SQL) is so square that it's three-dimensional. Every piece of code executes in a block—no, not the kind you walk around when you're angry with your old man or old lady. I'm talking about four keywords:

DECLARE: Every PL/SQL block has a declaration section. This is where you will allocate memory for cursors, data type definitions, variables, embedded functions, and procedures (don't worry—you'll learn about all of these in this book, beginning with functions and procedures in this chapter). Sometimes, when you code a PL/SQL program, you won't even use the declaration section, but it's still there.

BEGIN: Every PL/SQL block has an executable section. It starts with the keyword BEGIN. BEGIN marks the beginning of where you put your program logic. And every PL/SQL program must have at least one line of executable code, even if it's the keyword NULL, which in this context means no operation.

EXCEPTION: Every PL/SQL block has an exception-handling section. It starts with the keyword EXCEPTION. This is where you will catch any database or PL/SQL errors, or as they are affectionately known, *exceptions*. Like the declaration section, sometimes you won't even use an exception-handling section, but it's still there.

END: Every PL/SQL block ends with the keyword END.

■**Note** Before you get further into PL/SQL, you should re-create the relational schema for the example, just to make sure it's complete. To do so, log in to SQL*Plus from Chapter 2's downloaded source code directory, and then execute the script create_relational.sql. This script will delete and re-create the tables for the sample schema.

Anonymous Blocks

We'll start with an anonymous PL/SQL block. It's called *anonymous* because it's not going to be saved in the database, so it will never have a name. In practice, you won't find yourself using anonymous blocks in production, but you'll use them throughout the development process. They're perfect for creating test units that you'll eventually move into your stored PL/SQL blocks. You'll learn more about that in Chapter 8. For now, let's look at an example.

Anonymous Block Example

Listing 2-1 is an example of an anonymous PL/SQL block. Comments describe the different sections.

Listing 2-1. *An Anonymous PL/SQL Block, anonymous.sql*

```
01  -- This is an anonymous procedure, so it has no name
02  DECLARE
03    /*
04      You declare local cursors, variables, and methods here,
05      but you don't need to have a declaration section.
06    */
07  BEGIN
08    -- You write your executable code here
09
10    NULL;  -- Ahhh, you've got to have at least one command!
11  EXCEPTION
12    when NO_DATA_FOUND then
13      raise_application_error(-20000,
14        'Hey, This is in the exception-handling section!');
15  END;
16  /
17  -- the forward slash on a line by itself says execute this procedure
```

Let's go through Listing 2-1 line by line:

Line 1 is a single-line comment. Single-line comments start with a double-dash (--), but line 1 is not part of the PL/SQL block or program, because it exists outside the block structure.

Line 2 starts the block with the keyword DECLARE. This anonymous PL/SQL block could have started with the keyword BEGIN, because it doesn't have anything to declare.

Lines 3 through 6 are a multiline comment in the declaration section. Multiline comments start with a slash and asterisk (/*) and end with an asterisk and slash (*/).

Line 7 starts the PL/SQL executable section of the PL/SQL block with the keyword BEGIN.

Line 8 is a single-line comment in the executable section.

Line 10 is the PL/SQL keyword NULL followed by a single-line comment. NULL in this context means no operation. I put it there because every PL/SQL block must have at least one line of code, or it won't compile.

Line 11 starts the exception-handling section with the keyword EXCEPTION. If you code an exception-handling section, you must catch at least one exception. In this case, I've coded a NO_DATA_FOUND exception, which will raise an application error with my message should a NO_DATA_FOUND exception occur.

Line 15 ends the PL/SQL block or program with keyword END.

Line 16 has a *single forward slash (/), which is a signal to SQL*Plus* to execute the PL/SQL block. In this case—that is, with an anonymous PL/SQL block—the Oracle database will compile and then run the code in the PL/SQL block.

Line 17 is another single-line comment that, too, exists outside the PL/SQL block.

It's Your Turn to Execute an Anonymous Block

Now it's time for you to execute an anonymous PL/SQL block/program.

1. Open SQL*Plus and connect to the database.

2. At the SQL> prompt, type the following:

```
set serveroutput on size 1000000
begin
  SYS.DBMS_OUTPUT.put_line('Hi there genius!');
end;
/
```

After you typed the forward slash on a line by itself, you will have executed your very first PL/SQL procedure, and a very complimentary one at that.

The first line tells SQL*Plus to echo the database's output for your session to the screen after the PL/SQL procedure is finished executing:

```
set serveroutput on size 1000000
```

It is a SQL*Plus command and is not part of the anonymous block.

The line that starts with begin starts your PL/SQL procedure's executable code section. The next line calls the put_line procedure in package (library of stored procedures) DBMS_OUTPUT, owned by user SYS:

```
SYS.DBMS_OUTPUT.put_line('Hi there genius!');
```

put_line stores your text in a buffer until the PL/SQL procedure ends. Then SQL*Plus displays the text from that buffer on the screen for you to see.

The fourth line, which starts with end, ends the anonymous PL/SQL procedure. Finally, as stated earlier, the forward slash (/) on a line by itself tells SQL*Plus to execute the procedure.

In this example, you didn't code declaration or exception-handling sections, but they're still there! If an error occurs between the BEGIN and END keywords, PL/SQL will use the default (invisible) exception handler to raise the error to the enclosing program unit, which, in this case, is SQL*Plus.

Exceptions

Exceptions allow you to catch errors as your PL/SQL program executes, so you have control over what happens in response to those errors. PL/SQL predefines more than 20 named exceptions, but you'll probably use only a few.

■**Note** After you've gained more PL/SQL experience, you may even want to define your own named exceptions. For more information about custom exceptions, see Oracle's *PL/SQL User's Guide and Reference*.

Common Exceptions

As you'll learn in future chapters, there are a handful of commonly seen exceptions. The rest occur only when there are catastrophic problems with the database, the network, or your PL/SQL code (oh, not my code!).

Two exceptions are very common:

- NO_DATA_FOUND: You'll get a NO_DATA_FOUND exception anytime you code a SQL SELECT statement that does not return any rows.

- TOO_MANY_ROWS: If you code a SELECT statement where you expect only one row but you get more than one, you'll get a TOO_MANY_ROWS exception.

Catching an Exception

You add the keyword EXCEPTION between the keywords BEGIN and END in order to add an exception-handling section to your PL/SQL block. Once you do that, any error that occurs between the keywords BEGIN and EXCEPTION will be handled by your exception-handling section.

Functions

A FUNCTION is a PL/SQL block or method that returns a value, so it can be used on the right-hand side of an assignment. Here is an example:

```
n_value := to_number('123.45');
```

In this line of PL/SQL code, n_value is a numeric variable (we'll cover variables in the next chapter). n_value is followed by an assignment operator, which is a colon followed by an equal sign (:=). Next is the PL/SQL built-in function to_number(text in varchar2), which parses a varchar2 data type, and then returns its numeric value—that is, if the varchar2 represents a number; otherwise, the function raises an INVALID_NUMBER exception.

Since a FUNCTION returns a value, you can also use it in a SQL statement, as in this example:

```
SQL> select to_number('A') from dual;
select to_number('A') from dual
                  *
ERROR at line 1:
ORA-01722: invalid number
```

Look, there's that INVALID_NUMBER exception I was talking about!

Create a Function

Instead of dealing with errors when we try to convert a varchar2 (character string) to a number on the fly as in a SELECT statement, let's create an errorless to_number() function. Listing 2-2 is the DDL to do just that.

Listing 2-2. *An Errorless to_number() Function, to_number_or_null.fun*

```
01  CREATE OR REPLACE FUNCTION to_number_or_null (
02  aiv_number                      IN      varchar2 )
03  return                                  number is
04  /*
05  to_number_or_null.fun
06  by Donald J. Bales on 12/15/2006
07  An errorless to_number( ) method
08  */
09  begin
10    return to_number(aiv_number);
11  exception
12    when INVALID_NUMBER then
13      return NULL;
14  end to_number_or_null;
15  /
16  @fe.sql to_number_or_null;
```

The DDL syntax used in Listing 2-2 to create the function is as follows:

```
CREATE [OR REPLACE] FUNCTION <function_name> [(
<parameter_name_1>          [IN] [OUT] <parameter_data_type_1>,
<parameter_name_2>          [IN] [OUT] <parameter_data_type_2>,...
<parameter_name_N>          [IN] [OUT] <parameter_data_type_N> )]
RETURN                                 <return_data_type> IS
  --the declaration section
BEGIN
  -- the executable section
  return <return_data_type>;
EXCEPTION
  -- the exception-handling section
END;
/
```

where <function_name> is the name of the FUNCTION; <parameter_name> is the name of a parameter being passed IN, OUT, or IN and OUT; <parameter_data_type> is the PL/SQL data type of the corresponding parameter; and <return_data_type> is the PL/SQL data type of the value that will be returned by the FUNCTION when it completes its execution. The brackets ([ ]) around the keywords OR REPLACE denote that they are optional. The brackets around the parameters denote that they are optional, too.

The block structure of a FUNCTION is exactly the same as an anonymous procedure, except for the addition of the DDL CREATE FUNCTION keywords, the optional parameters, and the RETURN clause.

Let's take a look at Listing 2-2, line by line:

Line 1 has the DDL keywords to CREATE a stored FUNCTION. These take the place of the keyword DECLARE used earlier in the anonymous PL/SQL block.

Line 2 declares one parameter, aiv_number, a varchar2 value passed INto the FUNCTION.

Line 3 contains the RETURN clause. In this case, I'm returning a number.

Lines 4 through 8 contain a multiline comment that lists the function's source code filename, the name of the author, the date the function was written, and a description of the function's purpose. So the only thing in the declaration section of this PL/SQL block is the multiline comment.

On line 9, the keyword BEGIN starts the execution section of the PL/SQL block.

On line 10, I return the built-in to_number( )'s return value for converting the varchar2 variable aiv_number to a number. Then the program ends. However, if the built-in to_number( ) raises an exception, the program's execution branches to the exception-handling section.

On line 11, the keyword EXCEPTION starts the exception-handling section of this PL/SQL block.

On line 12, the exception handler checks to see if the raised exception is the named exception INVALID_NUMBER. If it is, it executes the code that follows it on line 13.

On line 13, I return NULL if there is an INVALID_NUMBER exception. That's what makes this an errorless to_number( ) function. If there are any other exceptions, the exception hander will raise the error to the enclosing PL/SQL block or program, which in this case, will be SQL*Plus.

On line 14, the keyword END denotes the end of the PL/SQL block, and hence the FUNCTION.

On line 15, the single slash character (/) tells SQL*Plus to execute the DDL, which stores the PL/SQL in the database and then compiles it.

Line 16 contains a helper SQL script that will list any compilation errors. Most of the time, this script will simply have one line of code that says show errors. However, if you're compiling into another schema (other than the username you're logged in with), you may need a more complex SQL script to display errors.

Now let's try using this errorless FUNCTION in a SELECT statement:

```
SQL> select to_number_or_null('A') from DUAL;
```

```
TO_NUMBER_OR_NULL('A')
----------------------
```

Ta da! It returned a NULL value since the letter *A* is not a number. Just in case you're a skeptic, here's a second test:

```
SQL> select to_number_or_null('234.56') from DUAL;
```

```
TO_NUMBER_OR_NULL('234.56')
---------------------------
                     234.56
```

Yes, indeed, it works correctly!

It's Your Turn to Create a Function

For this exercise, you'll create a function that returns a date value. You can use the function in Listing 2-2 as a model. This time, you'll pass this new function a varchar2 value that represents a date in the form *MM/DD/YYYY*. Your function will parse the varchar2 value and return a date data type if the varchar2 value is actually a date in the form *MM/DD/YYYY*; otherwise, it will return NULL.

You can use the PL/SQL built-in function to_date(text in varchar2, format in varchar2) in your function to do the actual parsing of the date. In the following form, to_date( ) will return a date value if it successfully parses the passed varchar2 value, or raise an exception if the passed varchar2 value is not a date in the format *MM/DD/YYYY*:

```
return to_date(aiv_date, 'MM/DD/YYYY');
```

Using this function, create your function by following these steps:

1. Warm up the old text editor, and code the DDL to create your function.

2. Save your new DDL script with the filename to_mmsddsyyyy_or_null.fun.

3. At your SQL*Plus prompt, type the at sign (@) followed by the name of your file in order to store and compile your new function.

4. Test your new function by using it in a SELECT statement against table DUAL.

Listing 2-3 shows my solution for this exercise.

Listing 2-3. *An Errorless to_date( ) Function, to_mmsddmyyyy_or_null.fun*

```
01  create or replace FUNCTION to_mmsddsyyyy_or_null (
02  aiv_date                    in      varchar2 )
03  return                              date is
04  /*
05  to_mmsddsyyyy_or_null.fun
```

```
06  by Donald J. Bales on 12/15/2006
07  An errorless to_date( ) method
08  */
09  begin
10    return to_date(aiv_date, 'MM/DD/YYYY');
11  exception
12    /*
13    There are too many possible errors, for example:
14      ORA-01830: date format picture ends before
15                 converting entire input string
16      ORA-01843: not a valid month
17      ORA-01847: day of month must be between 1
18                 and last day of month
19      ORA-01858: a non-numeric character was found
20                 where a numeric was expected
21    so I used the exception OTHERS
22    */
23    when OTHERS then
24      return NULL;
25  end to_mmsddsyyyy_or_null;
26  /
27  @fe.sql to_mmsddsyyyy_or_null;
```

First, I'll test it using a SELECT statement against DUAL:

```
SQL> select to_mmsddsyyyy_or_null('A') from DUAL;


TO_MMSDDSYYYY_OR
----------------
```

Well, that worked. The to_mmsddsyyyy_or_null() function returned a NULL because the letter *A* is not a date in the form *MM/DD/YYYY*. So let's try a date string. This time, however, I'll execute the anonymous PL/SQL block in Listing 2-4 as a test unit in order to test the function.

Listing 2-4. *A Test Unit for Function to_mmsddsyyyy_or_null( ), to_mmsddsyyyy_or_null.sql*

```
01  rem to_mmsddsyyyy_or_null.sql
02  rem by Donald J. Bales on 12/15/2006
03  rem FUNCTION to_mmsddsyyyy_or_null test unit
04
05  alter session set nls_date_format = 'SYYYYMMDD HH24MISS';
06  begin
07    sys.dbms_output.put_line(to_mmsddsyyyy_or_null('01/01/1980'));
08    sys.dbms_output.put_line(to_mmsddsyyyy_or_null('02/29/1980'));
09    sys.dbms_output.put_line(to_mmsddsyyyy_or_null('02/29/1981'));
10    sys.dbms_output.put_line(to_mmsddsyyyy_or_null('9/9/2006'));
11    sys.dbms_output.put_line(to_mmsddsyyyy_or_null('9/9/9999'));
```

```
12    sys.dbms_output.put_line(to_mmsddsyyyy_or_null('1/1/4712 BC'));
13  end;
14  /
```

The following output from executing function to_mmsddsyyyy_or_null()'s test unit shows that it's working great. The tests on lines 9 and 12 should have returned NULL, because I passed invalid date strings, and they did! Note that on line 5 in Listing 2-4, I changed the default date format used by the database, and hence SQL*Plus, to be YYYYMMDD HH24MISS in order to make it easier to see the full year and time in any date displayed by SQL*Plus.

```
SQL> @to_mmsddsyyyy_or_null.sql
```

```
Session altered.

19800101 000000
19800229 000000
20060909 000000
99990909 000000

PL/SQL procedure successfully completed.
```

Up to this point, you've seen an anonymous PL/SQL block and a function's PL/SQL block. The differences between the two are that an anonymous block is not permanently stored in the database with a name, nor can it return a value. Now let's take a look at PL/SQL blocks that do have names, but don't return values: procedures.

Procedures

"Just do it; don't give me any lip!" That's what Oracle is telling your PL/SQL block when it's a procedure. "Any lip," in this context, is a return value, and PL/SQL procedures don't return a value. They just do it—whatever *it* is. Of course, this means that you can't use procedures on the right-hand side of an assignment statement like a function (aw shucks!).

Create a Procedure

Listing 2-5 is a very simple example of a procedure. It's a wrapper around the Oracle SYS.DBMS_LOCK package's procedure sleep(seconds in number). This procedure will stop executing (or sleep) without using many CPU cycles for the number of seconds specified. I'll admit, it's kind of lame, but we're just starting out here, so I'm keeping things simple.

■**Note** By default, the SYS.DBMS_LOCK package is not accessible by non-DBA users. The username creation script in this book's appendix will grant you access, but if you don't use that script, you may need to ask your DBA to explicitly grant you execute access to package SYS.DBMS_LOCK.

Listing 2-5. *A Wrapper Procedure for SYS.DBMS_LOCK.sleep(), wait.prc*

```
01  CREATE OR REPLACE PROCEDURE wait(
02  ain_seconds                    IN      number) is
03  /*
04  wait.prc
05  by Donald J. Bales on 12/15/2006
06  Wrapper for SYS.DBMS_LOCK.sleep()
07  */
08  begin
09    SYS.DBMS_LOCK.sleep(ain_seconds);
10  end wait;
11  /
12  @pe.sql wait
```

The DDL syntax used by Listing 2-5 is as follows:

```
CREATE [OR REPLACE] PROCEDURE <procedure_name> [(
<parameter_name_1>          [IN] [OUT] <parameter_data_type_1>,
<parameter_name_2>          [IN] [OUT] <parameter_data_type_2>,...
<parameter_name_N>          [IN] [OUT] <parameter_data_type_N> )] IS
  --the declaration section
BEGIN
  -- the executable section
EXCEPTION
  -- the exception-handling section
END;
/
```

where `<procedure_name>` is the name of the `PROCEDURE`; `<parameter_name>` is the name of a parameter being passed `IN`, `OUT`, or `IN` and `OUT`; and `<parameter_data_type>` is the PL/SQL data type of the corresponding parameter. The brackets around the keywords `OR REPLACE` denote that they are optional. In addition, just as with a function, the brackets around the parameters denote that they are optional.

The block structure of a `PROCEDURE` is exactly the same as an anonymous block, except for the addition of the DDL `CREATE PROCEDURE` keywords and the optional parameters. A procedure differs from a function in that it does not have a `RETURN` parameter.

Let's take a look at Listing 2-5, line by line:

Line 1 contains the DDL keywords to `CREATE` a stored `PROCEDURE`.

Line 2 passes in one parameter: the number of seconds to wait.

Lines 3 through 7, in the declaration section, have a multiline comment that documents the procedure's source code filename, author, date the procedure was written, and finally a comment about what the procedure does.

On line 8, the keyword `BEGIN` starts the executable section.

On line 9, I call the procedure sleep() located in package DBMS_LOCK, owned by user SYS. sleep() calls the host operating system's sleep() or wait() function and then returns sometime after the specified period in seconds.

On line 10, the keyword END ends the executable section. Did you notice that there is no defined exception-handling section? Since I didn't code one, PL/SQL will use the default exception handler, which will simply raise the error to the enclosing program unit.

On line 11, the slash (/) tells Oracle to store and then compile the procedure.

Line 12 calls a helper script to show any compilation errors.

The PL/SQL block structure for the stored procedure in Listing 2-5 was really not that much different from the structure of the anonymous procedure and the stored function. The wait() procedure has a name and parameters, while an anonymous procedure does not. In addition, wait() does not return a value, while a stored function does.

It's Your Turn to Create a Procedure

Now you'll create a procedure that wraps the SYS.DBMS_OUTPUT.put_line() procedure, but uses a very short name. You'll end up using the SYS.DBMS_OUTPUT.put_line() procedure a lot. It gets tiresome to type a 24-character method name every time you want to display a line of text on the screen in SQL*Plus. So, to save keystrokes, you will give your SYS.DBMS_OUTPUT.put_line() wrapper procedure the name pl(), as in p for put and l for line.

You can use the procedure in Listing 2-5 as a model. Just replace the parameter on line 2 with aiv_text in varchar2, and write line 9 with a call to SYS.DBMS_OUTPUT.put_line(aiv_text).

1. Write the DDL to create your procedure.

2. Save your new DDL script with the filename pl.prc.

3. At your SQL*Plus prompt, type the at sign (@) followed by the name of your file to store and compile your new procedure.

4. Test your new procedure by using it in an anonymous procedure.

Listing 2-6 shows my solution for this exercise.

Listing 2-6. *A Lazy Typist's SYS.DBMS_OUTPUT.put_line(), pl.prc*

```
01  create or replace PROCEDURE pl(
02  aiv_text                    in      varchar2 ) is
03  /*
04  pl.prc
05  by Donald J. Bales on 12/15/2006
06  A wrapper procedure for SYS.DBMS_OUTPUT.put_line()
07  for the lazy typist.
08  */
09
```

```
10  begin
11    SYS.DBMS_OUTPUT.put_line(aiv_text);
12  end pl;
13  /
14  @pe.sql pl
```

Listing 2-7 is my test unit for procedure pl(). I've named it with the same filename as my procedure, except for the extension: I used .prc for the stored procedure and .sql for the anonymous procedure, its test unit. Since this is a wrapper procedure, I'm simply testing the known limits of procedure SYS.DBMS_OUTPUT.put_line(), to make sure pl() is working properly.

Listing 2-7. *A Test Unit for Procedure pl(), pl.sql*

```
01  rem pl.sql
02  rem by Donald J. Bales on 12/15/2006
03  rem Test unit for procedure pl
04
05  begin
06    pl('Test a line of text.');
07    pl('Test a number, such as 1?');
08    pl(1);
09    pl('Test a date, such as 01/01/1980?');
10    pl(to_date('19800101', 'YYYYMMDD'));
11    pl('Test a line <= 255');
12    pl('123456789012345678901234567890123456789012345678901234567890'||
13       '123456789012345678901234567890123456789012345678901234567890'||
14       '123456789012345678901234567890123456789012345678901234567890'||
15       '123456789012345678901234567890123456789012345678901234567890'||
16       '12345678901234567890123456789012345678901234567890123456789012345');
17    pl('Test a line  > 255');
18    pl('123456789012345678901234567890123456789012345678901234567890'||
19       '123456789012345678901234567890123456789012345678901234567890'||
20       '123456789012345678901234567890123456789012345678901234567890'||
21       '123456789012345678901234567890123456789012345678901234567890'||
22       '123456789012345678901234567890123456789012345678901234567890123456');
23    pl('Test a multi-line');
24    pl('123456789012345678901234567890123456789012345678901234567890'||
25       '123456789012345678901234567890123456789012345678901234567890'||chr(10)||
26       '123456789012345678901234567890123456789012345678901234567890'||
27       '123456789012345678901234567890123456789012345678901234567890'||chr(10)||
28       '123456789012345678901234567890123456789012345678901234567890'||
29       '123456789012345678901234567890123456789012345678901234567890');
30  end;
31  /
```

Here's the output from my test unit:

```
SQL> @pl.sql
```

```
Test a line of text.
Test a number, such as 1?
1
Test a date, such as 01/01/1980?
19800101 000000
Test a line <= 255
123456789012345678901234567890123456789012345678901234567890123456789012345678901...
Test a line  > 255
begin
*
ERROR at line 1:
ORA-20000: ORU-10028: line length overflow, limit of 255 chars per line
ORA-06512: at "SYS.DBMS_OUTPUT", line 35
ORA-06512: at "SYS.DBMS_OUTPUT", line 117
ORA-06512: at "BPS.PL", line 11
ORA-06512: at line 15
```

The line of text, number 1, date 01/01/1980, line < 255 characters, and > 255 tests ran, but the last test, multiline, didn't, because the > 255 test threw an exception that was not handled. Let's see how our code can handle this problem.

Nested Blocks

You can, and should when necessary, nest PL/SQL blocks. To nest a PL/SQL block means to embed one or more PL/SQL blocks inside another PL/SQL block. Nesting PL/SQL blocks allows you greater control over your PL/SQL program's execution. You can wrap one or more PL/SQL or SQL statements in their own PL/SQL block, so you can catch an exception that is generated within that block. I call this "blocking" code. Let's look at an example.

An Example of Nesting Blocks

As you saw, the test unit for procedure pl() in Listing 2-7 stopped executing after line 18, because line 18 caused the following error:

```
ORA-20000: ORU-10028: line length overflow, limit of 255 chars per line
```

In Listing 2-8, I've recoded the pl() test unit. This time, I've blocked the lines that I expect to fail, so the program will catch any raised exceptions and continue processing the code all the way to the end of the source code listing.

Listing 2-8. *The New, Improved pl() Test Unit, pl2.sql*

```
01  rem pl2.sql
02  rem by Donald J. Bales on 12/15/2006
03  rem Test unit for procedure pl
04
```

```
05  begin
06    pl('Test a line of text.');
07    pl('Test a number, such as 1?');
08    pl(1);
09    pl('Test a date, such as 01/01/1980?');
10    pl(to_date('19800101', 'YYYYMMDD'));
11    pl('Test a line <= 255');
12    pl('123456789012345678901234567890123456789012345678 90'||
13       '123456789012345678901234567890123456789012345678 90'||
14       '123456789012345678901234567890123456789012345678 90'||
15       '123456789012345678901234567890123456789012345678 90'||
16       '1234567890123456789012345678901234567890123456789012345');
17    pl('Test a line  > 255');
18    begin
19      pl('123456789012345678901234567890123456789012345678 90'||
20         '123456789012345678901234567890123456789012345678 90'||
21         '123456789012345678901234567890123456789012345678 90'||
22         '123456789012345678901234567890123456789012345678 90'||
23         '12345678901234567890123456789012345678901234567890123456');
24    exception
25      when OTHERS then
26        pl(SQLERRM);
27    end;
28    pl('Test a multi-line');
29    begin
30      pl('123456789012345678901234567890123456789012345678 90'||
31         '123456789012345678901234567890123456789012345678 90'||chr(10)||
32         '123456789012345678901234567890123456789012345678 90'||
33         '123456789012345678901234567890123456789012345678 90'||chr(10)||
34         '123456789012345678901234567890123456789012345678 90'||
35         '123456789012345678901234567890123456789012345678 90');
36    exception
37      when OTHERS then
38        pl(SQLERRM);
39    end;
40  end;
41  /
```

The changed lines (highlighted in the listing) are as follows:

Line 18 starts a nested block with the keyword BEGIN around the PL/SQL statement that will actually test > 255.

Line 24 contains a corresponding keyword EXCEPTION in order to create an exception-handling section for the nested PL/SQL block.

Line 25 has the phrase when OTHERS then in order to catch all exceptions that can be generated within the nested block.

On line 26, I once again call procedure pl(), but this time I display the exception error message: SQLERRM.

On line 27, the nested block ends with the keyword END.

Once again, on lines 29 and 36 through 40, I create a nested block around the next PL/SQL statement that I expect to fail.

Let's see the results of these changes:

```
SQL> @pl2.sql
```

```
Test a line of text.
Test a number, such as 1?
1
Test a date, such as 01/01/1980?
19800101 000000
Test a line <= 255
12345678901234567890123456789012345678901234567890123456789012345678901...
Test a line  > 255
ORA-20000: ORU-10028: line length overflow, limit of 255 chars per line
Test a multi-line
ORA-20000: ORU-10028: line length overflow, limit of 255 chars per line

PL/SQL procedure successfully completed.
```

Great! Now my test unit completed successfully, and it reported the errors I expected to see. As we move through the chapters ahead, you'll get plenty of experience nesting PL/SQL blocks.

Rules for Nesting

Here are the rules I employ when it comes to blocking PL/SQL code:

- Block every SQL statement except cursors (you'll learn about cursors in Chapter 5).

- Block any PL/SQL statement where you are converting from one data type to another, or moving a possibly larger character string into a smaller character string variable (you'll learn about variables in Chapter 3).

- Block any PL/SQL statement that you expect will raise an exception.

- Small branches, string, and mud make a good nest.

OK, forget the last item. The important point about these nesting rules is that blocking will enable you to identify the reason for and the location of an exception when it is raised. In turn, that will make your software development easier and the resulting programs more robust.

Packages

In practice, you'll rarely create a stand-alone stored function or procedure. Instead, you'll use a package. What is a package? A package is a means to organize related functions and procedures together, like creating a library, but in PL/SQL jargon the library is called a *package*.

A PL/SQL package has two parts:

- A package specification

- A package body

A package specification (spec) is the public face to the package. It lists any globally accessible constants, cursors, functions, procedures, and variables. By "globally accessible," I mean those procedures, functions, and other items that other PL/SQL programs can access. If you consider a package as a sort of library, then the package spec describes what you can read from that library, while the package body contains the behind-the-scenes code that implements the package spec.

Create a Package Specification

Listing 2-9 is an example of a package spec. It shows the package spec for the package DATES, which is a utility package for date-related constants and functions.

Listing 2-9. *The DATES Package Spec, dates.pks*

```
01  CREATE OR REPLACE PACKAGE DATES AS
02  /*
03  dates.pks
04  by Donald J. Bales on 12/15/2006
05  Additional DATE data type methods.
06  */
07
08  -- The maximum and minimum date values.
09
10  d_MAX                    constant date :=
11    to_date('99991231235959', 'YYYYMMDDHH24MISS');
12  d_MIN                    constant date :=
13    to_date('-47120101', 'SYYYYMMDD');
14
15
16  -- Returns the specified date with the time set to 23:59:59, therefore,
17  -- the end of the day.
18
19  FUNCTION end_of_day(
20  aid_date                 in      date )
21  return                           date;
22
23
```

```
24   -- Returns constant d_MAX. This is useful in SQL statements where the
25   -- constant DATES.d_MAX is not accessible.
26
27   FUNCTION get_max
28   return                                  date;
29
30
31   -- Returns constant d_MIN. This is useful in SQL statements where the
32   -- constant DATES.d_MIN is not accessible.
33
34   FUNCTION get_min
35   return                                  date;
36
37
38   -- Text-based help for this package. "set serveroutput on" in SQL*Plus.
39
40   PROCEDURE help;
41
42
43   -- Returns a randomly generated date that exists between the years specified.
44
45   FUNCTION random(
46   ain_starting_year           in      number,
47   ain_ending_year             in      number )
48   return                              date;
49
50
51   -- Returns the specified date with the time set to 00:00:00, therefore, the
52   -- start of the day.
53
54   FUNCTION start_of_day(
55   aid_date                    in      date )
56   return                              date;
57
58
59   -- Test unit for this package.
60
61   PROCEDURE test;
62
63
64   end DATES;
65   /
66   @se.sql DATES
```

The DDL syntax used to create the package spec in Listing 2-9 is as follows:

```
CREATE [OR REPLACE] PACKAGE <package_name> AS
-- one or more: constant, cursor, function, procedure, or variable declarations
END <package_name>;
```

where `<package_name>` is the name of the package you're creating.

Not much to a package spec? Sure there is. Now, instead of using the DDL `CREATE FUNCTION` or `CREATE PROCEDURE`, you'll use the keywords `FUNCTION` and `PROCEDURE` for each PL/SQL method you want to declare globally.

Let's take a look at the package spec in Listing 2-9:

Line 1 uses the DDL keywords to `CREATE` a stored `PACKAGE` specification.

Lines 10 and 12 declare two global constants (ones available to any other PL/SQL stored procedure), d_MAX and d_MIN, which are the current maximum and minimum date values supported by Oracle.

Lines 19, 27, 34, 45, and 54 declare five date functions. Please note that these are only declarations; they have no code. The code will be found in the package body.

Lines 40 and 61 declare two "helper" procedures. We will discuss these helper procedures in great length in Chapters 7, 8, and 9.

Line 64 ends the `PACKAGE` declaration with the keyword `END`.

On line 65, I tell Oracle to store and compile the package spec.

Line 66 calls a helper SQL script to show any errors.

You may also have noticed that I took the time to document the purpose of every declaration in the package spec. You should do the same. Documenting as you go is one of the major characteristics of a professional PL/SQL programmer.

It's Your Turn to Create a Package Specification

Do you remember the function `to_number_or_null()` in Listing 2-2? Now you will create a package called `NUMBERS` that has that as one of its methods. Mimic what I just showed you as you follow these steps:

1. Write the DDL to create a package spec called `NUMBERS`.

2. Save your DDL script as `numbers.pks`.

3. Execute your DDL script in SQL*Plus: `SQL> @numbers.pks`.

4. Type `desc numbers` at the SQL*Plus prompt to verify that your package spec exists.

As usual, if you get any errors, work on your script until you hate me, or figure out what's wrong so you can compile the script successfully. Remember to use the script in Listing 2-9 as a model.

Listing 2-10 shows my solution.

Listing 2-10. *The NUMBERS Package Spec, numbers.pks*

```
01  create or replace package NUMBERS as
02  /*
03  numbers.pks
04  by Donald J. Bales on 12/15/2006
05  A utility package for the data type NUMBER
06  */
07
08  /*
09  Returns the passed varchar2 as a number if it represents a number,
10  otherwise, it returns NULL
11  */
12  FUNCTION to_number_or_null (
13  aiv_number                      in      varchar2 )
14  return                                  number;
15
16  end NUMBERS;
17  /
18  @se.sql
```

There's no way to test the package spec, because there's no code yet. The code goes in the package body.

Create a Package Body

A package body is the implementation for a package spec. It must contain the code for any functions or procedures declared in its corresponding package spec. In addition, the body can also contain any constant, cursor, function, procedure, or variable that should be accessible within the package body (that is, not publicly accessible). Let's take a look at the corresponding package body for package DATES.

I'm about to show you a package body that has a lot of PL/SQL code that we haven't covered yet. Don't worry too much about the code itself. You won't understand it all now, but you'll be able to understand it after finishing this book. What you need to take away from this example is the package body structure, which is also a PL/SQL block structure. So go get a cup or glass of your favorite caffeine beverage, and then look at Listing 2-11.

Listing 2-11. *The DATES Package Body, dates.pkb*

```
001  CREATE OR REPLACE PACKAGE BODY DATES AS
002  /*
003  dates.pkb
004  by Donald J. Bales on 12/15/2006
005  Additional DATE data type methods
006  */
007
008
```

```
009   FUNCTION end_of_day(
010   aid_date                      in      date )
011   return                                date is
012
013   begin
014    return to_date(to_char(aid_date, 'SYYYYMMDD')||'235959',
015      'SYYYYMMDDHH24MISS');
016   end end_of_day;
017
018
019   FUNCTION get_max
020   return                                date is
021
022   begin
023    return d_MAX;
024   end get_max;
025
026
027   FUNCTION get_min
028   return                                date is
029
030   begin
031    return d_MIN;
032   end get_min;
033
034
035   FUNCTION random(
036   ain_starting_year             in      number,
037   ain_ending_year               in      number )
038   return                                date is
039
040   d_random                              date;
041   n_day                                 number;
042   n_month                               number;
043   n_year                                number;
044
045   begin
046     n_year    := round(DBMS_RANDOM.value(
047       ain_starting_year, ain_ending_year), 0);
048     --pl('n_year='||n_year);
049     loop
050       n_month := round(DBMS_RANDOM.value(1, 12), 0);
051       --pl('n_month='||n_month);
052       n_day   := round(DBMS_RANDOM.value(1, 31), 0);
053       --pl('n_day='||n_day);
054       begin
```

```
055        d_random := to_date(lpad(to_char(n_year),  4, '0')||
056                            lpad(to_char(n_month), 2, '0')||
057                            lpad(to_char(n_day),   2, '0'),
058                            'YYYYMMDD');
059        exit;
060      exception
061        when OTHERS then
062          if SQLCODE <> -1839 then
063            pl(SQLERRM);
064          --else
065          -- pl('29-31');
066          end if;
067      end;
068    end loop;
069    return d_random;
070 end random;
071
072
073 FUNCTION start_of_day(
074 aid_date                    in     date )
075 return                             date is
076
077 begin
078  return trunc(aid_date);
079 end start_of_day;
080
081
082 -- Write up the help text here in this help method
083 PROCEDURE help is
084
085 begin
086 --   123456789012345678901234567890123456789012345678901234567890
087   pl('============================= PACKAGE =============================');
088   pl(chr(9));
089   pl('DATES');
090   pl(chr(9));
091   pl('---------------------------- CONSTANTS ----------------------------');
092   pl(chr(9));
093   pl('d_MAX');
094   pl(chr(9)||'Represents the maximum value for the DATE data type.');
095   pl('d_MIN');
096   pl(chr(9)||'Represents the minimum value for the DATE data type.');
097   pl(chr(9));
098   pl('---------------------------- FUNCTIONS ----------------------------');
099   pl(chr(9));
100   pl('DATES.end_of_day(');
101   pl('aid_date                    in     date)');
```

```
102   pl('return                                  date;');
103   pl(chr(9)||'Returns the passed date with the time portion set to the end ');
104   pl(chr(9)||'of the day:');
105   pl(chr(9)||'23:59:59 (HH24:MI:SS).');
106   pl(chr(9));
107   pl('DATES.get_max( )');
108   pl('return                                  date;');
109   pl(chr(9)||'Returns the constant DATES.d_MAX.');
110   pl(chr(9));
111   pl('DATES.get_mim( )');
112   pl('return                                  date;');
113   pl(chr(9)||'Returns the constant DATES.d_MIN.');
114   pl(chr(9));
115   pl('DATES.random(');
116   pl('ain_starting_year            in     number,');
117   pl('ain_ending_year              in     number)');
118   pl('return                                  date;');
119   pl(chr(9)||'Returns a random date that exists between the specified years.');
120   pl(chr(9));
121   pl('DATES.start_of_day(');
122   pl('aid_date                     in     date)');
123   pl('return                                  date;');
124   pl(chr(9)||'Returns the passed date with the time portion set to the start');
125   pl(chr(9)||'of the day:');
126   pl(chr(9)||'00:00:00 (HH24:MI:SS).');
127   pl(chr(9));
128   pl('---------------------------- PROCEDURES ----------------------------');
129   pl(chr(9));
130   pl('DATES.help( );');
131   pl(chr(9)||'Displays this help text if set serveroutput is on.');
132   pl(chr(9));
133   pl('DATES.test( );');
134   pl(chr(9)||'Built-in test unit. It will report success or error for each');
135   pl(chr(9)||'test if set');
136   pl(chr(9)||'serveroutput is on.');
137   pl(chr(9));
138 end help;
139
140
141 PROCEDURE test is
142
143 d_date                          date;
144
145 begin
146   pl('============================ PACKAGE ============================');
147   pl(chr(9));
148   pl('DATES');
```

```
149    pl(chr(9));
150    pl('1. Testing constants d_MIN and d_MAX');
151    if d_MIN < d_MAX then
152     pl('SUCCESS');
153    else
154      pl('ERROR: d_MIN is not less than d_MAX');
155    end if;
156
157    pl('2. Testing end_of_day()');
158    if to_char(end_of_day(SYSDATE), 'HH24MISS') = '235959' then
159     pl('SUCCESS');
160    else
161      pl('ERROR: end_of_day is not 23:59:59');
162    end if;
163
164    pl('3. Testing get_max()');
165    if get_max() = d_MAX then
166     pl('SUCCESS');
167    else
168      pl('ERROR: get_max() is not equal to d_MAX');
169    end if;
170
171    pl('4. Testing get_min()');
172    if get_min() = d_MIN then
173     pl('SUCCESS');
174    else
175      pl('ERROR: get_min() is not equal to d_MIN');
176    end if;
177
178    pl('5. Testing random() 1000 times');
179    for i in 1..1000 loop
180      d_date := random(1, 9999);
181      --pl(to_char(d_date, 'YYYY-MM-DD HH24:MI:SS'));
182    end loop;
183    pl('SUCCESS');
184
185    pl('6. Testing start_of_day()');
186    if to_char(start_of_day(SYSDATE), 'HH24MISS') = '000000' then
187     pl('SUCCESS');
188    else
189      pl('ERROR: start_of_day is not 00:00:00');
190    end if;
191  end test;
192
193
194  end DATES;
195  /
196  @be.sql DATES
```

The DDL syntax used to create the package body in Listing 2-11 is as follows:

```
CREATE [OR REPLACE] PACKAGE BODY <package_name> AS
-- one or more constant, cursor, or variable declarations
-- one or more function, or procedure implementations
[BEGIN]
-- you can code a PL/SQL block called an initialization section that is
-- executed only once, when the package is first instantiated into memory
[EXCEPTION]
-- you can code an exception-handling section for the initialization section
END <package_name>;
```

where <package_name> is the name of the package body you're creating.

Did you notice the two optional sections? If you have some initialization code that you want to run the first time a package is loaded into memory, you can use the keyword BEGIN to start an initialization section. And if you want an exception-handling section for your initialization section, you can add it by using the keyword EXCEPTION. This is classic PL/SQL block structure.

Your implementations of functions and procedures are actually embedded functions and procedures in the declaration section of a PL/SQL block! Any constant, cursor, or variable that you declare in the declaration section of the package body is accessible to all the declared functions and procedures in that section, but not globally to other stored procedures. Only the items you declared in the package spec are accessible to other stored procedures.

As I noted at the beginning of this section, Listing 2-11 contains a lot of code that we haven't yet discussed, so I'll leave its explanation for later chapters.

Note In Listing 2-11, if I had declared any package body (or instance) functions or procedures—ones not accessible outside the package body—I would take time to document the purpose of the instance declaration in the package body. You should do the same. Once again, I declare that professional PL/SQL programmers document as they go.

It's Your Turn to Create a Package Body

You should already have a package spec created for the NUMBERS package, as in Listing 2-10. Now it's time to create the corresponding package body. It's almost like the package spec, except for the keyword BODY in the DDL and the function to_number_or_null()'s implementation, as in Listing 2-2. Create your package body by following these steps:

1. Write the DDL to create a package body called NUMBERS.

2. Save your DDL script as numbers.pkb.

3. Execute your DDL script in SQL*Plus: SQL> @numbers.pkb.

4. Test your function using a SELECT statement, just as you did way back in the section on functions. This time, however, you'll prefix the function name with the name of your package.

Again, if you get any errors, work on your script until you figure out what's wrong so you can compile the script successfully. Listing 2-12 shows my solution.

Listing 2-12. *The NUMBERS Package Body, numbers.pkb*

```
01  create or replace package body NUMBERS as
02  /*
03  numbers.pkb
04  by Donald J. Bales on 12/15/2006
05  A utility package for the data type NUMBER
06  */
07
08  FUNCTION to_number_or_null (
09  aiv_number                   in      varchar2 )
10  return                               number is
11  begin
12    return to_number(aiv_number);
13  exception
14    when OTHERS then
15      return NULL;
16  end to_number_or_null;
17
18  end NUMBERS;
19  /
20  @be.sql
```

Notice that on line 14 of Listing 2-12, I've changed the function implementation so it uses the named exception OTHERS instead of INVALID_NUMBER. I did so because when I tested it, I got the following error:

```
SQL> select numbers.to_number_or_null('A') from dual;
```

```
select numbers.to_number_or_null('A') from dual
       *
ERROR at line 1:
ORA-06502: PL/SQL: numeric or value error: character to number conversion error
ORA-06512: at "BPS.NUMBERS", line 12
```

So rather than pull my hair out just because PL/SQL treats a stored function and a packaged function differently, I changed the code to use OTHERS and tested it again:

```
SQL> select numbers.to_number_or_null('A') from dual;
```

```
NUMBERS.TO_NUMBER_OR_NULL('A')
------------------------------
```

Now, why it failed, I don't know, nor do I care. What I'm interested in is a function that solves my business problem and also passes my test unit. This problem highlights the need for test plans and test units that can be run every time code is changed in order to verify that your solutions continue to work properly. Thank goodness that's the subject of Chapter 8.

Benefits of Using Packages

As I mentioned earlier, anything declared in a package spec can be seen by any username that has execute privileges on the package. Package specs also reduce dependency invalidation issues. What does that mean?

Say that procedure1 calls function1 and is called by procedure2. Then if you change function1, function1 becomes invalid, and so do procedure1 and procedure2. This means you would need to recompile all three PL/SQL programs. This chain of dependency can be broken by using packages.

Now suppose that you use packages: package1.procedure1 calls package2.function1, and it is called by package3.procedure2. If you change the package implementation, or body, of package2.function1, it will not cause the invalidation of the function, nor any dependent PL/SQL blocks. You will cause dependent PL/SQL blocks to be invalidated only if you change the package spec.

Summary

Table 2-1 shows a side-by-side comparison of the syntax used for the various types of PL/SQL blocks covered in this chapter. The point here is that PL/SQL code always exists in a PL/SQL block, and that PL/SQL blocks are quite consistent in their structure. Even nested PL/SQL blocks are consistent with the ones shown in Table 2-1.

Table 2-1. *A Comparison of PL/SQL Block Syntax*

ANONYMOUS [DECLARE	CREATE FUNCTION	CREATE PROCEDURE	CREATE PACKAGE	CREATE PACKAGE BODY
	[parameters]	[parameters]		
	RETURN			
declaration section]	declaration section	declaration section	declaration section	declaration section
BEGIN	BEGIN	BEGIN		[BEGIN
executable section	executable section	executable section		executable section]
[EXCEPTION	[EXCEPTION	[EXCEPTION		[EXCEPTION
exception-handling section]	exception-handling section]	exception-handling section]		exception-handling section]
END;	END;	END;	END;	END;
/	/	/	/	/

Now that you have a firm understanding of the block structure of PL/SQL, you're ready to move on to the next step: learning about PL/SQL data types and variables. So clear your head, because next we're going to play with your memory. "Now where did my old (man or lady) go, man?"

CHAPTER 3

■ ■ ■

Now Where Did I Put That?

OK, now you're going to hear me start repeating myself. Now you're going to hear me start repeating myself. It's not necessarily because I'm old, although that may have something to do with it, but rather because I introduced some of the topics covered in this chapter in Chapters 1 and 2.

Have you ever noticed that when you try to figure something out you pull out a piece of paper and start jotting down things (OK, maybe you're more of a geek and open up Excel)? For example, if you want to figure out how much it will cost for you to buy every copy of this book so you can burn them, you'll need to know the price, less the volume discount, the cost for shipping, the cost to burn them, and the toxic waste disposal fee. That's a lot of variables to keep track of, and that's what this chapter is all about: how you keep track of variables in a PL/SQL program.

Before this chapter ends, you'll learn about PL/SQL data types, variables, scope, types, and parameters. So go get yourself a snack to keep your brain fueled (but no powdered sugar doughnuts—the sugar gets all over the keyboard), and let's get started.

PL/SQL Data Types

Given that PL/SQL is the Procedural Language extension for SQL, you would think that it supports and uses the same data types as SQL does for the database, right? Right! It turns out that is almost the case, but not quite. PL/SQL can handle any database data type and also some data types of its own.

Do you remember the "Data Definition Language (DDL)" section in Chapter 1? There, I talked about the three basic data types that you will use all the time: character (VARCHAR2), numeric (NUMBER), and time (DATE). Here's how those types work in PL/SQL:

VARCHAR2: Just as in the database, most of the time, you'll work with character strings in PL/SQL using the data type VARCHAR2. However, unlike the database VARCHAR2 type, a PL/SQL VARCHAR2 can hold as many as 32,767 characters, whereas the database type holds up to 4,000.

NUMBER: Just as in the database, most of the time, you'll work with numbers in PL/SQL using the data type NUMBER. And, just like the database, PL/SQL has additional numeric data types available. For example, you can use the type PLS_INTEGER, which has an integer range from −2147483648 to 2147483647. PLS_INTEGER also uses the computer's hardware to do its calculations instead of library routines, so it's faster. However, until you're comfortable writing stored procedures with PL/SQL, I don't think you need to bother with them. You can always take a look at them in Oracle's *PL/SQL User's Guide and Reference* in case you think, "He's messing with me."

DATE: Just as in the database, most of the time, you'll work with dates and times in PL/SQL using data type DATE. Like NUMBER, PL/SQL has additional time-related data types. Check them out in Oracle's reference once you're up and coding confidently.

PL/SQL also has a BOOLEAN data type that allows you to store the logical values FALSE or TRUE (you find it irritating when I say false and true instead or true and false, don't you?) in a variable. SQL has no equivalent. So you can pass BOOLEAN values between methods and use them as variables in your PL/SQL program units, but you can't store them in the database.

Of course, there are many more Oracle SQL and PL/SQL data types, but the ones we just covered are the ones you'll use most often.

Variables

Variables are named temporary storage locations that support a particular data type in your PL/SQL program. You must declare them in the declaration section of a PL/SQL block.

By "named," I mean that you give each of your variables a name. They are temporary, because the values you assign to variables typically exist only in memory (or are accessible in memory) while the PL/SQL block in which they are declared is executing. They are storage locations in memory. And they are declared to store a particular data type so PL/SQL knows how to create, store, access, and destroy them.

Let's start by looking at how to name your variables.

Variable Naming

Like a SQL or database data type, PL/SQL variables must follow the identifier naming rules:

- A variable name must be less than 31 characters in length.

- A variable name must start with an uppercase or lowercase ASCII letter: *A–Z* or *a–z*. PL/SQL is not case-sensitive.

- A variable name may be composed of 1 letter, followed by up to 29 letters, numbers, or the underscore (_) character. You can also use the number (#) and dollar sign ($) characters.

As a matter of fact, all PL/SQL identifiers, like stored function and procedure names, must follow these naming rules!

I like to use the following conventions when naming variables:

- Use the two-character prefix for each data type, as defined in Table 3-1.

- Make its purpose obvious. If the variable will hold a value from the database, use the same name as in the database, but with the appropriate prefix.

Table 3-1. *My PL/SQL Variable Naming Prefixes*

Prefix	Data Type
c_	CURSOR
d_	DATE

Table 3-1. *My PL/SQL Variable Naming Prefixes*

Prefix	Data Type
n_	NUMBER
r_	ROW
t_	TABLE
v_	VARCHAR2

For example, if I were to declare variables to hold data from the columns in the AUTHOR table, I would use the following identifier names:

- n_id

- v_name

- d_birth_date

- v_gender

The advantage of using these prefixes is that you'll always know the variable's data type and its scope. (We'll cover scope shortly.) In addition, since you made the name obvious, you'll also know where it comes from or where it's going.

By "obvious," I mean that you shouldn't use a synonym for an already existing identifier. For example, don't create variables named d_born, d_date_of_birth, and d_bday for a value from the birth_date column in the database. Why? All those name variations will just make what you're referring to unclear, and all professional PL/SQL programmers want to make it absolutely clear what is going on in their code!

Now that you know how to name your variables, let's look at how to declare them.

Variable Declarations

To declare a variable, type the variable name (identifier) followed by the data type definition, as you would use in SQL, terminated by a semicolon (;). The data type definition is the name of the data type, possibly followed by length constraints in a set of parentheses. For example, to declare variables to hold the data from columns in the AUTHOR table, I would code the following in a PL/SQL block's declaration section:

```
declare

  n_id                          number;
  v_name                        varchar2(100);
  d_birth_date                  date;
  v_gender                      varchar2(30);

begin
  ...
end;
```

The DDL syntax used to declare the preceding variables is as follows:

```
<variable_name>   <data_type>;
```

where `<variable_name>` is the name of the variable (or identifier), and `<data_type>` is one of the PL/SQL data types.

You'll notice that if you get rid of the data type prefixes, variable declarations look just like the SQL in the table definition for AUTHOR in Chapter 1, and that's the whole point. They should! It wouldn't make much sense to declare varchar2 variables that are smaller than the ones in the database, because that could cause an error. And it doesn't make much sense to name them differently than what they're named in the database, because that would just make things confusing. That's why I use those prefixes shown in Table 3-1.

Most of the time, you'll end up declaring variables that temporarily hold values from or that are going into the database, and PL/SQL has a keyword for simplifying just that situation: %TYPE.

Variable Anchors

"Anchors away my boys, anchors away . . ." An *anchor* is a term coined by Steven Feuerstein (high demigod of PL/SQL), which refers to the use of the keyword %TYPE to "anchor" a PL/SQL data type definition in a PL/SQL variable to the corresponding SQL data type definition of a column in a table. I've always liked the term *anchor*, so I use it whenever I talk about the keyword %TYPE.

Here's an example of our PL/SQL variables for the table AUTHOR declared using column anchors (the %TYPE keyword):

```
n_id                          AUTHOR.id%TYPE;
v_name                        AUTHOR.name%TYPE;
d_birth_date                  AUTHOR.birth_date%TYPE;
v_gender                      AUTHOR.gender%TYPE;
```

The syntax used to declare the preceding variables is as follows:

```
<variable_name>   <table_name>.<column_name>%TYPE;
```

where `<variable_name>` is the name of the variable (or identifier), `<table_name>` is the name of the table for which to anchor the data type, and `<column_name>` is the name of the column for which to anchor the data type.

Programming in PL/SQL just keeps getting better, doesn't it? By using anchors, you now know that the variables use the same data types and sizes as the table that will be the source of, or permanent storage for, each variable's value. Regardless, I still use those silly data type prefixes in order to remind me of the variables' data types.

Now that you've seen how to declare variables, let's talk about how to assign values to them.

Variable Assignments

To assign a literal value to a variable in PL/SQL, you use the assignment operator, which is a colon (`:`) followed by an equal sign (`=`): `:=`. For example, I can make the following assignments:

```
declare
  ...
begin

  n_id          := 400;
  v_name        := 'STEVEN FEUERSTEIN';
  d_birth_date := to_date('19800101', 'YYYYMMDD');
  v_gender      := 'M';

end;
```

What do I mean by "a literal value"? OK, let's back up a second:

- A numeric literal is just a number without any formatting, such as 400.

- A character literal is just a string of characters enclosed in a pair of tick (') characters (or single quotes), such as 'STEVEN FEUERSTEIN'.

There is no such thing as a date literal. You can assign a character literal and hope the format you decided to use matches the current NLS_DATE_FORMAT (automatic type conversion—dangerous, very dangerous), or you can use the built-in function:

```
to_date(aiv_date in varchar2. aiv_date_format in varchar2)
```

A second way to assign a value to a variable is to use an INTO clause in a SQL SELECT statement. Here's an example:

```
select id,
       name,
       birth_date,
       gender
into   n_id
       v_name,
       d_birth_date,
       v_gender
from   AUTHOR
where  AUTHOR.id = (
  select PUBLICATION.id
  from   PUBLICATION
  where  title = 'ORACLE PL/SQL PROGRAMMING');
```

In this example, the PL/SQL keyword INTO moves the values from the SELECT statement's column list into the corresponding PL/SQL variables. We'll talk a lot more about this in Chapter 4.

By default, variables are uninitialized and hence are NULL. You can initialize them to a value when they are declared by simply assigning them a value in the declaration section. For example, you could initialize the AUTHOR variables as follows:

```
declare

   n_id          AUTHOR.id%TYPE          := 400;
   v_name        AUTHOR.name%TYPE        := 'STEVEN FEUERSTEIN';
   d_birth_date  AUTHOR.birth_date%TYPE  := to_date('19800101', 'YYYYMMDD');
   v_gender      AUTHOR.gender%TYPE      := NULL;

begin
   ...
end;
```

The syntax used to declare the preceding variables is as follows:

```
<variable_name>  <table_name>.<column_name>%TYPE := <value>;
```

where `<variable_name>` is the name of the variable (or identifier), `<table_name>` is the name of the table for which to anchor the data type, `<column_name>` is the name of the column for which to anchor the data type, and `<value>` is the initial value for the variable. But what exactly is NULL?

NULL Value

The term *NULL value* is a bit of a misnomer. The keyword NULL means I don't know! The keyword NULL means you don't know! So how can there be something such as a NULL value? Let's further define NULL:

- NULL is not equal to anything, not even NULL.

- NULL is not less than or greater than anything else, not even NULL.

- NULL means nothing knows, not even NULL.

You can test for NULL values in a SQL statement or PL/SQL code by using one of two phrases:

```
is NULL
is not NULL
```

Although the PL/SQL compiler may let you, you cannot use a logical operator with NULL, like this:

```
= NULL
```

or this:

```
<> NULL
```

and get the logical results you're seeking.

You must use is NULL and is not NULL. Remember this lesson, grasshopper, and you will save yourself many hours of troubleshooting erratic behavior.

It's Your Turn to Declare Variables

Now that you're familiar with the declaration of variables, let's put you to work. Create an anonymous PL/SQL procedure where you declare variables using anchors, and with default values, for the columns in the WORKER_T table. Follow these steps:

1. Code your anonymous procedure.

2. Save it with the filename worker_t_variables.sql.

3. Execute your script in SQL*Plus: SQL> @worker_t_variables.sql.

Listing 3-1 is my solution for this problem.

Listing 3-1. *An Anonymous PL/SQL Procedure with Variable Declarations, worker_t_variables.sql*

```
01  declare
02  n_id               WORKER_T.id%TYPE              := 1;
03  n_worker_type_id   WORKER_T.worker_type_id%TYPE := 3;
04  v_external_id      WORKER_T.external_id%TYPE     := '6305551212';
05  v_first_name       WORKER_T.first_name%TYPE      := 'JANE';
06  v_middle_name      WORKER_T.middle_name%TYPE     := 'E';
07  v_last_name        WORKER_T.last_name%TYPE       := 'DOE';
08  v_name             WORKER_T.name%TYPE            := 'JANEDOEE';
09  d_birth_date       WORKER_T.birth_date%TYPE      :=
10    to_date('19800101', 'YYYYMMDD');
11  v_gender_id        WORKER_T.gender_id%TYPE       := 1;
12  begin
13    null;
14  end;
15  /
```

Let's break Listing 3-1 down, line by line:

Line 1 uses the keyword DECLARE to start an anonymous PL/SQL procedure.

Lines 2 through 11 declare variables to hold the contents of the columns from the WORKER_T table.

Line 12 starts the executable section of the procedure with the keyword BEGIN.

On line 13, I coded a no operation (NULL) so the block will compile.

Line 14 ends the procedure with the keyword END.

On line 15, I tell Oracle to compile and execute the procedure.

Now that you're an expert at declaring variables, let's take a look at when they are in scope.

Scope

No, I'm not talking about the mouthwash! In this context, *scope* refers to when a declared item can be seen by another PL/SQL block. And yes, I'm not just talking about variables here; I'm talking about any kind of declared item: a constant, cursor, function, procedure, or variable.

Scope Rules

The following is a list of rules for scope. As you go through the list, it may be helpful for you to examine Figure 3-1.

- Any item declared in the declaration section of a function or procedure is visible only within the same function or procedure.

- Any item declared in the declaration section of a package body is visible only within any other item in the same package body.

- Any item declared in a package specification is visible to any other stored function, stored procedure, and package for which the owner of the calling method has execute privileges.

- It's better to use mouthwash after brushing your teeth.

Figure 3-1. *Where an item is declared determines its scope.*

Listings 3-2 and 3-3 are a package spec and package body, respectively, to test scope. Listing 3-2 declares a global function, procedure, and variable in the package spec. Listing 3-3 declares an instance function, a procedure, and a variable. And, in the function and procedure implementations, I've declared local variables.

Listing 3-2. *A Package Spec to Test Scope, scopes.pks*

```
01  create or replace package SCOPES as
02  /*
03  scopes.pks
04  by Donald J. Bales on 12/15/2006
05  A package to test scope
06  */
07
08  -- Here's a global variable declaration
09  gv_scope                        varchar2(40) :=
10    'I''m a global (or package spec) variable';
11
12  -- Here's a global (or package spec) function declaration
13  FUNCTION my_scope_is_package_spec
14  return                          varchar2;
15
16  -- Here's a global (or package spec) procedure declaration
17  PROCEDURE my_scope_is_package_spec;
18
19
20  end SCOPES;
21  /
22  @se.sql SCOPES
```

Listing 3-3. *A Package Body to Test Scope, scope.pkb*

```
01  create or replace package body SCOPES as
02  /*
03  scopes.pkb
04  by Donald J. Bales on 12/15/2006
05  A package to test scope
06  */
07
08  -- Here's an instance (or package body) variable declaration
09  iv_scope                        varchar2(40) :=
10    'I''m an instance (or package body) variable';
11
12
13  -- Here's an instance (or package body) function declaration
14  FUNCTION my_scope_is_package_body
15  return                          varchar2 is
16  v_answer_1                      varchar2(3) := 'Yes';
17  begin
18    return v_answer_1;
```

```
19  end my_scope_is_package_body;
20
21
22  -- Here's a global (or package spec) function declaration
23  FUNCTION my_scope_is_package_spec
24  return                          varchar2 is
25  v_answer_2                      varchar2(3) := 'Yes';
26  begin
27    return v_answer_2;
28  end my_scope_is_package_spec;
29
30
31  -- Here's an instance (or package body) procedure declaration
32  PROCEDURE my_scope_is_package_body is
33  v_answer_3                      varchar2(3) := 'Yes';
34  begin
35    pl(v_answer_3);
36  end my_scope_is_package_body;
37
38
39  -- Here's a global (or package spec) procedure declaration
40  PROCEDURE my_scope_is_package_spec is
41  v_answer_4                      varchar2(3) := 'Yes';
42  begin
43    pl(v_answer_4);
44  end my_scope_is_package_spec;
45
46
47  end SCOPES;
48  /
49  @se.sql SCOPES
```

Take some time to look over the two code listings. At this point, you should be able to understand the PL/SQL block structure of the package and the methods declared and implemented in it, along with the variable declarations. The point now is to understand when a given function, procedure, or variable is in scope.

Listing 3-4 is an anonymous PL/SQL procedure that I wrote as a test unit for package SCOPES, specifically to help you understand when a declared item is in scope.

Listing 3-4. *A Test Unit for Package SCOPES, scopes.sql*

```
01  rem scopes.sql
02  rem by Donald J. Bales on 12/15/2006
03  rem Test unit for package scopes
04
05  declare
06
07  -- ANONYMOUS PL/SQL BLOCK'S DECLARATION SECTION --
```

```
08
09  v_scope                              varchar2(40) :=
10    'I''m a local variable';
11
12  -- This is a local (or embedded) function
13  FUNCTION my_scope_is_local
14  return                               varchar2 is
15  v_answer_0                           varchar2(3) := 'Yes';
16  begin
17    return v_answer_0;
18  end my_scope_is_local;
19
20  -- This is a local (or embedded) procedure
21  PROCEDURE my_scope_is_local is
22  v_answer                             varchar2(3) := 'Yes';
23  begin
24    pl(v_answer);
25  end my_scope_is_local;
26
27  begin
28
29  -- ANONYMOUS PL/SQL BLOCK'S EXECUTABLE SECTION --
30
31    pl('Can I access my local variable?');
32    pl(v_scope);
33    pl('Can I access SCOPES'' global variable?');
34    pl(SCOPES.gv_scope);
35    pl('Can I access SCOPES'' instance variable?');
36    --pl(SCOPES.iv_scope);
37    pl('No!');
38
39    pl('Can I access my local function?');
40    pl(my_scope_is_local());
41    pl('Can I access SCOPES'' global function?');
42    pl(SCOPES.my_scope_is_global());
43    pl('Can I access SCOPES'' instance function?');
44    --pl(SCOPES.my_scope_is_instance());
45    pl('No!');
46
47    pl('Can I access my local procedure?');
48    my_scope_is_local();
49    pl('Can I access SCOPES'' global procedure?');
50    SCOPES.my_scope_is_global();
51    pl('Can I access SCOPES'' instance procedure?');
52    --SCOPES.my_scope_is_instance();
53    pl('No!');
54
```

```
55  end;
56  /
```

When I execute `scopes.sql` from Listing 3-4, I get the following output from SQL*Plus:

```
SQL> @scopes.sql
```

```
Can I access my local variable?
I'm a local variable
Can I access SCOPES' global variable?
I'm a global (or package spec) variable
Can I access SCOPES' instance variable?
No!
Can I access my local function?
Yes
Can I access SCOPES' global function?
        Can function my_scope_is_global see variable iv_scope?
        I'm an instance (or package body) variable
Yes
Can I access SCOPES' instance function?
No!
Can I access my local procedure?
Yes
Can I access SCOPES' global procedure?
        Can procedure my_scope_is_global see variable iv_scope?
        I'm an instance (or package body) variable
Yes
Can I access SCOPES' instance procedure?
No!

PL/SQL procedure successfully completed.
```

If you examine all three code listings and the SQL*Plus output carefully, you'll see that you can access any item:

- Declared in a package specification, granted you have access to it

- Declared in a package body, if the calling declared item also exists in the same package body

- Declared in a function or procedure, if you're trying to access it from the same function or procedure

Perhaps you would like to try testing the scope rules yourself?

It's Your Turn to Scope Things Out

There's nothing like hacking to see how things work. So put on your hacker's hat and take the anonymous procedure in `scopes.sql` for a ride.

1. Compile `scopes.pks`.

2. Compile `scopes.pkb`.

3. Try alternatively removing the single-line comments characters on lines 36, 44, and 52 in `scopes.sql`, and then execute the script.

Each time you try to access a declared item that is out of scope, PL/SQL will let you know exactly where the coding problem exists in you source code.

Now that you have a firm understanding of scope, let's step it up a notch.

Types

No discussion of declaring variables would be complete, nor would any programming language itself be complete, without mentioning arrays. PL/SQL supports three kinds of arrays, or as they are known in PL/SQL jargon, *collections*. I will discuss only one kind here: *associative arrays*. Originally called PL/SQL tables, associative arrays provide you with the means to create a single-dimension array. Associative arrays can be based on almost any data type. However, you'll typically use one of the data types we've already covered.

Table Types

By table TYPEs, I'm not referring to SQL tables that are used to permanently store data, but PL/SQL tables (or associative arrays), which are used to temporarily store data in memory. Listing 3-5 is an anonymous PL/SQL procedure that demonstrates how you declare an associative array (or PL/SQL table). You'll see that declaring an associative array consists of two steps:

1. Declare the new TYPE.

2. Declare a new variable of that TYPE.

Listing 3-5. *Declaring a PL/SQL Table with a Column Data Type, table.sql*

```
01  rem table.sql
02  rem by Don Bales on 12/15/2006
03  rem An anonymous PL/SQL procedure to demonstrate
04  rem the elementary use of PL/SQL tables
05
06  declare
07
08  TYPE name_table IS TABLE OF WORKER_T.name%TYPE
09  INDEX BY BINARY_INTEGER;
10
11  t_name                          name_table;
12
13  n_name                          binary_integer;
14
15  begin
```

```
16    t_name(1)  := 'DOE, JOHN';
17    t_name(10) := 'DOE, JANE';
18
19    pl(t_name(1));
20    pl(t_name(10));
21    pl('There are '||t_name.count()||' elements.');
22    n_name := t_name.first();
23    pl('The first element is '||n_name||'.');
24    n_name := t_name.next(n_name);
25    pl('The next element is '||n_name||'.');
26    n_name := t_name.last();
27    pl('The last element is '||n_name||'.');
28    n_name := t_name.prior(n_name);
29    pl('The prior element is '||n_name||'.');
30    if t_name.exists(1) then
31      pl('Element 1 exists.');
32    end if;
33    pl('I''m deleting element 10');
34    t_name.delete(10);
35    pl('There are '||t_name.count()||' elements.');
36    if not t_name.exists(10) then
37      pl('Element 10 no longer exists.');
38    end if;
39    pl('There are '||t_name.count()||' elements.');
40    pl('I''m deleting all elements');
41    t_name.delete();
42    pl('There are '||t_name.count()||' elements.');
43  end;
44  /
```

The syntax used in Listing 3-5 on lines 8 and 9 to declare the associative array is as follows:

```
TYPE <plsql_table_type_name> IS TABLE OF <data_type>
INDEX BY BINARY_INTEGER;
```

where <plsql_table_type_name> is the name you are giving to the new PL/SQL table TYPE, and <data_type> is the data type to use for the elements in the table (or associative array).

Then, on line 11, I declare an associative array based on the new type with the following syntax:

```
<variable_name>                       <plsql_table_type_name>;
```

where <variable_name> is an identifier for the PL/SQL table, and <plsql_table_type_name> is the name of the TYPE.

One of the unique characteristics of an associative array is that it can be sparsely populated. That means you don't need to add items consecutively to the array. Instead, you can add them to any index value between –2,147,483,647 and 2,147,483,647. Did you notice how I did just that in Listing 3-5, on lines 16 and 17? This can be very handy when copying values from a database table into a PL/SQL table, because database tables are generally sparsely populated.

You can then use the commands FIRST and NEXT to iterate through the list consecutively, or look up a value using the index randomly. (You can find more information about the FIRST and NEXT commands in the *PL/SQL User's Guide and Reference*.)

Table 3-2 lists the PL/SQL table built-in functions and procedures. With PL/SQL tables, it's also possible to use a varchar2 data type as the index value. So anywhere you see a reference to binary_integer, you can replace it with varchar2 (up to 32,767 characters long).

Table 3-2. *PL/SQL Table (Associative Array) Built-in Functions and Procedures*

Method	Description
count()	Returns the number of elements
delete(ain_index in binary_integer)	Deletes the specified element
delete()	Deletes all elements
exists(ain_index in binary_integer)	Returns TRUE if the element exists; otherwise, FALSE
first()	Returns the index of the first element
last()	Returns the index of the last element
prior(ain_index in binary_integer)	Returns the index of the first element before the specified element
next(ain_index in binary_integer)	Returns the index of the first element after the specified element

The following is the output from SQL*Plus when I execute table.sql from Listing 3-5:

```
SQL> @table.sql
```

```
DOE, JOHN
DOE, JANE
There are 2 elements.
The first element is 1.
The next element is 10.
The last element is 10.
The prior element is 1.
Element 1 exists.
I'm deleting element 10
There are 1 elements.
Element 10 no longer exists.
There are 1 elements.
I'm deleting all elements
There are 0 elements.

PL/SQL procedure successfully completed.
```

As you can see from the output, the procedure in the `table.sql` script exercises each of the associative array's methods.

Do you remember that I said it was possible to declare a PL/SQL table of almost any data type? Let's look at creating one with a composite data type next. Listing 3-6 is an example of a PL/SQL table (associative array) based on a row-level anchor.

Listing 3-6. *Declaring a PL/SQL Table with a Row Type Anchor, row.sql*

```
01   rem row.sql
02   rem by Don Bales on 12/15/2006
03   rem An anonymous PL/SQL procedure to demonstrate
04   rem the elementary use of PL/SQL tables
05
06   declare
07
08   TYPE name_table IS TABLE OF WORKER_T%ROWTYPE
09   INDEX BY BINARY_INTEGER;
10
11   t_name                              name_table;
12
13   n_name                              binary_integer;
14
15   begin
16     t_name(1).name  := 'DOE, JOHN';
17     t_name(10).name := 'DOE, JANE';
18     pl(t_name(1).name);
19     pl(t_name(10).name);
20     pl('There are '||t_name.count()||' elements.');
21     n_name := t_name.first();
22     pl('The first element is '||n_name||'.');
23     n_name := t_name.next(n_name);
24     pl('The next element is '||n_name||'.');
25     n_name := t_name.last();
26     pl('The last element is '||n_name||'.');
27     n_name := t_name.prior(n_name);
28     pl('The prior element is '||n_name||'.');
29     if t_name.exists(1) then
30       pl('Element 1 exists.');
31     end if;
32     pl('I''m deleting element 10');
33     t_name.delete(10);
34     pl('There are '||t_name.count()||' elements.');
35     if not t_name.exists(10) then
36       pl('Element 10 no longer exists.');
37     end if;
38     pl('There are '||t_name.count()||' elements.');
39     pl('I''m deleting all elements');
```

```
40   t_name.delete();
41   pl('There are '||t_name.count()||' elements.');
42   end;
43   /
```

A couple of new things are happening in Listing 3-6. First, line 8 uses the keyword %ROWTYPE to anchor to a composite record type based on the columns in the WORKER table. Second, on lines 16 and 17, I appended the composite record's field name name with a dot operator (.) to the PL/SQL table's name and index, in order to store the name value in the associative array. Other than those items, the procedures in Listing 3-5 and Listing 3-6 are identical. I did this to point out how to address the fields in a PL/SQL record in a PL/SQL table, and also to show that the use of the PL/SQL table operators remains the same, regardless of which data type is used.

Perhaps you would like to declare your own composite record type. Let's see how you can do that next.

Record Types

Just as you can use the TYPE keyword to declare a new PL/SQL table, you can also use it to declare a PL/SQL record. Listing 3-7 is an example of doing just that.

Listing 3-7. *Declaring a PL/SQL Record, record.sql*

```
01   rem record.sql
02   rem by Don Bales on 12/15/2006
03   rem An anonymous PL/SQL procedure to demonstrate
04   rem the use of PL/SQL records
05
06   declare
07
08   TYPE name_record is record (
09   first_name                         WORKER_T.first_name%TYPE,
10   middle_name                        WORKER_T.middle_name%TYPE,
11   last_name                          WORKER_T.last_name%TYPE );
12
13   TYPE name_table is table of name_record
14   index by binary_integer;
15
16   t_name                             name_table;
17
18   begin
19   t_name(1).first_name  := 'JOHN';
20   t_name(1).last_name   := 'DOE';
21   t_name(2).first_name  := 'JANE';
22   t_name(2).last_name   := 'DOE';
23
24   pl(t_name(1).last_name||', '||t_name(1).first_name);
25   pl(t_name(2).last_name||', '||t_name(2).first_name);
26   end;
27   /
```

The syntax used in Listing 3-7 to declare a PL/SQL record is as follows:

```
TYPE <plsql_record_type_name> IS RECORD (
<field_name_1>                      <data_type_1>,
<field_name_2>                      <data_type_2>,...
<field_name_N>                      <data_type_N>);
```

where `<plsql_record_type_name>` is the name for the new PL/SQL record type, `<field_name>` is the name of a field in the record, and `<data_type>` is the data type for the corresponding field.

As with the program in Listing 3-6, on lines 19 through 25 in Listing 3-7, I use the dot operator (.) followed by the name of the field in the record to address the composite data type values in the PL/SQL table.

WHAT'S WITH THIS NOMENCLATURE INCONSISTENCY ANYWAY?

I like things, especially programming code, to be consistent. Consistency makes things obvious. Obvious makes program code easy to maintain. Along those lines, I would feel much better if Oracle had called the syntax for creating a composite data type in a PL/SQL block a *row* instead of a *record*. Then we could refer to a *field* as *column*. The syntax would then be as follows:

```
TYPE <plsql_row_type_name> IS ROW (
<column_name_1>                      <data_type_1>,
<column_name_2>                      <data_type_2>,...
<column_name_N>                      <data_type_N>);
```

OK, now I feel better. I just needed to share how much that irritates me!

Single Dimension My Foot!

Earlier, I said that associative arrays will support only a single dimension. In other words, you can't declare a multidimensional array and address it like this: `t_name(1, 7).name`. Well, there's a way around that limitation. Every good problem deserves a good hack. Listing 3-8 demonstrates how to use a PL/SQL table inside a PL/SQL record in order to work around the one-dimension limit.

Listing 3-8. *A Hack to Work Around the PL/SQL Table One-Dimension Limit, multidimensional.sql*

```
01   rem multidimensional.sql
02   rem Copyright by Don Bales on 12/15/2006
03   rem An anonymous PL/SQL procedure to demonstrate
04   rem the use of nested PL/SQL tables
05
06   declare
07
08   TYPE name_table is table of WORKER_T.name%TYPE
```

```
09  index by binary_integer;
10
11  TYPE name_record is record (
12  dim2 name_table );
13
14  TYPE dim1 is table of name_record
15  index by binary_integer;
16
17  t_dim1                              dim1;
18
19  begin
20    t_dim1(1).dim2(1) := 'DOE, JOHN';
21    t_dim1(1).dim2(2) := 'DOE, JANE';
22
23    t_dim1(2).dim2(1) := 'DOUGH, JAYNE';
24    t_dim1(2).dim2(2) := 'DOUGH, JON';
25
26    pl(t_dim1(1).dim2(1));
27    pl(t_dim1(1).dim2(2));
28    pl(t_dim1(2).dim2(1));
29    pl(t_dim1(2).dim2(2));
30  end;
31  /
```

Here's how Listing 3-8 works:

Lines 8 and 9 declare a table type, name_table, to hold a list of names.

Lines 11 and 12 declare a record type, name_record, with one field named dim2, where the data type is name_table, a PL/SQL table.

Lines 14 and 15 declare a second table type, dim1, which is based on record type dim2.

On lines 20 through 29, with the pseudo-two-dimension table in place, I exercise accessing it using two indexes.

As I said, "single dimension my foot!" Since the use of arrays is a rather advanced topic, I'm going to skip the exercise here.

Next, we'll look at the most temporary of variables, which aren't really variables at all: parameters.

Parameters

Parameters allow you to pass values into (IN), pass values out of (OUT), or pass values into and out of (IN OUT) a cursor, function, or procedure. (Cursors are covered in Chapter 5.) You've already seen parameters used in earlier code listings. I'm covering parameters here because they use declaration syntax similar to variables, and they themselves are variables.

Parameter Naming

Parameters follow the same PL/SQL identifier naming rules as variables. In practice, however, I like to use a couple of additional prefix characters on parameter names so I can also tell their scope, along with the data type. Table 3-3 is a list of those parameter prefix values.

Table 3-3. *My PL/SQL Parameter Naming Prefixes*

Prefix	Description
ai	Argument IN
ao	Argument OUT
aio	Argument IN OUT

For example, if I were to declare parameters to pass data from the columns in the AUTHOR table into and/or out of a method, I would use the identifier names in Table 3-4.

Table 3-4. *Parameter Name Examples Using My Prefixing Scheme*

Scope		
IN	**OUT**	**IN OUT**
ain_id	aon_id	aion_id
aiv_name	aov_name	aiov_name
aid_birth_date	aod_birth_date	aiod_birth_date
aiv_gender	aov_gender	aiov_gender

The advantage of using these prefixes is that you'll always know the scope and data type of the parameter with which you're working.

Parameter Declarations

Listings 3-9 and 3-10 create a package named PARAMETERS, which I'll use to explain the parameter declaration syntax and parameter scope.

Listing 3-9. *A Package Spec to Test Parameter Scope, parameters.pks*

```
01  create or replace package PARAMETERS as
02  /*
03  parameters.pks
04  by Donald J. Bales on 12/15/2006
05  A package to test parameter scope
06  */
```

```
07
08  -- A function that exercises the scope of parameters
09  FUNCTION in_out_inout(
10  aiv_in                      in      varchar2,
11  aov_out                         out varchar2,
12  aiov_inout                  in out  varchar2)
13  return                          varchar2;
14
15
16  -- A procedure that exercises the scope of parameters
17  PROCEDURE in_out_inout(
18  aiv_in                      in      varchar2,
19  aov_out                         out varchar2,
20  aiov_inout                  in out  varchar2);
21
22
23  end PARAMETERS;
24  /
25  @se.sql PARAMETERS
```

The syntax used to declare the parameters in the function and procedure in Listing 3-9 is as follows:

```
(
<parameter_name_1>          [IN][OUT] <data_type_1>,
<parameter_name_2>          [IN][OUT] <data_type_2>,...
<parameter_name_N>          [IN][OUT] <data_type_N>)
```

where <parameter_name> is the name of the parameter, the scope is IN, OUT, or IN OUT, and <data_type> is the data type of the parameter. As you have already seen in previous listings, you can use column or row anchors to specify the data type (you know—%TYPE or %ROWTYPE). However, the value of the parameter will not be constrained by the specified size in the anchor. Only the data type is used from the anchor.

Parameter Scope

The parameter keywords IN and OUT determine the accessibility, or scope, of the parameters:

- IN makes your parameters' data available to the called cursor, function, or procedure.

- OUT allows the called function or procedure to set the parameter's value within the called PL/SQL block.

- The combination of IN and OUT allows both levels of accessibility.

Seeing is believing, so take some time to study Listings 3-10 and 3-11, and the output of Listing 3-11.

Listing 3-10. *A Package Body to Test Parameter Scope, parameters.pkb*

```
01  create or replace package body PARAMETERS as
02  /*
03  parameters.pkb
04  by Donald J. Bales on 12/15/2006
05  A package to test parameter scope
06  */
07
08  FUNCTION in_out_inout(
09  aiv_in                      in      varchar2,
10  aov_out                         out varchar2,
11  aiov_inout              in out varchar2)
12  return                          varchar2 is
13  begin
14    pl(chr(9)||'Before assignments...');
15    pl(chr(9)||'Inside function in_out_inout, aiv_in    = '||aiv_in);
16    pl(chr(9)||'Inside function in_out_inout, aov_out   = '||aov_out);
17    pl(chr(9)||'Inside function in_out_inout, aiov_inout = '||aiov_inout);
18    -- You can only assign a value (write) to an OUT
19    -- parameter, you can't read it!
20    aov_out   := 'OUT';
21
22    -- You can only read an IN parameter
23    aiov_inout := aiv_in;
24
25    -- You can read and write an IN OUT parameter
26    aiov_inout := aiov_inout||'OUT';
27
28    pl(chr(9)||'After assignments...');
29    pl(chr(9)||'Inside function in_out_inout, aiv_in    = '||aiv_in);
30    pl(chr(9)||'Inside function in_out_inout, aov_out   = '||aov_out);
31    pl(chr(9)||'Inside function in_out_inout, aiov_inout = '||aiov_inout);
32    return 'OK'; -- a function must return a value!
33  end in_out_inout;
34
35
36  PROCEDURE in_out_inout(
37  aiv_in                      in      varchar2,
38  aov_out                         out varchar2,
39  aiov_inout              in out varchar2) is
40  begin
41    pl(chr(9)||'Before assignments...');
42    pl(chr(9)||'Inside procedure in_out_inout, aiv_in    = '||aiv_in);
43    pl(chr(9)||'Inside procedure in_out_inout, aov_out   = '||aov_out);
44    pl(chr(9)||'Inside procedure in_out_inout, aiov_inout = '||aiov_inout);
45    -- You can only assign a value (write) to an OUT
46    -- parameter, you can't read it!
```

```
47    aov_out    := 'OUT';
48
49    -- You can only read an IN parameter
50    aiov_inout := aiv_in;
51
52    -- You can read and write an IN OUT parameter
53    aiov_inout := aiov_inout||'OUT';
54    pl(chr(9)||'After assignments...');
55    pl(chr(9)||'Inside procedure in_out_inout, aiv_in     = '||aiv_in);
56    pl(chr(9)||'Inside procedure in_out_inout, aov_out    = '||aov_out);
57    pl(chr(9)||'Inside procedure in_out_inout, aiov_inout = '||aiov_inout);
58  end in_out_inout;
59
60
61  end PARAMETERS;
62  /
63  @be.sql PARAMETERS
```

Listing 3-11 is an anonymous PL/SQL procedure to test the scope defined by the use of IN, OUT, or IN OUT.

Listing 3-11. *A Test Unit for Package PARAMETERS, parameters.sql*

```
01  rem parameters.sql
02  rem Copyright by Donald J. Bales on 12/15/2006
03  rem A test unit for package PARAMETERS
04
05  declare
06
07  v_in                      varchar2(30) := 'IN';
08  v_out                     varchar2(30) :=
09    'Na na, you can''t see me!';
10  v_inout                   varchar2(30) :=
11    'But you can see me!';
12  v_return                  varchar2(30);
13
14  begin
15    pl('Before calling the function...');
16    pl('Inside test unit parameters v_in    = '||v_in);
17    pl('Inside test unit parameters v_out   = '||v_out);
18    pl('Inside test unit parameters v_inout = '||v_inout);
19    pl('Test function PARAMETERS.in_out_inout(v_in, v_out, v_inout).');
20    v_return := PARAMETERS.in_out_inout(v_in, v_out, v_inout);
21    pl(v_return);
22    pl('After calling the function...');
23    pl('Inside test unit parameters v_in    = '||v_in);
24    pl('Inside test unit parameters v_out   = '||v_out);
25    pl('Inside test unit parameters v_inout = '||v_inout);
```

```
26    pl('Resetting initial values...');
27    v_out   := 'Na na, you can''t see me!';
28    v_inout := 'But you can see me!';
29    pl('Before calling the procedure...');
30    pl('Inside test unit parameters v_in    = '||v_in);
31    pl('Inside test unit parameters v_out   = '||v_out);
32    pl('Inside test unit parameters v_inout = '||v_inout);
33    pl('Test procedure PARAMETERS.in_out_inout(v_in, v_out, v_inout).');
34    PARAMETERS.in_out_inout(v_in, v_out, v_inout);
35    pl('OK');
36    pl('After calling the procedure...');
37    pl('Inside test unit parameters v_in    = '||v_in);
38    pl('Inside test unit parameters v_out   = '||v_out);
39    pl('Inside test unit parameters v_inout = '||v_inout);
40  end;
41  /
```

Here's the SQL*Plus output from the parameters.sql script (Listing 3-11):

```
SQL> @parameters.sql
```

```
Before calling the function...
Inside test unit parameters v_in    = IN
Inside test unit parameters v_out   = Na na, you can't see me!
Inside test unit parameters v_inout = But you can see me!
Test function PARAMETERS.in_out_inout(v_in, v_out, v_inout).
        Before assignments...
        Inside function in_out_inout, aiv_in     = IN
        Inside function in_out_inout, aov_out    =
        Inside function in_out_inout, aiov_inout = But you can see me!
        After assignments...
        Inside function in_out_inout, aiv_in     = IN
        Inside function in_out_inout, aov_out    = OUT
        Inside function in_out_inout, aiov_inout = INOUT
OK
After calling the function...
Inside test unit parameters v_in    = IN
Inside test unit parameters v_out   = OUT
Inside test unit parameters v_inout = INOUT
Resetting initial values...
Before calling the procedure...
Inside test unit parameters v_in    = IN
Inside test unit parameters v_out   = Na na, you can't see me!
Inside test unit parameters v_inout = But you can see me!
```

```
Test procedure PARAMETERS.in_out_inout(v_in, v_out, v_inout).
        Before assignments...
        Inside procedure in_out_inout, aiv_in    = IN
        Inside procedure in_out_inout, aov_out   =
        Inside procedure in_out_inout, aiov_inout = But you can see me!
        After assignments...
        Inside procedure in_out_inout, aiv_in    = IN
        Inside procedure in_out_inout, aov_out   = OUT
        Inside procedure in_out_inout, aiov_inout = INOUT
OK
After calling the procedure...
Inside test unit parameters v_in    = IN
Inside test unit parameters v_out   = OUT
Inside test unit parameters v_inout = INOUT

PL/SQL procedure successfully completed.
```

As you can verify from studying Listing 3-11 and the output from test unit parameters.sql:

- An IN parameter can be used to pass a value into a cursor, function, or procedure.

- An OUT parameter can be used to pass a value out of a function or procedure.

- An IN OUT parameter can be used to do both.

It's Your Turn to Declare Parameters

You'll have plenty of practice declaring parameters in the coming chapters. So I want you to do this instead:

1. Go get a snack.

2. Eat it.

3. Take a quick nap.

4. Start on Chapter 4.

Summary

At this point, you should be a master of variable and parameter declarations. And you should understand the scope in which they are accessible. You should also be wary of any lunchtime conversation with someone who wants to sell you a NULL. There's nothing in it for you.

Next, let's start working with some SQL in our PL/SQL.

■ ■ ■

Whoa! One Statement at a Time, Please!

Now we begin our journey of using SQL in PL/SQL. We'll start out slowly, inserting one row at a time, then updating one row at a time, then deleting one row at a time, and finally selecting one row at a time. I take this approach because you first have to insert data into a database before you can update, delete or select it. I call these kinds of SQL statements *singletons*, because they return one set of results. So let's get started by putting some data into the database.

Inserts

No, I'm not talking about those annoying cards you find in books or magazines when you first open them. The context here is inserting data into a relational database. To insert data into a relational database from PL/SQL, you simply write a SQL INSERT statement, where the values are PL/SQL literals, PL/SQL variables, or SQL columns.

I'm going to start with the worst of all examples, and then continually improve its architecture and design as we progress through the chapter. To start out, you'll see what most PL/SQL programmers do, and then how to improve the code. Please keep in mind that there is a time and place for each of these solutions. In the end, you're the one who will need to make the decision about which is the best solution based on the business problem you're solving.

Rarely do you just perform a simple atomic INSERT statement in PL/SQL. You can do that using a SQL*Plus script, without using PL/SQL at all. More often, you'll want to insert or update depending on whether the data you intend to insert already exists in the database. If it does, you'll probably want to check to see if you need to update the values already in the database. So the process you decide to use to insert and/or update becomes a proverbial chicken vs. egg dilemma—which do you do first? Let's start by looking at what can happen if a duplicate row already exists.

You're going to have to put up with seeing me use SELECT when I INSERT, because, in a modern database design, you need to SELECT sequence and code ID values to use them in an INSERT statement. Let's check it out. Listing 4-1 is an anonymous PL/SQL procedure that inserts values into the WORKER_T table.

Listing 4-1. *An Insert Example Using PL/SQL Literals and Variables, insert.sql*

```
001   rem insert.sql
002   rem Donald J. Bales on 12/15/2006
003   rem An anonymous PL/SQL procedure to insert
004   rem values using PL/SQL literals and variables
005
006   set serveroutput on size 1000000;
007
008   declare
009
010   -- I declared these variables so I can get
011   -- the required ID values before I insert.
012   n_id                            WORKER_T.id%TYPE;
013   n_worker_type_id                WORKER_T.worker_type_id%TYPE;
014   v_external_id                   WORKER_T.external_id%TYPE;
015   n_gender_id                     WORKER_T.gender_id%TYPE;
016
017   -- I'll use this variable to hold the result
018   -- of the SQL insert statement.
019   n_count                         number;
020
021   begin
022
023     -- First, let's get the worker_type_id for a contractor
024     begin
025       select worker_type_id
026       into   n_worker_type_id
027       from   WORKER_TYPE_T
028       where  code = 'C';
029     exception
030       when OTHERS then
031         raise_application_error(-20002, SQLERRM||
032           ' on select WORKER_TYPE_T'||
033           ' in filename insert.sql');
034     end;
035
036     -- Next, let's get the gender_id for a male
037     begin
038       select gender_id
039       into   n_gender_id
040       from   GENDER_T
041       where  code = 'M';
042     exception
043       when OTHERS then
044         raise_application_error(-20004, SQLERRM||
045           ' on select GENDER_T'||
```

```
046            ' in filename insert.sql');
047    end;
048
049    -- Now, let's get the next id sequence
050    begin
051      select WORKER_ID_SEQ.nextval
052      into   n_id
053      from   SYS.DUAL;
054    exception
055      when OTHERS then
056        raise_application_error(-20001, SQLERRM||
057          ' on select WORKER_ID_SEQ.nextval'||
058          ' in filename insert.sql');
059    end;
060
061    -- And then, let's get the next external_id sequence
062    begin
063      select lpad(to_char(EXTERNAL_ID_SEQ.nextval), 9, '0')
064      into   v_external_id
065      from   SYS.DUAL;
066    exception
067      when OTHERS then
068        raise_application_error(-20003, SQLERRM||
069          ' on select EXTERNAL_ID_SEQ.nextval'||
070          ' in filename insert.sql');
071    end;
072
073    -- Now that we have all the necessary ID values
074    -- we can finally insert a row!
075    begin
076      insert into WORKER_T (
077            id,
078            worker_type_id,
079            external_id,
080            first_name,
081            middle_name,
082            last_name,
083            name,
084            birth_date,
085            gender_id )
086      values (
087            n_id,                   -- a variable
088            n_worker_type_id,       -- a variable
089            v_external_id,          -- a variable
090            'JOHN',                 -- a literal
091            'J.',                   -- a literal
092            'DOE',                  -- a literal
```

```
093                    'DOE, JOHN J.',                  -- a literal
094                    to_date('19800101', 'YYYYMMDD'), -- a function
095                    n_gender_id );                   -- a variable
096
097        n_count := sql%rowcount;
098      exception
099        when OTHERS then
100          raise_application_error(-20005, SQLERRM||
101            ' on insert WORKER_T'||
102            ' in filename insert.sql');
103      end;
104
105      pl(to_char(n_count)||' row(s) inserted.');
106    end;
107    /
108
109    commit;
```

The SQL INSERT syntax used in Listing 4-1 is as follows:

```
INSERT INTO <table_name> (
       <column_name_1>,
       <column_name_2>,...
       <column_name_N> )
VALUES (
       <column_value_1>,
       <column_value_2>,...
       <column_value_N> );
```

where <table_name> is the name of the table to INSERT VALUES INTO, <column_name> is the name of a column in the table, and <column_value> is the value for a corresponding <column_name>. The column values can be PL/SQL literals, variables, qualifying function results, or SQL column values.

You should always use a list of columns in your INSERT statements in order to maintain the validity of your code, in case someone later adds a column to a table definition (and, in practice, that happens).

Let's break down the code in Listing 4-1:

Lines 12 through 15 declare four variables to hold the ID values from related sequence and code tables.

Line 19 declares a number to hold the resulting row count from the INSERT statement.

Lines 25 through 28 contain a SELECT statement to get the worker_type_id value for a contractor.

On lines 24 through 34, I've blocked (put the code in a nested PL/SQL block) the SELECT statement so I can catch any catastrophic error, and report it to the presentation layer with an error number and message that are unique to the PL/SQL program. This practice greatly simplifies troubleshooting. You'll know exactly what went wrong and where it went wrong, and that's nice.

On lines 37 through 47, I get the gender_id value for a male.

On lines 50 through 59, I get the next id sequence value, storing that value in variable n_id.

On lines 62 through 71, I get the next external_id value. I use the SQL function to_char() to do an explicit data type conversion from numeric to character. I wrap the character value with the SQL function lpad() in order to left-pad the number string with zeros so it's nine characters long.

Lines 76 through 95 contain an INSERT statement to insert John Doe's data into the WORKER_T table.

Lines 77 through 85 list the names of the columns I'm going to insert values INTO. This is an important practice. If I didn't list the columns, the procedure would become invalid any time someone modified the WORKER_T table.

Lines 87 through 95 specify the column values using a combination of PL/SQL literals, PL/SQL variables, and even the return value of the SQL function to_date() for the value of column birth_date.

On line 97, I store the result value of the INSERT statement, which is the number of rows inserted. To accomplish this, I use the pseudo-cursor name sql% and its variable rowcount.

On lines 75 through 103 collectively, I've blocked the INSERT statement so I can detect and report the exact type and location of an error in the PL/SQL procedure.

The following is the output from the first time the insert.sql script is executed:

```
SQL> @insert.sql
```

```
1 row(s) inserted.

PL/SQL procedure successfully completed.
```

If you examine the code in Listing 4-1 and its output, you'll see that the procedure inserted one row into the database, as reported by the output from the INSERT statement through the sql%rowcount variable. But what happens if we run the script again? Here's the output from the script's second execution:

```
SQL> @insert.sql
```

```
declare
*
ERROR at line 1:
ORA-20005: ORA-00001: unique constraint (BPS.WORKER_T_UK2) violated
on insert WORKER_T in filename insert.sql
ORA-06512: at line 93
```

No PL/SQL procedure successfully completed message this time! An unhandled unique constraint exception was raised as an application error, number 20005, along with a meaningful message.

Now if you want to handle this particular kind of exception, you can use one of three tactics:

- Catch exception DUP_VAL_ON_INDEX (good)

- Use additional PL/SQL code to predetect the duplicate's presence (better)

- Use additional SQL code to predetect the duplicate's presence (best)

Let's take a look at these solutions, from good to best.

Catching a DUP_VAL_ON_INDEX Exception

When it comes to dealing with code that may raise a DUP_VAL_ON_INDEX exception (or any exception for that matter), catching the exception is the laziest of solutions, yet perfectly legitimate. Actually, catching a DUP_VAL_ON_INDEX exception during an INSERT is the only way to determine that a duplicate row exists. So regardless of which process you use to insert a row, you always need to catch any possible exceptions during the execution of a SQL statement and handle them appropriately.

Figure 4-1 shows a simple process flow diagram for inserting a row and catching a DUP_VAL_ON_INDEX exception if a duplicate row already exists in the database. The process in Figure 4-1 starts out by executing a SQL INSERT statement. When you do this, Oracle will check for duplicate values in any existing unique index or unique key entries for the table in question. If a duplicate entry is found, PL/SQL will raise a DUP_VAL_ON_INDEX exception. So how do you handle that?

What you know at this point in your program is that a duplicate entry existed at the moment the SQL engine tried to insert your row. But that does not guarantee that the same duplicate row exists microseconds later in the exception handler. Someone or something else using the database could have deleted it in the meantime.

So perhaps you decide to try to UPDATE the supposedly existing entry. If you choose that tactic, you can be 100% sure that the entry was updated only if you examine sql%rowcount for the number of rows updated after your attempted update. If the row count isn't equal to one, then you need to try to insert the row again.

This "classic" solution is perfectly legitimate and arguably the only correct way to insert values. Or is it? I don't like this approach because it's a reactive solution where you are not in complete control of the process. Is it better to gain control after an error or to maintain control all along? Let's look at an example in order to get a better understanding of the problem, before you decide on a solution. Listing 4-2 shows a modified version of Listing 4-1, where the ORA-00001: unique constraint ... violated, or DUP_VAL_ON_INDEX exception, is handled.

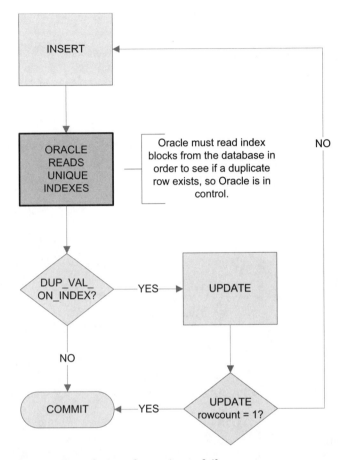

Figure 4-1. *Updating after an insert fails*

Note Listing 4-2 is a partial code listing. I'll use this technique whenever there's a lot of repeated code from one listing to the next. Because of this, you didn't have to pay as much for this book, nor did we have to kill as many trees; less paper, fewer dead trees, lower cost.

Listing 4-2. *An Insert Example, Modified to Catch DUP_VAL_ON_INDEX,*
insert_with_handled_exception.sql

```
073     -- Now that we have all the necessary ID values
074     -- we can finally insert a row!
075     begin
076       insert into WORKER_T (
077             id,
078             worker_type_id,
079             external_id,
080             first_name,
081             middle_name,
082             last_name,
083             name,
084             birth_date,
085             gender_id )
086       values (
087             n_id,                          -- a variable
088             n_worker_type_id,              -- a variable
089             v_external_id,                 -- a variable
090             'JOHN',                        -- a literal
091             'J.',                          -- a literal
092             'DOE',                         -- a literal
093             'DOE, JOHN J.',                -- a literal
094             to_date('19800101', 'YYYYMMDD'), -- a function
095             n_gender_id );                 -- a variable
096
097       n_count := sql%rowcount;
098     exception
099       when DUP_VAL_ON_INDEX then
100         n_count := 0;
101         pl('Caught a DUP_VAL_ON_INDEX exception');
102       when OTHERS then
103         raise_application_error(-20005, SQLERRM||
104           ' on insert WORKER_T'||
105           ' in filename insert_with_handled_exception.sql');
106     end;
```

So what changed?

Line 99 now has a WHEN DUP_VAL_ON_INDEX clause, which catches a DUP_VAL_ON_INDEX exception. The scope of the clause extends until the next use of the keyword WHEN or the keyword END for the enclosing PL/SQL block.

On line 100, I set the row count variable, n_count, to 0, because lines 96 and 97 are not executed when an exception occurs. Instead, the program's execution jumps from line 95, where the error takes place, directly to line 98, in order to start handling exceptions.

On line 101, I display a custom error message, but I don't raise the exception, so the program executes successfully.

Here's the output of the modified script, insert_with_handled_exception.sql:

```
SQL> @insert_with_handle_exception.sql
```

```
Caught a DUP_VAL_ON_INDEX exception
0 row(s) inserted.

PL/SQL procedure successfully completed.
```

But a nagging question remains. Is it better to gain control after an error or to maintain control all along? Let's take a look at tactic number two.

Using PL/SQL to Predetect a Duplicate

Using additional PL/SQL code to predetect the presence of duplicate values is, in my opinion, better than catching a DUP_VAL_ON_INDEX exception, for these reasons:

- You maintain control of your PL/SQL program's execution.
- You can conditionally decide how to handle duplicate values.
- You can use your detection scheme to acquire the primary key for the row that is a duplicate, and then update that row.

Figure 4-2 is a simple process flow diagram for predetecting a duplicate entry using PL/SQL, and then acting accordingly—that is, inserting or updating as needed. In this process, you start out by selecting the primary key value from the database for the table entry in question. If you find an existing entry, you can determine whether the entry needs to be updated, and then execute an UPDATE statement. Alternatively, you execute an INSERT statement if the SELECT statement raises a NO_DATA_FOUND exception.

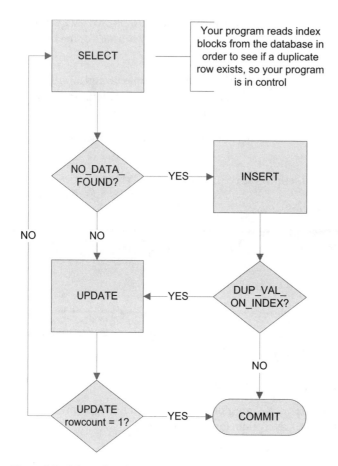

Figure 4-2. *Select, then insert or update as needed*

However, you cannot ignore the possibility that, even though a duplicate entry did not exist at the moment you executed a SELECT statement against the database, someone or something has since inserted a duplicate entry. This could happen in the microseconds between the raised exception and the execution of your INSERT statement, so you must still catch any possible exceptions on the execution of the INSERT statement and act accordingly.

This time, if the sql%rowcount variable is not equal to one, you need to try selecting the entry again.

So which solution is better? Once again, let's look at an example before you decide. Listing 4-3 is another modification of Listing 4-1. This time, I've added a nested block of PL/SQL code to detect possible duplicate values.

Listing 4-3. *An Insert Example, Modified to Detect Duplicates with PL/SQL, insert_with_plsql_detection.sql*

```
015  v_first_name                    WORKER_T.first_name%TYPE;
016  v_middle_name                   WORKER_T.middle_name%TYPE;
017  v_last_name                     WORKER_T.last_name%TYPE;
```

```
018   v_name                                WORKER_T.name%TYPE;
019   d_birth_date                          WORKER_T.birth_date%TYPE;
...
027     v_first_name  := 'JOHN';
028     v_middle_name := 'J.';
029     v_last_name   := 'DOE';
030     v_name        :=
031       rtrim(v_last_name||', '||v_first_name||' '||v_middle_name);
032     d_birth_date  :=
033       to_date('19800101', 'YYYYMMDD'); -- I'm guessing
...
061     -- Detect any existing entries with the unique
062     -- combination of columns as in this constraint:
063     -- constraint   WORKER_T_UK2
064     -- unique (
065     -- name,
066     -- birth_date,
067     -- gender_id )
068     begin
069       select count(1)
070       into   n_count
071       from   WORKER_T
072       where  name       = v_name
073       and    birth_date = d_birth_date
074       and    gender_id  = n_gender_id;
075     exception
076       when OTHERS then
077         raise_application_error(-20005, SQLERRM||
078           ' on select WORKER_T_T'||
079           ' in filename insert_with_plsql_detection.sql');
080     end;
081
082     -- Conditionally insert the row
083     if n_count = 0 then
084       -- Now, let's get the next id sequence
085       begin
086         select WORKER_ID_SEQ.nextval
087         into   n_id
088         from   SYS.DUAL;
089       exception
090         when OTHERS then
091           raise_application_error(-20001, SQLERRM||
092             ' on select WORKER_ID_SEQ.nextval'||
093             ' in filename insert_with_plsql_detection.sql');
094       end;
095
096       -- And then, let's get the next external_id sequence
```

```
097       begin
098         select lpad(to_char(EXTERNAL_ID_SEQ.nextval), 9, '0')
099         into   v_external_id
100         from   SYS.DUAL;
101       exception
102         when OTHERS then
103           raise_application_error(-20003, SQLERRM||
104             ' on select EXTERNAL_ID_SEQ.nextval'||
105             ' in filename insert_with_plsql_detection.sql');
106       end;
107
108       -- Now that we have all the necessary ID values
109       -- we can finally insert a row!
110       begin
111         insert into WORKER_T (
112                 id,
113                 worker_type_id,
114                 external_id,
115                 first_name,
116                 middle_name,
117                 last_name,
118                 name,
119                 birth_date,
120                 gender_id )
121         values (
122                 n_id,
123                 n_worker_type_id,
124                 v_external_id,
125                 v_first_name,
126                 v_middle_name,
127                 v_last_name,
128                 v_name,
129                 d_birth_date,
130                 n_gender_id );
131
132         n_count := sql%rowcount;
133       exception
134         when OTHERS then
135           raise_application_error(-20006, SQLERRM||
136             ' on insert WORKER_T'||
137             ' in filename insert_with_plsql_detection.sql');
138       end;
139     else
140       n_count := 0;
141     end if;
```

Let's review the modifications:

On lines 15 through 19, I've added variables to hold column values. I've done this because I need to specify the column values more than once. This way, I can set their values once, and then know that I will consistently use the same values twice.

Lines 27 through 33 initialize the variables I added on lines 15 through 19. A particularly troublesome issue is the variable v_name for column WORKER_T.name. It's a computed value that will be stored in the database in order to improve performance. This tactic will cause any relational database purist to have a hissy fit. But that's not what I find troublesome. Since it's a computed value, you must make sure it's always computed the same way. Hmm, that sounds like a job for a function dedicated to the WORKER_T table. We'll create one to handle this issue in Chapter 5, so don't sweat it yet.

Lines 68 through 80 contain a new nested PL/SQL block that queries the WORKER_T table against the columns that make up the unique constraint in question, to see if an entry with duplicate values already exists in the table. The SQL statement simply counts the number of rows with duplicate values, storing the count in variable n_count.

Line 83 has a new IF statement, which determines whether to insert a row. If the value of the variable n_count is 0, I go ahead and insert the row. Otherwise, on line 140, I set n_count to 0, in order to correctly report the number of rows inserted.

In Listing 4-3, I was able to maintain control of the execution of my PL/SQL program. But what if I wanted to update the row that already existed? Then I would have coded the detection block as shown in Listing 4-4.

Listing 4-4. *An Insert Example, Modified to Detect Duplicates with PL/SQL for Update, insert_with_plsql_detection_for_update.sql*

```
069    begin
070      select id
071      into    n_id
072      from    WORKER_T
073      where   name      = v_name
074      and     birth_date = d_birth_date
075      and     gender_id  = n_gender_id;
076    exception
077      when NO_DATA_FOUND then
078        n_id := NULL; -- Is this really needed?
079      when OTHERS then
080        raise_application_error(-20003, SQLERRM||
081          ' on select WORKER_T_T'||
082          ' in filename insert_with_plsql_detection_for_update.sql');
083    end;
084
```

```
085    -- Conditionally insert the row
086    if n_id is NULL then
087      -- Now, let's get the next id sequence
088      begin
089        select WORKER_ID_SEQ.nextval
090        into   n_id
091        from   SYS.DUAL;
092      exception
093        when OTHERS then
094          raise_application_error(-20004, SQLERRM||
095            ' on select WORKER_ID_SEQ.nextval'||
096            ' in filename insert_with_plsql_detection_for_update.sql');
097      end;
098
099      -- And then, let's get the next external_id sequence
100      begin
101        select lpad(to_char(EXTERNAL_ID_SEQ.nextval), 9, '0')
102        into   v_external_id
103        from   SYS.DUAL;
104      exception
105        when OTHERS then
106          raise_application_error(-20005, SQLERRM||
107            ' on select EXTERNAL_ID_SEQ.nextval'||
108            ' in filename insert_with_plsql_detection_for_update.sql');
109      end;
110
111      -- Now that we have all the necessary ID values
112      -- we can finally insert a row!
113      begin
114        insert into WORKER_T (
115               id,
116               worker_type_id,
117               external_id,
118               first_name,
119               middle_name,
120               last_name,
121               name,
122               birth_date,
123               gender_id )
124        values (
125               n_id,
126               n_worker_type_id,
127               v_external_id,
128               v_first_name,
```

```
129                 v_middle_name,
130                 v_last_name,
131                 v_name,
132                 d_birth_date,
133                 n_gender_id );
134
135        n_inserted := sql%rowcount;
136      exception
137        when OTHERS then
138          raise_application_error(-20006, SQLERRM||
139            ' on insert WORKER_T'||
140            ' in filename insert_with_plsql_detection_for_update.sql');
141      end;
142    else
143      begin
144        update WORKER_T
145        set    worker_type_id  = n_worker_type_id
146        where  id              = n_id;
147
148        n_updated := sql%rowcount;
149      exception
150        when OTHERS then
151          raise_application_error(-20007, SQLERRM||
152            ' on update WORKER_T'||
153            ' in filename insert_with_plsql_detection_for_update.sql');
154      end;
155    end if;
```

On lines 69 through 83, I've recoded the detection block to retrieve the primary key value for a row with duplicate values. If a duplicate row exists, variable n_id, initially NULL, will be set to the value of the primary key. Otherwise, if a duplicate row does not exist, a NO_DATA_FOUND exception will be raised. In turn, the exception will be handled by the WHEN NO_DATA_FOUND clause in the enclosing PL/SQL block's exception-handling section. There, in the EXCEPTION clause, I set the value of variable n_id to NULL, to flag that I did not find a duplicate. I actually don't need to set it to NULL, because it remained NULL when the exception was raised. But the Oracle PL/SQL documentation does not explicitly guarantee this behavior, so I set it to NULL.

Also, on line 86, now I use the n_id variable to determine if I found a duplicate row. If n_id is NULL, I insert the row. Otherwise, on lines 143 through 154, I update the duplicate row with the worker_type_id value.

So if this was a better tactic, what's best? Before I answer that question, let's first digress a moment so I can finally explain the syntax of all those IF statements I've been using all along!

IF I Don't Tell You Now, When ELSE Can I?

This seems as good a time as any to finally get around to defining just what an IF statement is. Let's look at the IF statement syntax used in Listing 4-4:

```
IF <boolean_evaluation> THEN
  -- do this if it's TRUE
[ELSE
  -- do this if it's not TRUE]
END IF;
```

where <boolean_evaluation> is PL/SQL that evaluates to a Boolean value. If the
<boolean_evaluation> is TRUE, then the lines of code between the THEN and ELSE keywords are
executed. Otherwise, if the <boolean_evaluation> is not TRUE, then the lines of code between
keywords ELSE and END IF are executed.

In Listing 4-4, on line 86, I evaluate id is NULL. If it's TRUE, PL/SQL executes lines 87
through 141; otherwise (ELSE), it executes lines 143 through 154. You can also use the following
syntaxes:

```
IF <boolean_evaluation> THEN
  -- do this if it's TRUE
END IF;
```

or

```
IF    <boolean_evaluation> THEN

  -- do this if it's TRUE
[ELSIF <boolean_evaluation> THEN
  -- do this if it's TRUE
ELSIF ...

ELSE
  -- do this if it's not TRUE]
END IF;
```

Now, let's get back to the subject of inserting.

Using SQL to Predetect a Duplicate

It's almost always best to let SQL simply do its job! You can't imagine how much PL/SQL code
I've seen that can be replaced by one SQL statement—for example, all the code you've seen so
far in this chapter in Listings 4-1 through 4-4.

Figure 4-3 is a simple process flow diagram for predetecting a duplicate entry using SQL.
In this process, SQL performs the work of predetection using an EXISTS clause. If a duplicate
entry does not exist at the moment the EXISTS clause is executed, the SQL engine immediately
follows with an INSERT. Regardless, this does not mean you can't get a DUP_VAL_ON_INDEX exception. In the microseconds between the evaluation of the EXISTS clause and the INSERT, it is
possible that someone or something has inserted a duplicate value into the database. So you
must still catch any exceptions from the SELECT...INTO statement and act accordingly.

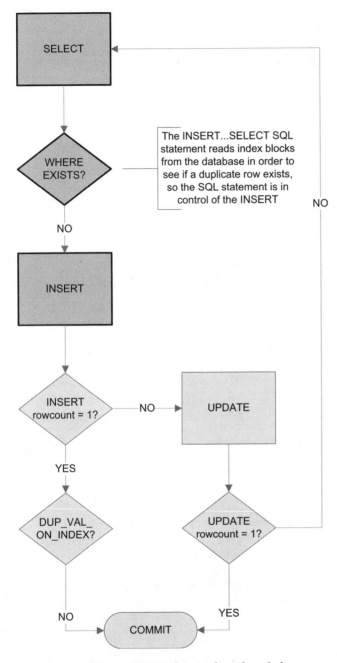

Figure 4-3. *INSERT...SELECT, then update if needed*

There appears to be no "perfect" solution, and indeed, that is the case. It's always possible that someone or something has deleted or inserted an entry in the database between your duplicate row detection and corresponding action. Now let's take a look at an example that uses SQL predetection.

Listing 4-5 is an example of letting SQL determine whether there's a duplicate row, and then conditionally inserting values into the WORKER_T table.

Listing 4-5. *An Insert Example, Modified to Detect Duplicates with SQL, insert_with_sql_detection.sql*

```
01  rem insert_with_sql_detection.sql
02  rem Donald J. Bales on 12/15/2006
03  rem An anonymous PL/SQL procedure to insert
04  rem values using PL/SQL literals and variables
05
06  set serveroutput on size 1000000;
07
08  declare
09
10  v_first_name                        WORKER_T.first_name%TYPE;
11  v_middle_name                       WORKER_T.middle_name%TYPE;
12  v_last_name                         WORKER_T.last_name%TYPE;
13  v_name                              WORKER_T.name%TYPE;
14  d_birth_date                        WORKER_T.birth_date%TYPE;
15
16  -- I'll use this variable to hold the result
17  -- of the SQL insert statement.
18  n_count                             number;
19
20  begin
21    -- Since I use these values more than once,
22    -- I set them here, and then use the variables
23    v_first_name  := 'JOHN';
24    v_middle_name := 'J.';
25    v_last_name   := 'DOE';
26    v_name        :=
27      rtrim(v_last_name||', '||v_first_name||' '||v_middle_name);
28    d_birth_date  :=
29      to_date('19800101', 'YYYYMMDD'); -- I'm guessing
30
31    -- Now I can just let SQL do all the work.  Who needs PL/SQL!
32    begin
33      insert into WORKER_T (
34            id,
35            worker_type_id,
36            external_id,
37            first_name,
38            middle_name,
39            last_name,
40            name,
41            birth_date,
```

```
42                gender_id )
43      select WORKER_ID_SEQ.nextval,
44               c1.worker_type_id,
45               lpad(to_char(EXTERNAL_ID_SEQ.nextval), 9, '0'),
46               v_first_name,
47               v_middle_name,
48               v_last_name,
49               v_name,
50               d_birth_date,
51               c2.gender_id
52      from    WORKER_TYPE_T c1,
53               GENDER_T c2
54      where   c1.code = 'C'
55      and     c2.code = 'M'
56      and not exists (
57        select 1
58        from    WORKER_T x
59        where   x.name       = v_name
60        and     x.birth_date = d_birth_date
61        and     x.gender_id  = c2.gender_id );
62
63      n_count := sql%rowcount;
64    exception
65      when OTHERS then
66        raise_application_error(-20006, SQLERRM||
67          ' on insert WORKER_T'||
68          ' in filename insert_with_sql_detection.sql');
69    end;
70
71    pl(to_char(n_count)||' row(s) inserted.');
72  end;
73  /
```

Listing 4-5 isn't a partial listing; it's the whole program! Where did all the PL/SQL go? Well, let's see. First, I'm using a different syntax for this program's INSERT statement, as follows:

```
INSERT INTO <insert_table_name> (
       <column_name_1>,
       <column_name_2>,...
       <column_name_N> )
SELECT <column_name_or_value_1>,
       <column_name_or_value_2>,...
       <column_name_or_value_N>
FROM   <select_table_name_1> <select_table_alias_1>,
       <select_table_name_2> <select_table_alias_2>,...
       <select_table_name_N> <select_table_alias_N>
WHERE  <where _clause>;
```

where `<insert_table_name>` is the name of the table to INSERT INTO, `<column_name>` is the name of a column in that table, `<column_name_or_value>` is the value for a corresponding `<column_name>` from one of the SELECT statement's tables, `<select_table_name>` is one of the tables being queried by the SELECT statement, `<select_table_alias>` is a corresponding table name alias, and `<where_clause>` is the SELECT statement's WHERE clause. The column values can be PL/SQL literals, variables, qualifying function results, or SQL column values.

I'll say it again: you should always use a list of columns in your INSERT statements in order to maintain the validity of your code in the event that someone later adds a column to the table.

Back to our super-duper SQL statement:

On lines 54 and 55, since the WHERE clause selects one row from the WORKER_TYPE_T and GENDER_T tables, the SELECT statement will return only one row of values.

On lines 56 through 61, the NOT EXISTS subquery performs the detection of a duplicate entry and accordingly, the conditional insert of a row.

All the work that was done by five other SQL SELECT statements is now accomplished in one INSERT SELECT statement. What's the moral of this story? Know thy SQL! Each solution presented here has its strengths and weaknesses. As I stated earlier, it's up to you to decide which is the best tactic to apply to each situation.

I favor predetection instead of postdetection (reacting to the DUP_VAL_ON_INDEX exception), because I can maintain control of my program. And I have never found a situation where my PL/SQL batch programs were working on inserting and/or updating the exact same set of data at the same time. So, in ten plus years of writing stored procedures, and after more than 30,000 stored procedures, I've never seen a DUP_VAL_ON_INDEX exception when using predetection. This means you must also consider the nature of the business environment in which you are going to run your stored procedures when deciding whether to use postdetection or predetection.

■Tip You should check out the functionality of the newer SQL DML statement MERGE. It can do a lot of what has already been covered in this chapter, using just SQL. However, it suffers from the same predetection issues I just covered.

It's Your Turn to Insert

Hey, are you just going to watch me do all the work? No way! Here's what I need you to do, and you've got to do it, or the coming examples won't work.

1. Use whatever PL/SQL insert technique you want to code a script to insert rows into the WORKER_T table for four workers: JANE J. DOE, her husband JOHN J. DOE, her daughter JANIE E. DOE, and her son JOHNNIE E. DOE.

2. Save your script as `insert_the_doe_family.sql`.

3. Execute your script.

4. Test your script by executing it again. Make sure you don't get any errors but still get the desired rows in the WORKER_T table.

Listing 4-6 is my solution to this exercise.

Listing 4-6. *An Anonymous Procedure to Insert the Doe Family into the Worker Table, insert_the_doe_family.sql*

```
01  rem insert_the_doe_family.sql
02  rem Donald J. Bales on 12/15/2006
03  rem An anonymous PL/SQL procedure to insert
04  rem values using PL/SQL literals and variables
05
06  set serveroutput on size 1000000;
07
08  declare
09
10  -- I'll use this variable to hold the result
11  -- of the SQL insert statement.
12  n_count                          number := 0;
13
14  -- I've declared this local (or embedded) function to
15  -- do the actual work of inserting values.  It uses
16  -- SQL detection to prevent DUP_VAL_ON_INDEX exceptions.
17  FUNCTION add_worker(
18  aiv_first_name                   WORKER_T.first_name%TYPE,
19  aiv_middle_name                  WORKER_T.middle_name%TYPE,
20  aiv_last_name                    WORKER_T.last_name%TYPE,
21  aid_birth_date                   WORKER_T.birth_date%TYPE,
22  aiv_gender_code                  GENDER_T.code%TYPE,
23  aiv_worker_type_code             WORKER_TYPE_T.code%TYPE)
24  return                           number is
25
26  v_name                           WORKER_T.name%TYPE;
27
28  begin
29    v_name        :=
30      rtrim(aiv_last_name||', '||aiv_first_name||' '||aiv_middle_name);
31
32    -- Now I can just let SQL do all the work.  Who needs PL/SQL!
33    begin
34      insert into WORKER_T (
35              id,
36              worker_type_id,
37              external_id,
38              first_name,
39              middle_name,
40              last_name,
41              name,
42              birth_date,
```

```
43            gender_id )
44     select WORKER_ID_SEQ.nextval,
45            c1.worker_type_id,
46            lpad(to_char(EXTERNAL_ID_SEQ.nextval), 9, '0'),
47            aiv_first_name,
48            aiv_middle_name,
49            aiv_last_name,
50            v_name,
51            aid_birth_date,
52            c2.gender_id
53     from   WORKER_TYPE_T c1,
54            GENDER_T c2
55     where  c1.code = aiv_worker_type_code
56     and    c2.code = aiv_gender_code
57     and not exists (
58       select 1
59       from   WORKER_T x
60       where  x.name       = v_name
61       and    x.birth_date = aid_birth_date
62       and    x.gender_id  = c2.gender_id );
63
64     return sql%rowcount;
65   exception
66     when OTHERS then
67       raise_application_error(-20001, SQLERRM||
68         ' on insert WORKER_T'||
69         ' in add_worker');
70   end;
71 end add_worker;
72
73 begin
74   -- All I have to do now is call the add_worker function
75   -- four times with each Doe family member's values.
76   n_count := n_count + add_worker(
77     'JOHN',   'J.', 'DOE', to_date('19800101', 'YYYYMMDD'), 'M', 'C');
78   n_count := n_count + add_worker(
79     'JANE',   'J.', 'DOE', to_date('19800101', 'YYYYMMDD'), 'F', 'E');
80   n_count := n_count + add_worker(
81     'JOHNNY', 'E.', 'DOE', to_date('19980101', 'YYYYMMDD'), 'M', 'E');
82   n_count := n_count + add_worker(
83     'JANIE',  'E.', 'DOE', to_date('19980101', 'YYYYMMDD'), 'F', 'E');
84
85   pl(to_char(n_count)||' row(s) inserted.');
86 end;
87 /
88
89 commit;
```

In practice, you'll find that you primarily use an INSERT statement in PL/SQL when you do the following:

- Move data from one application to another for data migration

- Transform data for data processing

Beyond those two applications, a program written in some other programming language like Java or a data-loading utility like SQL*Loader will be used to insert values into the database. Now that you have four entries in the WORKER_T table, let's update a couple of them!

Updates

No, I'm not referring to those annoying software revisions from a certain large software company that sometimes do more harm than good. I'm talking about updating a row or rows of data in a relational database from PL/SQL. Let's start with a simple update.

Updating a Row

Listing 4-7 is an example of using a SQL UPDATE statement in PL/SQL. It's just a good, old-fashioned UPDATE statement, where you can also use PL/SQL literals, PL/SQL variables, or SQL functions.

Listing 4-7. *An Update Example Using Variables, insert_with_plsql_detection_for_update.sql*

```
143     begin
144       update WORKER_T
145       set    worker_type_id  = n_worker_type_id
146       where  id              = n_id;
147
148       n_updated := sql%rowcount;
149     exception
150       when OTHERS then
151         raise_application_error(-20007, SQLERRM||
152           ' on update WORKER_T'||
153           ' in filename insert_with_plsql_detection_for_update.sql');
154     end;
```

The syntax used for the SQL UPDATE statement in Listing 4-7 is as follows:

```
UPDATE <table_name>
SET    <column_name_1> = <column_value_1>,
       <column_name_2> = <column_value_2>,...
       <column_name_N> = <column_value_N>
WHERE  <where_clause>;
```

where <table_name> is the name of the table to be updated, <column_name> is the name of a column to update, <column_value> is the corresponding value to use for the column, and <where_clause> is a WHERE clause that appropriately selects the rows to be updated.

I said it earlier, and I'll say it again: you should almost always have a WHERE clause with an UPDATE statement. I've seen some really catastrophic disasters in my day when someone has executed an UPDATE statement without a WHERE clause. I even go so far as to run a PL/SQL program against the database's source table, SYS.DBA_SOURCE, to look for UPDATE statements without WHERE clauses.

As for the code in this listing, well, there's nothing earth-shattering about it:

Lines 144 through 146 contain a SQL UPDATE statement to update a worker's type if a duplicate row already exists in the database.

Line 148 gets the result of the UPDATE statement: the number of rows updated.

On lines 143 through 154 collectively, I've blocked the UPDATE statement in order to capture and report the exact type and location of any unexpected error.

The number one abuse of PL/SQL when used for data-processing is using it to update values in a table in a row-by-row fashion. Why is that an abuse of PL/SQL? Because that's what SQL is for.

Using SQL to Perform Complex Updates

The SQL UPDATE statement is very powerful. While it can't leap tall buildings in a single bound, it can update one or more columns for a predetermined set of rows in a single bound. Why am I spending so much time on this soapbox about knowing SQL? The whole purpose of PL/SQL is to control when to execute an appropriate SQL statement. It is *not* intended to replace SQL with a bunch of poorly performing PL/SQL statements.

You can update multiple columns at a time in a SQL UPDATE statement, as demonstrated in Listing 4-8.

Listing 4-8. *Updating Multiple Columns with an UPDATE Statement, update_multiple.sql*

```
1  update WORKER_T u
2  set    ( u.worker_type_id,  u.gender_id ) = (
3  select c1.worker_type_id, c2.gender_id
4  from   WORKER_TYPE_T c1,
5         GENDER_T c2
6  where  c1.code = decode(instr(u.first_name, 'JOHN'), 0, 'E', 'C')
7  and    c2.code = decode(instr(u.first_name, 'JOHN'), 0, 'F', 'M') )
8  where  u.last_name = 'DOE';
```

The syntax used in the UPDATE statement in Listing 4-8 is as follows:

```
UPDATE <update_table_name>
SET ( <update_column_name_1>, <update_column_name_2>,... <update_column_name_N> ) =
SELECT <select_column_name_1>, <select_column_name_2>,... <select_column_name_N>
FROM   <select_table_name_1>,
       <select_table_name_2>,...
       <select_table_name_N>
```

```
WHERE    <select_column_name_3> = <update_column_name_3>
AND      <select_column_name_4> = <update_column_name_4>
AND      <select_column_name_N> = <update_column_name_N> )
WHERE    <update_column_name_4> = ... ;
```

The UPDATE statement in Listing 4-8 will set the worker type and gender to C (contractor) and M (male), respectively, for anyone with the first name John and the last name Doe. Yes, this is a silly example, but the point here is that the use of subqueries in the SET and WHERE clauses of a SQL UPDATE statement make it possible to update almost anything. All you should need PL/SQL for is deciding when to execute an appropriate SQL UPDATE statement.

Let's take a close look at Listing 4-8:

Line 1 specifies the name of the table to be updated.

Line 2 specifies a list of columns in that table to be updated. The list is enclosed in parentheses followed by an equal sign, and then an opening parenthesis, which is the start of a subquery.

Lines 3 through 7 contain a subquery that will conditionally select which values to update the columns with based on information in the table to be updated.

Line 3 has a list of the same number of values (columns) in the SELECT statement's column list as in the UPDATE statement's SET list.

Lines 4 and 5 specify two code tables from which to draw update values.

On line 6, I conditionally specify the code value for C (contractor) or E (employee), based on whether or not the worker's first_name contains the string 'JOHN'.

On line 7, I conditionally specify the code value for F (female) or M (male), based on whether or not the worker's first name contains the string 'JOHN'.

On line 8, I constrain the rows that will be updated to those with the last_name equal to 'DOE'.

The lesson here: know thy SQL!

As I stated earlier, in practice, you'll primarily use an UPDATE statement in PL/SQL in the following situations:

- The conditions for updating are too complex to be determined using a SQL WHERE clause; that is, you need a more procedural decision-making process.

- Deriving the values to use to update a table's column values is too complex to be done by SQL; that is, you need a more procedural decision-making process.

- You need to use a PL/SQL program unit's ability to formulate a larger and more complex multistatement transaction context.

Hence, the reason PL/SQL exists: to add procedure decision-making capabilities to the use of nonprocedural SQL statements!

Guess what? There's even less to say about deleting rows.

Deletes

In practice, the SQL DELETE command is rarely used when compared to its siblings: INSERT,
UPDATE, and SELECT. However, for completeness, let's look at how you use it in PL/SQL.
Listing 4-9 is an example of using a DELETE statement in PL/SQL, where I use a PL/SQL literal,
a SQL function, and a subquery that uses a PL/SQL variable.

Listing 4-9. *A Delete Example Using a PL/SQL Literal and Variable, delete.sql*

```
01  rem delete.sql
02  rem Donald J. Bales on 12/15/2006
03  rem An anonymous PL/SQL procedure to delete
04  rem rows using PL/SQL literals and variables
05
06  set serveroutput on size 1000000;
07
08  declare
09
10  -- I'll use this variable to hold the result
11  -- of the SQL delete statement.
12  n_count                        number;
13
14  v_code                         GENDER_T.code%TYPE := 'M';
15
16  begin
17
18    begin
19      delete from WORKER_T d
20      where  d.name        = 'DOE, JOHN J.'              -- a literal
21      and    d.birth_date = to_date('19800101', 'YYYYMMDD')  -- a function
22      and    d.gender_id  = (                           -- a sub-query
23      select c.gender_id
24      from   GENDER_T c
25      where  c.code        = v_code );                  -- a variable
26
27      n_count := sql%rowcount;
28    exception
29      when OTHERS then
30        raise_application_error(-20001, SQLERRM||
31          ' on delete WORKER_T'||
32          ' in filename delete.sql');
33    end;
34
35    pl(to_char(n_count)||' row(s) deleted.');
36  end;
37  /
```

The syntax for the SQL DELETE statement used in Listing 4-9 is as follows:

```
DELETE [FROM] <delete_table_name>
WHERE <where_clause> ;
```

Where <delete_table_name> is the name of the table from which to delete rows, and <where_clause> is a SQL WHERE clause that appropriately specifies the rows within the table to delete.

On line 27, I capture the result of the SQL DELETE statement: the number of rows deleted. Just as with an UPDATE statement, every DELETE statement should have a WHERE clause.

Let's discuss how you might apply a DELETE statement in PL/SQL. In practice, you'll primarily use a DELETE statement in PL/SQL when the conditions for deleting are too complex to be determined by using a WHERE clause. So you'll find that you rarely use DELETE at all!

Finally, let's look at the SELECT statement.

Selects

The SQL SELECT statement is the most used SQL statement in PL/SQL, and for a good reason. PL/SQL is all about encompassing set-based operations with procedural logic. Yet, a SQL SELECT statement is a nonprocedural construct; hence, the need for the PL in PL/SQL. In this section, I'll discuss the singleton SELECT statement—the one that is supposed to return one row.

You've seen me use SELECT statements over and over again at this point. As I've said, I assume you already know SQL. Regardless, I've tried to take some time to review what you know about SQL, so you'll be ready for PL/SQL. Most PL/SQL stored procedures you write will have one or more SELECT statements in them. So what you can accomplish using PL/SQL—whether it's object-oriented architecture, service-oriented architecture, data processing, data migration, or reporting—will be constrained by your competency in writing a SQL SELECT statement.

Let's look back at our first source code listing in this chapter, Listing 4-3. For your convenience (and mine), I'm going to show part of it to you again in Listing 4-10.

Listing 4-10. *An Example of Using Singleton SELECT Statements in PL/SQL, insert_with_plsql_detection.sql*

```
048    -- Next, let's get the gender_id for a male
049    begin
050      select gender_id
051      into   n_gender_id
052      from   GENDER_T
053      where  code = 'M';
054    exception
055      when OTHERS then
056        raise_application_error(-20004, SQLERRM||
057          ' on select GENDER_T'||
058          ' in filename insert_with_plsql_detection.sql');
059    end;
060
```

```
061    -- Detect any existing entries with the unique
062    -- combination of columns as in this constraint:
063    -- constraint   WORKER_T_UK2
064    -- unique (
065    -- name,
066    -- birth_date,
067    -- gender_id )
068    begin
069      select count(1)
070      into   n_count
071      from   WORKER_T
072      where  name       = v_name
073      and    birth_date = d_birth_date
074      and    gender_id  = n_gender_id;
075    exception
076      when OTHERS then
077        raise_application_error(-20005, SQLERRM||
078          ' on select WORKER_T_T'||
079          ' in filename insert_with_plsql_detection.sql');
080    end;
081
082    -- Conditionally insert the row
083    if n_count = 0 then
084      -- Now, let's get the next id sequence
085      begin
086        select WORKER_ID_SEQ.nextval
087        into   n_id
088        from   SYS.DUAL;
089      exception
090        when OTHERS then
091          raise_application_error(-20001, SQLERRM||
092            ' on select WORKER_ID_SEQ.nextval'||
093            ' in filename insert_with_plsql_detection.sql');
094      end;
```

The syntax used for the SQL SELECT statements in Listing 4-10 is as follows:

```
SELECT <column_name_1>,
       <column_name_2>,...
       <column_name_N>
INTO   <plsql_variable_1>,
       <plsql_variable_2>,...
       <plsql_variable_N>
FROM   <table_name_1>,
       <table_name_2>,...
       <table_name_N>
WHERE  <where_clause>... ;
```

where `<column_name>` is the name of a column in one of the tables in the FROM list, `<plsql_variable>` is the corresponding variable to copy the column value to, `<table_name>` is a table to query, and `<where_clause>` is an appropriate WHERE clause.

Let's examine the three SQL SELECT INTO statements in Listing 4-10:

Lines 50 through 53 get the corresponding gender_id value for the code 'M'.

Line 50 selects the column name, gender_id.

Line 51 specifies the PL/SQL variable n_gender_id in the INTO clause.

Line 52 specifies the code table's name, GENDER_T.

Line 53 specifies a WHERE clause, where the code is equal to 'M'.

On lines 49 through 59 collectively, I block the SQL SELECT statement in order to catch and report any catastrophic errors (WHEN OTHERS). This is a SELECT statement where I don't expect any exceptions. I always expect the corresponding values to exist in the database.

On lines 69 through 74, I use a SQL group operator, count(), to determine the number of rows in the table that match the criteria of the associated WHERE clause.

On lines 68 through 80 collectively, I block the SQL SELECT statement for OTHERS. This is a safe SQL SELECT statement. It will always have a result, except for in the case of some unforeseeable database error.

Lines 86 through 88 get the next sequence value for the column id from sequence WORKER_ID_SEQ.

On lines 85 through 94 collectively, I block the SQL SELECT statement for any unforeseeable errors, but I never expect this SQL SELECT statement to raise an exception.

But what do you do if you expect an error? For example, perhaps a row matching the WHERE clause criteria is not in the table! Or maybe too many rows match the WHERE clause criteria. What do you do then?

What Do You Mean, "No Data Found?"

As I stated earlier when I first discussed exceptions in Chapter 2, there are two very commonly used exceptions. The most commonly used exception is NO_DATA_FOUND. When a singleton SELECT statement can't find a row to match its WHERE clause's criteria, it will raise a NO_DATA_FOUND exception. You saw an example of this earlier in Listing 4-4. Listing 4-11 highlights the SELECT statement in question.

Listing 4-11. *An Example of a SELECT Statement That May Raise a NO_DATA_FOUND Exception, insert_with_plsql_detection_for_update.sql*

```
069    begin
070       select id
071       into   n_id
072       from   WORKER_T
073       where  name       = v_name
```

```
074      and     birth_date = d_birth_date
075      and     gender_id  = n_gender_id;
076   exception
077     when NO_DATA_FOUND then
078       n_id := NULL; -- Is this really needed?
079     when OTHERS then
080       raise_application_error(-20003, SQLERRM||
081         ' on select WORKER_T_T'||
082         ' in filename insert_with_plsql_detection_for_update.sql');
083   end;
```

This SELECT statement may raise a NO_DATA_FOUND exception because the database might not contain a matching row. As a matter of fact, that's just what we're trying to determine here. If the SELECT statement returns an id value, then the program knows that an entry already exists, so it will update the existing entry. Otherwise, the program will insert a new entry. It's the otherwise condition that will raise the exception.

When the NO_DATA_FOUND exception is raised, program execution jumps from the SELECT statement directly to the enclosing WHEN NO_DATA_FOUND clause. In this case, I set the n_id to NULL in that clause, and then later in the program, I use that fact to conditionally insert a new row.

Since the SELECT statement returns one set of columns—one row—from the database, there's no way for it to report the number of rows found, right? No, you can still get the number of rows returned from sql%rowcount. Take a look at Listing 4-12.

Listing 4-12. *An Example of a SELECT Statement That Captures the Selected Row Count, select_no_data_found.sql*

```
40   begin
41     select id
42     into   n_id
43     from   WORKER_T
44     where  name       = v_name
45     and    birth_date = d_birth_date
46     and    gender_id  = n_gender_id;
47
48     n_selected := sql%rowcount;
49   exception
50     when NO_DATA_FOUND then
51       n_selected := sql%rowcount;
52       pl('Caught raised exception NO_DATA_FOUND');
53     when OTHERS then
54       raise_application_error(-20002, SQLERRM||
55         ' on select WORKER_T'||
56         ' in filename select_no_data_found.sql');
57   end;
```

In Listing 4-12, I initially set the value of n_selected to –1, just so I can prove the value is changed later in the program. If the SELECT statement executes successfully, n_selected is equal

to 1, because its value is set on line 48. However, if the SELECT statement raises the
NO_DATA_FOUND exception, n_selected is equal to 0, because I set its value on line 51.

The number of rows returned from the SELECT statement is reported by the database, so
why do we need a NO_DATA_FOUND exception? Why does it even exist? Quite frankly, I don't know.
I think the exception exists as a matter of programming convenience. It's syntactic sugar. So
even though it breaks my "You should always maintain control in your program" rule, it's
commonly used to detect that no matching row was found for a WHERE clause's criteria. Even I
use it.

I'll show you another tactic for detecting no data found for a singleton in the next chapter
when we cover cursors. If you're going to rely on the NO_DATA_FOUND exception, you must keep
in mind that any code that comes after your SELECT statement will not be executed if your SELECT
statement raises NO_DATA_FOUND.

Next, let's look at the other singleton SELECT issue: too many rows are returned.

Too Many Rows—You're Kidding, Right?

Hey, I'm an American! How can any amount of rows be too many? Well, in the context of a
singleton SELECT, PL/SQL is always going to expect your SELECT statement to return one and
only one row. We just finished discussing what happens when a SELECT statement doesn't get
at least one row. So what happens when a SELECT statement gets one (or more) too many? It
raises the exception TOO_MANY_ROWS. Listing 4-13 is an example of a SELECT statement that will
raise the exception TOO_MANY_ROWS.

Listing 4-13. *An Example of a SELECT Statement That Raises a TOO_MANY_ROWS Exception,*
select_too_many_rows.sql

```
40    begin
41      select id
42      into   n_id
43      from   WORKER_T;
44  --    where name      = v_name
45  --      and   birth_date = d_birth_date
46  --      and   gender_id  = n_gender_id;
47      n_selected := sql%rowcount;
48    exception
49      when NO_DATA_FOUND then
50        n_selected := sql%rowcount;
51        pl('Caught raised exception NO_DATA_FOUND');
52      when TOO_MANY_ROWS then
53        n_selected := sql%rowcount;
54        pl('Caught raised exception TOO_MANY_ROWS');
55      when OTHERS then
56        raise_application_error(-20002, SQLERRM||
57          ' on select WORKER_T'||
58          ' in filename select_too_many_rows.sql');
59    end;
```

In Listing 4-13, I've commented out the WHERE clause so the SELECT statement will see all four Doe family entries, and accordingly, will raise a TOO_MANY_ROWS exception. On lines 52 through 54, I've also added a WHEN TOO_MANY_ROWS clause to catch the raised exception, and in turn, capture the number of rows returned by the SELECT statement.

Guess what? On line 53, sql%rowcount reports that only one row was selected. So PL/SQL has no idea how many rows actually match the query. It only knows that more than one exists, and that's a problem—where will PL/SQL put the data from rows 2 and on? There's actually no place for the data, so PL/SQL appropriately throws an exception. After all, the query was supposed to be a singleton query!

You can add PL/SQL code to predetect too many rows, similar to the technique demonstrated in Listing 4-3, when I was trying to predetect a duplicate row.

If count() returns a value greater than one, the program will know that there's more than one row. But once again, PL/SQL provides us with some syntactic sugar that allows us to use an exception to detect a condition. Yes, again that syntactic sugar—catching a TOO_MANY_ROWS exception—breaks my rule "You should always maintain control over your program!" I'll admit it, I use it. I catch the exception. I don't like it. But as I'll show you in the next chapter, you'll need to write a lot of extra code to maintain control, so PL/SQL programmers commonly use the exception TOO_MANY_ROWS.

Once again, if you're going to rely on the TOO_MANY_ROWS exception, you must keep in mind that any code that comes after your SELECT statement will not be executed if your SELECT statement raises TOO_MANY_ROWS!

That's enough of that. Now let's see you put what I just said to work.

It's Your Turn to Select

Your assignment is to write an anonymous procedure that displays the first name of each of the Doe family members from the WORKER_T table—remember, the ones you added in the previous exercise? To that end, follow these steps:

1. Write your script using at least one singleton SELECT.

2. Save your script as select_the_doe_family.sql.

3. Execute your script.

4. Test your script by executing it again. Make sure you don't get any errors but still get the desired rows from the WORKER_T table.

Listing 4-14 is my lousy solution. Why lousy? Because my solution involves repeatedly executing a singleton SELECT statement in order to read multiple rows from the WORKER_T table. We really need a better way to handle this situation, and a better solution for this problem is just what we'll cover in the next chapter.

Listing 4-14. *A Really Bad Way to Select Multiple Rows from a Table, select_the_doe_family.sql*

```
01  rem select_the_doe_family.sql
02  rem Donald J. Bales on 12/15/2006
03  rem An anonymous PL/SQL procedure to select
04  rem the first names for the Doe family from
```

```
05  rem the Worker table.
06
07  set serveroutput on size 1000000;
08
09  declare
10
11  v_first_name                        WORKER_T.first_name%TYPE;
12  n_id                                WORKER_T.id%TYPE;
13
14  -- A local function that will be called over and over again
15  -- to find the next first_name for the specified id
16  -- and last_name.
17  FUNCTION get_first_name(
18  aion_id                     in out WORKER_T.id%TYPE,
19  aiv_last_name               in     WORKER_T.last_name%TYPE)
20  return                             WORKER_T.first_name%TYPE is
21
22  v_first_name                        WORKER_T.first_name%TYPE;
23
24  begin
25    -- Use SQL pseudo-column rownum in order
26    -- to limit the SELECT to the first row
27    select id,
28           first_name
29    into   aion_id,
30           v_first_name
31    from   WORKER_T
32    where  id > aion_id
33    and    last_name like aiv_last_name||'%'
34    and    rownum = 1;
35
36    return v_first_name;
37  exception
38    when NO_DATA_FOUND then
39      return v_first_name;
40    when OTHERS then
41      raise_application_error(-20001, SQLERRM||
42        ' on select WORKER_T'||
43        ' in show_worker');
44  end get_first_name;
45
46  begin
47    -- Keep track of the primary key so you
48    -- only retrieve the SELECTed row once
49    n_id := 0;
50    -- Loop until there's NO_DATA_FOUND
51    loop
```

```
52      -- get the first name from the local function
53      v_first_name := get_first_name(n_id, 'DOE');
54      -- detect NO_DATA_FOUND
55      if v_first_name is NULL then
56         exit;  -- Exit the loop
57      end if;
58      -- show the first_name
59      pl(v_first_name);
60    end loop;
61  end;
62  /
```

In practice, you'll find that you primarily use a singleton SELECT statement in PL/SQL when you want to do the following:

- Select the IDs for some code values that you will reference repeatedly

- Allocate a sequence value for a new primary key value

- Predetect the presence of a matching row

Let's review what you've learned.

Summary

At this point, it should be evident that a singleton is a SQL statement that returns one set of results. Table 4-1 is a side-by-side comparison of the results returned by each of the singletons I've covered: INSERT, UPDATE, DELETE, and SELECT.

Table 4-1. *Singleton Results for INSERT, UPDATE, DELETE, and SELECT*

Statement	Returns	Common Exceptions
INSERT INTO	Row count	DUP_VAL_ON_INDEX
UPDATE	Row count	
DELETE FROM	Row count	
SELECT...INTO	Row count and column values	NO_DATA_FOUND, TOO_MANY_ROWS

When you're working with the INSERT INTO and SELECT...INTO statements, you may as well expect an exception, and write your PL/SQL accordingly. Of the four singletons, you'll use the SELECT statement the most. After all, you are working with a database.

Our last exercise left us begging for a better solution to selecting more than one row at a time. In the next chapter, we'll look at the PL/SQL solution to this problem: a CURSOR.

CHAPTER 5

■ ■ ■

Next Please, One Row at a Time!

In our last episode, we left off with our "would-be" PL/SQL programmer trying to retrieve the first names of the Doe family members from table WORKER_T using a singleton SELECT. Little did our programmer know that Oracle has already solved this problem, and the magic required to pull off such a feat was already in his hands.

Cursors

And I don't mean the four-letter ones either! A *cursor* in this context is a named SQL SELECT statement that you can use in your PL/SQL program to access multiple rows from a table, yet retrieve them one row at a time.

Cursor Declarations

You declare cursors in the declaration section of a PL/SQL block just as you declare functions, procedures, and variables. And you should declare them with parameters, if required, just as you do with functions and procedures.

Listing 5-1 is a better solution to our last exercise in Chapter 4, where you were assigned the task of listing the Doe family's first names.

Listing 5-1. *An Example of Using a Cursor to Select Multiple Rows from a Table, cursor_the_doe_family.sql*

```
01  rem cursor_the_doe_family.sql
02  rem by Donald J. Bales on 12/15/2006
03  rem An anonymous PL/SQL procedure to select
04  rem the first names for the Doe family from
05  rem the Worker table.
06
07  set serveroutput on size 1000000;
08
09  declare
10
```

```
11  CURSOR c_worker(
12  aiv_last_name                    IN      WORKER_T.last_name%TYPE) is
13  select first_name
14  from    WORKER_T
15  where   last_name like aiv_last_name||'%'
16  order by id;
17
18  v_first_name                             WORKER_T.first_name%TYPE;
19
20  begin
21    OPEN c_worker('DOE');
22    LOOP
23      FETCH c_worker INTO v_first_name;
24
25      if c_worker%notfound then
26        CLOSE c_worker;
27        EXIT;
28      end if;
29
30      pl(v_first_name);
31    END LOOP;
32  end;
33  /
```

There's a lot of new PL/SQL in this example. Let's start with syntax. The syntax used in Listing 5-1 to declare CURSOR c_worker is as follows:

```
CURSOR <cursor_name> [(
<parameter_name_1>        [IN]        <parameter_data_type_1>,
<parameter_name_2>        [IN]        <parameter_data_type_2>,...
<parameter_name_N>        [IN]        <parameter_data_type_N> )] IS
<select_statement>;
```

where <cursor_name> is the name of the CURSOR; <parameter_name> is the name of a parameter being passed IN; <parameter_data_type> is the PL/SQL data type of the corresponding parameter; and <select_statement> is a SQL SELECT statement. The brackets ([ ]) around the parameters denote that they are optional.

Of course, there's more to using cursors than just declaring them. Read on, as the next few subsections tell you all about what you can accomplish using cursors.

Fetching Rows from a Cursor Manually

The procedural PL/SQL, or control structure, syntax used to retrieve rows using the declared CURSOR in Listing 5-1 is as follows:

```
OPEN <cursor_name> [(
  <parameter_value_1,
  <parameter_value_2>,...
  <parameter_value_N> )];

LOOP
  -- loop until you manually EXIT;
END LOOP;

FETCH <cursor_name> INTO
  <variable_name_1>,
  <variable_name_2>,...
  <variable_name_N>;

CLOSE <cursor_name>;

EXIT;
```

where <cursor_name> is the name of a declared CURSOR; <parameter_value> is a value to pass in to the CURSOR that will be utilized somewhere in its SQL SELECT statement; and <variable_name> is a PL/SQL variable to receive one of the SQL SELECT statement's column values from the CURSOR.

The keyword OPEN is used to pass parameters to, and then execute, the cursor's SQL SELECT statement. FETCH retrieves one row of column values from the cursor's SELECT statement into a comma-separated list of PL/SQL variables. CLOSE does just that—it closes a CURSOR, releasing the cursor's resources back to PL/SQL and the database.

The keyword LOOP is used to start an unconstrained loop. In this context, any PL/SQL code between the keywords LOOP and END LOOP will continue to be executed over and over again until you manually exit the loop with the keyword EXIT. It's what I call a manual loop.

Here's the output from the cursor_the_doe_family.sql script (Listing 5-1):

```
SQL> @cursor_the_doe_family


JOHN
JANE
JOHNNY
JANIE

PL/SQL procedure successfully completed.
```

It's the same output you got from doing the last exercise in Chapter 4, right? Let's take a moment to look at Listing 5-1, line by line:

Lines 11 through 16 declare CURSOR c_worker, which will select the first name column from the table WORKER_T, where the last name is like the one passed in.

Line 18 declares a variable to hold the column value from the cursor.

On line 21, I open the cursor, passing it the last name 'DOE'. This should give me all the first names for anyone with a name like "DOE."

Line 22 starts a manual loop. Lines 23 through 30 will be repeated endlessly, until I exit manually, as I do on line 27.

On line 23, I fetch the value of the column first_name into variable v_first_name.

On line 25, I test the cursor c_worker for %notfound. If the SELECT statement did not find a row in the database for the current loop, the cursor c_worker will report no data found through the cursor variable %notfound.

On line 26, if there is no data found, I CLOSE the cursor, and then EXIT the loop on line 27.

On line 30, if a row is found, I display the first name on the screen using pl().

On line 31, the keywords END LOOP signifies the end of the LOOP.

Using a cursor for this type of problem—that is, retrieving multiple rows one row at a time—is definitely a better solution, if for no other reason than it was easier to maintain control over the program. But PL/SQL's solutions to this problem are going to get even better.

Cursor Records

On line 18 in Listing 5-1, I declared the variable v_first_name, to hold the value from the database during each iteration of the LOOP. You can also use the keyword %ROWTYPE to declare a record for a cursor. So with one declaration, you can declare a record that has as many columns as the cursor it is defined for, with the same field names as the column names in the SELECT statement of the cursor. For example, I could have declared a record for CURSOR c_worker on line 18 as follows:

```
r_worker                          c_worker%ROWTYPE;
```

Pretty neat, huh? You'll see an example of this later in the chapter, in Listing 5-7. Now let's take a look at using a cursor as a singleton SELECT.

A Singleton Cursor

By using a cursor, you can eliminate having to give up control of your programs when a NO_DATA_FOUND exception is raised, because one is never raised. Instead, you can check the cursor variable for the status %notfound. Listing 5-2 is an example of using a cursor for a singleton SELECT. As you will see as we review the listing, sometimes using a cursor to retrieve one row can cost more in code than it's worth.

Listing 5-2. *An Example of Using a Cursor for a Singleton SELECT,*
insert_with_plsql_cursor_detection_for_update.sql

```
001   rem insert_with_plsql_cursor_detection_for_update.sql
002   rem by Donald J. Bales on 12/15/2006
003   rem An anonymous PL/SQL procedure to insert
004   rem values using PL/SQL literals and variables
005
006   set serveroutput on size 1000000;
007
008   declare
009
010   cursor c_worker_type(
011   aiv_code                    in      WORKER_TYPE_T.code%TYPE) is
012   select id
013   from   WORKER_TYPE_T
014   where  code = aiv_code;
015
016   cursor c_gender(
017   aiv_code                    in      GENDER_T.code%TYPE) is
018   select id
019   from   GENDER_T
020   where  code = aiv_code;
021
022   cursor c_worker(
023   aiv_name                    in      WORKER_T.name%TYPE,
024   aid_birth_date              in      WORKER_T.birth_date%TYPE,
025   ain_gender_id               in      WORKER_T.gender_id%TYPE) is
026   select id
027   from   WORKER_T
028   where  name       = aiv_name
029   and    birth_date = aid_birth_date
030   and    gender_id  = ain_gender_id;
031
032   cursor c_worker_id is
033   select WORKER_ID_SEQ.nextval worker_id
034   from   SYS.DUAL;
035
036   cursor c_external_id is
037   select lpad(to_char(EXTERNAL_ID_SEQ.nextval), 9, '0') external_id
038   from   SYS.DUAL;
039
040   -- I declared these variables so I can get
041   -- the required ID values before I insert.
042   n_ id                          WORKER_T. id%TYPE;
043   n_worker_type_id               WORKER_T.worker_type_id%TYPE;
044   v_external_id                  WORKER_T.external_id%TYPE;
045   v_first_name                   WORKER_T.first_name%TYPE;
```

```
046  v_middle_name                        WORKER_T.middle_name%TYPE;
047  v_last_name                          WORKER_T.last_name%TYPE;
048  v_name                               WORKER_T.name%TYPE;
049  d_birth_date                         WORKER_T.birth_date%TYPE;
050  n_gender_id                          WORKER_T.gender_id%TYPE;
051
052  -- I'll use these variables to hold the result
053  -- of the SQL insert and update statements.
054  n_inserted                           number := 0;
055  n_updated                            number := 0;
056
057  begin
058    v_first_name  := 'JOHN';
059    v_middle_name := 'J.';
060    v_last_name   := 'DOE';
061    v_name        :=
062      rtrim(v_last_name||', '||v_first_name||' '||v_middle_name);
063    d_birth_date  :=
064      to_date('19800101', 'YYYYMMDD'); -- I'm guessing
065
066    -- First, let's get the worker_type_id for a contractor
067    begin
068      open  c_worker_type('C');
069      fetch c_worker_type
070      into  n_worker_type_id;
071      if    c_worker_type%notfound then
072       raise_application_error(-20001,
073         'Can''t find the worker type ID for Contractor.'||
074         ' on select WORKER_TYPE_T'||
075         ' in filename insert_with_plsql_cursor_detection_for_update.sql');
076      end if;
077      close c_worker_type;
078    exception
079      when OTHERS then
080        raise_application_error(-20002, SQLERRM||
081          ' on select WORKER_TYPE_T'||
082          ' in filename insert_with_plsql_cursor_detection_for_update.sql');
083    end;
084
085    -- Next, let's get the gender_id for a male
086    begin
087      open  c_gender('M');
088      fetch c_gender
089      into  n_gender_id;
090      if    c_gender%notfound then
091       raise_application_error(-20003,
092         'Can''t find the gender ID for Male.'||
```

```
093           ' on select GENDER_T'||
094           ' in filename insert_with_plsql_cursor_detection_for_update.sql');
095      end if;
096      close c_gender;
097   exception
098      when OTHERS then
099        raise_application_error(-20004, SQLERRM||
100           ' on select GENDER_T'||
101           ' in filename insert_with_plsql_cursor_detection_for_update.sql');
102   end;
103
104   -- Detect any existing entries with the unique
105   -- combination of columns as in this constraint:
106   -- constraint    WORKER_T_UK2
107   -- unique (
108   -- name,
109   -- birth_date,
110   -- gender_id )
111   begin
112     open  c_worker(v_name, d_birth_date, n_gender_id);
113     fetch c_worker
114     into  n_id;
115     if    c_worker%notfound then
116       n_id := NULL;
117     end if;
118     close c_worker;
119   exception
120      when OTHERS then
121        raise_application_error(-20005, SQLERRM||
122           ' on select WORKER_T'||
123           ' in filename insert_with_plsql_cursor_detection_for_update.sql');
124   end;
125
126   -- Conditionally insert the row
127   if n_id is NULL then
128     -- Now, let's get the next worker id sequence
129     begin
130     open  c_worker_id;
131     fetch c_worker_id
132     into  n_id;
133     close c_worker_id;
134     exception
135        when OTHERS then
136          raise_application_error(-20006, SQLERRM||
137             ' on select WORKER_ID_SEQ.nextval'||
138             ' in filename insert_with_plsql_cursor_detection_for_update.sql');
139     end;
140
```

```
141        -- And then, let's get the next external_id sequence
142        begin
143        open  c_external_id;
144        fetch c_external_id
145        into  v_external_id;
146        if    c_external_id%notfound then
147          v_external_id := NULL;
148        end if;
149        close c_external_id;
150        exception
151          when OTHERS then
152            raise_application_error(-20006, SQLERRM||
153              ' on select EXTERNAL_ID_SEQ.nextval'||
154              ' in filename insert_with_plsql_cursor_detection_for_update.sql');
155        end;
156
157        -- Now that we have all the necessary ID values
158        -- we can finally insert a row!
159        begin
160          insert into WORKER_T (
161                id,
162                worker_type_id,
163                external_id,
164                first_name,
165                middle_name,
166                last_name,
167                name,
168                birth_date,
169                gender_id )
170          values (
171                n_id,
172                n_worker_type_id,
173                v_external_id,
174                v_first_name,
175                v_middle_name,
176                v_last_name,
177                v_name,
178                d_birth_date,
179                n_gender_id );
180
181          n_inserted := sql%rowcount;
182        exception
183          when OTHERS then
184            raise_application_error(-20007, SQLERRM||
185              ' on insert WORKER_T'||
186              ' in filename insert_with_plsql_cursor_detection_for_update.sql');
187        end;
```

```
188    else
189      begin
190        update WORKER_T
191        set    worker_type_id = n_worker_type_id
192        where  id             = n_id;
193
194        n_updated := sql%rowcount;
195      exception
196        when OTHERS then
197          raise_application_error(-20008, SQLERRM||
198            ' on update WORKER_T'||
199            ' in filename insert_with_plsql_cursor_detection_for_update.sql');
200      end;
201    end if;
202
203    pl(to_char(n_inserted)||' row(s) inserted.');
204    pl(to_char(n_updated)||' row(s) updated.');
205  end;
206  /
```

Listing 5-2 doesn't have any new syntax, but it does show a different utilization of the keywords OPEN, FETCH, and CLOSE. You may recall seeing a form of this source code originally in Listing 4-4. Now it has been modified to use cursors for its singleton SELECT statements, so I can argue when it's a good idea to use cursors for singletons and when it's not.

Let's break down the listing:

Lines 10 through 14 declare a cursor for table WORKER_TYPE_T.

Lines 16 through 20 declare a cursor for table GENDER_T.

Lines 22 through 30 declare a cursor for table WORKER_T. Later in the executable section, I'll pass parameters for the worker's name, birth date, and gender in order to try to find an existing row in the database.

Lines 32 through 34 declare a cursor for allocating the next worker ID sequence value.

Lines 36 through 38 I declare a cursor for allocating the external ID sequence value.

On line 68, I open the cursor for the worker type, passing the code value C as a parameter.

On line 69 and 70, I try to fetch the corresponding worker_type_id value into variable n_worker_type_id.

On line 71, I test the cursor variable c_worker_type%notfound to see if a corresponding ID value was found. If not, I raise an application error, which stops the execution of the program.

Line 77 closes the cursor (that's a mandatory programming task).

On lines 68 through 83 collectively, I've blocked OPEN, FETCH, and CLOSE in order to capture any unusual errors.

On lines 86 through 102 collectively, I do the same for table GENDER_T as I have done for table WORKER_TYPE_T. *My assessment: using a cursor for getting the code IDs gains me nothing.* I don't expect there to be an exception, so I really don't gain any more control over the program by using a cursor for singleton SELECT as in this situation.

On lines 111 through 124 collectively, I use a cursor to select a matching id from WORKER_T. *This time, there is an advantage in using a cursor for a singleton SELECT.* Since I expect that the SELECT may not find any data, I can query the cursor variable c_worker%notfound to determine this. If the SELECT statement did not find a matching entry in the table, I set variable n_id to NULL to flag that no matching entry exists. In this instance, I no longer needed to code a WHEN NO_DATA_FOUND exception.

On lines 129 through 139, and 142 through 155 collectively, I've used cursors to select the next sequence values from the database. Once again, since I don't expect any possible errors, using cursors for singleton SELECT statements adds a lot of code but little value.

The moral of the story is that you may want to use a cursor for a singleton SELECT if you expect a NO_DATA_FOUND exception may be raised; otherwise, you may as well stick to a simple SELECT statement. In practice, I personally have no problem with utilizing the exception NO_DATA_FOUND, syntactic sugar that it is, but the choice is now yours.

It's Your Turn to Fetch Manually

Yes, your head is growing with knowledge, and if you don't put it to use soon, it may swell (and you'll forget everything). In this section, I'll give you an assignment to write a program using cursors. But first, I'll present a point of view on why good use of cursors is so important.

Do you ever think about how many times you've written a given SQL statement? Do you ever find yourself writing the same statement more than once in your program? Just how many times should you write the same SQL statement? In my opinion, the answer is just once! There are a lot of reasons to avoid writing the same statement more than once. Let's start with these:

- One SQL statement to accomplish one goal means fewer cursors in use on your database, and that means better performance.

- One SQL statement to accomplish one task means consistent behavior across your application's presentation layers.

- One SQL statement to accomplish one requirement means it will be easier to maintain and modify your application's code.

- One SQL statement to attain the goals just mentioned means saving money, and saved money is profit.

To attain better performance, consistent behavior, more maintainable code, and profit, you're going to have to start thinking like an object-oriented programmer.

What's your assignment? Write three packages for three tables. I'll show you two out of the three so you have some models for your coding, but I expect you to stretch during your third exercise and do number three all on your own. Let's start by *modularizing* a code table.

A Code Table Package

In the listings in Chapter 4 and now Chapter 5, I've repeatedly coded the same SQL SELECT statement, in order to get the corresponding ID value for a given code. So rather than keep writing the same code over and over, I've created a package called WORKER_TYPE_TS, for table WORKER_TYPE_T. This is what I call a pseudo-object-oriented approach to programming in PL/SQL.

Listing 5-3 is the worker type codes package spec, and Listing 5-4 is its implementation, or package body.

Listing 5-3. *The WORKER_TYPE_TS Package Spec, worker_type_ts.pks*

```
01  create or replace PACKAGE WORKER_TYPE_TS as
02  /*
03  worker_type_ts.pks
04  by Donald J. Bales on 12/15/2006
05  Code Table WORKER_TYPE_T's methods.
06  */
07
08
09  -- Returns the id for the specified code value.
10
11  FUNCTION get_id(
12  aiv_code                    in      WORKER_TYPE_T.code%TYPE )
13  return                              WORKER_TYPE_T.id%TYPE;
14
15
16  end WORKER_TYPE_TS;
17  /
18  @se.sql WORKER_TYPE_TS
```

In Listing 5-3, I've declared one function, get_id(aiv_code) return id. Now if programmers—whether they are coding in a PL/SQL program, a JDBC program, C, C++, Perl, PowerScript, and so on—want to get the id value for a corresponding code value, all they need to do is call the PL/SQL function WORKER_TYPE_TS.get_id(), passing it an existing code value.

Listing 5-4. *The WORKER_TYPE_TS Package Body, worker_type_ts.pkb*

```
01  create or replace PACKAGE BODY WORKER_TYPE_TS as
02  /*
03  worker_type_ts.pkb
04  by Donald J. Bales on 12/15/2006
05  Table WORKER_TYPE_T's methods
06  */
07
08
09  -- FUNCTIONS
10
```

```
11  FUNCTION get_id(
12  aiv_code                        in        WORKER_TYPE_T.code%TYPE )
13  return                                    WORKER_TYPE_T.id%TYPE is
14
15  n_id                                      WORKER_TYPE_T.id%TYPE;
16
17  begin
18    select id
19    into   n_id
20    from   WORKER_TYPE_T
21    where  code = aiv_code;
22
23    return n_id;
24  end get_id;
25
26
27  end WORKER_TYPE_TS;
28  /
29  @be.sql WORKER_TYPE_TS
```

Let's look at the implementation in Listing 5-4:

Line 11 declares the implementation for function get_id().

Line 12 specifies that a calling program must pass in a code value.

Line 13 specifies that the function will return a worker type ID value.

Line 15 declares a local variable, n_id to hold the ID value retrieved from the database.

Lines 18 through 21 contain a SQL SELECT statement to retrieve a corresponding ID value for the given code value in parameter aiv_code.

On line 23, I return the retrieved ID value to the calling program unit.

Lines 11 through 24 collectively implement a SQL SELECT statement to retrieve an ID value for a corresponding code value. I have not blocked this SQL statement, so it will raise a NO_DATA_FOUND exception should one occur. This means the calling program may want to block the call to WORKER_TYPE_TS.get_id() in order to be able to report the exact error and the location where it occurred in the program.

Now, anywhere I would have coded another SQL statement to select an ID from table WORKER_TYPE_T for a given code, I can simply code:

```
n_worker_type_id := WORKER_TYPE_TS.get_id('C');
```

or better yet:

```
begin
  n_worker_type_id := WORKER_TYPE_TS.get_id('C');
exception
  when OTHERS then
```

```
    raise_application_error(-20???, SQLERRM||
      ' on call WORKERT_TYPE_TS.get_id()'||
      ' in <my_program_unit>');
end;
```

The latter example, although more code, will make it easier to troubleshoot your program when an error does occur.

So what's part one of your assignment? Create a codes package for table GENDER_T, and that includes compiling and testing it. When you're finished, continue reading for part two.

A Worker Table Package

In a similar fashion to the code tables, I've written SQL SELECT statements numerous times in order to allocate database-generated sequence values. So I've created package WORKER_TS to hold functions and procedures for table WORKER_T. The first function I've added is get_id(). However, this time, get_id() is called without parameters and returns the next available sequence number for the WORKER_T id column.

Take a look at package WORKER_TS. Listing 5-5 is its package spec, and Listing 5-6 is its implementation.

Listing 5-5. *The WORKER_TS Package Spec, worker_ts.pks*

```
01  create or replace PACKAGE WORKER_TS as
02  /*
03  worker_ts.pks
04  by Donald J. Bales on 12/15/2006
05  Table WORKER_T's methods.
06  */
07
08
09  -- Return the next ID sequence value
10
11  FUNCTION get_id
12  return                          WORKER_T.id%TYPE;
13
14
15  end WORKER_TS;
16  /
17  @se.sql WORKER_TS
```

In Listing 5-5, I've declared one function: get_id(). It will return the next WORKER_ID_SEQ sequence value.

Listing 5-6. *The WORKER_TS Package Body, worker_ts.pkb*

```
01  create or replace PACKAGE BODY WORKER_TS as
02  /*
03  worker_ts.pkb
04  by Donald J. Bales on 12/15/2006
```

```
05  Table WORKER_T's methods
06  */
07
08
09  -- FUNCTIONS
10
11  FUNCTION get_id
12  return                          WORKER_T.id%TYPE is
13
14  n_id                            WORKER_T.id%TYPE;
15
16  begin
17    select WORKER_ID_SEQ.nextval
18    into   n_id
19    from   SYS.DUAL;
20
21    return n_id;
22  end get_id;
23
24
25  end WORKER_TS;
26  /
27  @be.sql WORKER_TS
```

In Listing 5-6, I've coded a function that queries and returns the sequence value from WORKER_ID_SEQ.nextval. Remember that the SYS.DUAL table has one row, so selecting any value against it will return one value.

Your assignment for part two is to add three functions to package WORKER_TS:

- A get_external_id() function, which will return a value from sequence EXTERNAL_ID_SEQ as a properly zero-left-padded varchar2.

- A get_unformatted_name() function, which will return a concatenated value for three parameters: aiv_first_name, aiv_middle_name, and aiv_last_name. Use the concatenation operator—two vertical bars (||)—to concatenate the varchar2 values together. (Hint: I've already coded this concatenation time and time again in the previous listings.)

- An is_duplicate() function, which you will pass three parameters: aiv_name, aid_birth_date, and ain_gender_id. It should return a Boolean value of TRUE if a duplicate exists; otherwise, it should return FALSE.

Remember to test all three functions. Yes, write a test unit for each one!
Let's move on to part three of your assignment.

Write a Modularized Version of Insert with PL/SQL Detection

Do you remember Listing 4-3? Now that you have functions for five out of the five blocked singleton SELECT statements, rewrite Listing 4-3 (insert_with_plsql_detection.sql), but this time replace all the singletons and the creation of the value for v_name with function calls to the appropriate packages. Oh yeah, baby, you're a real PL/SQL programmer now! Save your script as insert_with_modularity.sql. Then execute it until it works.

My Solution?

If I show you my solution, you may not do the assignment. Do you promise not to look until you're finished? OK, then Listing 5-7 is my solution to this third part of the exercise.

Listing 5-7. *A Modular Approach to Inserting, insert_with_modularity.sql*

```
01  rem insert_with_modularity.sql
02  rem by Donald J. Bales on 12/15/2006
03  rem An anonymous PL/SQL procedure to insert
04  rem values using PL/SQL functions
05
06  set serveroutput on size 1000000;
07
08  declare
09
10  -- I declared this record, so I can get
11  -- the required ID values before I insert.
12  r_worker                         WORKER_T%ROWTYPE;
13
14  -- I'll use this variable to hold the result
15  -- of the SQL insert statement.
16  n_count                          number := 0;
17
18  begin
19    r_worker.first_name  := 'JOHN';
20    r_worker.middle_name := 'J.';
21    r_worker.last_name   := 'DOE';
22    -- Using the same function to get this derived value
23    -- from all programs will ensure its value is consistent
24    r_worker.name        := WORKER_TS.get_formatted_name(
25      r_worker.first_name, r_worker.middle_name, r_worker.last_name);
26    r_worker.birth_date  :=
27      to_date('19800101', 'YYYYMMDD'); -- I'm guessing
28
29    -- First, let's get the worker_type_id for a contractor
30    begin
31      r_worker.worker_type_id := WORKER_TYPE_TS.get_id('C');
32    exception
33      when OTHERS then
34        raise_application_error(-20001, SQLERRM||
35          ' on call WORKER_TYPE_TS.get_id(''C'')'||
36          ' in filename insert_with_modularity.sql');
37    end;
38
```

```
39    -- Next, let's get the gender_id for a male
40    begin
41      r_worker.gender_id := GENDER_TS.get_id('M');
42    exception
43      when OTHERS then
44        raise_application_error(-20002, SQLERRM||
45          ' on call GENDER_TS.get_id(''M'')'||
46          ' in filename insert_with_modularity.sql');
47    end;
48
49    -- Detect any existing entries, and
50    -- then conditionally insert the row
51    if not WORKER_TS.is_duplicate(
52      r_worker.name, r_worker.birth_date, r_worker.gender_id) then
53      -- I'm not going to block the next two calls,
54      -- because it's highly unlikely that I could
55      -- ever get an error allocating a sequence.
56
57      -- Now, let's get the next worker id sequence;
58      -- no parameters, so no parentheses needed
59      r_worker.id := WORKER_TS.get_id;
60
61      -- And then, let's get the next external_id sequence;
62      -- no parameters, so no parentheses needed
63      r_worker.external_id := WORKER_TS.get_external_id;
64
65      -- Now that we have all the necessary ID values
66      -- we can finally insert a row!
67      begin
68        -- Since I declared r_worker based on WORKER_T, I
69        -- can skip the column list and just use the record.
70        insert into WORKER_T values r_worker;
71
72        n_count := sql%rowcount;
73      exception
74        when OTHERS then
75          raise_application_error(-20003, SQLERRM||
76            ' on insert WORKER_T'||
77            ' in filename insert_with_modularity.sql');
78      end;
79    end if;
80
81    pl(to_char(n_count)||' row(s) inserted.');
82  end;
83  /
```

I'm not going to explain Listing 5-7 in detail, because it's well commented and you should be able to understand it by now. But I will say that, unless there's more you have to do between the selection of codes and sequences and before the insert, you're probably still better off using SQL to do all the work!

Now let me introduce you to the star of the PL/SQL show: CURSOR FOR LOOP.

Fetching Rows from a Cursor Automatically

Introducing, from the far away shores of Redwood Shores, California, the star of our show, the one, the only: the CURSOR FOR LOOP! "Why all the fanfare?" you ask. It's because the CURSOR FOR LOOP is the heart and soul of PL/SQL's abilities. The CURSOR FOR LOOP allows you to work with a cursor that returns multiple rows, one row at a time, using a very nice and neat structure that does everything for you automatically.

Listing 5-8 is a revision of Listing 5-1. The difference is that Listing 5-8 utilizes the "automatic" CURSOR FOR LOOP, instead of the manually coded loop involving OPEN, FETCH, and CLOSE.

Listing 5-8. *An Example of Using a CURSOR FOR LOOP, cursor_for_loop_the_doe_family.sql*

```
01   rem cursor_for_loop_the_doe_family.sql
02   rem by Donald J. Bales on 12/15/2006
03   rem An anonymous PL/SQL procedure to select
04   rem the first names for the Doe family from
05   rem the Worker table.
06
07   set serveroutput on size 1000000;
08
09   declare
10
11   cursor c_worker(
12   aiv_last_name                in      WORKER_T.last_name%TYPE) is
13   select first_name
14   from   WORKER_T
15   where  last_name like aiv_last_name||'%'
16   order by id;
17
18   begin
19     FOR r_worker IN c_worker('DOE') LOOP
20       pl(r_worker.first_name);
21     END LOOP;
22   end;
23   /
```

The CURSOR FOR LOOP syntax used in Listing 5-8 is as follows:

```
FOR <record_name> IN <cursor_name> [(<cursor_parameters>)] LOOP
  -- Put your PL/SQL to be executed for each row here
END LOOP;
```

where <record_name> is the name of the record that will contain fields that correspond to columns in the associated cursor's SELECT statement; <cursor_name> is the name of the associated CURSOR; and <cursor_parameters> is a list of zero or more parameters to be passed to the CURSOR. The brackets around the parameters denote that they are optional; they are needed only if the associated CURSOR was declared with parameters.

Listing 5-8 is short but powerful. In lines 11 through 16, I declare a CURSOR c_worker. Then, on line 19, I use the CURSOR FOR LOOP syntax to automatically OPEN the CURSOR and LOOP until there's no data found, placing any column values in an automatically declared record r_worker that is in scope only inside the FOR LOOP. If at least one row was retrieved from the database, the CURSOR FOR LOOP automatically CLOSEs the OPEN CURSOR when the LOOP ENDs. As I documented earlier in Table 3-1, I use the prefix c_ for cursors and the prefix r_ for records. This naming convention makes it easy to see exactly what is going on in PL/SQL.

I told you PL/SQL's solution to the last exercise in Chapter 4 was going to get even better. As you can see, the CURSOR FOR LOOP represents some powerfully compact syntax!

You can use a CURSOR FOR LOOP as long as you don't need the values of the fields in the automatically declared record outside the loop. And it will do you no good to declare the record outside the loop, because the CURSOR FOR LOOP will still declare its own. If you do need the cursor values beyond the fetch, you'll need to assign the record values to variables declared outside the loop or use a manual loop, as I did earlier in Listing 5-1.

Enough talk—it's time you put CURSOR FOR LOOP to work for you.

It's Your Turn to Fetch Automatically

In the development process, you'll eventually need to test what you've built with some realistic data; otherwise, you won't know how your code will perform in production. So your assignment here is to create a PL/SQL procedure that will populate table WORKER_T with test data.

If you combine 100 last names, 100 first names, and 26 different middle initials, you get 260,000 entries for table WORKER_T. A quarter of a million entries in a table is a fair amount of data for testing.

To help you out with this assignment, the create_relational.sql script created the TOP_100_FIRST_NAME, TOP_100_LAST_NAME, and A_THRU_Z tables for you when you ran it at the beginning of Chapter 2. I've also placed these table scripts in the downloaded source code directory for Chapter 5, as top_100_first_name.tab, top_100_last_name.tab, and a_thru_z.tab, respectively.

In order to populate table WORKER_T, I suggest you create a PL/SQL procedure that uses nested CURSOR FOR LOOPs to iterate through each table's entries, inserting an entry into the table for each loop, in the most nested FOR LOOP. Your executable code will look something like this:

```
begin
  for r_last in c_last loop
    for r_first in c_first loop
      for r_middle in c_middle loop
        -- initialize the variables to be used in the insert statement here.
        insert into WORKER_T ...
      end loop;
    end loop;
  end loop;
end;
```

Of course, you'll need to supply values for other columns. For those, I suggest you do the following:

- For id, call function WORKER_TS.get_id().

- For worker_type_id, use an IF statement to flip back and forth between the ID values for an employee vs. contractor, on every other entry.

- For external_id, call function WORKER_TS.get_external_id().

- For birth_date, call function DATES.random(1940, 1990); this will give you a randomly generated date between the years 1940 and 1990.

- For gender_id, use an IF statement to specify the correct ID value for the corresponding code found in the TOP_100_FIRST_NAME table.

Add a variable to keep track of how many inserts you've made, and then display that number on the screen when you're finished inserting. Save the script as worker_t_cursor_for_loop.ins, and then execute it. I know this is a hard assignment, but you have everything you need to get it done.

Listing 5-9 is my solution to this exercise. When I ran this script on my computer, it inserted 260,000 rows in an average time of 98 seconds—that's about 2,660 rows per second.

Listing 5-9. *Using CURSOR FOR LOOPs to Insert Test Data, worker_t_cursor_for_loop.ins*

```
001  rem worker_t_cursor_for_loop.ins
002  rem by Donald J. Bales on 12/15/2006
003  rem Seed the Worker table with the top 100 names
004  rem 100 last x 100 first x 26 middle = 260,000 entries
005
006  set serveroutput on size 1000000;
007
008  declare
009
010  -- This is the cursor for the last names.
011  cursor c_last is
012  select last_name
013  from   TOP_100_LAST_NAME;
014
015  -- This is the cursor for the first names.
016  cursor c_first is
017  select first_name,
018         gender_code
019  from   TOP_100_FIRST_NAME;
020
021  -- This is the cursor for the middle initials.
022  cursor c_middle is
023  select letter
024  from   A_THRU_Z;
025
026  -- This is the number of seconds since midnight.
027  -- I'll use it to profile my code's performance.
```

```
028   n_start                                  number :=
029     to_number(to_char(SYSDATE, 'SSSSS'));
030
031   -- Here, I declare four pseudo-constants to hold the
032   -- ID values from the code tables, rather than look
033   -- them up repeatedly during the insert process.
034   n_G_FEMALE                               GENDER_T.gender_id%TYPE;
035   n_G_MALE                                 GENDER_T.gender_id%TYPE;
036   n_WT_CONTRACTOR                          WORKER_TYPE_T.worker_type_id%TYPE;
037   n_WT_EMPLOYEE                            WORKER_TYPE_T.worker_type_id%TYPE;
038
039   -- I'll use this to keep track of the number of
040   -- rows inserted.
041   n_inserted                               number := 0;
042
043   -- Here, I declare a record anchored to the table so
044   -- I can set the column values and then insert using
045   -- the record.
046   r_worker                          WORKER_T%ROWTYPE;
047
048   begin
049     -- Get the ID values for the codes
050     n_G_FEMALE      := GENDER_TS.get_id('F');
051     n_G_MALE        := GENDER_TS.get_id('M');
052     n_WT_CONTRACTOR := WORKER_TYPE_TS.get_id('C');
053     n_WT_EMPLOYEE   := WORKER_TYPE_TS.get_id('E');
054
055     -- Loop through the last names
056     for r_last in c_last loop
057
058       -- While looping through the last names,
059       -- loop through the first names
060       for r_first in c_first loop
061
062         -- While looping through the last and first names,
063         -- loop through the 26 letters in the English
064         -- alphabet in order to get middle initials.
065         -- As an alternative, I could have used a FOR LOOP:
066   --        for i in ascii('A')..ascii('Z') loop
067         for r_middle in c_middle loop
068
069           -- Initialize the record
070
071           -- Get the PK using the table's package
072           r_worker.id              := WORKER_TS.get_id();
073
```

```
074           -- Flip flop from contractor to employee and back again
075           if r_worker.worker_type_id = n_WT_CONTRACTOR then
076             r_worker.worker_type_id := n_WT_EMPLOYEE;
077           else
078             r_worker.worker_type_id := n_WT_CONTRACTOR;
079           end if;
080
081           -- Get the External ID using the table's package
082           r_worker.external_id     := WORKER_TS.get_external_id();
083
084           -- The first, middle, and last names come from the cursors
085           r_worker.first_name      := r_first.first_name;
086   --        r_worker.middle_name      := chr(i)||'.';
087           r_worker.middle_name     := r_middle.letter||'.';
088           r_worker.last_name       := r_last.last_name;
089
090           -- Get the name using the table's package
091           r_worker.name            := WORKER_TS.get_formatted_name(
092             r_worker.first_name, r_worker.middle_name, r_worker.last_name);
093
094           -- Get a random date for a birth date
095           r_worker.birth_date      := DATES.random(
096             to_number(to_char(SYSDATE, 'YYYY')) - 65,
097             to_number(to_char(SYSDATE, 'YYYY')) - 18);
098
099           -- Select the corresponding ID value
100           if r_first.gender_code = 'F' then
101             r_worker.gender_id   := n_G_FEMALE;
102           else
103             r_worker.gender_id   := n_G_MALE;
104           end if;
105
106           -- Insert the row into the database
107           insert into WORKER_T values r_worker;
108
109           -- Keep track of the number of inserts
110           n_inserted := n_inserted + sql%rowcount;
111         end loop; -- c_middle
112   --      end loop; -- for i
113         commit;   -- commit every 26 rows
114
115       end loop; -- c_first
116
117     end loop; -- c_last
```

```
118    -- Display the results
119    pl(to_char(n_inserted)||' rows inserted in '||
120      (to_number(to_char(SYSDATE, 'SSSSS')) - n_start)||
121      ' seconds.');
122  end;
123  /
```

I won't elaborate on my solution here, because I've commented the code heavily. Notice that I've added a variable to hold the start time in seconds, so I can test the performance of this solution against others. You'll see me profile code this way as we move forward. It's part of the testing process. The question now is, "Can we make this PL/SQL procedure faster?"

In Oracle8, some additional functionality was added to PL/SQL to improve performance. Let's look at one of those additions next.

Bulk Collect

No, it's not that you're getting out of shape from sitting there learning about PL/SQL. In this context, BULK COLLECT is about reducing the number of transitions between the PL/SQL engine and SQL engine, in order to improve efficiency and speed of your PL/SQL program. (Although, if I look down, it appears that sitting and writing this book all day long, every day, has led to some bulk collection of another kind.)

The idea is simple. Every time you execute SQL from your PL/SQL program, PL/SQL must hand off the SQL statement to the Oracle database's SQL engine. When the SQL engine is finished, it returns its result to the PL/SQL engine. Flip-flopping back and forth from PL/SQL to SQL and back again takes time.

Since version 8 of Oracle, you can reduce the number of transitions between PL/SQL and SQL by using the BULK COLLECT command. Rather than fetch one row at a time from the SQL engine, you can fetch perhaps one hundred at a time into a PL/SQL collection, which can be a PL/SQL table (or array).

Although three types of PL/SQL collections exist, I'm going to cover only the use of associative arrays, or as they were once called, PL/SQL tables. Once you're comfortable programming in PL/SQL, I recommend you go back and learn about the other two in a good reference (such as *PL/SQL Programming* by Steven Feuerstein and Bill Pribyl).

Bulk Collect with a Cursor

Since we've been working with cursors, let's continue to talk about them. Listing 5-10 is yet another incarnation of Listing 5-1, the "select the Doe family" assignment. This time, however, it has been coded to use BULK COLLECT.

Listing 5-10. *An Example of Using BULK COLLECT with a CURSOR, cursor_bulk_collect_the_doe_family.sql.*

```
01  rem cursor_bulk_collect_the_doe_family.sql
02  rem by Donald J. Bales on 12/15/2006
03  rem An anonymous PL/SQL procedure to select
```

```
04  rem the first names for the Doe family from
05  rem the Worker table.
06
07  set serveroutput on size 1000000;
08
09  declare
10
11  cursor c_worker(
12  aiv_last_name                   in      WORKER_T.last_name%TYPE) is
13  select first_name
14  from    WORKER_T
15  where  last_name like aiv_last_name||'%'
16  order by id;
17
18  TYPE c_worker_table is table of c_worker%ROWTYPE
19  index by binary_integer;
20
21  t_worker                            c_worker_table;
22
23  begin
24    open c_worker('DOE');
25    loop
26      FETCH c_worker BULK COLLECT INTO t_worker limit 10;
27
28      exit when t_worker.count = 0;
29
30      FOR i IN t_worker.first..t_worker.last LOOP
31        pl(t_worker(i).first_name);
32      END LOOP;
33    end loop;
34  end;
35  /
```

The FETCH syntax used in the manual loop in Listing 5-10 is as follows:

```
FETCH <cursor_name> BULK COLLECT INTO <plsql_table_name> LIMIT <limit>;
```

where <cursor_name> is the name of an open cursor from which to fetch, and <plsql_table_name> is the name of the associative array in which to fetch the <limit> number of rows.

And the FOR LOOP syntax used in the listing is as follows:

```
FOR <index> IN <from_index>..<through_index> LOOP
  -- Put your PL/SQL code to execute during the loop here.
END LOOP
```

where <index> is an index value to use in the loop to address PL/SQL table elements, <from_index> is a valid index value to start with, and <through_index> is a valid index value to end with.

There's nothing like dissecting a program line by line to help explain it, so here it is:

Lines 11 through 16 declare a cursor to select the first names of a specified family. There's nothing new here. You've seen this time and again.

Lines 18 and 19 declare an associative array, or PL/SQL table, based on the row type of CURSOR c_worker.

Line 21 declares a variable of TYPE c_worker_table that will be the target of the FETCH ... BULK COLLECT command.

Line 24 opens the cursor c_worker.

Line 25 starts a manual LOOP.

On line 26, I fetch rows from the database, ten rows at a time, into table t_worker. Because I've reduced the number of transitions, or context switches, by ten, this PL/SQL program will run roughly ten times as fast. I specified the number of rows to retrieve with the LIMIT clause at the end of the FETCH ... BULK COLLECT statement. I could have set the limit to 100, 1000, 9999, or whatever. But keep in mind that the limit also determines how much memory will be consumed by holding the rows in memory between each call, so you need to use a reasonable value or bring your database to a screeching halt—it's your choice.

On line 28, instead of checking the cursor variable c_worker%notfound, I need to check the PL/SQL table t_worker's %count variable to see how many rows were inserted into the table from the last FETCH. If t_worker%count is zero, there are no more rows to retrieve from the cursor, so I EXIT the LOOP.

On line 30, now that the fetched data resides in PL/SQL table t_worker, I use a FOR LOOP to iterate through the entries, from the first, t_worker.first through (..) the last, t_worker.last. In this context, first and last are PL/SQL table variables that tell you the first and last rows in the table, respectively.

Line 31, inside the FOR LOOP, displays the first names on the screen. However, this time, since the PL/SQL table was based on a cursor's row type, I need to use the form table name, index, dot, field name—t_worker(i).first_name—in order to address the field.

Using BULK COLLECT with a FETCH statement for a cursor can lead to a significant performance improvement if you set a moderately sized LIMIT. If you specify too large of a LIMIT, you'll use up memory needed for other database sessions.

Another thing to consider is that using BULK COLLECT requires additional programming. So is the extra memory consumption and additional programming worth the investment? Or will a simple CURSOR FOR LOOP do the job?

In practice, I always start out with a CURSOR FOR LOOP. If I find that a particular PL/SQL program is a performance bottleneck, or needs to run faster for business purposes, I take the extra time to transform the PL/SQL module to use BULK COLLECT. But then I test its performance gains against every other PL/SQL program's performance loss due to the additional consumption of memory. Yes, I test, test, and test again.

Note Oracle Database 10*g* introduces an "auto bulk collect " feature. I suggest you investigate this later by reading Oracle's PL/SQL *User's Guide and Reference* for a version of Oracle Database 10*g*.

Bulk Collect with a Select Statement

If you know that the result of your SQL SELECT statement will always be a small number of rows, you can simplify your PL/SQL programming by using BULK COLLECT with a SELECT statement. The result is a SELECT statement that looks a lot like a singleton SELECT, with the difference being that rather than returning only one row at a time, your use of BULK COLLECT allows the statement to return a number of rows at a time.

Listing 5-11 demonstrates the use of BULK COLLECT with a SELECT statement. The difference with this listing compared to Listing 5-10 is that I no longer use an explicit CURSOR.

Listing 5-11. *An Example of Using BULK COLLECT with a SELECT statement,* *bulk_collect_the_doe_family.sql*

```
01  rem bulk_collect_the_doe_family.sql
02  rem by Donald J. Bales on 12/15/2006
03  rem An anonymous PL/SQL procedure to select
04  rem the first names for the Doe family from
05  rem the Worker table.
06
07  set serveroutput on size 1000000;
08
09  declare
10
11  TYPE worker_table is table of WORKER_T.first_name%TYPE
12  index by binary_integer;
13
14  t_worker                        worker_table;
15
16  begin
17    select first_name
18    BULK COLLECT
19    into   t_worker
20    from   WORKER_T
21    where  last_name like 'DOE%'
22    order by id;
23
24    for i in t_worker.first..t_worker.last loop
25      pl(t_worker(i));
26    end loop;
27  end;
28  /
```

The BULK COLLECT syntax used in Listing 5-11 is as follows:

```
SELECT <column_list>
BULK COLLECT
INTO    <plsql_table_name>
FROM    <table_name>
WHERE   <where_clause>
ORDER BY <order_by_colunmn_list>;
```

where <column_list> is a single column name from the table or an asterisk (*) to denote all columns from the table (or row); <plsql_table_name> is the name of one or more associative array(s) declared to match the column list's data types; <table_name> is the name of the table to query, <where_clause> is an appropriate WHERE clause for the query; and <order_by_column_list> is a list of column(s) by which to order the SELECT statement's results.

Let's break down Listing 5-11:

Lines 11 and 12 declare a TYPE based on the first_name column of the WORKER_T table.

Line 14 declares a table for the TYPE worker_table specified on lines 11 and 12.

On lines 17 through 22, the magic occurs. This is where I've used the SELECT BULK COLLECT INTO syntax to load all the resulting rows from the query into the PL/SQL table t_worker in just one context switch!

Lines 24 through 26 contain a FOR LOOP to iterate through the rows in PL/SQL table t_worker, displaying the results on the screen.

Sweet and simple, from disk to memory in one context switch, this is indeed a powerful syntax. However, it has all the same baggage as its CURSOR-based sibling in the previous section. So use it carefully, if at all.

In practice, I never use this syntax, because I can't guarantee that the tables I'm coding against won't grow to require an unreasonable amount of memory for the BULK COLLECT. Instead, I play it safe and use the CURSOR BULK COLLECT syntax. But now it's your choice.

It's Your Turn to Bulk Collect

Now that you know how to make your code more efficient by using BULK COLLECT, put it to the test by taking your solution to the last exercise and modifying it to use BULK COLLECT. This means you'll get rid of the three cursors you declared in that solution and replace them with three TYPE and three PL/SQL table declarations. Next, you'll change your CURSOR FOR LOOPs to FOR LOOPs, as in the following example:

```
begin
  for l in t_last.first..t_last.last loop
    for f in t_first.first..t_first.last loop
      for m in t_middle.first..t_middle.last loop
        -- initialize the variables to be used in the insert statement here.
        insert into WORKER_T ...
      end loop;
    end loop;
  end loop;
end;
```

Listing 5-12 is my solution to this exercise. When I ran this script on my computer, it inserted 260,000 rows in an average time of 94 seconds—that's about 2,750 rows per second, for a 3% improvement. The small amount of improvement is understandable here, because while there were 223 context switches saved by using BULK COLLECT, there were still 260,000 context switches due to inserts.

Listing 5-12. *Using BULK COLLECT to Improve the Insertion of Test Data, worker_t_bulk_collect.ins*

```
001  rem worker_t_bulk_collect.ins
002  rem by Donald J. Bales on 12/15/2006
003  rem Seed the Worker table with the top 100 names
004  rem 100 last x 100 first x 26 middle = 260,000 entries
005
006  set serveroutput on size 1000000;
007
008  declare
009
010  -- Declare a type for a PL/SQL table of last names
011  TYPE last_name_table is table of TOP_100_LAST_NAME%ROWTYPE
012  index by binary_integer;
013
014  -- Declare a type for a PL/SQL table of first names
015  TYPE first_name_table is table of TOP_100_FIRST_NAME%ROWTYPE
016  index by binary_integer;
017
018  -- Declare a type for a PL/SQL table of middle initials
019  TYPE middle_name_table is table of A_THRU_Z%ROWTYPE
020  index by binary_integer;
021
022  -- This is the number of seconds since midnight.
023  -- I'll use it to profile my code's performance.
024  n_start                        number :=
025    to_number(to_char(SYSDATE, 'SSSSS'));
026
027  -- Here, I declare four pseudo-constants to hold the
028  -- ID values from the code tables, rather than look
029  -- them up repeatedly during the insert process.
030  n_G_FEMALE                     GENDER_T.gender_id%TYPE;
031  n_G_MALE                       GENDER_T.gender_id%TYPE;
032  n_WT_CONTRACTOR                WORKER_TYPE_T.worker_type_id%TYPE;
033  n_WT_EMPLOYEE                  WORKER_TYPE_T.worker_type_id%TYPE;
034
035  -- I'll use this to keep track of the number of
036  -- rows inserted.
037  n_inserted                     number := 0;
038
```

```
039  -- Here, I declare a record anchored to the table so
040  -- I can set the column values and then insert using
041  -- the record.
042  r_worker                              WORKER_T%ROWTYPE;
043
044  -- Declare the three PL/SQL tables that replace cursors
045  t_first                               first_name_table;
046  t_middle                              middle_name_table;
047  t_last                                last_name_table;
048
049  begin
050    -- Get the ID values for the codes
051    n_G_FEMALE       := GENDER_TS.get_id('F');
052    n_G_MALE         := GENDER_TS.get_id('M');
053    n_WT_CONTRACTOR  := WORKER_TYPE_TS.get_id('C');
054    n_WT_EMPLOYEE    := WORKER_TYPE_TS.get_id('E');
055
056    -- Bulk collect the tables into the PL/SQL tables
057    select * bulk collect into t_last   from TOP_100_LAST_NAME;
058    select * bulk collect into t_first  from TOP_100_FIRST_NAME;
059    select * bulk collect into t_middle from A_THRU_Z;
060
061    -- Loop through the last names
062    for l in t_last.first..t_last.last loop
063
064      -- While looping through the last names,
065      -- loop through the first names
066      for f in t_first.first..t_first.last loop
067
068        -- While looping through the last and first names,
069        -- loop through the 26 letters in the English
070        -- alphabet in order to get middle initials
071        for m in t_middle.first..t_middle.last loop
072
073          -- Initialize the record
074
075          -- Get the PK using the table's package
076          r_worker.id                 := WORKER_TS.get_id();
077
078          -- Flip flop from contractor to employee and back again
079          if r_worker.worker_type_id = n_WT_CONTRACTOR then
080            r_worker.worker_type_id := n_WT_EMPLOYEE;
081          else
082            r_worker.worker_type_id := n_WT_CONTRACTOR;
083          end if;
084
```

```
085           -- Get the External ID using the table's package
086           r_worker.external_id      := WORKER_TS.get_external_id();
087
088           -- The first, middle, and last names come from the cursors
089           r_worker.first_name       := t_first(f).first_name;
090           r_worker.middle_name      := t_middle(m).letter||'.';
091           r_worker.last_name        := t_last(l).last_name;
092
093           -- Get the name using the table's package
094           r_worker.name             := WORKER_TS.get_formatted_name(
095            r_worker.first_name, r_worker.middle_name, r_worker.last_name);
096
097           -- Get a random date for a birth date
098           r_worker.birth_date       := DATES.random(
099            to_number(to_char(SYSDATE, 'YYYY')) - 65,
100            to_number(to_char(SYSDATE, 'YYYY')) - 18);
101
102           -- Select the corresponding ID value
103           if t_first(f).gender_code = 'F' then
104             r_worker.gender_id      := n_G_FEMALE;
105           else
106             r_worker.gender_id      := n_G_MALE;
107           end if;
108
109           -- Insert the row into the database
110           insert into WORKER_T values r_worker;
111
112           -- Keep track of the number of inserts
113           n_inserted := n_inserted + sql%rowcount;
114         end loop; -- t_middle
115         commit;   -- commit every 26 rows
116
117       end loop; -- t_first
118
119     end loop; -- t_last
120     -- Display the results
121     pl(to_char(n_inserted)||' rows inserted in '||
122       (to_number(to_char(SYSDATE, 'SSSSS')) - n_start)||
123       ' seconds.');
124   end;
125   /
```

Once again, I won't elaborate on my solution here, because I've commented the code heavily. The question remains, "Can we make this PL/SQL procedure faster?"

Well, we've already used BULK COLLECT. What else is in PL/SQL's bag of tricks?

For All

For the sake of completeness, I'm going to mention the FORALL statement here. It's kind of like the inverse of the BULK COLLECT statement. Given that you have a populated collection, like an associative array, you can bulk execute the same SQL statement for every entry or for selected entries in your collection(s).

For example, if you have 26 entries in your PL/SQL table, you can write a FORALL statement that will execute the same SQL statement 26 times, once for each row in your PL/SQL table. The assumption here is that you'll use the values from your PL/SQL table in each SQL statement.

The problem I have with FORALL is that the data for a collection usually comes from a table in the database in the first place. If that's the case, then a complex SQL statement can do everything a FORALL statement can do, with one context switch, just like FORALL, but using less memory. So why does FORALL exist? Frankly, I don't know. Perhaps it's syntactic sugar for PL/SQL programmers that have weak SQL skills. Or maybe I've just never run across a need for it. That's always possible. However, in practice, I never use it. I always seem to find a better solution using a complex SQL statement.

Let me show you what I mean. Listing 5-13 is a rewrite of our "populate the Worker table" assignment, where I use FORALL to bind 26 SQL statements per context switch. I could have rearranged my code some more so I could do 100 at a time, but the improvement from doing so is not significant.

Listing 5-13. *Using FORALL to Improve the Insertion of Test Data, worker_t_forall.ins*

```
001  rem worker_t_forall.ins
002  rem by Donald J. Bales on 12/15/2006
003  rem Seed the Worker table with the top 100 names
004  rem 100 last x 100 first x 26 middle = 260,000 entries
005
006  set serveroutput on size 1000000;
007
008  declare
009
010  -- Declare a type for a PL/SQL table of last names
011  TYPE last_name_table   is table of TOP_100_LAST_NAME%ROWTYPE
012  index by binary_integer;
013
014  -- Declare a type for a PL/SQL table of first names
015  TYPE first_name_table  is table of TOP_100_FIRST_NAME%ROWTYPE
016  index by binary_integer;
017
018  -- Declare a type for a PL/SQL table of middle initials
019  TYPE middle_name_table is table of A_THRU_Z%ROWTYPE
020  index by binary_integer;
021
022  -- Declare a type for a PL/SQL table of workers
023  TYPE worker_table      is table of WORKER_T%ROWTYPE
024  index by binary_integer;
025
```

```
026  -- This is the number of seconds since midnight.
027  -- I'll use it to profile my code's performance.
028  n_start                          number :=
029    to_number(to_char(SYSDATE, 'SSSSS'));
030
031  -- Here, I declare four pseudo-constants to hold the
032  -- ID values from the code tables, rather than look
033  -- them up repeatedly during the insert process.
034  n_G_FEMALE                       GENDER_T.gender_id%TYPE;
035  n_G_MALE                         GENDER_T.gender_id%TYPE;
036  n_WT_CONTRACTOR                  WORKER_TYPE_T.worker_type_id%TYPE;
037  n_WT_EMPLOYEE                    WORKER_TYPE_T.worker_type_id%TYPE;
038
039  -- I'll use this to keep track of the number of
040  -- rows inserted.
041  n_inserted                       number := 0;
042
043  -- Declare the four PL/SQL tables that replace cursors
044  -- and the worker record
045  t_first                          first_name_table;
046  t_middle                         middle_name_table;
047  t_last                           last_name_table;
048  t_worker                         worker_table;
049
050  begin
051    -- Get the ID values for the codes
052    n_G_FEMALE      := GENDER_TS.get_id('F');
053    n_G_MALE        := GENDER_TS.get_id('M');
054    n_WT_CONTRACTOR := WORKER_TYPE_TS.get_id('C');
055    n_WT_EMPLOYEE   := WORKER_TYPE_TS.get_id('E');
056
057    -- Bulk collect the tables into the PL/SQL tables
058    select * bulk collect into t_last   from TOP_100_LAST_NAME;
059    select * bulk collect into t_first  from TOP_100_FIRST_NAME;
060    select * bulk collect into t_middle from A_THRU_Z;
061
062    -- Loop through the last names
063    for l in t_last.first..t_last.last loop
064
065      -- While looping through the last names,
066      -- loop through the first names
067      for f in t_first.first..t_first.last loop
068
069        -- While looping through the last and first names,
070        -- loop through the 26 letters in the English
071        -- alphabet in order to get middle initials
072        for m in t_middle.first..t_middle.last loop
073
```

```
074             -- Initialize the table's rows
075
076             -- Get the PK using the table's package
077             t_worker(m).id              := WORKER_TS.get_id();
078
079             -- Flip flop from contractor to employee and back again
080             if t_worker(m).worker_type_id = n_WT_CONTRACTOR then
081               t_worker(m).worker_type_id := n_WT_EMPLOYEE;
082             else
083               t_worker(m).worker_type_id := n_WT_CONTRACTOR;
084             end if;
085
086             -- Get the External ID using the table's package
087             t_worker(m).external_id     := WORKER_TS.get_external_id();
088
089             -- The first, middle, and last names come from the cursors
090             t_worker(m).first_name      := t_first(f).first_name;
091             t_worker(m).middle_name     := t_middle(m).letter||'.';
092             t_worker(m).last_name       := t_last(l).last_name;
093
094             -- Get the name using the table's package
095             t_worker(m).name            := WORKER_TS.get_formatted_name(
096               t_worker(m).first_name,
097               t_worker(m).middle_name,
098               t_worker(m).last_name);
099
100             -- Get a random date for a birth date
101             t_worker(m).birth_date      := DATES.random(
102               to_number(to_char(SYSDATE, 'YYYY')) - 65,
103               to_number(to_char(SYSDATE, 'YYYY')) - 18);
104
105             -- Select the corresponding ID value
106             if t_first(f).gender_code = 'F' then
107               t_worker(m).gender_id    := n_G_FEMALE;
108             else
109               t_worker(m).gender_id    := n_G_MALE;
110             end if;
111
112         end loop; -- t_middle
113
114         -- Now bulk bind the 26 insert statements
115         forall i in t_worker.first..t_worker.last
116           insert into WORKER_T values t_worker(i);
117
118         n_inserted := n_inserted + sql%rowcount;
119
120     end loop; -- t_first
121
```

```
122    end loop; -- t_last
123    commit;
124    -- Display the results
125    pl(to_char(n_inserted)||' rows inserted in '||
126      (to_number(to_char(SYSDATE, 'SSSSS')) - n_start)||
127      ' seconds.');
128  end;
129  /
```

In Listing 5-13, the magic happens on lines 74 through 110, where I populate a PL/SQL table's records with values, and then, on lines 115 and 166, where I bulk bind the insert statements, so I have only one context switch for each set of 26 records. Using FORALL, my program now inserts 260,000 rows in an average time of 62 seconds. That's about 4,200 rows per second, for a 37% improvement. That's great, right? Well, what if I just use SQL?

Listing 5-14 is our "populate the Worker table" assignment, where I use a single SQL statement. How does it fare?

Listing 5-14. *Using SQL to Improve the Insertion of Test Data, worker_t.ins*

```
01  rem worker_t.ins
02  rem by Donald J. Bales on 12/15/2006
03  rem Seed the Worker table with the top 100 names
04  rem 100 last x 100 first x 26 middle = 260,000 entries
05
06  set serveroutput on size 1000000;
07
08  declare
09
10  -- This is the number of seconds since midnight.
11  -- I'll use it to profile my code's performance.
12  n_start                          number :=
13    to_number(to_char(SYSDATE, 'SSSSS'));
14
15  -- Here, I declare four pseudo-constants to hold the
16  -- ID values from the code tables, rather than look
17  -- them up repeatedly during the insert process.
18  n_G_FEMALE                       GENDER_T.gender_id%TYPE;
19  n_G_MALE                         GENDER_T.gender_id%TYPE;
20  n_WT_CONTRACTOR                  WORKER_TYPE_T.worker_type_id%TYPE;
21  n_WT_EMPLOYEE                    WORKER_TYPE_T.worker_type_id%TYPE;
22
23  -- I'll use this to keep track of the number of
24  -- rows inserted.
25  n_inserted                       number := 0;
26
27  begin
28    -- Get the ID values for the codes
29    n_G_FEMALE      := GENDER_TS.get_id('F');
```

```
30    n_G_MALE        := GENDER_TS.get_id('M');
31    n_WT_CONTRACTOR := WORKER_TYPE_TS.get_id('C');
32    n_WT_EMPLOYEE   := WORKER_TYPE_TS.get_id('E');
33
34    -- Use an INSERT...SELECT SQL statement
35    insert into WORKER_T (
36          id,
37          worker_type_id,
38          external_id,
39          first_name,
40          middle_name,
41          last_name,
42          name,
43          birth_date,
44          gender_id)
45    select WORKER_ID_SEQ.nextval,
46          decode(mod(WORKER_ID_SEQ.currval, 2),
47            0, n_WT_EMPLOYEE, n_WT_CONTRACTOR),
48          lpad(to_char(EXTERNAL_ID_SEQ.nextval), 9, '0'),
49          first_name,
50          letter||'.',
51          last_name,
52          WORKER_TS.get_formatted_name(
53            first_name, letter||'.', last_name),
54          DATES.random(
55            to_number(to_char(SYSDATE, 'YYYY')) - 65,
56            to_number(to_char(SYSDATE, 'YYYY')) - 18),
57          decode(gender_code, 'F', n_G_FEMALE, n_G_MALE)
58    from  TOP_100_LAST_NAME,
59          TOP_100_FIRST_NAME,
60          A_THRU_Z;
61
62    n_inserted := n_inserted + sql%rowcount;
63
64    commit;
65
66    pl(to_char(n_inserted)||' rows inserted in '||
67      (to_number(to_char(SYSDATE, 'SSSSS')) - n_start)||
68      ' seconds.');
69    end;
70    /
```

In Listing 5-14, a single INSERT ... SELECT statement, albeit a complex one, does almost all the work done by lines and lines of PL/SQL. But how does it perform? It inserts 260,000 rows in an average time of 53 seconds. That's about 4,900 rows per second, for a 46% improvement. And you can't get any faster than using plain-old SQL. So what's the moral of this story? Let me hear you say it. Know thy SQL!

When you're comfortable with PL/SQL and are up to challenging yourself, pull out a good PL/SQL reference and read up on FORALL. For now, I think you'll do better by improving your SQL skills instead.

Summary

In this chapter, we've gone from curs(or)ing, to fetching, to bulk collecting, to bulk binding, and then back to SQL again. CURSORs allow you to FETCH multiple rows from a SQL SELECT statement. You can FETCH rows manually or automatically, using a CURSOR FOR LOOP. You can use BULK COLLECT to improve the efficiency of loading an array with values from the database, and you can use FORALL to improve the efficiency of executing SQL statements with values from an array. But most important, you probably realize by now that when I stated in Chapter 1, "knowing SQL is a prerequisite to learning PL/SQL," I wasn't joking.

All too often, I see poorly performing PL/SQL programs that are bloated with PL/SQL code that tries to do what SQL can simply do better. After all, it is the Procedural Language extension to SQL. PL/SQL's job is to handle the procedural tasks, while SQL's job is to handle manipulating data. Keep that in mind whenever you write a PL/SQL program.

Up to this point, although we've been keeping functions and procedures in a package for each table, we've still been acting as though these behaviors were something apart from the data they work with. In fact, in the real world, the opposite is true. Things in the real world don't keep their behavior or actions someplace away from themselves; they are part of a whole, and that's what we are going to look at next. We'll explore storing the behavior with the attributes, or as I like to think of it: object-relational technology.

CHAPTER 6

■ ■ ■

Just Like It Is in the Real World!

It was the philosopher George Santayana who stated, "Those who cannot remember the past are condemned to repeat it." Philosophy is an interesting pursuit from my point of view, because it looks at very high-level abstract patterns of behavior. Patterns are repeated data or behavior of a simple or complex nature.

When we build an application, we attempt to model the workflow of the real world in order to automate or organize the workflow to improve how quickly or accurately we can perform its associated work. However, modeling is not only representing what data is used, but also recognizing the patterns of usage: behavior. Restated simply, we attempt to model the real world, and those who get modeling right, profit from it the most.

Information Modeling

As business analysts and computer scientists, we have come a long way. Relational database technology has freed us from the tyranny of the high priests of database administration so we are all capable of storing and retrieving data in sets of highly organized two-dimensional tables. But, up to this point, we store only the data we use, for the most part ignoring the behavior.

As an analyst, I know that the accuracy of a real-world model depends on its use of the following:

Current data: Data (words, numbers, and dates) about what happened last. I say "last" because usually, by the time you record the information, it's data about what just happened, not what's about to happen.

Hierarchical data: Data about the relationships of like datum. For example, in a business organization, a department may belong to a subdivision, which may in turn belong to a division, which may in turn belong to a particular operating company; these are all levels of organization that have a hierarchical relationship to each other.

Historical data: Multiple occurrences of "current" data; that is, data about what has happened over time, not just the last occurrence of behavior. Yes, data is about behavior.

Current behavior: Methods (functions or procedures) used to accomplish the last act of work. Once again, I say "last" because, by the time the act of work is recorded, these are the methods just used, not what will be used in the future.

Hierarchical behavior: Methods used with hierarchical data.

Historical behavior: Multiple occurrences of "current" methods; that is, methods used to accomplish acts of work at a particular point in time.

So I submit that in order for you to have an accurate model of the real world, you need to employ all six facets of information in your model. Is that what we do today? For the most part, no.

Today, simple applications store current data in a database and store current methods (behavior) in a presentation layer's codebase. When I say presentation layer, I mean the software you use to enter data into the application (data entry) or to view data from an application (reporting).

More sophisticated applications may store hierarchical data and try to separate the code (program logic) used to present information from the rules of work, or so-called business (busyness) rules. Then they have one database and two codebases: a database for the persistence of data, a codebase for the "current" business rules or behavior, and a second codebase for presenting or interfacing with a human role player. When business rules are changed in the mid-tier codebase, the old rules are lost forever.

Rarely do applications store the behavior that belongs to an entity with the entity. And even more rarely is the behavior that is stored with an entity temporal in nature; that is, sensitive to at what time the behavior takes place. Yet, that's how the real world is. No wonder business people have problems with our software solutions. We're not modeling the real world as it is!

To make matters worse, there's a disturbing trend toward the presentation layer defining the model. Mapping tools like Java Data Objects (JDO) will create database entities for you. That's very convenient. However, what may be a convenient way to pass current data for data entry is not necessarily an accurate model of the real world.

Often, using the presentation layer to build the underlying real-world model leads to denormalized data, which leads to fat rows in a database, which because of physics, leads to poor performance. The mantra behind tools like Enterprise JavaBeans (EJB), JDO, and so on is database independence—as if to suggest that all databases are created equal, which they certainly are not.

Oracle is dominant among its peers because it is superior. It's that simple. If you're not going to use Oracle, I suggest checking out PostgreSQL, which is a high-quality, object-relational, open source alternative, but it's not Oracle by any stretch of imagination.

We've had the capability of modeling the real world accurately in object-relational databases for some time now, so why don't we? The following are my answers to that question:

"Lex I: Corpus omne perseverare in statu suo quiescendi vel movendi uniformiter in directum, nisi quatenus a viribus impressis cogitur statum illum mutare." Newton's first law translated for our purposes: everyone uses relational databases, so everyone will continue to use relational databases unless there is a compelling enough reason to move in a different direction.

Ignorance, not stupidity (business community). The level of awareness that the real world is a combination of fact and action, or data and methods, and the value of that information is not commonly understood by business people. Yet, they are the ones who drive the need for applications. If the business community doesn't understand its own work problems, then no information technology department within that community will ever understand the associated work problems either, because the business community defines applications of business.

Ignorance, not stupidity (technical community). The level of awareness that technology developers have currently attained does not commonly include object-relational technology. Hell, most techies I talk to don't even know what object-relational means. You'll hear more evidence about this in this chapter.

In order for you to understand and communicate these newer ideas (my answers), you need to come up to speed on some technology jargon. Let's start with object orientation.

Object Orientation

What's the big deal about object orientation anyway? First and foremost, it's about modeling the real world. Here are some examples:

- Rather than being concerned about a particular process, the emphasis is on independent entities that can actually perform the process.

- Rather than write one large procedure that does everything, and would also need to be tossed if the process in question changed, it's about assigning the appropriate parts of a procedure to the various role players in the procedure.

- Instead of having one large program, it's about modularity—having multiple, independent, and reusable components that act appropriately together to complete an act of work.

So it's about teamwork.

Key Tenets

Object orientation has three key tenets:

Encapsulation: This refers to packaging related data and methods together. Object orientation is the natural way to think about things; natural, as in nature. It's the way nature does it. Nature creates things that have both attributes and behavior. For example, I don't think about eating, and then you go eat what I want. It doesn't work that way. My thoughts about food affect me, not you. We are separate entities. All my attributes and behaviors are encapsulated in me. All your attributes and behaviors are encapsulated in you. If someone tells each of us to do something, odds are, we'll do it differently, or may not do it at all. How's that for modularity?

Inheritance: This is the ability to reuse the data and methods of a more abstract type. If we continue on about the idea of asking each of us to perform a particular task, we'll most likely do it differently because we inherited different genetic attributes from our parents, and they taught us different behaviors, too. So we inherited different attributes and behaviors from our parents, upon which we will add new ones, or override what our parents taught us and do it our own way.

Polymorphism: This refers to hiding different implementations behind a common interface. Polymorphism is the use of the same name for a particular behavior, yet knowing that each object, or person in our case, may perform the behavior differently. If I'm asked to clean the floor, I'll get out the vacuum cleaner, and then follow up by washing the floor with a bucket of clear water, while you may hire someone to do the job. All the same, the floor gets cleaned, and that's the behavior that was requested.

Using these three tenets, you can naturally model both the attributes and behavior, or data and methods, for any real-world entity. Let's talk more about reuse.

Reuse

Just what the heck is reuse anyway? I consider it reuse any time you can abstract multiple lines of code into a larger block of code that will then be called by more than one actor. I also think there are multiple levels of reuse. Let's start with the smallest unit of reuse: method-level reuse.

Method-Level Reuse

I always tell programmers who I work with that if they must code the same lines of code more than once to accomplish the same task, then they need to create a method. That's what I call method-level reuse.

The trick is where to put the method. That's an easy question to answer for an object-oriented programmer: put the method with the entity that's executing the behavior! That's what object-orientation is all about.

Next up is what I call component-level reuse.

Component-Level Reuse

Component-level reuse is when you can reuse a particular class of an entity, or in SQL jargon, a TYPE. You can reuse a class in two ways: through direct application (composition) or inheritance. Direct application would be where you create a TYPE called PERSON_O, and then create a table based on that type, called PERSON_OT. In this case, you'll have used the TYPE PERSON_O directly.

On the other hand, you could create a sub-TYPE called WORKER_O based on TYPE PERSON_O. Now TYPE WORKER_O would inherit all the data attributes and methods from its parent PERSON_O, possibly adding some of its own attributes and methods. This would be a case where you reused component PERSON_O by using inheritance.

Finally, if you define these TYPEs, and then reuse them in more than one application, that's also an example of component reuse, and an example of reuse at the most intriguing level. For example, if a human resource information system (HRIS) uses the TYPE PERSON_O in its TYPE hierarchy for TYPE EMPLOYEE_O, and then a safety application on the same database uses PERSON_O in its TYPE hierarchy for TYPE VICTIM, then both applications can TREAT their sub-TYPEs as a PERSON_O in order to share (or reuse) related information.

The last example sounds like it could also be called application-level reuse.

Application-Level Reuse

You can also design an entire set of applications such that they all use the same underlying abstract TYPEs. This allows each application to share a common set of applications that act as infrastructure for more complex applications. The use of common TYPEs in the inheritance hierarchy of sub-TYPEs would allow the common use of the same tables for all related applications. Now that's what I call reuse, baby!

Service Orientation

Service schmervice. Service-oriented architecture (SOA) is today's silver bullet that's going to fix all business problems. Yeah, right. Not long ago, it was XML, and then before that . . . Who cares! Object-oriented programmers have been building service-oriented applications for ages. That's the entire nature of object-oriented programming. You build independent components that provide supporting services through their method calls. You test them, and then you don't have to recode the same service ever again.

Even if you continue to build relational instead of object-relational databases, you can still provide service-oriented routines by properly associating your methods with your data. That's what I've been having you do up to this point. I've asked you to create what I called a "table package" for each table. Each "table package" contains a set of methods that logically belong to the data that is stored in the associated table.

For example, I named the relational Worker table WORKER_T. Then I asked you to create a package called WORKER_TS that contained a method for allocating a new primary key value. I've been using this pseudo-object orientation since PL/SQL became available, and it's a tactic that has worked well. Every programmer I've worked with has quickly come up to speed on the technique, and then reused the methods in the table package over and over again to accomplish the same logical task consistently every time.

In addition, although applications have been written in multiple programming languages and tools, all of them call the same "table package" methods to perform a particular service. Once again, even though different presentation layers are coded in different languages by different programmers, the same consistent behavior is seen across all presentations for all services—and that, my friend, is reuse of the best kind.

Do these varying presentation layers recode the same behavior in varying languages? Hell, no! They all use the same code stored with the data. That's object orientation and service orientation in use. So how do you get there from here?

A Roadmap to Reality

So how do you get to using object-relational technology from relational technology? It's not as hard as you might think. Just like the function of life, $f(l)$, you'll get out whatever you put in to it. You can fully implement object-relational technology in four easy steps:

1. Create table packages.

2. Create user-defined types.

3. Create object views.

4. Create object tables.

Yes, you can implement four different levels of object orientation in your database, and based on what you implement, gain a level of consistency and reusability equal to your level of implementation.

Step 1: Table Packages

The first step is to start thinking in an object-oriented fashion, or as I call it, thinking naturally. This means organizing your data and methods in a related fashion, as I had you do earlier with table packages. I always name tables with a singular name, and then name their related packages with an S suffix, so the package names are the plural of the table names. You can use whatever convention you want. By doing so, you should at least be able to employ encapsulation and polymorphism.

Table Method Encapsulation

You'll be employing encapsulation by gathering behavior and hiding it behind a public method call specification. Create a table package for every table in your database that has the same SQL statement executed on it more than once. Create a method for such a SQL statement, so the same behavior can be shared by multiple program units. Also add any other related methods that perform calculations, concatenations, or locale-specific behavior.

Table Method Polymorphism

Next, look at the bigger picture. Notice the patterns of use of your table package methods, and use the same names for a particular pattern of use across all table packages.

For example, I use a FUNCTION named get_id() in every table package where I need a method that allocates a new primary key sequence value. Then, for a code table like WORKER_TYPE_T, if I need to get an ID value for a new entry, I call WORKER_TYPE_TS.get_id(). Similarly, getting an ID value for a new WORKER_T table entry will be a different package name, but the same method name: WORKER_TS.get_id().

That's polymorphism in action.

Step 2: User-Defined Types

The second step is to create a new object type, a user-defined type, which encapsulates both data attributes and method call specifications in a permanent new "data" or object type in the database.

Gather the list of column names you use in the relational table, and then collect the methods you specify in each table's package specification. Use this information along with the keyword TYPE to create a new object type in the database.

Unlike the table's associated package specification, where all methods are essentially STATIC (always available), you'll need to decide whether methods will operate on an instance of an object, a MEMBER method, or will be available through the object's TYPE definition, a STATIC method. In addition, you may want to add your own CONSTRUCTOR method(s) in order to make it easier to create a new object instance. And you may also want to define a MAP MEMBER method to specify how objects are sorted.

When you create user-defined types, you have the opportunity to use all three facets of object orientation. As with table packages, you'll be employing encapsulation and polymorphism. But you may also be able to leverage inheritance, so keep on the lookout for higher-level patterns between user-defined types. If you see a high-level pattern, consider defining a super-TYPE, and then inheriting from that super-TYPE for similar sub-TYPEs.

If you stop at this level of implementation, you'll still be able to use data from relational tables as objects by TREATing the relational data as objects on the fly in your SQL statements. But, if you get this far, I would at least do step 3.

Step 3: Object Views

The third step involves creating object views for your relational tables. An object view presents the underlying relational table data as a table of the newly created user-defined object type.

If you use more than one table in an object view, you can write INSTEAD OF triggers that will then appropriately update the underlying relational tables if you execute a SQL INSERT, UPDATE, or DELETE statement against an object view.

One of the advantages to using object views is that you can still use object-relational-ignorant tools against the relational tables. But if I were you, and you went this far, I would go all the way and reap the full benefit of object-oriented technology in an Oracle database; I would do step 4.

Step 4: Object Tables

The last step is where you create an object-relational database or *objectbase*, one where real-world entities are accurately modeled for both attributes and behavior. I'm not advocating moving all of an application's code into the database—I mean objectbase—actually, just the opposite. The only items that should reside in the objectbase are the entities, along with their data attributes and methods that are in scope for the particular application.

This means that what is normally thought of as data in a relational database should be stored in the objectbase, along with its associated business rules. Whatever code is used to present the object-relational model—data-entry screens, reports, graphics, and so on—should continue to reside in an external codebase. Regardless of the presentation layer, any business rule should be executed in the objectbase, not in the presentation layer.

That may seem like a radical departure from what you're currently doing, or perhaps not. If you're using EJBs, you're already making a remote procedure call to employ business rules in a so-called middle tier. Why not do it correctly, and employ the authoritative rules that permanently reside side by side with the data attributes, instead of supposedly recoding the same rules again and again (with inconsistency) in another codebase?

A Change in Order

Building an object-relational database, or objectbase, calls for a change in order. When building a relational database, you follow this order:

1. Create tables with columns (attributes).

2. Create table packages with methods (behavior).

3. Code presentation by accessing the data in tables and the behaviors in their associated packages.

When you build an object-relational database, or objectbase, you follow this order:

1. Create user-defined types with attributes and behaviors.

2. Create tables based on your user-defined types.

3. Code presentation by accessing attributes and behaviors in user-defined type tables.

With that change of order in mind, I think it's time I actually show you what the heck I'm talking about. Enough philosophy—it's time for action. We'll begin with how to create a new user-defined type, an object type.

Object Types

You remember the keyword TYPE from Chapter 3, right? We used it to declare the equivalent of an array in PL/SQL: a PL/SQL table. Well in this context, you're going to use it to permanently create a new user-defined data type in the database. Using the term *data type* is a bit of a misnomer. You're really going to be creating new types of classes of entities, or object types. Yes, here's a new word for your vocabulary: *object type.* An object type defines both data attributes and related methods. So the SQL keywords you'll use to create user-defined object types are CREATE TYPE.

By creating a user-defined type, you'll permanently marry data and its associated methods in the database so they can't be separated, not even accidentally. It's a marriage for life; no divorce allowed. Of course, you'll be able to change data and behavior over time, but you'll be coding behavior so it will be time-dependent, and therefore be coding behavior over time. Cool, huh?

Some day, we will store universal behavioral executables the same way we store data. But today, the best we can do is to store our code with our data, not as separate entities, and to modify our code to be point-in-time-dependent, so we can reproduce behavior as it existed at any point in time.

Since you probably have little experience with this form of SQL, I'm going to show you two examples, with you doing some of the coding along the way. First, let's create a user-defined TYPE for one of our code tables: Gender.

Create a User-Defined Type Specification

Creating a user-defined type has two steps. First, you create a specification, and then you create a type body, or implementation, similar to creating a package.

Listing 6-1 is an example of a CREATE TYPE specification script for creating a user-defined type for code table Gender.

Listing 6-1. *An Example of a CREATE TYPE Statement for a Code Table, gender_o.tps*

```
01  create or replace TYPE GENDER_O as object (
02  /*
03  gender_o.tps
04  by Donald J. Bales on 12/15/2006
05  Type GENDER's attributes and methods.
```

```
06  */
07  id                              number,
08  code                            varchar2(30),
09  description                     varchar2(80),
10  active_date                     date,
11  inactive_date                   date,
12  /*
13  A constructor for creating a new instance of type GENDER_O with NULL
14  values.
15  */
16  CONSTRUCTOR FUNCTION gender_o(
17  self                      in out gender_o)
18  return                          self as result,
19  /*
20  A constructor for creating a new instance of type GENDER_O for insert.
21  */
22  CONSTRUCTOR FUNCTION gender_o(
23  self                      in out gender_o,
24  aiv_code                        varchar2,
25  aiv_description                 varchar2)
26  return                          self as result,
27  /*
28  Gets the code and description values for the specified gender_id.
29  */
30  STATIC PROCEDURE get_code_descr(
31  ain_id                    in     number,
32  aov_code                  out varchar2,
33  aov_description           out varchar2),
34  /*
35  Verifies that the passed code value is an exact or like match on the
36  date specified.
37  */
38  STATIC PROCEDURE get_code_id_descr(
39  aiov_code                 in out varchar2,
40  aon_id                    out number,
41  aov_description           out varchar2,
42  aid_on                    in     date),
43  /*
44  Verifies that the passed code value is currently an exact or like match.
45  */
46  STATIC PROCEDURE get_code_id_descr(
47  aiov_code                 in out varchar2,
48  aon_id                    out number,
49  aov_description           out varchar2),
50  /*
51  Returns a new primary key id value for a row.
52  */
```

```
53  MEMBER FUNCTION get_id
54  return                               number,
55  /*
56  Returns the gender_id for the specified code value.
57  */
58  STATIC FUNCTION get_id(
59  aiv_code                    in     varchar2)
60  return                               number,
61  /*
62  Test-based help for this package.   "set serveroutput on" in SQL*Plus.
63  */
64  MEMBER PROCEDURE help,
65  /*
66  Test units for this package.
67  */
68  MEMBER PROCEDURE test,
69  /*
70  A MAP function for sorting at the object level.
71  */
72  MAP MEMBER FUNCTION to_varchar2
73  return                               varchar2
74  );
75  /
76  @se.sql GENDER_O
```

The CREATE TYPE specification syntax used by Listing 6-1 is as follows:

```
CREATE [OR REPLACE] TYPE <type_name> AS OBJECT (
<attribute_name_1>                   <attribute_type_1>,
<attribute_name_2>                   <attribute_type_2>,...
<attribute_name_N>                   <attribute_type_N>,
[MAP]MEMBER or STATIC FUNCTION or PROCEDURE <method_name> [(
SELF                        [IN OUT][NOCOPY]<type_name>,
<parameter_name_1>          [IN OUT] <parameter_type_1>,
<parameter_name_2>          [IN OUT] <parameter_type_2>,...
<parameter_name_N>          [IN OUT] <parameter_type_N>)]
[RETURN                              <return_type>],
CONSTRUCTOR FUNCTION <type_name> (
SELF                        [IN OUT][NOCOPY]<type_name>,[
<parameter_name_1>          [IN OUT] <parameter_type_1>,
<parameter_name_2>          [IN OUT] <parameter_type_2>,...
<parameter_name_N>          [IN OUT] <parameter_type_N>)],
);
```

where:

<type_name> is the name of your user-defined TYPE.

<attribute_name> is the name of a data item in your user-defined TYPE.

<attribute_type> is a predefined scalar data type or a user-defined type.

<method_name> is the name of a MEMBER or STATIC, FUNCTION or PROCEDURE.

<parameter_name> is the name of a parameter being passed into or out of a method.

<parameter_type> is a predefined scalar data type or a user-defined type.

<return_type> is also a predefined scalar data type or a user-defined type to be returned by an associated FUNCTION.

Wow! As you can see by Listing 6-1, I've added a lot of methods to my Gender code user-defined TYPE. Let's take a look at the listing line by line:

Line 1 uses the DDL keywords CREATE TYPE ... AS OBJECT to declare a new user-defined TYPE specification for my schema in the database. I call my new type GENDER_O, as in it's the Gender code's user-defined Object type.

Lines 2 through 6 contain my usual source code preamble that documents the name of the source file, the author, date written, and purpose.

On lines 7 through 11, I list the attributes for the TYPE. Theses are the names of the columns from the original relational table. Did you notice that I ended the last attribute with a comma (,), which means I intend to continue specifying attributes or methods for the TYPE?

Lines 12 through 18 declare a user-defined CONSTRUCTOR method. You'll call a CONSTRUCTOR any time you want to create a new instance of a TYPE. For example, all user-defined TYPEs come with a default CONSTRUCTOR, where you pass in attribute values in the order they are specified in the TYPE specification. So to create a new instance of Gender using the default CONSTRUCTOR, you would code something like this:

```
o_gender := GENDER_O(3, 'U', 'Unknown', SYSDATE, NULL);
```

The CONSTRUCTOR I've declared here will create an instance of the TYPE with all its attributes initialized to NULL values. This is handy when I want to access a member function without actually working with a permanent instance of a TYPE.

Lines 12 through 15 hold a multiline comment that documents the purpose of the method. Remember to document as you go,

Lines 19 through 26 declare a user-defined CONSTRUCTOR for coding convenience. Using it, you can create a new instance of Gender by simply passing the code and description like this:

```
o_gender := GENDER_O('U', 'Unknown');
```

On lines 27 through 33, I specify my first STATIC method for the TYPE. If I specify a method as STATIC, it's available for execution through the TYPE's name, like a package, but not available through an instance of the type. For example, to execute PROCEDURE get_code_descr(), I would code GENDER_O.get_code_desc(...), not using a variable of the TYPE in the method call like this: o_gender.get_code_desc(...).

Skipping down, lines 50 through 54 declare a MEMBER method, get_id(), to allocate the next primary key value. This is the same method I asked you to create in a table package in Chapter 5. Now it has become a MEMBER method for the TYPE.

Finally, lines 69 through 73 declare a MAP MEMBER FUNCTION. This method will be used by the Oracle database any time it needs to sort object-level instances of the TYPE.

Let's review. How did I get here, to a TYPE specification, from there, a relational table and associated table package? Here's what I did:

1. Took the columns from the relational table and made them the attributes of the TYPE.

2. Took the methods from the relational table's package specification and made them MEMBER or STATIC methods of the TYPE.

3. Added a MAP MEMBER FUNCTION for sorting.

4. Added user-defined CONSTRUCTOR FUNCTIONs for convenience.

Now that you've seen the specification, let's look at the implementation!

Create a User-Defined Type Implementation

Listing 6-2 is a CREATE TYPE BODY ... AS (implementation) script for the TYPE GENDER_O specification shown in Listing 6-1. We'll cover all the methods implemented in this TYPE in subsequent chapters, when we take a polymorphic look at methods required by the TYPE and presentation layers: data entry, data migration, data processing, reporting, graphing, and so on. For now, it's important for you to focus on the method implementations that are unique to a TYPE, namely the MAP MEMBER and CONSTRUCTOR FUNCTIONs.

Listing 6-2. *An Example of a CREATE TYPE BODY Statement for a Code Table, gender_o.tpb*

```
001  create or replace TYPE BODY gender_o as
002  /*
003  gender_o.tpb
004  by Donald J. Bales on 12/15/2006
005  Type GENDER_O's attributes and methods
006  */
007
008  CONSTRUCTOR FUNCTION gender_o(
009  self                          in out gender_o)
010  return                            self as result is
011
012  begin
013    id           := NULL;
014    code         := NULL;
015    description  := NULL;
016    active_date  := NULL;
017    inactive_date := NULL;
018    return;
019  end gender_o;
020
021
```

```
022  CONSTRUCTOR FUNCTION gender_o(
023  self                         in out gender_o,
024  aiv_code                            varchar2,
025  aiv_description                     varchar2)
026  return                              self as result is
027
028  begin
029    id            := get_id();
030    code          := aiv_code;
031    description   := aiv_description;
032    active_date   := SYSDATE;
033    inactive_date := NULL;
034    return;
035  end gender_o;
036
037
038  STATIC PROCEDURE get_code_descr(
039  ain_id                       in     number,
040  aov_code                            out varchar2,
041  aov_description                     out varchar2 ) is
042
043  begin
044    select code,
045           description
046    into   aov_code,
047           aov_description
048    from   GENDER_OT
049    where  id = ain_id;
050  end get_code_descr;
051
052
053  STATIC PROCEDURE get_code_id_descr(
054  aiov_code                    in out varchar2,
055  aon_id                              out number,
056  aov_description                     out varchar2,
057  aid_on                       in     date ) is
058
059  v_code                              varchar2(30);
060
061  begin
062    select id,
063           description
064    into   aon_id,
065           aov_description
066    from   GENDER_OT
067    where  code = aiov_code
068    and    aid_on between active_date and nvl(inactive_date, DATES.d_MAX);
```

```
069  exception
070    when NO_DATA_FOUND then
071      select id,
072             code,
073             description
074      into   aon_id,
075             v_code,
076             aov_description
077      from   GENDER_OT
078      where  code like aiov_code||'%'
079      and    aid_on between active_date and nvl(inactive_date, DATES.d_MAX);
080      aiov_code := v_code;
081  end get_code_id_descr;
082
083
084  STATIC PROCEDURE get_code_id_descr(
085  aiov_code                    in out varchar2,
086  aon_id                       out number,
087  aov_description              out varchar2 ) is
088
089  begin
090   get_code_id_descr(
091     aiov_code,
092     aon_id,
093     aov_description,
094     SYSDATE );
095  end get_code_id_descr;
096
097
098  MEMBER FUNCTION get_id
099  return                       number is
100
101  n_id                         number;
102
103  begin
104    select GENDER_ID_SEQ.nextval
105    into   n_id
106    from   SYS.DUAL;
107
108    return n_id;
109  end get_id;
110
111
112  STATIC FUNCTION get_id(
113  aiv_code                 in     varchar2 )
114  return                       number is
115
```

```
116  n_id                            number;
117
118  begin
119    select  id
120    into    n_id
121    from    GENDER_OT
122    where   code = aiv_code;
123
124    return n_id;
125  end get_id;
126
127
128  MEMBER PROCEDURE help is
129
130  begin
...
184  end help;
185
186
187  MEMBER PROCEDURE test is
188
189  begin
...
195  end test;
196
197
198  MAP MEMBER FUNCTION to_varchar2
199  return                          varchar2 is
200
201  begin
202    return description||to_char(active_date, 'YYYYMMDDHH24MISS');
203  end to_varchar2;
204
205
206  end;
207  /
208  @be.sql GENDER_O
```

The CREATE TYPE BODY syntax used by Listing 6-2 is as follows:

```
CREATE [OR REPLACE] TYPE BODY <type_name> AS
[MAP]MEMBER or STATIC FUNCTION or PROCEDURE <method_name> [(
SELF                     [IN OUT][NOCOPY]<type_name>,
<parameter_name_1>       [IN OUT] <parameter_type_1>,
<parameter_name_2>       [IN OUT] <parameter_type_2>,...
<parameter_name_N>       [IN OUT] <parameter_type_N>),]
[RETURN                            <return_type>],
CONSTRUCTOR FUNCTION <type_name> (
```

```
SELF                    [IN OUT][NOCOPY]<type_name>,[
<parameter_name_1>      [IN OUT] <parameter_type_1>,
<parameter_name_2>      [IN OUT] <parameter_type_2>,...
<parameter_name_N>      [IN OUT] <parameter_type_N>),]
END;
```

where:

> \<type_name> is the name of your user-defined TYPE.

> \<method_name> is the name of a MEMBER or STATIC, FUNCTION or PROCEDURE.

> \<parameter_name> is the name of a parameter being passed INto or OUT of a method.

> \<parameter_type> is a predefined scalar data type or a user-defined type.

> \<return_type> is also a predefined scalar data type or a user-defined type to be returned by an associated FUNCTION.

As you can see by Listing 6-2, I've added quite a bit of behavior to my Gender code user-defined type. Let's break down the listing:

Line 1 uses the DDL keywords CREATE TYPE BODY ... AS to create a TYPE BODY for TYPE specification GENDER_O. The BODY consists of method implementations for the methods declare in the TYPE specification.

Lines 9 through 19 implement a CONSTRUCTOR FUNCTION that will return an instance of a Gender object initialized to NULL values.

Lines 22 through 35 implement a CONSTRUCTOR FUNCTION for coding convenience that requires you to pass in only a code and description in order to create a new Gender object instance. As you can see on line 29, the method initializes the id attribute using the MEMBER FUNCTION get_id().

Lines 98 through 109 implement the MEMBER FUNCTION get_id() in order to allocate the next primary key value.

Lines 198 through 203 implement the MAP MEMBER FUNCTION to_varchar2(), which returns the description for a given code along with its creation date, all as one long varchar2 value. Oracle will use this value to determine precedence when ordering object instances in a SQL SELECT statement. You don't need to declare and implement a MAP MEMBER FUNCTION, but I always do.

Which came first, the chicken or the egg? Now, if you're real sharp, you may have noticed that I have some dependency issues with the implementation. In order for the TYPE BODY to compile, an object table named GENDER_OT must already exist! Yes, the STATIC methods refer to an object table GENDER_OT, based on object TYPE GENDER_O. This isn't a big problem, I can address it one of two ways:

- Compile the TYPE specification, create the object table based on the TYPE specification, and then compile the TYPE BODY.

- Use dynamic SQL in the STATIC methods so the dependent table name in the SQL statements doesn't get resolved until runtime.

I normally choose the first alternative, for performance reasons.

It's Your Turn to Create a User-Defined Type

Now that you've seen me transform the Gender table and table package into a user-defined TYPE, it's time for you to do the same for the Worker Type table.

1. Get the list of columns from the WORKER_TYPE_T table, and at least the one method you created in table package WORKER_TYPE_TS, and use that information to code a WORKER_TYPE_O TYPE specification.

2. Save your specification script as worker_type_o.tps.

3. Compile your specification: @worker_type_o.tps.

4. Create a WORKER_TYPE_O TYPE BODY script, which will contain the implementation for your method get_id().

5. Save you body script as worker_type_o.tpb.

6. Compile your body: @worker_type_o.tpb.

7. Test your user-defined type, to at least see that it compiled.

To test your user-defined type, you can use an anonymous PL/SQL procedure like the following.

```
declare
-- Declare a worker_type_o variable
o_worker_type                    WORKER_TYPE_O;

begin
  -- Now use the default constructor to create a new instance
  -- of the object
  o_worker_type := new WORKER_TYPE_O(
    NULL, 'H', 'A hard worker', SYSDATE, NULL);
  -- Now allocate a new ID using the member function get_id()
  o_worker_type.id := o_worker_type.get_id();
  -- Now show the values of the attributes in the instance
  pl('o_worker_type.id            = '||o_worker_type.id);
  pl('o_worker_type.code          = '||o_worker_type.code);
  pl('o_worker_type.description   = '||o_worker_type.description);
  pl('o_worker_type.active_date   = '||o_worker_type.active_date);
  pl('o_worker_type.inactive_date = '||o_worker_type.inactive_date);
end;
/
```

Your results should look something like this:

```
o_worker_type.id            = 111
o_worker_type.code          = H
o_worker_type.description   = A hard worker
o_worker_type.active_date   =  20070223 100918
o_worker_type.inactive_date =

PL/SQL procedure successfully completed.
```

Listings 6-3 and 6-4 demonstrate my solution for this exercise. Once again, I'm showing you a fully implemented TYPE.

Listing 6-3. *A Worker Type Used-Defined TYPE Specification, worker_type_o.tps*

```
01  create or replace TYPE WORKER_TYPE_O as object (
02  /*
03  worker_type_o.tps
04  by Donald J. Bales on 12/15/2006
05  Type WORKER_TYPE_O's attributes and methods.
06  */
07  id                          number,
08  code                        varchar2(30),
09  description                 varchar2(80),
10  active_date                 date,
11  inactive_date               date,
12  -- Gets the code and description values for the specified work_type_id.
13  STATIC PROCEDURE get_code_descr(
14  ain_id                      in    number,
15  aov_code                        out varchar2,
16  aov_description                 out varchar2 ),
17  -- Verifies the passed aiov_code value is an exact or like match on the
18  -- date specified.
19  STATIC PROCEDURE get_code_id_descr(
20  aiov_code                   in out varchar2,
21  aon_id                          out number,
22  aov_description                 out varchar2,
23  aid_on                      in    date ),
24  -- Verifies the passed aiov_code value is currently an exact or like match.
25  STATIC PROCEDURE get_code_id_descr(
26  aiov_code                   in out varchar2,
27  aon_id                          out number,
28  aov_description                 out varchar2 ),
29  -- Returns a newly allocated id value.
30  MEMBER FUNCTION get_id
31  return                          number,
32  -- Returns the id for the specified code value.
33  STATIC FUNCTION get_id(
```

```
34  aiv_code                        in      varchar2 )
35  return                                  number,
36  -- Test-based help for this package.  "set serveroutput on" in SQL*Plus.
37  MEMBER PROCEDURE help,
38  -- Test units for this package.
39  MEMBER PROCEDURE test,
40  -- A MAP function for sorting at the object level.
41  MAP MEMBER FUNCTION to_varchar2
42  return                                  varchar2,
43  -- A constructor for creating a new instance of type WORKER_TYPE_O
44  -- with NULL values.
45  CONSTRUCTOR FUNCTION worker_type_o(
46  self                      in out worker_type_o)
47  return                                  self as result,
48  -- A constructor for creating a new instance of type WORKER_TYPE_O
49  -- for insert.
50  CONSTRUCTOR FUNCTION worker_type_o(
51  self                      in out worker_type_o,
52  aiv_code                  in      varchar2,
53  aiv_description           in      varchar2)
54  return                                  self as result
55  );
56  /
57  @se.sql WORKER_TYPE_O
```

Listing 6-4. *A Worker Type User-Defined TYPE BODY, worker_type_o.tpb*

```
001  create or replace TYPE BODY WORKER_TYPE_O as
002  /*
003  worker_type_o.tpb
004  by Donald J. Bales on 12/15/2006
005  Type WORKER_TYPE_O's methods
006  */
007
008
009  MEMBER FUNCTION get_id
010  return                                  number is
011
012  n_id                                    number;
013
014  begin
015    select WORKER_TYPE_ID_SEQ.nextval
016    into   n_id
017    from   SYS.DUAL;
018
019    return n_id;
020  end get_id;
```

```
021
022
023   STATIC FUNCTION get_id(
024   aiv_code                      in     varchar2 )
025   return                               number is
026
027   n_id                                 number;
028
029   begin
030     select id
031     into   n_id
032     from   WORKER_TYPE_OT
033     where  code = aiv_code;
034
035     return n_id;
036   end get_id;
037
038
039   STATIC PROCEDURE get_code_descr(
040   ain_id                        in     number,
041   aov_code                             out varchar2,
042   aov_description                      out varchar2 ) is
043
044   begin
045     select code,
046            description
047     into   aov_code,
048            aov_description
049     from   WORKER_TYPE_OT
050     where  id = ain_id;
051   end get_code_descr;
052
053
054   STATIC PROCEDURE get_code_id_descr(
055   aiov_code                     in out varchar2,
056   aon_id                               out number,
057   aov_description                      out varchar2,
058   aid_on                        in     date ) is
059
060   v_code                               varchar2(30);
061
062   begin
063     select id,
064            description
065     into   aon_id,
066            aov_description
067     from   WORKER_TYPE_OT
068     where  code = aiov_code
```

```
069    and     aid_on between active_date and nvl(inactive_date, DATES.d_MAX);
070  exception
071    when NO_DATA_FOUND then
072      select id,
073             code,
074             description
075      into   aon_id,
076             v_code,
077             aov_description
078      from   WORKER_TYPE_OT
079      where  code like aiov_code||'%'
080      and    aid_on between active_date and nvl(inactive_date, DATES.d_MAX);
081
082      aiov_code := v_code;
083  end get_code_id_descr;
084
085
086  STATIC PROCEDURE get_code_id_descr(
087  aiov_code                      in out varchar2,
088  aon_id                         out number,
089  aov_description                out varchar2 ) is
090
091  begin
092   get_code_id_descr(
093    aiov_code,
094    aon_id,
095    aov_description,
096    SYSDATE );
097  end get_code_id_descr;
098
099
100  MEMBER PROCEDURE help is
101
102  begin
...
156  end help;
157
158
159  MEMBER PROCEDURE test is
160
161  begin
...
173  end test;
174
175
176  MAP MEMBER FUNCTION to_varchar2
177  return                          varchar2 is
```

```
178
179   begin
180     return description||to_char(active_date, 'YYYYMMDDHH24MISS');
181   end to_varchar2;
182
183
184   CONSTRUCTOR FUNCTION worker_type_o(
185   self                          in out worker_type_o)
186   return                                self as result is
187
188   begin
189     id              := NULL;
190     code            := NULL;
191     description     := NULL;
192     active_date     := NULL;
193     inactive_date := NULL;
194     return;
195   end worker_type_o;
196
197
198   CONSTRUCTOR FUNCTION worker_type_o(
199   self                          in out worker_type_o,
200   aiv_code                      in      varchar2,
201   aiv_description               in      varchar2)
202   return                                self as result is
203
204   begin
205     id              := get_id();
206     code            := aiv_code;
207     description     := aiv_description;
208     active_date     := SYSDATE;
209     inactive_date := NULL;
210     return;
211   end worker_type_o;
212
213
214   end;
215   /
216   @be.sql WORKER_TYPE_O
```

Just think, you are able to test the TYPE, yet you haven't even created a view or table that utilizes it. Speaking of that, why don't we create an object view next!

Object Views

It's time to turn a sow's ear into a silk purse! OK, maybe just a whole pig. Think of this as a cloning project. You can seamlessly transition into the use of user-defined objects by intelligently overlaying your relational database structure with a set of object views. An object view takes the columns from one or more relational tables and morphs them into a pseudo-table of user-defined objects, complete with attributes and behavior. Sorry, no I'm not smoking anything funny here. I don't blow smoke.

Create an Object View

Listing 6-5 is a script to create an object view for the relational Gender code table GENDER_T. This view automatically maps the column values in table GENDER_T to the attributes of user-defined TYPE GENDER_O, producing what appears to be a table of GENDER_O objects called GENDER_OV.

Listing 6-5. *An Example of an Object View Script for Table GENDER_T, gender_ow.vw*

```
01   rem gender_ov.vw
02   rem by Donald J. Bales on 12/15/2006
03   rem Create an object view for table GENDER_T
04
05   create view GENDER_OV of GENDER_O
06   with object identifier (id) as
07   select id,
08          code,
09          description,
10          active_date,
11          inactive_date
12   from    GENDER_T;
```

The CREATE VIEW syntax used in Listing 6-5 is as follows:

```
CREATE [OR REPLACE] VIEW <view_name> OF <type_name>
WITH OBJECT IDENTIFIER (<primary_key_attributes>) AS
SELECT <column_name_1>,
       <column_name_2>,...
       <column_name_N>
FROM   <table_name>;
```

where:

<view_name> is the name of the view to create.

<type_name> is the user-defined TYPE to map the columns to in the relational table.

<primary_key_attributes> is one or more attributes in the user-defined TYPE that map to the primary key column(s) of the underlying table.

<column_name> is the name of a column in the table to map to the attributes of the user-defined TYPE.

<table_name> is the underlying table to map to the user-defined TYPE.

Now that wasn't much work was it? OK, now let's test the view. Listing 6-6 is an anonymous PL/SQL procedure to test the object view. It's well commented, so you can see what is being tested. Note that you can execute INSERT, UPDATE, DELETE, and SELECT statements against an object view or its underlying table and get the same results. An object view therefore provides a means for your database to be both relational and object-oriented at the same time!

Listing 6-6. *A Test Unit for View GENDER_OV, gender_ov.sql*

```
01  rem gender_ov.sql
02  rem by Donald J. Bales on 12/15/2006
03  rem test unit for object view GENDER_OV
04
05  declare
06  -- Declare a variable of the user-defined type
07  o_gender                        GENDER_O;
08  -- Declare a variable for the underlying table
09  r_gender                        GENDER_T%ROWTYPE;
10
11  begin
12    -- Insert a test object using the convenience constructor
13    insert into GENDER_OV
14    values ( GENDER_O( 'T', 'Test') );
15
16    -- Now update the inactive date on the object
17    update GENDER_OV
18    set    inactive_date = SYSDATE
19    where  code          = 'T';
20
21    -- Retrieve the object in order to show its values
22    select value(g)
23    into   o_gender
24    from   GENDER_OV g
25    where  code          = 'T';
26
27    -- Show the object's values
28    pl('o_gender.id            = '||o_gender.id);
29    pl('o_gender.code          = '||o_gender.code);
30    pl('o_gender.description   = '||o_gender.description);
31    pl('o_gender.active_date   = '||o_gender.active_date);
32    pl('o_gender.inactive_date = '||o_gender.inactive_date);
33
34    -- Delete the test object
35    delete GENDER_OV
36    where  code          = 'T';
37
38    -- This time insert the test object using the instance variable
39    insert into GENDER_OV
40    values ( o_gender );
41
```

```
42     -- Now, select the values from the underlying relational table
43     select *
44     into    r_gender
45     from    GENDER_T
46     where   code           = 'T';
47
48     -- Show the record's values
49     pl('r_gender.id            = '||r_gender.id);
50     pl('r_gender.code          = '||r_gender.code);
51     pl('r_gender.description   = '||r_gender.description);
52     pl('r_gender.active_date   = '||r_gender.active_date);
53     pl('r_gender.inactive_date = '||r_gender.inactive_date);
54
55     -- Last, delete the object from the relational table
56     delete GENDER_T
57     where   code           = 'T';
58
59     -- Commit all these operations
60     commit;
61
62     -- Confirm that the test completed successfully
63     pl('Test completed successfully.');
64   end;
65   /
```

And, here are the results of the test unit in Listing 6-6:

```
SQL> @gender_ov.sql
```

```
o_gender.id            = 131
o_gender.code          = T
o_gender.description   = Test
o_gender.active_date   =  20070223 140020
o_gender.inactive_date =  20070223 140020
r_gender.id            = 131
r_gender.code          = T
r_gender.description   = Test
r_gender.active_date   =  20070223 140020
r_gender.inactive_date =  20070223 140020
Test completed successfully.

PL/SQL procedure successfully completed.
```

It's Your Turn to Create an Object View

Yes, it's your turn. Can you guess what I'm going to ask you to do next? I thought so.

1. Create a script to create an object view for table WORKER_TYPE_T that maps its values to user-defined type WORKER_TYPE_O. You know, the TYPE you just finished creating in the previous exercise.

2. Save your script as worker_type_ov.vw.

3. Execute your script to create the object view: @worker_type_ov.vw.

4. Create a test unit script and test your new object view.

Nope, I'm not going to show you my solution. This is so simple you don't need my help! Next, instead of turning a sow's ear into a pig, just pass me the pig!

Object Tables

Pass me the pig, please. Have you ever heard that at the dinner table before? Who wants to settle for a sow's ear when you can have the whole pig, bacon and all. Yum, bacon, the candy of meats! Anyway, once you've created a TYPE, it's no harder to create an object (-relational) table than it is to build a relational table.

Create an Object Table

As a matter of fact, Listing 6-7 is nothing more than my table-creation script for the Gender table, gender_t.tab, renamed to gender_ot.tab, with a few minor changes.

Listing 6-7. *An Example of an Object Table Script for GENDER_OT, gender_ot.tab*

```
01  rem gender_ot.tab
02  rem by Donald J. Bales on 12/15/2006
03  rem create an object table for the Gender codes
04
05  --drop   table GENDER_OT;
06  create table GENDER_OT of GENDER_O
07  tablespace USERS pctfree 20
08  storage (initial 10K next 10K pctincrease 0);
09
10  --drop   sequence GENDER_ID_SEQ;
11  --create sequence GENDER_ID_SEQ
12  --start with 1;
13
14  alter  table GENDER_OT add
15  constraint   GENDER_OT_PK
16  primary key ( id )
17  using index
18  tablespace USERS pctfree 20
19  storage (initial 10K next 10K pctincrease 0);
20
21  alter  table GENDER_OT add
```

```
22   constraint    GENDER_OT_UK
23   unique ( code )
24   using index
25   tablespace USERS pctfree 20
26   storage (initial 10K next 10K pctincrease 0);
```

The CREATE TABLE syntax used in Listing 6-7 is as follows:

```
CREATE TABLE <table_name> OF <type_name>;
```

where <table_name> is the name of the table to create, and <type_name> is the user-defined TYPE to use instead of column names for the table.

There isn't a lot of extra work to creating an object table vs. a relational table, now is there? Here's the rundown:

On lines 6 through 8, I use the new syntax to create a table of one user-defined TYPE instead of one or more predefined scalar data types.

I've commented out lines 10 through 12, because I've already created this sequence for the relational table.

On lines 14 through 19, I create a primary key on the object table, just as I did on the relational table.

On lines 21 through 26, I create a unique key on the object table, just as I did on the relational table.

It's Your Turn to Create an Object Table

Once again, it's your turn. For this exercise, create an object table named WORKER_TYPE_OT for the Worker Type code table.

1. Write a script to create an object table based on user-defined TYPE WORKER_TYPE_O.

2. Save your script as worker_type_ot.tab.

3. Execute your script to create the object view: @worker_type_ot.tab.

4. Create a test unit script and test your new object view.

I'll indulge you. Listing 6-8 is my solution to this exercise.

Listing 6-8. *An Example of an Object Table Script for WORKER_TYPE_OT, worker_type_ot.tab*

```
01   rem worker_type_ot.tab
02   rem by Donald J. Bales on 12/15/2006
03   rem Create an object table for the Worker Type codes
04
05   --drop    table WORKER_TYPE_OT;
06   create table WORKER_TYPE_OT of WORKER_TYPE_O
07   tablespace USERS pctfree 20
```

```
08   storage (initial 10K next 10K pctincrease 0);
09
10   --drop    sequence WORKER_TYPE_ID_SEQ;
11   --create sequence WORKER_TYPE_ID_SEQ
12   --start with 1;
13
14   alter  table WORKER_TYPE_OT add
15   constraint   WORKER_TYPE_OT_PK
16   primary key ( id )
17   using index
18   tablespace USERS pctfree 20
19   storage (initial 10K next 10K pctincrease 0);
20
21   alter  table WORKER_TYPE_OT add
22   constraint   WORKER_TYPE_OT_UK
23   unique ( code )
24   using index
25   tablespace USERS pctfree 20
26   storage (initial 10K next 10K pctincrease 0);
```

To test this object table, I just save my object view test unit as worker_type_ot.sql, change the object view name to the object table name, and get rid of the relational table tests, and then ta da! Listing 6-9 shows my test unit for WORKER_TYPE_OT.

Listing 6-9. *A Test Unit for Table WORKER_TYPE_OT, worker_type_ot.sql*

```
01   rem worker_type_ot.sql
02   rem by Donald J. Bales on 12/15/2006
03   rem test unit for object table WORKER_TYPE_OT
04
05   declare
06   -- Declare a variable of the user-defined type
07   o_worker_type                     WORKER_TYPE_O;
08
09   begin
10     -- Insert a test object using the convenience constructor
11     insert into WORKER_TYPE_OT
12     values ( WORKER_TYPE_O( 'T', 'Test') );
13
14     -- Now update the inactive date on the object
15     update WORKER_TYPE_OT
16     set    inactive_date = SYSDATE
17     where  code          = 'T';
18
19     -- Retrieve the object in order to show its values
20     select value(t)
21     into   o_worker_type
22     from   WORKER_TYPE_OT t
```

```
23     where  code          = 'T';
24
25     -- Show the object's values
26     pl('o_worker_type.id               = '||o_worker_type.id);
27     pl('o_worker_type.code             = '||o_worker_type.code);
28     pl('o_worker_type.description       = '||o_worker_type.description);
29     pl('o_worker_type.active_date       = '||o_worker_type.active_date);
30     pl('o_worker_type.inactive_date     = '||o_worker_type.inactive_date);
31
32     -- Delete the test object
33     delete WORKER_TYPE_OT
34     where  code          = 'T';
35
36     -- This time insert the test object using the instance variable
37     insert into WORKER_TYPE_OT
38     values ( o_worker_type );
39
40     -- Last, delete the object from the relational table
41     delete WORKER_TYPE_T
42     where  code          = 'T';
43
44     -- Commit all these operations
45     commit;
46
47     -- Confirm that the test completed successfully
48     pl('Test completed successfully.');
49 end;
50 /
```

The results of the test unit in Listing 6-9 should look something like this:

```
SQL> @worker_type_ot
```

```
o_worker_type.id              = 112
o_worker_type.code            = T
o_worker_type.description     = Test
o_worker_type.active_date     =  20070223 155157
o_worker_type.inactive_date   =  20070223 155157
Test completed successfully.

PL/SQL procedure successfully completed.
```

Come on, you have to admit it. It's pretty easy to make a transition to object orientation, right? Perhaps, or perhaps not. Some argue that there is a problem between how object-oriented languages represent data and how data is stored in a relational database, calling it an *impedance mismatch*.

Impedance Mismatch My Foot!

I argue that if done properly, there is little so-called "mismatch" between the classes used in an object-oriented language like Java and object-relational user-defined types in Oracle—that is, if they both properly model the real world.

I have an entire section dedicated to the use of Java Database Connectivity (JDBC) and object-relational user-defined types in one of my previous books (*Java Programming with Oracle JDBC*). My 20 plus years of experience in both programming with object-oriented languages and using relational and now object-relational databases has led me to the conclusion that the mismatch is one of improper analysis vs. the reality of the problem domain.

The only time I see a mismatch is when one of the following occurs:

- "Catchall" classes are used in the presentation layer that make it easy to represent and move objects around in the presentation layer, but they don't actually model the real world at all.

- Denormalized attributes in classes that once again make it easier to work with data in the presentation layer, but don't even remotely represent the cardinality of the real world.

- No time is taken to do a proper analysis. It's build a presentation and then create a database that fits it, or restated, shoot, ready, aim! Right.

- Target databases use a different programming language from the presentation layer's object-oriented programming environment, so the database programming language is misunderstood, misused, or ignored altogether.

Don't take these in any particular order, because there are more reasons than I am willing to list. I seem to remember the same phenomena—you know, all the reasons not to adopt better technology—years ago when relational technology first appeared, say 1984?

So what haven't I told you? There are, in fact, a few topics I have not covered yet. Let's delve into those next.

Nested Types and Collections

First, I haven't shown any examples with nested types. For example, I could create a TYPE ADDRESS_O for address information, and then use that TYPE as an attribute in another TYPE like CONTACT_O. You can do that; it's not a problem.

Nor have I shown you any examples of a TYPE that contain arrays of other TYPEs. That's certainly possible. You can create what is called a nested TYPE, and implement it as a nested table where you can have an unlimited number of entries, or as a varying array that has a fixed number of entries. I don't like the sound of the latter. It's not very relational in nature. And nesting is where all the so-called impedance mismatch occurs.

In the minds of some object-oriented programmers, it's necessary to create huge, complex, object types that contain everything remotely similar. You know, if you're an object-oriented programmer, you've seen them, or worse, created them.

Consider Figure 6-1, a class diagram to replace the ERD for our problem domain from Chapter 1. Are all three historical entities—LocgicalAssignment, PhysicalAssignment, and WorkAssignment—part of Worker in an object-oriented setting? No, they may be related, but you won't find them on any particular worker, will you? They are actually stand-alone entities.

However, in most cases, someone would create a class `Worker` that contained these three entities as arrays. There's the mismatch. It's a break between reality and programming convenience.

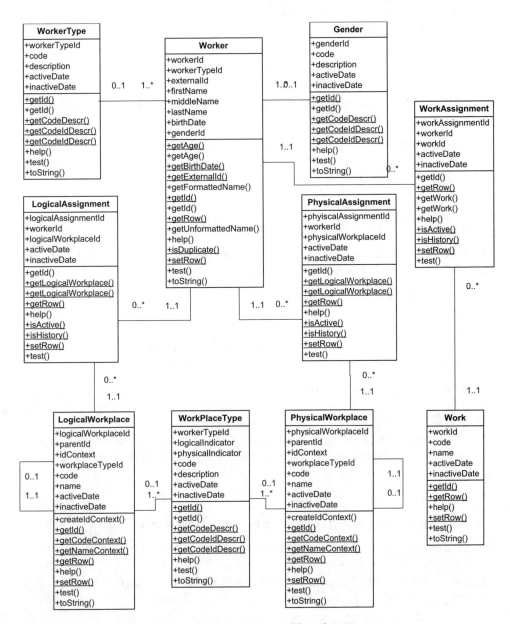

Figure 6-1. *A partial class diagram for our sample problem domain*

It's Your Turn to Prove There's No Impedance Mismatch

At this point, I've coded the scripts to create the Gender code object table, and you've done the same for the Worker Type object table. Now you can put these to work as you code the scripts for and create a Worker object table. Here's what to do:

1. Verify that you successfully executed the following scripts: gender_o.tps, gender_o.tpb, gender_ot.tab, and gender_ot.ins.

2. Verify that you successfully coded and executed the following scripts: worker_type_o. tps, worker_type_o.tpb, worker_type_ot.tab, and worker_type_ot.ins.

3. Write a script to create a TYPE specification for the Worker entity. You can get the attributes from the column names in file worker_type_t.tab. You can get the method names from package file worker_type_ts.pks.

4. Save your script as worker_o.tps.

5. Compile your script: @worker_o.tps.

6. Write a script to create an object table named WORKER_OT using the user-defined type WORKER_O you just created.

7. Save your script as worker_ot.tab.

8. Compile your script: @worker_ot.tab.

9. Write a script to implement the TYPE BODY for the Worker entity. You can get the method implementations from package file worker_type_ts.pkb.

10. Save your script as worker_o.tpb.

11. Compile your script: @worker_o.tps.

12. At this point, you should have a valid WORKER_OT object table. So now modify the script we used to populate the WORKER_T table, worker_t.ins, to populate the WORKER_OT object table.

13. Save your script as worker_ot.ins.

14. Execute your script in order to populate the object table: @worker_ot.ins.

15. Create a test unit script and test your new object table.

Listings 6-10 through 6-13 show my solutions for this exercise. Listing 6-10 is my specification for the TYPE WORKER_O.

Listing 6-10. *The Specification Script for User-Defined TYPE WORKER_O, worker_o.tps*

```
001  create or replace type WORKER_O as object (
002  /*
003  worker_o.tps
004  by Donald J. Bales on 12/15/2006
```

```
005   Type WORKER_O's attributes and methods.
006   */
007   id                              number,
008   worker_type_id                  number,
009   external_id                     varchar2(30),
010   first_name                      varchar2(30),
011   middle_name                     varchar2(30),
012   last_name                       varchar2(30),
013   name                            varchar2(100),
014   birth_date                      date,
015   gender_id                       number,
016   /*
017   Get the worker's current age.
018   */
019   MEMBER FUNCTION get_age
020   return                          number,
021   /*
022   Get the worker's age on the specified date.
023   */
024   MEMBER FUNCTION get_age(
025   aid_on                          date)
026   return                          number,
027   /*
028   Calculate a worker's age for the given birth date
029   and point in time.
030   */
031   STATIC FUNCTION get_age(
032   aid_birth_date        in        date,
033   aid_on                in        date)
034   return                          number,
035   /*
036   Calculate a worker's current age for the given birth date.
037   */
038   STATIC FUNCTION get_age(
039   aid_birth_date        in        date)
040   return                          number,
041   /*
042   Get the specified worker's age at the given point in time.
043   */
044   STATIC FUNCTION get_age(
045   ain_id                in        number,
046   aid_on                in        date)
047   return                          number,
048   /*
049   Get the specified worker's current age.
050   */
051   STATIC FUNCTION get_age(
```

```
052  ain_id                       in     number)
053  return                              number,
054  /*
055  Get the specified worker's birth date.
056  */
057  STATIC FUNCTION get_birth_date(
058  ain_id                       in     number)
059  return                              date,
060  /*
061  Get the specified worker's external ID.
062  */
063  STATIC FUNCTION get_external_id
064  return                              varchar2,
065  /*
066  Calculate the locale specific formatted name.
067  */
068  STATIC FUNCTION get_formatted_name(
069  aiv_first_name               in     varchar2,
070  aiv_middle_name              in     varchar2,
071  aiv_last_name                in     varchar2)
072  return                              varchar2,
073  /*
074  Get the specified worker's formatted name.
075  */
076  STATIC FUNCTION get_formatted_name(
077  ain_id                       in     number)
078  return                              varchar2,
079  /*
080  Get the next primary key value for the table.
081  */
082  STATIC FUNCTION get_id
083  return                              number,
084  /*
085  Get the specified worker's internal ID.
086  */
087  STATIC FUNCTION get_id(
088  aiv_external_id              in     varchar2)
089  return                              number,
090  /*
091  Get the specified worker's row object.
092  */
093  STATIC FUNCTION get_row(
094  aio_worker                   in     WORKER_O)
095  return                              WORKER_O,
096  /*
097  Calculate the non-locale specific unformatted name.
098  */
```

```
099  STATIC FUNCTION get_unformatted_name(
100  aiv_first_name              in      varchar2,
101  aiv_middle_name             in      varchar2,
102  aiv_last_name               in      varchar2)
103  return                              varchar2,
104  /*
105  Display the help text for this TYPE.
106  */
107  MEMBER PROCEDURE help,
108  /*
109  Check to see if a worker with the same name, birth_date and
110  gender already exists in the database.
111  */
112  STATIC FUNCTION is_duplicate(
113  aiv_name                    in      varchar2,
114  aid_birth_date              in      varchar2,
115  ain_gender_id               in      varchar2)
116  return                              boolean,
117  /*
118  Set the specified worker's row object.
119  */
120  STATIC PROCEDURE set_row(
121  aioo_worker                 in out WORKER_O),
122  /*
123  Execute the test unit for this TYPE.
124  */
125  MEMBER PROCEDURE test,
126  /*
127  The MAP function for this TYPE.
128  */
129  MAP MEMBER FUNCTION to_varchar2
130  return                              varchar2,
131  /*
132  A convenience constructor for this TYPE.
133  */
134  CONSTRUCTOR FUNCTION worker_o(
135  self                        in out worker_o,
136  ain_worker_type_id          in      number,
137  aiv_first_name              in      varchar2,
138  aiv_middle_name             in      varchar2,
139  aiv_last_name               in      varchar2,
140  aid_birth_date              in      date,
141  ain_gender_id               in      number)
142  return                              self as result,
143  /*
144  A NULL values constructor for this TYPE.
145  */
```

```
146  CONSTRUCTOR FUNCTION worker_o(
147  self                          in out worker_o)
148  return                              self as result
149  );
150  /
151  @se.sql
```

Listing 6-11. *The CREATE TABLE Script for Object Table WORKER_OT, worker_ot.tab*

```
01  rem worker_ot.tab
02  rem  by Donald J. Bales on 12/15/2006
03  rem Create an object table for Workers
04
05  --drop   table WORKER_OT;
06  create table WORKER_OT of WORKER_O
07  tablespace USERS pctfree 20
08  storage (initial 10K next 10K pctincrease 0);
09
10  --drop   sequence WORKER_ID_SEQ;
11  --create sequence WORKER_ID_SEQ
12  --start with 1;
13
14  --drop    sequence EXTERNAL_ID_SEQ;
15  --create sequence EXTERNAL_ID_SEQ
16  --start with 100000000 order;
17
18  alter  table WORKER_OT add
19  constraint   WORKER_OT_PK
20  primary key ( id )
21  using index
22  tablespace USERS pctfree 20
23  storage (initial 10K next 10K pctincrease 0);
24
25  alter  table WORKER_OT add
26  constraint   WORKER_OT_UK1
27  unique ( external_id )
28  using index
29  tablespace USERS pctfree 20
30  storage (initial 10K next 10K pctincrease 0);
31
32  alter  table WORKER_OT add
33  constraint    WORKER_OT_UK2
34  unique (
35  name,
36  birth_date,
37  gender_id )
38  using index
```

```
39  tablespace USERS pctfree 20
40  storage (initial 10K next 10K pctincrease 0);
41
42  alter  table WORKER_OT add
43  constraint   WORKER_OT_FK1
44  foreign key              ( worker_type_id )
45  references   WORKER_TYPE_OT ( worker_type_id );
46
47  alter  table WORKER_OT add
48  constraint   WORKER_OT_FK2
49  foreign key              ( gender_id )
50  references   GENDER_OT    ( gender_id );
```

Listing 6-12. *The BODY Implementation Script for TYPE WORKER_O, worker_o.tpb*

```
001  create or replace type body WORKER_O as
002  /*
003  worker_o.tpb
004  by Donald J. Bales on 12/15/2006
005  TYPE WORKER's methods
006  */
007
008  MEMBER FUNCTION get_age(
009  aid_on                   in     date)
010  return                          number is
011
012  begin
013    return WORKER_O.get_age(birth_date, aid_on);
014  end get_age;
015
016
017  MEMBER FUNCTION get_age
018  return                          number is
019
020  begin
021    return WORKER_O.get_age(birth_date, SYSDATE);
022  end get_age;
023
024
025  STATIC FUNCTION get_age(
026  aid_birth_date           in     date,
027  aid_on                   in     date)
028  return                          number is
029
030  begin
031   if aid_birth_date is not NULL and
032      aid_on        is not NULL then
```

```
033       return trunc(months_between(aid_on, aid_birth_date) / 12);
034    else
035      return NULL;
036    end if;
037  exception
038    when OTHERS then
039      return NULL;
040  end get_age;
041
042
043  STATIC FUNCTION get_age(
044  aid_birth_date              in     date)
045  return                             number is
046
047  begin
048    return WORKER_O.get_age(aid_birth_date, SYSDATE);
049  end get_age;
050
051
052  STATIC FUNCTION get_age(
053  ain_id                      in     number,
054  aid_on                      in     date)
055  return                             number is
056
057  begin
058    return WORKER_O.get_age(WORKER_O.get_birth_date(ain_id), aid_on);
059  end get_age;
060
061
062  STATIC FUNCTION get_age(
063  ain_id                      in     number)
064  return                             number is
065
066  begin
067    return WORKER_O.get_age(WORKER_O.get_birth_date(ain_id));
068  end get_age;
069
070
071  STATIC FUNCTION get_birth_date(
072  ain_id                      in     number)
073  return                             date is
074
075  d_birth_date                       date;
076
077  begin
078    select birth_date
079    into   d_birth_date
```

```
080    from   WORKER_T
081    where  id = ain_id;
082
083    return d_birth_date;
084  end get_birth_date;
085
086
087  STATIC FUNCTION get_external_id
088  return                              varchar2 is
089
090  v_external_id                       varchar2(30);
091
092  begin
093    select lpad(to_char(EXTERNAL_ID_SEQ.nextval), 9, '0')
094    into   v_external_id
095    from   SYS.DUAL;
096
097    return v_external_id;
098  end get_external_id;
099
100
101  STATIC FUNCTION get_id
102  return                              number is
103
104  n_id                                number;
105
106  begin
107    select WORKER_ID_SEQ.nextval
108    into   n_id
109    from   SYS.DUAL;
110
111    return n_id;
112  end get_id;
113
114
115  STATIC FUNCTION get_id(
116  aiv_external_id            in    varchar2)
117  return                           number is
118
119  n_id                             number;
120
121  begin
122    select id
123    into   n_id
124    from   WORKER_T
125    where  external_id = aiv_external_id;
126
```

```
127    return n_id;
128  end get_id;
129
130
131  STATIC FUNCTION get_formatted_name(
132  aiv_first_name                 in      varchar2,
133  aiv_middle_name                in      varchar2,
134  aiv_last_name                  in      varchar2)
135  return                                 varchar2 is
136
137  begin
138   return aiv_last_name||', '||aiv_first_name||' '||aiv_middle_name;
139  end get_formatted_name;
140
141
142  STATIC FUNCTION get_formatted_name(
143  ain_id                         in      number)
144  return                                 varchar2 is
145
146  v_first_name                           varchar2(30);
147  v_middle_name                          varchar2(30);
148  v_last_name                            varchar2(30);
149
150  begin
151    select first_name,
152           middle_name,
153           last_name
154    into   v_first_name,
155           v_middle_name,
156           v_last_name
157    from   WORKER_OT
158    where  id = ain_id;
159
160    return get_formatted_name(
161           v_first_name,
162           v_middle_name,
163           v_last_name);
164  end get_formatted_name;
165
166
167  STATIC FUNCTION get_row(
168  aio_worker                     in      WORKER_O)
169  return                                 WORKER_O is
170
171  o_worker                               WORKER_O;
172
173  begin
```

```
174    if    aio_worker.id is not NULL then
175      -- retrieve the row by the primary key
176      select value(w)
177      into   o_worker
178      from   WORKER_OT w
179      where  id = aio_worker.id;
180    elsif aio_worker.external_id is not NULL then
181      -- retrieve the row by the external unique key
182      select value(w)
183      into   o_worker
184      from   WORKER_OT w
185      where  external_id = aio_worker.external_id;
186    else
187      -- retrieve the row by the name, birth_date, and gender
188      select value(w)
189      into   o_worker
190      from   WORKER_OT w
191      where  name       = worker_o.get_formatted_name(
192                              aio_worker.first_name,
193                              aio_worker.middle_name,
194                              aio_worker.last_name)
195      and    birth_date = aio_worker.birth_date
196      and    gender_id  = aio_worker.gender_id;
197    end if;
198    return o_worker;
199  exception
200    when NO_DATA_FOUND then
201      raise;
202    when OTHERS then
203      raise_application_error(-20001, SQLERRM||
204        ' on select WORKER_OT'||
205        ' in WORKER_O.get_row()');
206  end get_row;
207
208
209  STATIC FUNCTION get_unformatted_name(
210  aiv_first_name             in      varchar2,
211  aiv_middle_name            in      varchar2,
212  aiv_last_name              in      varchar2)
213  return                             varchar2 is
214
215  begin
216    return upper(replace(replace(replace(replace(replace(
217      aiv_last_name||aiv_first_name||aiv_middle_name,
218        '''', NULL), ',', NULL), '-', NULL), '.', NULL), ' ', NULL));
219  end get_unformatted_name;
220
```

```
221
222   STATIC FUNCTION is_duplicate(
223   aiv_name                        in      varchar2,
224   aid_birth_date                  in      varchar2,
225   ain_gender_id                   in      varchar2)
226   return                                  boolean is
227
228   n_selected                              number;
229
230   begin
231     execute immediate
232       'select count(1)
233        from    WORKER_OT
234        where   name      = aiv_name
235        and     birth_date = aid_birth_date
236        and     gender_id  = ain_gender_id'
237        into    n_selected
238        using   in aiv_name,
239                in aid_birth_date,
240                in ain_gender_id;
241
242     if nvl(n_selected, 0) > 0 then
243       return TRUE;
244     else
245       return FALSE;
246     end if;
247   end is_duplicate;
248
249
250   MEMBER PROCEDURE help is
251
252   begin
...
306   end help;
307
308
309   STATIC PROCEDURE set_row(
310   aioo_worker                     in out WORKER_O) is
311
312   d_null                          constant date        := DATES.d_MIN;
313   n_null                          constant number      := 0;
314   v_null                          constant varchar2(1) := ' ';
315   o_worker                        WORKER_O;
316
317   begin
318     -- set the formatted name
319     aioo_worker.name := worker_o.get_formatted_name(
```

```
320                          aioo_worker.first_name,
321                          aioo_worker.middle_name,
322                          aioo_worker.last_name);
323    -- get the existing row
324    begin
325      o_worker := get_row(aioo_worker);
326    exception
327      when NO_DATA_FOUND then
328        o_worker := NULL;
329    end;
330    -- if a row exists, update it if needed
331    if o_worker is not NULL then
332      aioo_worker.id := o_worker.id;
333      if nvl(o_worker.worker_type_id, n_null) <>
334           nvl(aioo_worker.worker_type_id, n_null) or
335         nvl(o_worker.external_id,    n_null) <>
336           nvl(aioo_worker.external_id,    n_null) or
337         nvl(o_worker.first_name,     v_null) <>
338           nvl(aioo_worker.first_name,     v_null) or
339         nvl(o_worker.middle_name,    v_null) <>
340           nvl(aioo_worker.middle_name,    v_null) or
341         nvl(o_worker.last_name,      v_null) <>
342           nvl(aioo_worker.last_name,      v_null) or
343         nvl(o_worker.birth_date,     d_null) <>
344           nvl(aioo_worker.birth_date,     d_null) or
345         nvl(o_worker.gender_id,      n_null) <>
346           nvl(aioo_worker.gender_id,      n_null) then
347        begin
348          update WORKER_OT
349          set    worker_type_id = aioo_worker.worker_type_id,
350                 external_id    = aioo_worker.external_id,
351                 first_name     = aioo_worker.first_name,
352                 middle_name    = aioo_worker.middle_name,
353                 last_name      = aioo_worker.last_name,
354                 name           = aioo_worker.name,
355                 birth_date     = aioo_worker.birth_date,
356                 gender_id      = aioo_worker.gender_id
357          where  id             = aioo_worker.id;
358
359    --       n_updated := nvl(n_updated, 0) + nvl(sql%rowcount, 0);
360        exception
361          when OTHERS then
362            raise_application_error( -20002, SQLERRM||
363              ' on update WORKER_OT'||
364              ' in WORKER_TS.set_row()' );
365        end;
366      end if;
```

```
367     else
368     -- add the row if it does not exist
369       begin
370         aioo_worker.id := get_id();
371         insert into WORKER_OT
372         values ( aioo_worker );
373
374  --       n_inserted := nvl(n_inserted, 0) + nvl(sql%rowcount, 0);
375       exception
376         when OTHERS then
377           raise_application_error( -20003, SQLERRM||
378             ' on insert WORKER_OT'||
379             ' in WORKER_O.set_row()' );
380       end;
381     end if;
382  end set_row;
383
384
385  MEMBER PROCEDURE test(
386  self                             in out nocopy worker_o) is
387
388  begin
...
400  end test;
401
402
403  MAP MEMBER FUNCTION to_varchar2
404  return                           varchar2 is
405
406  begin
407    return rtrim(name||to_char(birth_date, 'YYYYMMDDHH24MISS'));
408  end to_varchar2;
409
410
411  CONSTRUCTOR FUNCTION worker_o(
412  self                     in out worker_o,
413  ain_worker_type_id       in     number,
414  aiv_first_name           in     varchar2,
415  aiv_middle_name          in     varchar2,
416  aiv_last_name            in     varchar2,
417  aid_birth_date           in     date,
418  ain_gender_id            in     number)
419  return                          self as result is
420
421  begin
422    id             := WORKER_O.get_id();
423    worker_type_id := ain_worker_type_id;
```

```
424    external_id    := WORKER_O.get_external_id();
425    first_name     := aiv_first_name;
426    middle_name    := aiv_middle_name;
427    last_name      := aiv_last_name;
428    name           := WORKER_O.get_formatted_name(
429      first_name, middle_name, last_name);
430    birth_date     := aid_birth_date;
431    gender_id      := ain_gender_id;
432    return;
433  end worker_o;
434
435
436  CONSTRUCTOR FUNCTION worker_o(
437  self                         in out worker_o)
438  return                           self as result is
439
440  begin
441    id             := NULL;
442    worker_type_id := NULL;
443    external_id    := NULL;
444    first_name     := NULL;
445    middle_name    := NULL;
446    last_name      := NULL;
447    name           := NULL;
448    birth_date     := NULL;
449    gender_id      := NULL;
450    return;
451  end worker_o;
452
453
454  end; --WORKER;
455  /
456  @be.sql WORKER
```

Listing 6-13. *The Populate Table Script for Object Table WORKER_OT, worker_ot.ins*

```
01  rem worker_ot.ins
02  rem by Donald J. Bales on 12/15/2006
03  rem Seed the Worker table with the top 100 names
04  rem 100 last x 100 first x 26 middle = 260,000 entries
05
06  set serveroutput on size 1000000;
07
08  declare
09
10  -- This is the number of seconds since midnight
11  -- I'll use it to profile my code's performance.
```

```
12  n_start                              number :=
13    to_number(to_char(SYSDATE, 'SSSSS'));
14
15  -- Here, I declare four pseudo-constants to hold the
16  -- ID values from the code tables, rather than look
17  -- them up repeatedly during the insert process.
18  n_G_FEMALE                      GENDER_OT.gender_id%TYPE;
19  n_G_MALE                        GENDER_OT.gender_id%TYPE;
20  n_WT_CONTRACTOR                 WORKER_TYPE_OT.worker_type_id%TYPE;
21  n_WT_EMPLOYEE                   WORKER_TYPE_OT.worker_type_id%TYPE;
22
23  -- I'll use this to keep track of the number of
24  -- rows inserted.
25  n_inserted                      number := 0;
26
27  begin
28    -- Get the ID values for the codes
29    n_G_FEMALE      := GENDER_O.get_id('F');
30    n_G_MALE        := GENDER_O.get_id('M');
31    n_WT_CONTRACTOR := WORKER_TYPE_O.get_id('C');
32    n_WT_EMPLOYEE   := WORKER_TYPE_O.get_id('E');
33
34    -- Use an INSERT INTO SELECT SQL statement
35    insert into WORKER_OT
36    select WORKER_O(
37          WORKER_ID_SEQ.nextval,
38          decode(mod(WORKER_ID_SEQ.currval, 2),
39            0, n_WT_EMPLOYEE, n_WT_CONTRACTOR),
40          lpad(to_char(EXTERNAL_ID_SEQ.nextval), 9, '0'),
41          first_name,
42          letter||'.',
43          last_name,
44          WORKER_O.get_formatted_name(
45            first_name, letter||'.', last_name),
46          DATES.random(
47            to_number(to_char(SYSDATE, 'YYYY')) - 65,
48            to_number(to_char(SYSDATE, 'YYYY')) - 18),
49          decode(gender_code, 'F', n_G_FEMALE, n_G_MALE))
50    from  TOP_100_LAST_NAME,
51          TOP_100_FIRST_NAME,
52          A_THRU_Z;
53
54    n_inserted := n_inserted + sql%rowcount;
55
56    commit;
57
58    pl(to_char(n_inserted)||' rows inserted in '||
```

```
59      (to_number(to_char(SYSDATE, 'SSSSS')) - n_start)||
60      ' seconds.');
61  end;
62  /
```

If you compare our three object tables—GENDER_OT, WORKER_TYPE_OT, and WORKER_OT—against the class diagram in Figure 6-1, you'll see that you've fully implemented both the attributes and methods of the classes: Gender, WorkerType, and Worker in the database using user-defined TYPEs. Congratulations.

Summary

To sum it all up, the real world is made up of things, or objects. Objects have both attributes and behaviors. Using attributes alone, you can answer only the question "What was that?" But with behaviors, you can also answer the question "When did it behave that way?" So you decide which way to go. Try one, then the other!

Table 6-1 is a summary of the SQL and PL/SQL objects that are used in order to fully model a business, scientific, or any, real-world problem accurately.

Table 6-1. *A Summary of SQL and PL/SQL Objects Used to Model the Real World*

Item	Data	Behavior
Relational table (SQL)	Columns	
Relational view (SQL)	Columns	
Table package (PL/SQL)		Methods
User-defined type (SQL and PL/SQL)	Attributes	Methods
Object view (SQL)	Columns mapped to attributes	Methods
Object table (SQL)	Attributes	Methods

The single most important point of this chapter is that you can't accurately model anything without attributes and behavior, or data and methods. And as the saying goes, "Those who cannot remember the past are condemned to repeat it." We, the business and technical community, can now accurately model the real world. So we can remember the past and no longer repeat our mistakes. We can profit from our knowledge, the information we have gathered, as we all move through time and space.

Now that you know how to write some PL/SQL, let's look at how you can see what's going on as your PL/SQL program executes.

CHAPTER 7

■■■

So Just What's Happening Here?

I believe programmers are no better than their knowledge of the debugging tools available for the programming language they're using. Why? Well first, all programmers make coding mistakes. I often remark that the day I code something that compiles and runs correctly the first time, I'm going to retire, because that would be the peak of my programming career. Second, programmers make logic mistakes. When is the last time you had to write some parsing code? That's one of the toughest types of programming to get right the first, second, third, or nth time around.

To find and solve our mistakes, we need a means to be able to discover exactly what is going on in our programs at that point in time when an error occurs. Sadly enough, when PL/SQL first appeared and for quite some time after, there was virtually no way to debug a stored PL/SQL program unit. The best we could do was to use SYS.DBMS_OUTPUT.put_line() to display a bunch of messages on the screen after the stored procedure finished executing.

Then along came the package SYS.DBMS_PIPE, where the most adventurous of us could write our own utilities to monitor an executing stored PL/SQL program unit in "real-time" from a second session. That was an improvement, but not one that most PL/SQL programmers could use. Next, the pragma autonomous transaction showed up, which allowed us to write logging utilities that used a second session in order to monitor a stored PL/SQL program unit, and could permanently save the monitoring messages to a table. That was better, but still not very good.

More recently, the package SYS.DBMS_DEBUG became available. It allows us to write our own programs to actually run a remote debugging utility against a stored PL/SQL program unit. And now, Oracle has made a PL/SQL debugger freely available to its programming communities with a product (written in Java) called Oracle SQL Developer. Other vendors have followed suit, and now you can remotely debug from graphical user interface (GUI) integrated development environments (IDEs) like TOAD for Oracle and Visual Studio, to name just a few. With a real remote debugger in our hands, we can actually see just what's happening in our PL/SQL programs.

When it comes to SQL, we've had access to EXPLAIN PLAN and TKPROF for as long as I can remember. Both give us the means to see the plans that the Oracle SQL Optimizer is going to use to access the underlying objects that are part of our SQL statements. Once again, using these tools, we can actually see just what's happening in our SQL.

However, having access to these fine troubleshooting tools is not enough. You also need to prepare for trouble ahead of time. You need to build troubleshooting capabilities into your program units. To that end, I'm going to show you how to do the following:

- Prevent trouble in the first place

- Prepare for trouble so you're ready for troubleshooting when an error does occur

- Use SYS.DBMS_OUTPUT.put_line() to provide meaningful troubleshooting information after a program unit finishes executing

- Use a logging utility to provide meaningful troubleshooting information "real time"

- Use a remote debugger to walk through a program unit as it executes

- Use EXPLAIN PLAN to troubleshoot the performance of your SQL statements

Let's start out with some prevention techniques.

Prevention

If you want to prevent problems, then assume nothing. A handful of capabilities built into PL/SQL are nothing but an invitation for trouble. They are all centered on data types and implicit conversion. What's implicit conversion? Let's say you have a number held in a varchar2 data type variable, v_value. You try assigning n_value, a number data type variable, that value with the following line of code:

```
n_value := v_value;
```

That should work, right? Yes, it should, but when it doesn't, because you don't actually have a numeric literal stored in variable v_value, the implicit data type conversion will raise an "unexpected" exception in your program unit, which will be hard to identify. By "identify," I mean determine which line of code caused the error and why. Before we get to the solution for this problem, let's look at another example.

This time, let's say you want to pass a date value to a function that will return the time in seconds since midnight, January 1, 1980. The function requires the date be passed as a varchar2 parameter in the form DD-MON-YY. Hey, no problem. Just pass the date variable:

```
...
d_value                              date := SYSDATE;
n_value                              number;

begin
  n_value := date_to_long(d_value);
...
```

Oracle's default date format is DD-MON-YY, so it will work fine, right? Not exactly. If the current NLS_DATE_FORMAT for the session is DD-MON-YY (the default), it will work, but not if it is YYYYMMDD HH24MISS, as I set mine every time I log in to SQL*Plus.

What's the solution? Use a combination of anchors, data type prefixes, and explicit conversions with blocking.

Anchors

I've already discussed anchors in Chapter 3. They are those wacky looking data type declarations that use the %TYPE or %ROWTYPE keyword. For example, here's a list of variables declared in a manner so they match the data types of their corresponding table columns:

```
...
d_birth_date                        WORKER_T.birth_date%TYPE;
n_gender_id                         WORKER_T.gender_id%TYPE;
v_name                              WORKER_T.name%TYPE;
...
```

How does using anchors help prevent errors? Since each variable is anchored to the data type of the column in a table for which it will be used to temporarily hold a value, SQL and PL/SQL will not need to perform an implicit data type conversion when values are moved between the SQL and PL/SQL. Explicitly anchoring the data types of variables to their database counterparts prevents implicit conversions. Preventing implicit conversions prevents errors.

But if you're going to anchor variables to their corresponding database columns or attributes, why use data type prefixes?

Data Type Prefixes

Data type prefixes help prevent errors in two ways. One is that when you declare a variable with a data type prefix, you're documenting that you understand that the data type is a date, number, or varchar2. You're saying, "Hey, I know what this is!" From that point in your coding forward, you can work with that assertion in place, to make sure that you're not doing any implicit conversions. Preventing implicit conversions prevents errors.

Data type prefixes also make it clear that a data type conversion is necessary. If you find yourself coding away in the far recesses of your stored procedure, and you come to a line where you're going to make an assignment and the data type prefixes are not the same, you know that you need to code an explicit data type conversion. In turn, coding an explicit data type conversion will prevent an implicit conversion. Again, preventing implicit conversions prevents errors.

So let's look at how you code an explicit data type conversion.

Explicit Conversions

When you perform an explicit conversion, you can wrap your PL/SQL statements in their own PL/SQL block, or as I like to say, "block your code." This allows you to catch any exceptions raised during the data type conversion, so you can do something intelligent with your newfound knowledge of the error.

You perform an explicit data type conversion by using one of the following functions:

to_char(): Used to convert a date or number to a varchar2 data type

to_date(): Used to convert a varchar2 to a date data type

to_number(): Used to convert a varchar2 to a number data type

For example, to convert the value January 1, 1980 in variable d_date to a varchar2 data type for variable v_date in the form YYYYMMDD, you could use the following code:

```
v_date := to_char(d_date, 'YYYYMMDD');
```

It's unlikely that converting from a date (or number) to a varchar2 is ever going to cause an error, but, on the other hand, it's very likely an error will occur if you convert from a varchar2 to a date, as in the following:

```
...
  begin
    d_date := to_date(v_date, 'YYYYMMDD');
  exception
    when OTHERS then
      pl(SQLERRM);
      pl('Converting "'||v_date||'" to a date using format YYYYMMDD');
      raise_application_error(-20001, SQLERRM||
        ' converting v_date to d_date'||
        ' in my_program_unit.method');
  end;
...
```

In this example, if the character representation of the date in variable v_date is not in the format YYYYMMDD, the to_date() function will raise an appropriate exception. The enclosing PL/SQL block will echo the details to the screen using put_line() via pl(), and then raise an application error that will report exactly where the error occurred in the program. This, in turn, will give you details as to why there was an error, so you are armed with good error information when you start troubleshooting, not some time after you are well into troubleshooting.

Just as to_date() and to_char() have formats they can use to specify the conversion parameters, so does to_number(). You can find the details on these formats in the freely available *PL/SQL User's Guide and Reference*. You can find this and the rest of the Oracle documentation set online at http://otn.oracle.com.

So the proper use of the combination of anchors, data type prefixes, and explicit conversion functions will prevent many unexpected errors. Next, let's see how you can better prepare for those that will still eventually arrive.

Preparation

Preparing for trouble ahead of time means preparing for troubleshooting ahead of time. How do you prepare for troubleshooting? You can do that by using blocks and bread crumbs.

You can block (wrap code in its own PL/SQL block) risky code ahead of time. When I say "risky code," I mean:

- Explicit data type conversions

- Movement of larger character strings to shorter character variables

- Singleton SQL statements

And what about bread crumbs? You know the fairy tale about Hansel and Gretel, right? They dropped bread crumbs on the ground as they walked through the forest, so they could find their way back. Well, I want you to drop code on your listings as you type through your program, so you, too, can find your way back—back to the source of a problem.

Let's start our discussion of blocking and bread crumbs with the former.

Blocking

I just showed you an example of blocking—wrapping a small piece of your PL/SQL in its own PL/SQL block in order to catch a raised exception and dealing with it—when I discussed explicit conversions. Now I'll show you another example, where I move a larger character string into a smaller character variable.

It's not uncommon when coding a data migration or data processing program to move a larger varchar2 variable into a smaller one. In such a situation, you can substring the larger variable in order to blindly truncate the larger string, or you can block the assignment so it raises an exception that you can deal with intelligently. Here's an example of the latter:

```
declare

v_large                          varchar2(80);
v_small                          varchar2(30);

begin
  -- I'm assigning the variable in the executable section, because
  -- assignment errors in the declaration section are also very hard
  -- to troubleshoot!
  -- 12345678901234567890123456789012345678901234567890123456789012345678
  v_large :=
    'This is a large string of characters, at least longer than 30 bytes!';

  -- Now let's raise an exception
  begin
    -- This won't work!  68 bytes won't fit in 30 bytes!
    v_small := v_large;
  exception
    when OTHERS then
      pl(SQLERRM);
      pl('Moving v_large, length '||
        to_char(length(v_large))||' into v_small.');
    raise_application_error(-20001, SQLERRM||
      ' on v_small := v_large'||
      ' in my anonymous procedure');
  end;

  pl(v_small);
end;
/
```

Executing this example results in the following output from SQL*Plus:

```
ORA-06502: PL/SQL: numeric or value error: character string buffer too small
Moving v_large, length 68 into v_small.
declare
*
ERROR at line 1:
ORA-20001: ORA-06502: PL/SQL: numeric or value error: character string
buffer too small on v_small := v_large in my anonymous procedure
ORA-06512: at line 23
```

As you can see from the output, the first three lines come from the pl() messages, while the last four come from the raised application error. The important point here is that without the "extra" information displayed by pl() or the raised application error, you wouldn't know where in the program the assignment error occurred. So by "blocking" the code, you can use pl() or raise_application_error(), or both, in order to identify the location and reason for an error in your PL/SQL program.

This is invaluable information when troubleshooting. And, by now, you're probably tired of me stating that, but I can't impress on you enough how taking the time to add a few additional lines of PL/SQL code while you're programming can later drastically reduce the amount of time it takes to test and troubleshoot your code.

So how about those bread crumbs?

Bread Crumbs

So just what do I mean by "bread crumbs"? I mean adding columns to staging tables, adding logging from your PL/SQL programs, and so on, as you initially write your code, in preparation for trouble. I suppose you may think, "That's not a very optimistic way to think about my work." However, programming is highly detailed logical work. Therefore, human beings are bound to make mistakes, since we are, by nature, emotionally "big picture" thinkers.

With that in mind, here are some ideas for leaving behind bread crumbs:

- Never use WHEN OTHERS NULL in an exception-handling section. OK, how about almost never use WHEN OTHERS NULL. It's a rare occasion when you'll actually want to suppress all errors and do nothing. Think about it. The only example I've ever run into is my errorless to_number_or_null() and to_date_or_null() functions. If there are errors, you need to know, and you need to fix your program's logic so it deals with the errors intelligently, which means predictably.

- Never handle exceptions in a table package's methods or a type's methods. You want these to show up in the presentation layer so the end user (the programmer) can deal with them appropriately, which means predictably.

- Use SYS.DBMS_OUTPUT.put_line() to display success and error messages as the output of any data migration or data processing program unit.

- Use a procedure that utilizes pragma autonomous transaction to log your data migration or data processing program's progress to a table so you can see where in the process your program is currently executing or later review the program's execution.

- If you're involved in building interfaces that migrate data from another system into yours, add columns to the interface's staging tables, with the same names as the primary key columns in the destination tables. Then store the mappings used by your PL/SQL program (the primary key values) in the corresponding staging table columns when moving the data. This will allow you to see where your program moved the data.

You'll see some of these ideas in action in Chapter 10, when we talk about the polymorphic use of method names among the various table package methods and TYPE methods.

I'll talk more about the use of put_line() and logging next. put_line() was the original means of debugging available to PL/SQL programmers, and even though it's not as powerful as a full-blown debugger, it remains useful. Let's see why.

After the Fact

Up to this point, you've seen the stored package procedure SYS.DBMS_OUTPUT.put_line() in action time and time again. Do you remember how, back in Chapter 2, we wrapped SYS.DBMS_OUTPUT.put_line() with a stored procedure named pl() so we wouldn't have to type that long name every time we wanted to display something on the screen?

Just because put_line() is the simplest of debugging tools in your arsenal does not by any means make it useless. If fact, because of its simplicity, it will probably be the first tool you use to debug any PL/SQL program unit. However, keep in mind that when you use put_line(), you're saying: "I can't wait to find out what's going on. OK, maybe I can." Why? Because you don't see any output from put_line() until your PL/SQL program unit has finished executing.

All the output from put_line() is stored in a temporary buffer until your PL/SQL program unit completes its execution, successfully or not. Then whatever tool you are using to execute your PL/SQL must query the DBMS_OUTPUT buffer and display your buffered messages on its screen. SQL*Plus does this for you automatically. However, if you were to write your own PL/SQL execution tool, you would need to program it to pull the messages from the DBMS_OUTPUT buffer after your PL/SQL program completed executing. The point is that put_line() messages appear after the fact.

In addition, you may be limited to the amount of message text you can output during any PL/SQL program unit's execution. You set this value in SQL*Plus using this command:

```
set serveroutput on size 1000000;
```

The size you specify is the maximum amount of memory to use for the DBMS_OUTPUT buffer. It used to be that you could specify 1,000,000 bytes at most, as in the preceding line. However, now you can use an unlimited amount, but is that a good idea?

And then there's the third limitation to put_line(). No single message can be more that 32,767 bytes in length. While that's not much of limitation, large messages can easily use up the buffer, so you must be careful about how you specify your messages.

In the end, the value of the information you get from put_line() is going to be equal to the quality of the messages you add to your PL/SQL code. So let's discuss that next.

Success Messages

It's just as important to display messages of successful operation as it is those related to failure. If you're writing a data processing or data migration program, it's likely that you'll leave your put_line() message in place. The thoughtful placement of success messages will narrow down the number of lines to investigate if an error does occur. For example, in Listing 7-1, I have five success messages. When an application error is raised on line 14, these messages will narrow the location of where the error actually took place.

Listing 7-1. *An Example of Success Messages Narrowing the Scope of an Error, success.sql*

```
01  rem success.sql
02  rem by Donald J. Bales on 12/15/2006
03  rem a script with success messages
04
05  declare
06
07  n_number                            number;
08
09  begin
10    pl('begin');
11
12    n_number := -1;
13
14    pl('No error here!');
15
16    n_number := 0;
17
18    pl('Still no error here!');
19
20    n_number := 'one';
21
22    pl('After the error.');
23
24    pl('end');
25  exception
26    when OTHERS then
27      raise_application_error(-20000, SQLERRM||
28        ' on assigning a value to n_number'||
29        ' in success.sql');
30  end;
31  /
```

When the script success.sql is executed, SQL*Plus outputs the following:

```
SQL> @success.sql
```

```
begin
No error here!
Still no error here!
declare
*
ERROR at line 1:
ORA-20000: ORA-06502: PL/SQL: numeric or value error: character to number
conversion error on assigning a value to n_number in success.sql
ORA-06512: at line 23
```

So, PL/SQL is reporting an ERROR at line 1:? That doesn't make much sense. Yet, further down it reports an error at line 23. Hey, that doesn't help much either. It's just a line number by the exception, but it can't be the error—it's a blank line! Where did the error occur? It took place somewhere in the block of PL/SQL code in scope for the exception-handling section.

Regardless, if we rely on our success messages, we can see that the error took place some time after the message Still no error here! and before After the error, and thus narrow down our search to lines 19 through 21. That helps.

In addition to using success messages to narrow the scope of an error, I like to keep track of the number of inserts, updates, deletes, and selects and display them at the end of the procedure to verify that something has actually happened.

If, on the other hand, you're writing table package or TYPE service methods, you may use put_line() messages during the development process, and then manually comment them out before going into production. Why just comment them out and not delete them altogether? By leaving them commented out, you give support programmers a clue about a hard-to-understand or an error-prone section of code, and give them an opportunity to comment the put_line() back into play to help them debug your code in the future.

So how can we use failure messages?

Failure Messages

In practice, I rely on method raise_application_error() to send a meaningful error number and message to the presentation layer. I simply number application error messages from -20000 to -20199, from top down in my package body. The messages include the variable SQLERRM, a very brief note about what I was doing in the section of code, and the package and/or function or procedure name as a location of the error. The description in the message needs to be brief, because raise_application_error() allows a maximum message size of only 2,048 bytes (255 bytes in earlier versions).

Since my message size is limited by raise_application_error(), I supplement the error message with extra lines of output using put_line() before the call to raise_application_error(). With the "extra" lines of output, I list the values of variables. By including the extra lines of error information, I can call the PL/SQL program unit that raised an error message with the same values as the presentation layer in order to re-create and then correct my code defect.

Now that you have some idea how to go about using put_line(), let's see you put it to use.

It's Your Turn to Use put_line()

It's your turn to put your knowledge of put_line() and raise_application_error() to work by following these steps:

1. Write an anonymous PL/SQL procedure that adds a number in a number variable to a "number" in a varchar2 variable together. Here's the hitch: you should spell out the second number in the varchar2 variable so it will raise an exception when added.

2. "Block" the line of code where you do your addition and then catch the error, list the contents of the variables with pl(), and then raise an application error.

3. Save your script as failure.sql.

4. Execute your script: @failure.sql.

Did your script and results turn out similar to mine? Listing 7-2 is my solution to this exercise.

■**Note** You won't get any output if you haven't executed the SQL*Plus command: set serveroutput on size 1000000;, which I have already placed in the script login.sql that SQL*Plus executes every time it starts.

Listing 7-2. *An Example of Using put_line() to List Variable Values, failure.sql*

```
01   rem failure.sql
02   rem by Donald J. Bales on 12/15/2006
03   rem a script that fails on purpose
04
05   declare
06
07   n_number                          number;
08   v_number                          varchar2(30);
09
10   begin
11     pl('begin');
12
13     pl('before n_number assignment');
14
15     n_number := 1;
16
17     pl('after n_number assignment');
18
19     pl('before v_number assignment');
20
21     v_number := 'two';
```

```
22
23     pl('after v_number assignment');
24
25     pl('before addition');
26     begin
27       pl('n_number + v_number = '||to_char(n_number + to_number(v_number)));
28     exception
29       when OTHERS then
30         pl('n_number = '||to_char(n_number));
31         pl('v_number = '||v_number);
32         raise_application_error(-20000, SQLERRM||
33           ' on n_number + v_number'||
34           ' in failure.sql');
35     end;
36     pl('after addition');
37
38     pl('end');
39   end;
40   /
```

And here are the results from executing the failure.sql script:

```
SQL> @failure.sql
```

```
begin
before n_number assignment
after n_number assignment
before v_number assignment
after v_number assignment
before addition
n_number = 1
v_number = two
declare
*
ERROR at line 1:
ORA-20000: ORA-06502: PL/SQL: numeric or value error: character to
number conversion error on n_number + v_number in failure.sql
ORA-06512: at line 28
```

This time, since I blocked the one line where I'm performing the addition, the line number for the error reported by PL/SQL is fairly accurate. Still, the success messages do more to narrow the location of the error than does the error message from PL/SQL's raise_application_error(). In addition, since I use pl() to display the variable values, it's fairly easy to discern the reason for the program's error.

But what happens if you have a long-running procedure, and you want to get some ongoing feedback about its success? Then it's time to take advantage of logging from another session.

As It Happens

By utilizing the PL/SQL `pragma autonomous transaction`, you can build your own logging utility that can do the following:

- Insert and commit messages into a logging table from your PL/SQL program unit without committing your PL/SQL program's own transaction context

- Select the committed messages from a log table immediately after they are written from any other session

In essence, it's as if you're saying, "No, I've changed my mind. I can't wait after all." This technique of logging from another transaction context using an autonomous transaction allows you to see what's happening in your PL/SQL program unit almost in "real time." Let's start by building our own logging utility, and then putting it to work in an example. First, we'll need a table to store messages.

A DEBUG Table

Should I build a relational example or an object-relational example? I know, this time I'll build an object-relational example, and then you'll build its relational equivalent. So what do I need to store about a message? How about the list of attributes in Table 7-1?

Table 7-1. *Attributes for a Debugging Message Table*

Attribute	Description
id	A primary key column for the object table
text	The message to log from the calling PL/SQL program unit
unique_session_id	The unique session ID from the calling PL/SQL program unit
insert_user	The user from the calling PL/SQL program unit
insert_date	The date and time (SYSDATE) from the calling PL/SQL program unit

And don't forget about the behavior! What will my debug TYPE or package need to do for me? How about the list of behaviors in Table 7-2?

Table 7-2. *Behaviors for a Debugging Message Table*

Behavior	Description
get_id()	Allocate a primary key from the corresponding sequence
Null constructor	Return an object initialized to NULL values
Convenience constructor	Return an object initialized and ready for INSERT
Map method	Return a value to sort an object by
enable()	Enable set_text() for the specified program unit

Table 7-2. *Behaviors for a Debugging Message Table*

Behavior	Description
disable()	Disable set_text() for the specified program unit
set_text()	Log the text to the debug table

Since I'm building the object-relational version, I need to create the TYPE first, the table second, and then the TYPE BODY last. Listing 7-3 is my source code for the object TYPE DEBUG_O.

Listing 7-3. *Type DEBUG_O's Specification, debug_o.tps*

```
01  create type DEBUG_O as object (
02  /*
03  debug_o.tps
04  by Donald Bales on 12/15/2006
05  Type DEBUG_O's specification:
06  A type for logging debug information
07  */
08  id                            number,
09  text                          varchar2(256),
10  unique_session_id             varchar2(24),
11  insert_user                   varchar2(30),
12  insert_date                   date,
13  -- Get the next primary key value
14  STATIC FUNCTION get_id
15  return                        number,
16  -- A NULL values constructor
17  CONSTRUCTOR FUNCTION debug_o(
18  self                   in out nocopy debug_o)
19  return                        self as result,
20  -- A convenience constructor
21  CONSTRUCTOR FUNCTION debug_o(
22  self                   in out nocopy debug_o,
23  ain_id                 in    number,
24  aiv_text               in    varchar2)
25  return                        self as result,
26  -- Override the default constructor
27  CONSTRUCTOR FUNCTION debug_o(
28  self                   in out nocopy debug_o,
29  id                     in    number,
30  text                   in    varchar2,
31  unique_session_id      in    varchar2,
32  insert_user            in    varchar2,
33  insert_date            in    date)
34  return                        self as result,
```

```
35   -- Write to the debug object table
36   STATIC PROCEDURE set_text(
37   aiv_program_unit                in      varchar2,
38   aiv_text                        in      varchar2),
39   -- A map function
40   MAP MEMBER FUNCTION to_map
41   return                                  number
42   ) not final;
43   /
44   @se.sql
```

Let's take a close look at Listing 7-3:

Lines 8 through 12 declare the five attributes for the TYPE.

Lines 14 and 15 declare a static function get_id() to allocate the next primary key value. Since it's a static method, the function is executed using the TYPE rather than an instance of the TYPE.

Lines 17 and 18 declare a constructor that returns an instance of the TYPE initialized to NULL values.

Lines 21 through 25 declare a convenience constructor that will return a fully initialized instance of the TYPE, ready to be inserted into the DEBUG_OT table.

Lines 27 through 34 declare a constructor that will override the default constructor definition provided by SQL.

Lines 36 through 38 declare a static procedure set_text(), which will insert an entry into the DEBUG_OT table using an autonomous transaction. This will allow me to commit the log entry without committing anything in the session where I'm using this method to log debug information.

Lines 40 and 41 declare a MAP method used by SQL to compare and sort objects of this TYPE.

The next step in the development process is to create an object table based on the TYPE. You may have thought that I needed to code the TYPE's implementation first. In this case, I'm going to reference the object table in the TYPE BODY, so I must create the table first. Listing 7-4 is the DDL for creating an object table based on TYPE DEBUG_O.

Listing 7-4. *DDL for Creating an Object Table Based on Type DEBUG_O, debug_ot.tab*

```
01   rem debug_ot.tab
02   rem by Donald Bales on 12/15/2006
03   rem Create debugging message table
04
05   --drop    table DEBUG_OT;
06   create table DEBUG_OT of DEBUG_O
07   tablespace USERS pctfree 0
08   storage (initial 1M next 1M pctincrease 0);
09
```

```
10  alter  table DEBUG_OT add
11  constraint   DEBUG_OT_PK
12  primary key (
13  id )
14  using index
15  tablespace USERS pctfree 0
16  storage (initial 1M next 1M pctincrease 0);
17
18  drop   sequence DEBUG_ID_SEQ;
19  create sequence DEBUG_ID_SEQ
20  start with 1 order;
21
22  analyze table DEBUG_OT estimate statistics;
23
24  grant all on DEBUG_OT to PUBLIC;
```

Let's look at Listing 7-4 line by line:

Lines 6 through 8 create object table DEBUG_OT based on TYPE DEBUG_O.

Lines 10 through 16 create a primary key on the object table DEBUG_OT.

Lines 18 through 20 declare a sequence to be used to allocate primary key values for table DEBUG_OT.

On line 22, I analyze table DEBUG_OT to give the Optimizer some initial statistics to work with.

On line 24, I grant all privileges to PUBLIC so anyone on the database can use the debug table facility I'm creating.

Now that the table exists, I can compile the TYPE BODY without dependency errors. Listing 7-5 is the TYPE BODY for TYPE DEBUG_O.

Listing 7-5. *Type DEBUG_O's Implementation, debug_o.tpb*

```
001  create or replace type body DEBUG_O as
002  /*
003  debug_o.tpb
004  by Donald Bales on 12/15/2006
005  Type DEBUG_O's implementation
006  A type for logging debug information
007  */
008
009  STATIC FUNCTION get_id
010  return                              number is
011
012  n_id                                number;
013
014  begin
```

```
015    select DEBUG_ID_SEQ.nextval
016    into   n_id
017    from   SYS.DUAL;
018
019    return n_id;
020  end get_id;
021
022
023  CONSTRUCTOR FUNCTION debug_o(
024  self                          in out nocopy debug_o)
025  return                            self as result is
026
027  begin
028    pl('debug_o(zero param)');
029    self.id                :=  NULL;
030    self.text              :=  NULL;
031    self.unique_session_id :=  NULL;
032    self.insert_user       :=  NULL;
033    self.insert_date       :=  NULL;
034
035    return;
036  end debug_o;
037
038
039  CONSTRUCTOR FUNCTION debug_o(
040  self                          in out nocopy debug_o,
041  ain_id                        in      number,
042  aiv_text                      in      varchar2)
043  return                            self as result is
044
045  begin
046    pl('debug_o(two params)');
047    self.id                := ain_id;
048    self.text              := aiv_text;
049    self.unique_session_id := SYS.DBMS_SESSION.unique_session_id;
050    self.insert_user       := USER;
051    self.insert_date       := SYSDATE;
052
053    return;
054  end debug_o;
055
056
057  -- Override the default constructor.  To do so, you must
058  -- use the same attribute names for the parameter names
059  -- and use them in the order specified in the type spec.
060  CONSTRUCTOR FUNCTION debug_o(
061  self                          in out nocopy debug_o,
```

```
062  id                           in      number,
063  text                         in      varchar2,
064  unique_session_id            in      varchar2,
065  insert_user                  in      varchar2,
066  insert_date                  in      date)
067  return                               self as result is
068
069  begin
070    pl('debug_o(five params)');
071    self.id                := id;
072    self.text              := text;
073    self.unique_session_id := unique_session_id;
074    self.insert_user       := insert_user;
075    self.insert_date       := insert_date;
076
077    return;
078  end debug_o;
079
080
081  STATIC PROCEDURE set_text(
082  aiv_program_unit             in      varchar2,
083  aiv_text                     in      varchar2) is
084
085  pragma autonomous_transaction;
086
087  v_text                               varchar2(256);
088
089  begin
090    v_text := substrb(aiv_program_unit||': '||aiv_text, 1, 256);
091
092    insert into DEBUG_OT
093    values (DEBUG_O(DEBUG_ID_SEQ.nextval, aiv_text));
094  -- A defect in SQL prevents me from using the function
095  -- get_id() as follows:
096  --values (DEBUG_O(DEBUG_O.get_id(), aiv_text));
097    commit;
098  end set_text;
099
100
101  MAP MEMBER FUNCTION to_map
102  return                               number is
103
104  begin
105    return id;
106  end to_map;
107
108
```

```
109   end;
110   /
111   @be.sql DEBUG_O
```

Listing 7-5 doesn't have any new code, so I'll just point out two details. The first centers around the second constructor found on lines 39 through 51. In this constructor, I should be able to code line 47 to read as follows:

```
self.id                        := DEBUG_O.get_id();
```

However, in SQL the constructor is called repeatedly, seemingly the number of times that there are attributes in the TYPE. Accordingly, SQL calls the constructor for this TYPE five times. I consider this a defect. It causes extra CPU and memory consumption, along with the wasted allocation of sequence values that will not be used if implemented in a reasonably object-oriented fashion. I've left in some troubleshooting pl() statements to prove that the constructors are called multiple times. To work around this defect, I've added parameter ain_id on line 41, and used the sequence directly in the SQL—for example, on line 93.

How long it will take Oracle to getting around to fixing this problem is anyone's guess, so for the time being, I'm coding the convenience constructor for two parameters instead of one. So, I've just shown you an example of using pl() to help troubleshoot a problem.

The second item to notice is the use of the following on line 85:

```
pragma autonomous_transaction;
```

This effectively executes method set_text() in its own session, so committing the inserted debugging information will not affect the transaction state in the calling program unit.

My next step is to test what I've coded. To do that, I actually have three listings. Listing 7-6 is a test unit for TYPE DEBUG_O.

Listing 7-6. *Type DEBUG_O's Test Unit, debug_o.sql*

```
01   rem debug_o.sql
02   rem by Donald J. Bales on 12/15/2006
03   rem A test unit for type DEBUG_O
04
05   declare
06
07   begin
08     DEBUG_O.set_text('DEBUG_O.SQL', 'before the loop');
09     for i in 1..10 loop
10       DEBUG_O.set_text('DEBUG_O.SQL', 'loop '||to_char(i)||' before sleep');
11       SYS.DBMS_LOCK.sleep(3);
12       DEBUG_O.set_text('DEBUG_O.SQL', 'loop '||to_char(i)||' after sleep');
13     end loop;
14     DEBUG_O.set_text('DEBUG_O.SQL:', 'after the loop');
15   end;
16   /
```

When executed, Listing 7-6 will log debug messages to object table DEBUG_OT. But before you execute it, you may want to determine your session's unique ID so you can specify that value from a second session in order to filter the debug messages that appear as your program executes.

Listing 7-7 is a very short anonymous PL/SQL program to get your session's unique ID. Then when you want to see what's going on with the program from which you're debug logging, you can specify your first session's unique session ID on the SQL*Plus command line when you execute the SQL query from Listing 7-8.

Listing 7-7. *An Example of How to Get Your Unique Session ID, usi.sql*

```
1  rem usi.sql
2  rem by Donald J. Bales on 12/15/2007
3  rem Show me my unique session ID
4
5  execute pl('unique_session_id='||SYS.DBMS_SESSION.unique_session_id);
```

For example, if I execute usi.sql in SQL*Plus from my first session, session 1, it reports the following:

```
SQL> @usi.sql
```

```
unique_session_id=01800B510001

PL/SQL procedure successfully completed.
```

Next, I open a second session, session 2. I execute the following at the SQL> prompt:

```
@debug_ot.sql 01800B510001
```

Of course, I get no rows selected, because I haven't started my test unit in session 1. So I go back to session 1 and execute the following at the SQL> prompt:

```
@debug_o.sql
```

Then I switch back to session 2 and simply type a forward slash at the SQL> prompt to see the PL/SQL program in session 1's progress:

```
SQL> @debug_ot.sql 01800B510001
```

```
old   4: where  unique_session_id = upper('&unique_session_id')
new   4: where  unique_session_id = upper('01800B510001')

no rows selected
```

```
SQL> /
```

```
old   4: where  unique_session_id = upper('&unique_session_id')
new   4: where  unique_session_id = upper('01800B510001')

      ID TEXT
---------- --------------------------------------------------------
     203 before the loop
     204 loop 1 before sleep
     205 loop 1 after sleep
     206 loop 2 before sleep
```

```
SQL> /
```

```
old   4: where  unique_session_id = upper('&unique_session_id')
new   4: where  unique_session_id = upper('01800B510001')

      ID TEXT
---------- --------------------------------------------------------
     203 before the loop
     204 loop 1 before sleep
     205 loop 1 after sleep
     206 loop 2 before sleep
     207 loop 2 after sleep
     208 loop 3 before sleep
     209 loop 3 after sleep
     210 loop 4 before sleep
     211 loop 4 after sleep
     212 loop 5 before sleep
     213 loop 5 after sleep
     214 loop 6 before sleep

12 rows selected.
```

```
SQL> /
```

```
old   4: where  unique_session_id = upper('&unique_session_id')
new   4: where  unique_session_id = upper('01800B510001')

      ID TEXT
---------- --------------------------------------------------------
     203 before the loop
     204 loop 1 before sleep
     205 loop 1 after sleep
     206 loop 2 before sleep
```

```
207 loop 2 after sleep
208 loop 3 before sleep
209 loop 3 after sleep
210 loop 4 before sleep
211 loop 4 after sleep
212 loop 5 before sleep
213 loop 5 after sleep
214 loop 6 before sleep
215 loop 6 after sleep
216 loop 7 before sleep
217 loop 7 after sleep
218 loop 8 before sleep
219 loop 8 after sleep
220 loop 9 before sleep
221 loop 9 after sleep
222 loop 10 before sleep
223 loop 10 after sleep
224 after the loop
```

22 rows selected.

As you can see from the preceding output, I reexecuted the SQL SELECT statement three times (using the forward slash, /) during the 33 seconds it took to run the test unit, and I got more debug information as the program unit executed.

If you examine Listing 7-8, which I used to query the table DEBUG_OT, you can see that I am limiting the information to a specified unique session ID and for the last ten minutes (the expression (10/(24*60)) means ten minutes).

Listing 7-8. *An Example of How to Check on Progress in "Real Time," debug_ot.sql*

```
01  rem debug_ot.sql
02  rem by Donald J. Bales on 12/15/2006
03  rem Query DEBUG_OT the specified unique session ID
04
05  define unique_session_id=&1;
06
07  select id,
08         text
09  from   DEBUG_OT
10  where  unique_session_id = upper('&unique_session_id')
11  and    insert_date       > SYSDATE - (10/(24*60))
12  order by id;
```

A debug table can be very handy. It gives you the kind of information you get from put_line(), but as it happens. Now you can just add the following command to your code as needed:

```
DEBUG_O.set_text(<aiv_program_unit>, <aiv_text>);
```

However, you'll need to wrap set_text() in an IF statement if you want to turn it on or off as needed. I have a better solution. How about a debug package?

A DEBUG Package

I'm going to create a DEBUG_OTS package in order to extend the table DEBUG_OT and its underlying TYPE DEBUG_O's functionality. I have two methods that I wasn't able to add to TYPE DEBUG_O, because there's no way to maintain temporary state in a TYPE's BODY. That's not the case for a package, so I'm going to create a table package DEBUG_OTS for table DEBUG_OT, which will implement methods disable(), enable(), and a conditional set_text().

Method enable() will add a specified program unit to a list of program units for which to log debug information to table DEBUG_OT. If a program calls DEBUG_OTS.enable(), passing its name, then any calls to DEBUG_OTS.set_text() will be logged to table DEBUG_OT. If a program doesn't enable debug logging, nothing will happen when it calls DEBUG_OTS.set_text(). Conversely, method DEBUG_OTS.disable() will remove a specified program unit from the "debug logging enabled" list. Listing 7-9 is the package specification, and Listing 7-10 is its corresponding package body.

Listing 7-9. *A Table Package Specification for Object Table DEBUG_OT, debug_ots.pks*

```
01  create or replace package DEBUG_OTS as
02  /*
03  debug_ots.pks
04  by Donald J. Bales on 12/15/2006
05  Object Table DEBUG_OT's package
06  */
07
08  -- Disable debug logging for the specified program unit
09  PROCEDURE disable(
10  aiv_program_unit              in      varchar2);
11
12  -- Enable debug logging for the specified program unit
13  PROCEDURE enable(
14  aiv_program_unit              in      varchar2);
15
16  -- Conditionally log the debug information for the specified
17  -- program unit, if it is enabled
18  PROCEDURE set_text(
19  aiv_program_unit              in      varchar2,
20  aiv_text                      in      DEBUG_OT.text%TYPE);
21
22
23  end DEBUG_OTS;
24  /
25  @se.sql DEBUG_OTS;
```

Listing 7-10. *A Table Package Body for Object Table DEBUG_OT, debug_ots.pkb*

```
01  create or replace package body DEBUG_OTS as
02  /*
03  debug_ots.pkb
04  by Donald J. Bales on 12/15/2006
05  Object Table DEBUG_OT's package
06  */
07
08  -- Declare a table type and then table to hold the
09  -- enabled program units
10  TYPE program_unit_table is table of varchar2(1)
11  index by varchar2(30);
12
13  t_program_unit                         program_unit_table;
14
15
16  PROCEDURE disable(
17  aiv_program_unit               in      varchar2) is
18
19  v_program_unit                         varchar2(30);
20
21  begin
22    v_program_unit := upper(aiv_program_unit);
23
24    if t_program_unit.exists(v_program_unit) then
25      t_program_unit.delete(v_program_unit);
26    end if;
27  end disable;
28
29
30  PROCEDURE enable(
31  aiv_program_unit               in      varchar2) is
32
33  v_program_unit                         varchar2(30);
34
35  begin
36    v_program_unit := upper(aiv_program_unit);
37
38    if not t_program_unit.exists(v_program_unit) then
39      t_program_unit(v_program_unit) := NULL;
40    end if;
41  end enable;
42
43
```

```
44  PROCEDURE set_text(
45  aiv_program_unit              in      varchar2,
46  aiv_text                      in      DEBUG_OT.text%TYPE) is
47
48  v_program_unit                        varchar2(30);
49
50  begin
51    v_program_unit := upper(aiv_program_unit);
52
53    if t_program_unit.exists(v_program_unit) then
54      DEBUG_O.set_text(v_program_unit, aiv_text);
55    end if;
56  end set_text;
57
58
59  end DEBUG_OTS;
60  /
61  @be.sql DEBUG_OTS;
```

Let's take a detailed look at Listing 7-10:

Lines 10 and 11 declare a PL/SQL table TYPE indexed by a varchar2. You couldn't do this with older versions of Oracle, but you can now. I'm taking advantage of that fact, so PL/SQL can do the work, instead of me writing a lot more code.

Line 13 declares an "enabled program unit list" table, which will temporarily hold a list of program units for which to log debug information to table DEBUG_OT.

Lines 16 through 27 implement method disable(). This method looks to see if an entry exists in the "enabled program unit" PL/SQL table for the specified program unit. If it does exist, it deletes the PL/SQL table entry, effectively disabling debug logging for the specified program unit.

Lines 30 through 41 implement the enable() method. This method looks to see if an entry exists in the "enabled program unit" PL/SQL table for the specified program unit. If it does not exist, the method adds an entry to the PL/SQL table, effectively enabling debug logging for the specified program unit.

Lines 44 through 56 implement the set_text() method. This method simply calls the autonomous procedure set_text() in the underlying TYPE DEBUG_O if the program unit in question is enabled.

"Big deal—so what?" you say. The implications are staggering. You can add DEBUG_OTS. set_text() calls to your long-running or complicated PL/SQL programs and leave them there to be enabled as needed when trouble rears its ugly head!

Listing 7-11 is a test unit for package DEBUG_OTS that turns debug logging on then off, repeating the same test twice.

Listing 7-11. *A Test Unit for Package DEBUG_OTS, debug_ots.sql*

```
01  rem debug_ots.sql
02  rem by Donald J. Bales on 12/15/2006
03  rem A test unit for type DEBUG_O's package
04
05  declare
06
07  begin
08    -- Enable debug output
09    DEBUG_OTS.enable('DEBUG_OTS.SQL');
10    -- Test
11    DEBUG_OTS.set_text('DEBUG_OTS.SQL', 'before the loop ');
12    for i in 1..10 loop
13      DEBUG_OTS.set_text('DEBUG_OTS.SQL', 'loop '||to_char(i)||' before sleep');
14      SYS.DBMS_LOCK.sleep(3);
15      DEBUG_OTS.set_text('DEBUG_OTS.SQL', 'loop '||to_char(i)||' after sleep');
16    end loop;
17    DEBUG_OTS.set_text('DEBUG_OTS.SQL', 'after the loop ');
18
19    -- Disable debug output
20    DEBUG_OTS.disable('DEBUG_OTS.SQL');
21    -- Test
22    DEBUG_OTS.set_text('DEBUG_OTS.SQL', 'before the loop ');
23    for i in 1..10 loop
24      DEBUG_OTS.set_text('DEBUG_OTS.SQL', 'loop '||to_char(i)||' before sleep');
25      -- SYS.DBMS_LOCK.sleep(3);
26      DEBUG_OTS.set_text('DEBUG_OTS.SQL', 'loop '||to_char(i)||' after sleep');
27    end loop;
28    DEBUG_OTS.set_text('DEBUG_OTS.SQL', 'after the loop ');
29  end;
30  /
```

Given that you have your unique session ID and start debug_ots.sql in session 1, and then switch to session 2 and query table DEBUG_OT with debug_ot.sql, you'll see output like this:

```
SQL> @debug_ot.sql 01800B510001


old  4: where  unique_session_id = upper('&unique_session_id')
new  4: where  unique_session_id = upper('01800B510001')

     ID TEXT
---------- ------------------------------------------------------------
    225 before the loop
    226 loop 1 before sleep
    227 loop 1 after sleep
    228 loop 2 before sleep
```

```
4 rows selected.
```

```
SQL> /
```

```
old   4: where  unique_session_id = upper('&unique_session_id')
new   4: where  unique_session_id = upper('01800B510001')

        ID TEXT
---------- -------------------------------------------------------
       225 before the loop
       226 loop 1 before sleep
       227 loop 1 after sleep
       228 loop 2 before sleep
       229 loop 2 after sleep
       230 loop 3 before sleep
       231 loop 3 after sleep
       232 loop 4 before sleep
       233 loop 4 after sleep
       234 loop 5 before sleep
       235 loop 5 after sleep
       236 loop 6 before sleep
       237 loop 6 after sleep
       238 loop 7 before sleep
       239 loop 7 after sleep
       240 loop 8 before sleep
       241 loop 8 after sleep
       242 loop 9 before sleep
       243 loop 9 after sleep
       244 loop 10 before sleep
       245 loop 10 after sleep
       246 after the loop

22 rows selected.
```

In the preceding output, you see the first half of the test unit where the program unit was enabled, but not the second half of the program unit where it was disabled. This means you can turn debug logging on and off programmatically as needed. That's a powerful troubleshooting tool!

Now that you've seen me do the object-relational version, it's your turn to do the relational version.

It's Your Turn to Use Debug Logging

Your assignment is to create a relational debug table and table package that incorporate the same functionality as the object-relational example I just showed you. Yes, you should also include the test unit. Follow these steps to debug logging happiness:

1. Write a DDL script to create a relational table called DEBUG_T with the same columns as the attributes found in TYPE DEBUG_O.

2. Save your script as debug_t.tab.

3. Create your table DEBUG_T by executing your script: @debug_t.tab.

4. Write a DDL script to create a table package specification for DEBUG_T. You should have three methods: disable(), enable(), and set_text().

5. Save your script as debug_ts.pks.

6. Create your package specification by executing your script: @debug_ts.pks.

7. Write a DDL script to create a table package body for DEBUG_T. Remember to use the pragma autonomous_transaction; in set_text()!

8. Save your script as debug_ts.pkb.

9. Create your package body by executing your script: @debug_ts.pkb.

10. Write a test unit for package DEBUG_TS, saving your script as debug_ts.sql.

11. Open two SQL*Plus sessions. Get the unique session ID from the first session by executing script usi.sql. Then start your test unit in the first session by executing your script: @debug_ts.sql.

12. Quickly switch to session 2, and then execute a SELECT statement against table DEBUG_T so you can see the output of your test unit as it executes.

Listings 7-12 through 7-16 are my solution to this exercise. Listing 7-12 is a script to create a relational table for debug logging output.

Listing 7-12. *A DDL Script to Create Table DEBUG_T, debug_t.tab*

```
01  rem debug_t.tab
02  rem by Donald Bales on 12/15/2006
03  rem Create debugging message table
04
05  drop   table DEBUG_T;
06  create table DEBUG_T (
07  id                       number                        not null,
08  text                     varchar2(256),
09  unique_session_id        varchar2(24)                  not null,
10  insert_user              varchar2(30) default USER     not null,
11  insert_date              date         default SYSDATE  not null )
12  tablespace USERS pctfree 0
13  storage (initial 1M next 1M pctincrease 0);
14
15  alter  table DEBUG_T add
16  constraint   DEBUG_T_PK
17  primary key (
```

```
18  id )
19  using index
20  tablespace USERS pctfree 0
21  storage (initial 1M next 1M pctincrease 0);
22
23  drop    sequence DEBUG_ID_SEQ;
24  create sequence DEBUG_ID_SEQ
25  start with 1 order;
26
27  analyze table DEBUG_T estimate statistics;
28
29  grant all on DEBUG_T to PUBLIC;
```

Listing 7-13 is the specification for the table package for table DEBUG_T. I've declared three methods: disable(), enable(), and conditional set_text().

Listing 7-13. *A DDL Script to Create Table Package Spec DEBUG_TS, debug_ts.pks*

```
01  create or replace package DEBUG_TS as
02  /*
03  debug_ts.pks
04  by Donald J. Bales on 12/15/2006
05  Table DEBUG_T's package
06  */
07
08  -- Gets the next primary key value for the table
09  FUNCTION get_id
10  return                          DEBUG_T.id%TYPE;
11
12  -- Enable debug output for the specified program unit
13  PROCEDURE enable(
14  aiv_program_unit             in      varchar2);
15
16  -- Disable debug output for the specified program unit
17  PROCEDURE disable(
18  aiv_program_unit             in      varchar2);
19
20  -- Log debug output if enabled for the specified program unit
21  PROCEDURE set_text(
22  aiv_program_unit             in      varchar2,
23  aiv_text                     in      DEBUG_T.text%TYPE);
24
25
26  end DEBUG_TS;
27  /
28  @se.sql DEBUG_TS;
```

Listing 7-14 is the body for table package DEBUG_TS. In it, I've declared a PL/SQL table TYPE
and PL/SQL table to hold the "enabled program units," and then implemented methods
disable(), enable(), and set_text().

Listing 7-14. *A DDL Script to Create Table Package Body DEBUG_TS, debug_ts.pkb*

```
01  create or replace package body DEBUG_TS as
02  /*
03  debug_ts.pkb
04  by Donald J. Bales on 12/15/2006
05  Table DEBUG_T's package
06  */
07
08  -- A table to hold the list of program units for which
09  -- to store debug information
10  TYPE program_unit_table is table of varchar2(1)
11  index by varchar2(30);
12
13  t_program_unit                      program_unit_table;
14
15
16  FUNCTION get_id
17  return                              DEBUG_T.id%TYPE is
18
19  n_id                                DEBUG_T.id%TYPE;
20
21  begin
22    select DEBUG_ID_SEQ.nextval
23    into   n_id
24    from   SYS.DUAL;
25
26    return n_id;
27  end get_id;
28
29
30  PROCEDURE disable(
31  aiv_program_unit                in      varchar2) is
32
33  begin
34    if t_program_unit.exists(upper(aiv_program_unit)) then
35      t_program_unit.delete(upper(aiv_program_unit));
36    end if;
37  end disable;
38
39
40  PROCEDURE enable(
41  aiv_program_unit                in      varchar2) is
```

```
42
43  begin
44    if not t_program_unit.exists(upper(aiv_program_unit)) then
45      t_program_unit(upper(aiv_program_unit)) := NULL;
46    end if;
47  end enable;
48
49
50  PROCEDURE set_text(
51  aiv_program_unit              in      varchar2,
52  aiv_text                      in      DEBUG_T.text%TYPE) is
53
54  pragma autonomous_transaction;
55
56  begin
57    if not t_program_unit.exists(upper(aiv_program_unit)) then
58      insert into DEBUG_T (
59            id,
60            text,
61            unique_session_id )
62      values (
63            DEBUG_TS.get_id(),
64            substrb(aiv_program_unit||': '||aiv_text, 1, 256),
65            SYS.DBMS_SESSION.unique_session_id);
66    end if;
67    commit;
68  end set_text;
69
70
71  end DEBUG_TS;
72  /
73  @be.sql DEBUG_TS;
```

In Listing 7-14, method set_text() logs information to table DEBUG_T only if the specified program unit is "enabled." Listing 7-15 is a test unit for table package DEBUG_TS.

Listing 7-15. *An Anonymous PL/SQL Script to Test Table Package DEBUG_TS, debug_ts.sql*

```
01  rem debug_ts.sql
02  rem by Donald J. Bales on 12/15/2006
03  rem Test unit for package DEBUG_TS
04
05  declare
06
```

```
07   v_program_unit                          varchar2(30) :=
08     'debug_ts.sql';
09
10   begin
11     DEBUG_TS.enable(v_program_unit);
12     DEBUG_TS.set_text(v_program_unit, 'before the loop ');
13     for i in 1..10 loop
14       DEBUG_TS.set_text(v_program_unit, 'loop '||to_char(i)||' before sleep');
15       SYS.DBMS_LOCK.sleep(3);
16       DEBUG_TS.set_text(v_program_unit, 'loop '||to_char(i)||' after sleep');
17     end loop;
18     DEBUG_TS.set_text(v_program_unit, 'after the loop ');
19     DEBUG_TS.disable(v_program_unit);
20     DEBUG_TS.set_text(v_program_unit, 'before the loop ');
21     for i in 1..10 loop
22       DEBUG_TS.set_text(v_program_unit, 'loop '||to_char(i)||' before sleep');
23       -- SYS.DBMS_LOCK.sleep(3);
24       DEBUG_TS.set_text(v_program_unit, 'loop '||to_char(i)||' after sleep');
25     end loop;
26     DEBUG_TS.set_text(v_program_unit, 'after the loop ');
27   end;
28   /
```

The following is the output from a query against the debug table DEBUG_T.

```
SQL> select * from debug_t;
```

```
        ID TEXT
---------- -------------------------------------------------
       313 DEBUG_TS.SQL: before the loop
       314 DEBUG_TS.SQL: loop 1 before sleep
       315 DEBUG_TS.SQL: loop 1 after sleep
       316 DEBUG_TS.SQL: loop 2 before sleep
```

```
SQL> /
```

```
        ID TEXT
---------- -------------------------------------------------
       313 DEBUG_TS.SQL: before the loop
       314 DEBUG_TS.SQL: loop 1 before sleep
       315 DEBUG_TS.SQL: loop 1 after sleep
       316 DEBUG_TS.SQL: loop 2 before sleep
```

```
SQL> /
```

```
        ID TEXT
---------- ------------------------------------------------
       313 DEBUG_TS.SQL: before the loop
       314 DEBUG_TS.SQL: loop 1 before sleep
       315 DEBUG_TS.SQL: loop 1 after sleep
       316 DEBUG_TS.SQL: loop 2 before sleep
       317 DEBUG_TS.SQL: loop 2 after sleep
       318 DEBUG_TS.SQL: loop 3 before sleep
       319 DEBUG_TS.SQL: loop 3 after sleep
       320 DEBUG_TS.SQL: loop 4 before sleep
       321 DEBUG_TS.SQL: loop 4 after sleep
       322 DEBUG_TS.SQL: loop 5 before sleep
       323 DEBUG_TS.SQL: loop 5 after sleep
       324 DEBUG_TS.SQL: loop 6 before sleep

12 rows selected.
```

```
SQL> /
```

```
        ID TEXT
---------- ------------------------------------------------
       313 DEBUG_TS.SQL: before the loop
       314 DEBUG_TS.SQL: loop 1 before sleep
       315 DEBUG_TS.SQL: loop 1 after sleep
       316 DEBUG_TS.SQL: loop 2 before sleep
       317 DEBUG_TS.SQL: loop 2 after sleep
       318 DEBUG_TS.SQL: loop 3 before sleep
       319 DEBUG_TS.SQL: loop 3 after sleep
       320 DEBUG_TS.SQL: loop 4 before sleep
       321 DEBUG_TS.SQL: loop 4 after sleep
       322 DEBUG_TS.SQL: loop 5 before sleep
       323 DEBUG_TS.SQL: loop 5 after sleep
       324 DEBUG_TS.SQL: loop 6 before sleep
       325 DEBUG_TS.SQL: loop 6 after sleep
       326 DEBUG_TS.SQL: loop 7 before sleep
       327 DEBUG_TS.SQL: loop 7 after sleep
       328 DEBUG_TS.SQL: loop 8 before sleep
       329 DEBUG_TS.SQL: loop 8 after sleep
       330 DEBUG_TS.SQL: loop 9 before sleep
       331 DEBUG_TS.SQL: loop 9 after sleep
       332 DEBUG_TS.SQL: loop 10 before sleep
       333 DEBUG_TS.SQL: loop 10 after sleep
       334 DEBUG_TS.SQL: after the loop

22 rows selected.
```

As you can see from this output, you are able to view the progress of the test unit as it executes. Armed with this troubleshooting tool, you can monitor your long-running or short-running data processing or data migration programs.

In practice, I've even found this technique useful in some table package or TYPE methods that are called by the presentation layer. One example is when I worked with a table package that built SQL statements dynamically using information from the database, and then passed them back to the presentation layer. If a user got an error, we could see what SQL was passed back to his web page by looking in the debug table in the database. It didn't take long for us to figure out that we had some data-entry errors in the tables used to build the dynamic queries, but it would have been next to impossible to identify the problem in the presentation layer.

As an alternative to debug logging, you may decide to use package SYS.DBMS_TRACE to trace the execution of a session to a file that you can later examine, line by line, or using a utility like TKPROF. However, I've found that DBMS_TRACE creates too much information to be useful. With it, you have limited control of the volume of information collected. In contrast, with a debug logging utility, you determine what information is logged and when.

Another alternative package you may want to investigate is SYS.DBMS_ERRLOG. With this package, you can write debug information to a table anytime an exception occurs in your PL/SQL program unit. I still find the use of my "homegrown" debug logging to be more useful.

Debug logging is a good tool, but in some situations, a real debugging tool is more appropriate. Let's look at Oracle's debugger next.

One Step at a Time

After what seems an eternity, PL/SQL programmers now have a real, honest-to-goodness debugger. What's a debugger? It allows you to step through your PL/SQL code as it executes, one step at a time, line by line, inspecting the value of variables, and seeing how your program executes your logic. It's a remote debugger—remote in the fact that your PL/SQL program unit must be stored in the database, and it must be executable. By "executable," I mean it must be a stored: function, procedure, or packaged function or procedure.

So how did this revolution come about? It started with a PL/SQL package called SYS.DBMS_DEBUG. Oracle database PL/SQL package DBMS_DEBUG provides communication hooks into the PL/SQL debugger layer in the database. Using this package, you can build your own remote debugger, but it's much easier to use Oracle SQL Developer.

Debugging with Oracle SQL Developer

Oracle SQL Developer is a long overdue SQL and PL/SQL development tool for the Oracle database. You can download a free copy from the Oracle Technology Network site: http://otn.oracle.com.

In the past, Oracle's Developer 2000 product had a tool called Procedure Builder, but it pretty much stunk up the place. Procedure Builder would allow you to debug client-side code, but not server-side code. Oracle SQL Developer not only provides an easy-to-use interface for creating SQL DDL and PL/SQL stored procedures, but it also has a built-in remote debugger!

I'm not going to give you a lesson on how to use Oracle SQL Developer here, because that would be a book in itself, but I will show you some highlights to debugging with it.

Your first step in using a remote debugger with Oracle is to grant debugging rights to the username for which you intend to debug a stored program unit. That's done by the system administrator or DBA using the following syntax:

```
grant debug connect session to <username>;
grant debug any procedure to <username>;
```

where `<username>` is the name of the user for which to grant the debug privileges.

Your next step is to recompile the stored program units in question with the DEBUG option, using the appropriate syntax for the object type from the following list:

```
alter function  <name> compile debug;
alter package   <name> compile debug package;
alter package   <name> compile debug specification;
alter package   <name> compile debug body;
alter procedure <name> compile debug;
alter trigger   <name> compile debug;
alter type      <name> compile debug specification;
alter type      <name> compile debug body;
```

Alternatively, you can recompile the code from Oracle SQL Developer! Let me show you an example of debugging (of all things) the DEBUG_O TYPE and the DEBUG_OTS package. In this example, I've already started Oracle SQL Developer and logged in to database ORA1012, where, incidentally, I have already granted debug connect session and debug any procedure rights to the username.

In Figure 7-1, I used the tree view on the left side of the screen to drill down and select the BODY for TYPE DEBUG_O. From there, I right-clicked and chose Edit. That action displayed the tab DEBUG_O Body, where I subsequently added a breakpoint to the constructor. Next, I clicked the compile with debug icon. Just to prove a point, I then clicked the debug (ladybug) icon. Oracle SQL Developer responded with the message "Source does not have a runnable target." See, I told you it had to be a function, procedure, or packaged procedure! That's doesn't mean we can't debug this item; it means we'll have to execute a runnable target to do so, which I'll get to shortly.

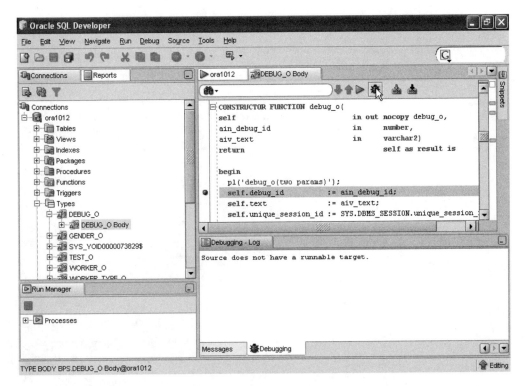

Figure 7-1. *Setting a breakpoint in TYPE DEBUG_O's constructor*

In Figure 7-2, I used the tree view to find the package body for DEBUG_OTS. Next, I right-clicked and selected Edit. That action displayed the tab DEBUG_OTS Body, where I added a breakpoint for procedure set_text(). Then I clicked the icon to recompile the item with debug.

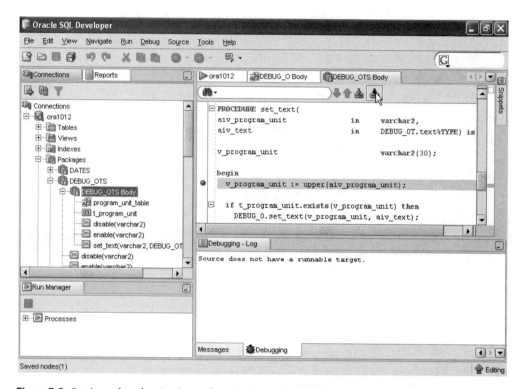

Figure 7-2. *Setting a breakpoint in package body method DEBUG_OTS.set_text()*

At this point, I've set two breakpoints: one in TYPE DEBUG_O's constructor and a second in package body DEBUG_OTS's set_text() method. Now when I execute a program unit that calls either DEBUG_O's constructor or DEBUG_OTS.set_text(), the debugger will stop execution so I can inspect variable values or single-step through each line of code.

My next task is to select an executable target and then debug it. That's what I did in Figure 7-3. Once again, I used the tree view to select the package specification for DEBUG_OTS. Then I right-clicked and selected Edit. That action displayed the tab DEBUG_OTS. From there, I clicked the debug icon. This time, since I'm in a package specification, the target is runnable, so Oracle SQL Developer prompted me for an anonymous procedure that I can use to execute the target.

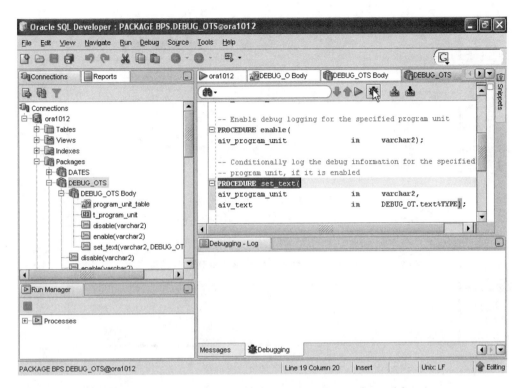

Figure 7-3. *Editing the package specification for DEBUG_OTS in order to debug it*

When I clicked the debug icon in Figure 7-3, the Debug PL/SQL dialog box appeared, as shown in Figure 7-4. Here, I selected the target method to debug—in this case, set_text. Next, I needed to modify the anonymous PL/SQL procedure stub presented by Oracle SQL Developer or select one from the file system by clicking the From File button. Since I already had a test unit script written, debug_ots.sql, I selected it from the file system, deleted the remark lines and the trailing compile slash, and then clicked the OK button to start the procedure, hence starting the debugging session.

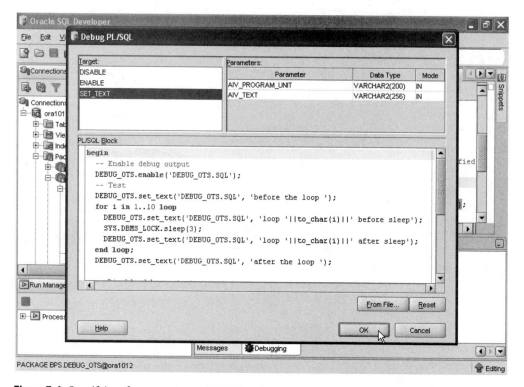

Figure 7-4. *Specifying the anonymous PL/SQL script to execute the runnable target*

In Figure 7-5, the debugger stopped the execution of the program when it encountered the breakpoint set on method set_text(). From there, I clicked the step into icon in order to execute the code line by line. In the lower-right corner of the screen, you can see the value of variable v_program_unit because I set up a watch on that variable.

As you can see from this short example, you have total access to both the values of variables and how program logic is being executed when you're in a debugger. This is the ultimate troubleshooting tool. Or is it?

For a simple troubleshooting task, you are probably better off using put_line(). For a long-running program unit, you're probably better off using debug logging. Then once you've narrowed down the problem, if you haven't already solved it, you may want to use a debugger. Why?

Using a debugger requires a great deal of setup, arranging access to the username of the stored program unit and grants for debugging. And it can take a lot of time to use for the simple fact that stepping through a program line by line can be extremely time-consuming. It's up to you to use the appropriate tool at the appropriate time.

Figure 7-5. *Stepping into code after a breakpoint has been encountered*

Debugging Anonymous PL/SQL

So far, I've been talking only about debugging stored program units. What about anonymous PL/SQL procedures? Sorry, you cannot debug anonymous PL/SQL program units. And that should not be a big deal. If you have an anonymous PL/SQL program that's so big that it needs debugging, it probably needs to be permanently stored in the database. Once you store it in the database. You can use Oracle SQL Developer to debug it.

Debugging with TOAD for Oracle

TOAD for Oracle is a very popular SQL and PL/SQL development tool by Quest Software. There's a freeware version available for download from Quest Software at http://www.toadsoft.com/ toad_oracle.htm. However, the free version does not include debugging capability. To get a copy of TOAD with a debugger, you must download the trial version.

The TOAD debugger is currently not capable of debugging user-defined TYPEs. Other than that, it has almost the same set of debugging features as Oracle SQL Developer.

Debugging with Visual Studio

Oracle has a plug-in module that allows you to use the remote debugger from Microsoft's Visual Studio. Once again, you can download this plug-in from Oracle's Technology Network web site at `http://otn.oracle.com`.

It's Your Turn to Use a Debugger

I know I haven't taken the time to show you how to use the PL/SQL debugger; I've only walked through an example, As a professional, it will be invaluable for you to know how to use the PL/SQL debugger. So, follow these somewhat loosely defined steps to install the PL/SQL debugger and get some experience using it:

1. Go to `http://otn.oracle.com` and search for "Oracle SQL Developer download." This should bring you to the Oracle SQL Developer page, where you can download a copy of the software, get its installation instructions, and access tutorials for using the product.

2. Download Oracle SQL Developer.

3. Print a copy of the tutorials "Creating a database connection" and "Loading, executing and debugging PL/SQL."

4. Install Oracle SQL Developer.

5. Run Oracle SQL Developer and create a connection to the database you're using for working on your exercises.

6. Using the "Loading, executing and debugging PL/SQL" tutorial as your guide, find table package `DEBUG_TS` in the tree view.

7. Edit the package body by right-clicking its name in the tree view, and then recompile it with debug.

8. Create breakpoints in `DEBUG_TS`'s three methods: `disable()`, `enable()`, and `set_text()`.

9. Edit the package specification, and click the ladybug icon to run the debugger.

10. When the Debug PL/SQL dialog box appears, click the From File button, and then load your test unit script: `debug_ts.sql`.

11. Remove the comment lines at the top of the test unit script and the trailing compile slash at the end of the script, and then click OK to start your debug session.

12. After the first breakpoint is triggered, click the Step Into icon to walk through the code line by line.

13. Add some watches so you can see the variable's values change as the program executes.

14. Sit back and think how helpful this tool can be in your future.

At this point, you should now have three tools in your troubleshooting arsenal: `put_line()`, table package `DEBUG_TS`, and a real live debugger! With these tools, you should be able to trouble-shoot any logic problem, but what about performance?

If you have a long-running or large stored procedure, how do you know where in its code it's slow? You can get this information with runtime profiling, our next topic.

Profiling

Profiling in this context is about collecting runtime statistics from your PL/SQL program units in order to determine which lines of code are consuming the most resources, usually in a unit of time. Armed with these statistics, you can quickly see what part of your PL/SQL program is taking the most time to execute, so you can concentrate your efforts on improving performance on those lines of code that are poor performers.

In days of yore, you had to write your own profiling package in order to collect runtime statistics. Then you had to sprinkle your code with calls to your profiling package in order to collect the statistics. In fact, I did just that, creating a profiling package with architecture similar to the debug logging package.

Nowadays, you have access to a built-in profiling package, SYS.DBMS_PROFILER, which can hook itself into your session and profile your PL/SQL code line by line, without you needing to add many lines of code to your listings. Here, we'll look at the three tables where DBMS_PROFILER stores its collected statistics, the package's methods, and an example of its use. Then we'll finish up this section by having you profile your own code.

Profiler's Tables

The profiling package DBMS_PROFILER stores the statistics it collects during its use in memory, until you call its flush_data() method, at which point, it moves the statistics to three tables:

PLSQL_PROFILER_RUNS: Holds information about a particular run.

PLSQL_PROFILER_UNITS: Holds the names of program units for a particular run.

PLSQL_PROFILE_DATA: Holds the profiling statistics for every line of each program unit accessed in a particular run.

Your Oracle system administrator or DBA must create these tables globally using the profload.sql script, or in the schema you're logged in to using the proftab.sql script, before you try to use the profiler. In addition, you must have the same rights granted to your username as you need for debugging.

You can find detailed information about the DBMS_PROFILER package and these three tables in Oracle's PL/SQL Packages and Types Reference. Let's look at the package's methods next.

Profiler's Methods

The DBMS_PROFILER package has seven methods, of which you must use at least three to profile an application. Here are the three I am referring to:

start_profiler(): Initializes and starts a profiling "run" in order to collect statistics. You can specify a description for the run so you can identify the run number after the run, or you can use an overloaded version of the method that returns the run number when you start the run.

stop_profile(): Stops a previously started run.

flush_data(): Stores the statistics for the current run into three tables: PLSQL_PROFILER_RUNS, PLSQL_PROFILER_UNITS, and PLSQL_PROFILER_DATA.

To start a profiling session, you need to execute procedure start_profiler() in your PL/SQL program unit where you want to start collecting performance statistics. To stop collecting statistics, you need to execute stop_profile(), usually followed by flush_data(), in order to permanently store the statistics in the profiler's tables.

Listing 7-16 is a SQL*Plus script that can run any anonymous PL/SQL script with profiling turned on.

Listing 7-16. *A Script to Execute Another Script with Profiling, run_profile.sql*

```
01  rem run_profile.sql
02  rem by Donald J. Bales on 12/15/2006
03  rem Capture DBMS_PROFILER information for the specified script
04
05  define script="&1";
06
07  set verify off;
08
09  declare
10
11  n_run_number                           number;
12
13  begin
14    DBMS_PROFILER.start_profiler(
15      '&script'||' on '||to_char(SYSDATE, 'YYYYMMDD HH24MISS'),
16      ' ',
17      n_run_number);
18
19    pl('DBMS_PROFILER run_number = '||to_char(n_run_number));
20  end;
21  /
22
23  @&script
24
25  execute DBMS_PROFILER.stop_profiler;
26  execute DBMS_PROFILER.flush_data;
27
28  set verify on;
```

To execute the script, type the name of the script in Listing 7-16 followed by the name of the script you wish to execute after the SQL*Plus prompt, as follows:

```
SQL> @run_profile.sql <script_name>
```

For example, to profile TYPE DEBUG_O and table package DEBUG_OTS, I executed the script passing in the name of my test unit script, debug_ots.sql:

```
SQL> @run_profile.sql debug_ots.sql
```

Here's the output from executing the script in SQL*Plus:

```
SQL> @run_profile debug_ots.sql
```

```
DBMS_PROFILER run_number = 4

PL/SQL procedure successfully completed.


PL/SQL procedure successfully completed.


PL/SQL procedure successfully completed.


PL/SQL procedure successfully completed.
```

---

run_profile.sql displays the run number for a profile run on the screen, so you can then run a report to view the profiling data.

Profiling Reports

I find two profiling reports helpful: one to display the average percent of processing time in descending order, and another to order average time consumption by program unit and line number.

The SQL*Plus script avg_profile.sql, shown in Listing 7-17, displays what percent of processing time was consumed by each program unit and line of code, in the descending order of time consumption.

Listing 7-17. *A Script to Create an Average Percent Profiling Report, avg_profile.sql*

```
01  rem avg_profile.sql
02  rem by Donald J. Bales on 12/15/2006
03  rem Create a DBMS_PROFILER report by avg desc
04
05  define runid="&1";
06
07  column avg_pct    format 990.99;
08  column line#      format 9999;
09  column occur      format 9999
10  column text       format a42 trunc;
11  column unit_name  format a11;
12
```

```
13  set linesize  1000;
14  set newpage    1;
15  set pagesize   32767;
16  set trimspool on;
17  set verify     off;
18
19  spool avg_profile_&runid..txt;
20
21  select v.unit_name,
22         round(v.avg_time/t.avg_time*100, 2) avg_pct,
23         v.occur,
24         v.line#,
25         ltrim(s.text) text
26  from   SYS.DBA_SOURCE s,
27       ( select u.runid,
28                u.unit_owner,
29                u.unit_type,
30                u.unit_name,
31                d.min_time,
32                to_number(decode(d.total_occur,
33                  NULL, NULL,
34                  0,    0,
35                  round(d.total_time/d.total_occur))) avg_time,
36                d.max_time,
37                d.total_time,
38                d.total_occur occur,
39                d.line#
40         from   PLSQL_PROFILER_UNITS u,
41                PLSQL_PROFILER_DATA d
42         where  u.runid       = d.runid
43         and    u.unit_number = d.unit_number
44         and    d.runid       = &runid ) v,
45       ( select sum(to_number(decode(d.total_occur,
46                  NULL, NULL,
47                  0,    0,
48                  round(d.total_time/d.total_occur)))) avg_time
49         from   PLSQL_PROFILER_UNITS u,
50                PLSQL_PROFILER_DATA d
51         where  u.runid       = d.runid
52         and    u.unit_number = d.unit_number
53         and    d.runid       = &runid ) t
54  where  v.unit_owner = s.owner(+)
55  and    v.unit_type  = s.type(+)
56  and    v.unit_name  = s.name(+)
57  and    v.line#      = s.line(+)
58  and    v.avg_time   > 0
59  order by v.avg_time desc,
```

```
60          v.unit_name,
61          v.line#;
62
63  spool off;
64
65  set verify on;
```

■Note To run the `avg_profile.sql` script, you will need `SELECT` privileges on table `SYS.DBA_SOURCE`, or you can try changing the table in the script to `SYS.ALL_SOURCE`.

The `avg_profile.sql` script produces a report that shows the following information:

- The program unit's name

- Its average consumption of time

- How many times the line was executed during the run

- The line number and text from the PL/SQL program unit in question

Listing 7-18 is an example of a report created by `avg_profile.sql` from Listing 7-17.

Listing 7-18. *An Average Percent Time Consumption Report for Test Unit, debug_ots.sql*

```
UNIT_NAME    AVG_PCT OCCUR LINE# TEXT
----------- ------- ----- ----- --------------------------------------------
DEBUG_O       83.03    22    92 insert into DEBUG_OT
DEBUG_O        3.98    22    97 commit;
<anonymous>    2.29     1    11
<anonymous>    1.24    12     1
<anonymous>    1.00     2     1
<anonymous>    0.84     1     5
<anonymous>    0.70    10    11
DEBUG_OTS      0.59     1    36 v_program_unit := upper(aiv_program_unit);
<anonymous>    0.53     2     1
<anonymous>    0.49    10     9
DEBUG_OTS      0.43     1    22 v_program_unit := upper(aiv_program_unit);
DEBUG_OTS      0.39     1    39 t_program_unit(v_program_unit) := NULL;
DEBUG_OTS      0.35    44    51 v_program_unit := upper(aiv_program_unit);
DEBUG_O        0.31    22    98 end set_text;
DEBUG_OTS      0.27     1    38 if not t_program_unit.exists(v_program_uni
DEBUG_O        0.26    22    90 v_text := substrb(aiv_program_unit||': '||
DEBUG_OTS      0.24     1    25 t_program_unit.delete(v_program_unit);
DEBUG_OTS      0.22     1    24 if t_program_unit.exists(v_program_unit) t
<anonymous>    0.20    10    10
DEBUG_O        0.19    22    89 begin
```

```
DEBUG_O        0.17    132    53 return;
DEBUG_OTS      0.17     44    53 if t_program_unit.exists(v_program_unit) t
DEBUG_OTS      0.16      1    16 PROCEDURE disable(
DEBUG_OTS      0.15      1    30 PROCEDURE enable(
DEBUG_OTS      0.14     44    44 PROCEDURE set_text(
DEBUG_O        0.14     22    81 STATIC PROCEDURE set_text(
DEBUG_O        0.13    132    39 CONSTRUCTOR FUNCTION debug_o(
DEBUG_OTS      0.12     22    54 DEBUG_O.set_text(v_program_unit, aiv_text)
DEBUG_O        0.11    132    49 self.unique_session_id := SYS.DBMS_SESSION
DEBUG_O        0.11    132    50 self.insert_user        := USER;
<anonymous>    0.10     10    20
<anonymous>    0.10      1    16
DEBUG_OTS      0.09      1    41 end enable;
PL             0.08    133    11 SYS.DBMS_OUTPUT.put_line(aiv_text);
<anonymous>    0.08      1    13
DEBUG_O        0.08    132    46 pl('debug_o(two params)');
<anonymous>    0.06      1    25
<anonymous>    0.06     10    22
DEBUG_OTS      0.05     44    56 end set_text;
DEBUG_O        0.05    132    51 self.insert_date        := SYSDATE;
DEBUG_O        0.05    132    54 end debug_o;
<anonymous>    0.04      1    18
<anonymous>    0.04     11     8
<anonymous>    0.03      1    12
<anonymous>    0.03      1     7
DEBUG_OTS      0.03      1    27 end disable;
PL             0.02    133    12 end pl;
DEBUG_O        0.02    132    47 self.id                 := ain_id;
<anonymous>    0.02      1    24
DEBUG_O        0.02    132    48 self.text               := aiv_text;
<anonymous>    0.01     11    19

51 rows selected.
```

Looking at Listing 7-18, it's easy to see that the bulk of time consumption is taken by the INSERT statement. This is typical. The slowest portion of any PL/SQL procedure is usually one or more SQL statements. That's why it's important to always maximize the efficiency of your SQL statements. You'll learn about one of the tools you can use to do that shortly, in the section about EXPLAIN PLAN. For now, it's important for you to understand just how valuable this report is when considering how to approach performance enhancements to your PL/SQL program units. With data like this, you can significantly narrow down the lines of code for which you need to improve performance, and not waste a lot of time guessing which ones are the poor performers.

A second report I like to use orders the average time consumption by program unit and line number. The script I execute for this report is named ord_profile.sql (you can find the listing for this report in the downloadable source code for the book). Just as with avg_profile.sql, you execute the script at the SQL*Plus prompt, passing in the run number as a parameter. Here's an example:

```
SQL> @ord_profile.sql 3
```

This command produced the report example shown in Listing 7-19. This report is helpful because it shows which lines in your program were actually executed. And even more interesting, you can add up the statistics for a function or procedure call by totaling the statistics from the line where the method is defined down to the line where it ends. For example, doing this for the constructor debug_o in Listing 7-19, you can calculate that it consumed 11,716 nanoseconds of processing time.

Listing 7-19. *An Average Time Consumption Report by Program Unit and Line Number for Test Unit, debug_ots.sql*

UNIT_NAME	AVG_TIME	OCCUR	LINE#	TEXT
<anonymous>	0	0	1	
<anonymous>	15912	2	1	
<anonymous>	0	0	1	
<anonymous>	8331	2	1	
<anonymous>	19592	12	1	
<anonymous>	13302	1	5	
<anonymous>	0	0	6	
<anonymous>	542	1	7	
<anonymous>	658	11	8	
<anonymous>	7808	10	9	
<anonymous>	3093	10	10	
<anonymous>	36312	1	11	
<anonymous>	11041	10	11	
<anonymous>	547	1	12	
<anonymous>	1292	1	13	
<anonymous>	1569	1	16	
<anonymous>	664	1	18	
<anonymous>	146	11	19	
<anonymous>	1584	10	20	
<anonymous>	953	10	22	
<anonymous>	297	1	24	
<anonymous>	989	1	25	
DEBUG_O	0	0	9	STATIC FUNCTION get_id
DEBUG_O	0	0	14	begin
DEBUG_O	0	0	15	select DEBUG_ID_SEQ.nextval
DEBUG_O	0	0	19	return n_id;
DEBUG_O	0	0	20	end get_id;
DEBUG_O	0	0	23	CONSTRUCTOR FUNCTION debug_o(
DEBUG_O	0	0	27	begin
DEBUG_O	0	0	28	pl('debug_o(zero param)');
DEBUG_O	0	0	29	self.id := NULL;
DEBUG_O	0	0	30	self.text := NULL;
DEBUG_O	0	0	31	self.unique_session_id := NULL;
DEBUG_O	0	0	32	self.insert_user := NULL;

```
DEBUG_O              0      0    33 self.insert_date        := NULL;
DEBUG_O              0      0    35 return;
DEBUG_O              0      0    36 end debug_o;
DEBUG_O           2113    132    39 CONSTRUCTOR FUNCTION debug_o(
DEBUG_O              0    132    45 begin
DEBUG_O           1190    132    46 pl('debug_o(two params)');
DEBUG_O            320    132    47 self.id                 := ain_id;
DEBUG_O            276    132    48 self.text               := aiv_text;
DEBUG_O           1790    132    49 self.unique_session_id := SYS.DBMS_SESSI
DEBUG_O           1787    132    50 self.insert_user        := USER;
DEBUG_O            768    132    51 self.insert_date        := SYSDATE;
DEBUG_O           2710    132    53 return;
DEBUG_O            762    132    54 end debug_o;
DEBUG_O              0      0    60 CONSTRUCTOR FUNCTION debug_o(
DEBUG_O              0      0    69 begin
DEBUG_O              0      0    70 pl('debug_o(five params)');
DEBUG_O              0      0    71 self.id                 := id;
DEBUG_O              0      0    72 self.text               := text;
DEBUG_O              0      0    73 self.unique_session_id := unique_session
DEBUG_O              0      0    74 self.insert_user        := insert_user;
DEBUG_O              0      0    75 self.insert_date        := insert_date;
DEBUG_O              0      0    77 return;
DEBUG_O              0      0    78 end debug_o;
DEBUG_O           2145     22    81 STATIC PROCEDURE set_text(
DEBUG_O           3002     22    89 begin
DEBUG_O           4056     22    90 v_text := substrb(aiv_program_unit||': '
DEBUG_O        1315546     22    92 insert into DEBUG_OT
DEBUG_O          63073     22    97 commit;
DEBUG_O           4922     22    98 end set_text;
DEBUG_O              0      0   101 MAP MEMBER FUNCTION to_map
DEBUG_O              0      0   104 begin
DEBUG_O              0      0   105 return id;
DEBUG_O              0      0   106 end to_map;
DEBUG_OTS            0      0     1 package body DEBUG_OTS as
DEBUG_OTS         2537      1    16 PROCEDURE disable(
DEBUG_OTS            0      1    21 begin
DEBUG_OTS         6814      1    22 v_program_unit := upper(aiv_program_unit
DEBUG_OTS         3492      1    24 if t_program_unit.exists(v_program_unit)
DEBUG_OTS         3767      1    25 t_program_unit.delete(v_program_unit);
DEBUG_OTS            0      1    26 end if;
DEBUG_OTS          402      1    27 end disable;
DEBUG_OTS         2387      1    30 PROCEDURE enable(
DEBUG_OTS            0      1    35 begin
DEBUG_OTS         9349      1    36 v_program_unit := upper(aiv_program_unit
DEBUG_OTS         4297      1    38 if not t_program_unit.exists(v_program_u
DEBUG_OTS         6209      1    39 t_program_unit(v_program_unit) := NULL;
DEBUG_OTS            0      1    40 end if;
```

DEBUG_OTS	1482	1	41 end enable;
DEBUG_OTS	2246	44	44 PROCEDURE set_text(
DEBUG_OTS	0	44	50 begin
DEBUG_OTS	5498	44	51 v_program_unit := upper(aiv_program_unit
DEBUG_OTS	2642	44	53 if t_program_unit.exists(v_program_unit)
DEBUG_OTS	1851	22	54 DEBUG_O.set_text(v_program_unit, aiv_tex
DEBUG_OTS	0	44	55 end if;
DEBUG_OTS	781	44	56 end set_text;
DEBUG_OTS	0	0	59 end DEBUG_OTS;
PL	0	0	1 PROCEDURE pl(
PL	1337	133	11 SYS.DBMS_OUTPUT.put_line(aiv_text);
PL	327	133	12 end pl;

93 rows selected.

Utilizing the statistics provided by DBMS_PROFILER, you can easily determine any bottlenecks in your PL/SQL programs and approach performance tuning in an efficient manner. DBMS_PROFILER data can also be used to detect defects in your code, in a fashion similar to debug logging.

Did you notice that, in both reports, the constructor for DEBUG_O was called 132 times, yet the INSERT statement was executed only 22 times? That means that SQL executed the constructor six times during each insert, clearly a defect in the SQL layer of the database, and subsequently a performance problem.

Now that I've profiled the object-relational version of the debug logger, it's your turn to profile the relational version.

It's Your Turn to Profile

The value of profiling code grows with the number of lines of code you're profiling. Still, you'll start out small by using DBMS_PROFILER on a smaller set of program units: your own code.

Before you begin, it's a good idea to see if DBMS_PROFILER is installed and if there are tables that it can store its data into when method flush_data() is called. To that end, execute a script like is_profiler.sql, as shown in Listing 7-20.

Listing 7-20. *A Script to Determine If SYS.DBMS_PROFILER Is Installed Properly, is_profiler.sql*

```
01  rem is_profiler.sql
02  rem by Donaled J. Bales on 12/15/2006
03  rem Check to see if the profiler is installed and accessible
04
05  declare
06
07  n_major                        number;
08  n_minor                        number;
09  n_package                      number;
10  n_local                        number;
11  n_global                       number;
12
13  begin
```

```
14    select count(1)
15    into   n_package
16    from   SYS.ALL_OBJECTS
17    where  object_type = 'PACKAGE'
18    and    object_name = 'DBMS_PROFILER'
19    and    owner        = 'SYS';
20
21    if n_package > 0 then
22      SYS.DBMS_PROFILER.get_version(n_major, n_minor);
23
24      pl('DBMS_PROFILER Version '||
25        to_char(n_major)||'.'||
26        to_char(n_minor));
27
28      pl('DBMS_PROFILER.internal_version_check = '||
29        to_char(SYS.DBMS_PROFILER.internal_version_check));
30    else
31      pl('Sorry, either the profile does not exist, or you'||
32          'don''t have access to it.  Contact your DBA!');
33    end if;
34
35    select count(1)
36    into   n_local
37    from   SYS.ALL_OBJECTS
38    where  object_type = 'TABLE'
39    and    object_name in (
40      'PLSQL_PROFILER_RUNS',
41      'PLSQL_PROFILER_UNITS',
42      'PLSQL_PROFILER_DATA')
43    and    owner = USER;
44
45    if n_local = 3 then
46      pl('You have access to locally defined profiler tables '||
47          'for your current username: '||USER);
48    end if;
49
50    select count(1)
51    into   n_global
52    from   SYS.ALL_OBJECTS
53    where  object_type = 'TABLE'
54    and    object_name in (
55      'PLSQL_PROFILER_RUNS',
56      'PLSQL_PROFILER_UNITS',
57      'PLSQL_PROFILER_DATA')
58    and    owner = 'SYS';
```

```
59
60    if n_global = 3 then
61      pl('You have access to globally defined profiler tables '||
62        'under username SYS');
63    end if;
64
65    if n_local  <> 3 and
66        n_global <> 3 then
67      pl('Sorry, either the profile tables do not exist, or you'||
68        'don''t have access to them.  Contact your DBA!');
69    end if;
70
71  end;
72  /
```

You should see SQL*Plus output like this:

```
SQL> @is_profiler
```

```
DBMS_PROFILER Version 2.0
DBMS_PROFILER.internal_version_check = 0
You have access to locally defined profiler
tables for your current username: BPS

PL/SQL procedure successfully completed.
```

Given that you have access to the profiler, profile your relational version of the debug logger by following these steps:

1. Profile your debug logger by executing the following at the SQL*Plus prompt:

   ```
   SQL> @run_profiler.sql debug_ts.sql
   ```

   This profiles your debug logging table package by executing your test unit for said package. The run_profiler.sql script should have displayed the run number on the screen. Jot down this number, because you'll need it to run the two profiling reports next.

2. Create an "average percent consumption" report by executing the following at the SQL*Plus prompt:

   ```
   SQL> @avg_profile.sql <run_number>
   ```

   where <run_number> is the run number you got from executing script run_profiler.sql.

3. Examine the file avg_profile_<run_number>.txt. Ask yourself, "What's the biggest consumer of resources?"

4. Create an "order by program unit and line number" report by executing the following at the SQL*Plus prompt:

```
SQL> @ord_profile.sql <run_number>
```

5. Examine the file ord_profile_<run_number>.txt. Scan down the report. Find where your methods start and stop. Add up the average time consumption in nanoseconds. Ask yourself, "What's the biggest consumer of resources?"

Interestingly enough, in both cases, when you ask yourself to identify the biggest consumer of resources, you'll see that the answer is your SQL statements. Yes, we're back to dealing with SQL again. It's important to verify that your PL/SQL program logic is sound and it performs well, but it's even more important to make sure that your SQL is efficient. So let's see how you can determine just what's going on in a SQL statement next.

Hey, Don't Forget SQL!

It's undeniable. You must make sure your SQL statements are as efficient as possible and that they are doing as much of the data manipulation work as is possible, because SQL is more efficient at manipulating data than PL/SQL. So how do you see what's going on when it comes to a SQL statement?

Oracle provides two tools that you can use to examine the underlying access plan generated by the Oracle SQL Optimizer:

EXPLAIN PLAN: Shows the execution plan generated by the Optimizer for a SQL statement you execute under the Oracle keywords EXPLAIN PLAN.

TKPROF: A utility program that can produce execution plans for all SQL statements executed against a database.

Let's start out by looking at EXPLAIN PLAN.

Explain Plan

"Explain this mess to me, please." Often, that's how you feel by the time you get around to using EXPLAIN PLAN. Before that point, you sit there scratching your head, talking to yourself out loud, "Why does this take so long to run?" Meanwhile, those sitting around you wonder if it's time for you to visit a mental health professional.

EXPLAIN PLAN will tell you, in just a bit more time than it takes you wrap your SQL statement in the keywords EXPLAIN PLAN FOR, exactly how the database intends to execute your SQL statement. Armed with this information, you can quickly determine if you need to do any of the following:

- Add an index to a table (or remove it)

- Rewrite your SQL statement

- Break your data processing into smaller chunks of work

- Just live with what you have

So why scratch your head?

Given what you just learned in the section on profiling about performance in a PL/SQL program, your first step should always be to use EXPLAIN PLAN on every SQL statement in your PL/SQL program unit. So how do you do that?

1. Execute your SQL statement prefixed with the keywords EXPLAIN PLAN FOR.

2. Query the table PLAN_TABLE to extract the statistics.

In the olden days, you had to write your own SQL statements to query the PLAN_TABLE, but now you have access to package SYS.DBMS_XPLAN, which will do all the work of formatting the statistics for you.

Listing 7-21 is a SQL*Plus script named xp.sql that will explain the Optimizer's plan for a SQL statement stored in a file, with the filename passed to the script as the first parameter.

Listing 7-21. *A Script to Explain the Optimizer Plan for SQL Statements, xp.sql*

```
01  rem xp.sql
02  rem by Donald J. Bales on 12/15/2006
03  rem Display the execution plan for the last executed cursor
04
05  define script="&1";
06
07  set linesize  1000;
08  set newpage   1;
09  set pagesize  0;
10  set trimspool on;
11  set verify    off;
12
13  EXPLAIN PLAN FOR
14  select 1 from DUAL;
15
16  spool &script..pln;
17
18  EXPLAIN PLAN FOR
19  @&script
20
21  set echo off;
22
23  select * from table(SYS.DBMS_XPLAN.DISPLAY);
24
25  spool off;
26
27  set pagesize  32767;
28  set verify    on;
```

For example, first I save the following simple query in file select_worker_ot_equlato.sql.

```
select *
from    WORKER_OT
where   name = 'DOE, JOHN J.'
order by 1;
```

Next, I execute xp.sql in SQL*Plus, passing it the filename as follows:

```
SQL> xp.sql select_worker_ot_equalto.sql
```

This produces the following plan:

```
Explained.

Plan hash value: 2430037530


---------------------------------------------------------------------
| Id | Operation                    | Name          | Rows | Bytes |
---------------------------------------------------------------------
|  0 | SELECT STATEMENT             |               |    1 |   61 |
|  1 |  SORT ORDER BY               |               |    1 |   61 |
|  2 |   TABLE ACCESS BY INDEX ROWID| WORKER_OT     |    1 |   61 |
|* 3 |    INDEX RANGE SCAN          | WORKER_OT_UK2 |    1 |      |
---------------------------------------------------------------------


----------------------
Cost (%CPU)| Time     |
----------------------
    5  (20)| 00:00:01 |
    5  (20)| 00:00:01 |
    4   (0)| 00:00:01 |
    3   (0)| 00:00:01 |
----------------------


Predicate Information (identified by operation id):
---------------------------------------------------

   3 - access("NAME"='DOE, JOHN J.')

15 rows selected.
```

If you examine the plan, you'll see that the query is retrieving the values from the database by first scanning index WORKER_OT_UK2. Since I know how the indexes were built, I can be assured by looking at the plan that the Optimizer has chosen the best plan for accessing the WORKER_OT table. Now let's see what the Optimizer decides to do when I change the query from an "equal to" to a "like literal ending with a wildcard" query.

First, I save the following query in file select_worker_ot_likepct.sql.

```
select *
from    WORKER_OT
where   name like 'DOE%'
order by 1;
```

Next, I execute xp.sql against that filename as follows:

```
SQL> xp.sql select_worker_ot_likepct.sql
```

This produces the following plan:

Explained.

Plan hash value: 2430037530

```
---------------------------------------------------------------------
| Id | Operation                     | Name          | Rows | Bytes |
---------------------------------------------------------------------
|  0 | SELECT STATEMENT              |               |    1 |    61 |
|  1 |  SORT ORDER BY                |               |    1 |    61 |
|  2 |   TABLE ACCESS BY INDEX ROWID | WORKER_OT     |    1 |    61 |
|* 3 |    INDEX RANGE SCAN           | WORKER_OT_UK2 |    1 |       |
---------------------------------------------------------------------
```

```
----------------------
Cost (%CPU)| Time     |
----------------------
   6  (17)| 00:00:01 |
   6  (17)| 00:00:01 |
   5   (0)| 00:00:01 |
   3   (0)| 00:00:01 |
----------------------
```

Predicate Information (identified by operation id):
```
---------------------------------------------------
```

```
   3 - access("NAME" LIKE 'DOE%')
       filter("NAME" LIKE 'DOE%')
```

16 rows selected.

The Optimizer chose the same plan for this query as it did that last one.

Now let's try a worst-case scenario for any LIKE statement. I'll use the (%) wildcard on both sides of the literal. I would assume that this SQL statement will lead to a *full index scan*, instead of an *index range scan*. Does it?

First, I save the following query in file select_worker_ot_pctlikepct.sql.

```
select *
from    WORKER_OT
where   name like '%DOE%'
order by 1;
```

Next, I pass the filename to xp.sql as follows:

```
SQL> xp.sql select_worker_ot_pctlikepct.sql
```

This produces the following plan:

```
Explained.

Plan hash value: 2955220684


-------------------------------------------------------------------
| Id  | Operation          | Name      | Rows  | Bytes |TempSpc|
-------------------------------------------------------------------
|   0 | SELECT STATEMENT   |           | 13026 |   775K|       |
|   1 |  SORT ORDER BY     |           | 13026 |   775K|  2168K|
|*  2 |   TABLE ACCESS FULL| WORKER_OT | 13026 |   775K|       |
-------------------------------------------------------------------


----------------------
Cost (%CPU)| Time    |
----------------------
 1022   (3)| 00:00:13 |
 1022   (3)| 00:00:13 |
  824   (4)| 00:00:10 |
----------------------


Predicate Information (identified by operation id):
---------------------------------------------------

   2 - filter("NAME" LIKE '%DOE%')

14 rows selected.
```

No, it doesn't use an index at all. Instead, it resorted to the worst of all options: a *full table scan*. Ouch! The cost went from 6 to 1022. That means it will take about 170 times longer for this query to respond than the first two. It looks like if I want to maintain performance in my application, I'm going to have to devise another solution for allowing my end users to find someone with a name like %<name>%. Is there something I can do in Oracle to improve this situation? Yes, sometimes there is.

Physics vs. Explain Plan

If you have a table that has much larger row sizes than an applicable index, you can use simple physics to improve your query response time. For example, the average row size for the table

WORKER_OT is 87 bytes. The average row size for index WORKER_OT_UK2 is 17 bytes. If I add a hint to the query forcing it to full scan the index WORKER_OT_UK2, the database will be able to retrieve five times as many index blocks per retrieval that it can table blocks. What does the Optimizer have to say about this plan? Let's find out.

First, I save the following query as select_worker_ot_pctlikepct2.sql:

```
select /*+ INDEX(WORKER_OT WORKER_OT_UK2) */
       *
from   WORKER_OT
where  name like '%DOE%'
order by 1;
```

In this query, I've added the hint /*+ INDEX(WORKER_OT WORKER_OT_UK2) */, which tells the Optimizer to use index WORKER_OT_UK2. Next, I use xp.sql to explain the Optimizer's plan as follows:

```
SQL> xp.sql select_worker_ot_pctlikepct.sql
```

This produces the following plan:

```
Explained.

Plan hash value: 4066707113
```

Id	Operation	Name	Rows	Bytes	TempSpc
0	SELECT STATEMENT		13026	775K	
1	SORT ORDER BY		13026	775K	2168K
2	TABLE ACCESS BY INDEX ROWID	WORKER_OT	13026	775K	
* 3	INDEX FULL SCAN	WORKER_OT_UK2	12364		

Cost (%CPU)	Time
14877 (1)	00:02:59
14877 (1)	00:02:59
14679 (1)	00:02:57
1635 (1)	00:00:20

```
Predicate Information (identified by operation id):
---------------------------------------------------

   3 - filter("NAME" LIKE '%DOE%')

15 rows selected.
```

Indeed, the Optimizer understands my hint and is prepared to scan the index, but the cost is astronomical! Well guess what—*the Optimizer is wrong*. It doesn't understand the underlying physics involved.

Since there are 260,000 rows of data, with an average length of 87 bytes, if the Oracle database retrieves the data in 4KB blocks, it will require the retrieval of at least 5,500 blocks from the disk drive. On the other hand, it will require the retrieval of only about 1,080 blocks to identify which data rows to retrieve. Since, in this context, searching for part of a name will return a small set of rows, the application's performance can permanently benefit from the use of the hint, regardless of how the Optimizer feels about it. But the proof is in testing.

If I execute the first query `select_worker_ot_pctlikepct.sql`, which does not have the hint, against 260,000 rows, it takes on average three seconds to retrieve the matching rows. If I execute the second query, `select_worker_ot_pctlikepct2.sql`, which does have the hint to scan the index, it takes on average one second to retrieve the matching rows.

What's the moral of this story? The Optimizer doesn't always know the best way to retrieve data. It works with what it knows—basically statistics gathered when you analyze a table. On the other hand, you're an intelligent programmer who is much more knowledgeable and can therefore consider things like physics.

It's Your Turn to Use Explain Plan

Do you remember the section on `FORALL` in Chapter 5? That's where I nailed down the value of using the power of SQL instead of writing a whole lot of PL/SQL code to do the same work. The following SQL statement comes from Listing 5-14.

```
insert into WORKER_T (
        worker_id,
        worker_type_id,
        external_id,
        first_name,
        middle_name,
        last_name,
        name,
        birth_date,
        gender_id)
select WORKER_ID_SEQ.nextval,
        decode(mod(WORKER_ID_SEQ.currval, 2),
          0, n_WT_EMPLOYEE, n_WT_CONTRACTOR),
        lpad(to_char(EXTERNAL_ID_SEQ.nextval), 9, '0'),
        first_name,
        letter||'.',
        last_name,
        WORKER_TS.get_formatted_name(
          first_name, letter||'.', last_name),
        DATES.random(
          to_number(to_char(SYSDATE, 'YYYY')) - 65,
          to_number(to_char(SYSDATE, 'YYYY')) - 18),
        decode(gender_code, 'F', n_G_FEMALE, n_G_MALE)
```

```
from   TOP_100_LAST_NAME,
       TOP_100_FIRST_NAME,
       A_THRU_Z;
```

In this code, I use pseudo-constants n_WT_EMPLOYEE, n_WT_CONTRACTOR, n_G_FEMALE, and n_G_MALE, which were preselected from the database, instead of selecting those values from the database in the SQL INSERT statement. Why?

It's another one of those tricks I've learned along the way. After years of using EXPLAIN PLAN on every SQL statement I've written, I noticed that I can improve the performance of a SQL statement if I reduce the number of tables accessed in the statement. If a SQL statement has three or less tables being selected, it performs pretty well. Add more tables, and its performance goes downhill fast.

So, if I have fairly limited number of constant values, I select them into pseudo-constant variables ahead of time, and then use those pseudo-constants in my SQL statement. Here's the Optimizer's plan for the preceding SQL INSERT statement:

```
Explained.

Plan hash value: 2041463127
```

Id	Operation	Name	Rows	Bytes
0	INSERT STATEMENT		260K	4316K
1	SEQUENCE	WORKER_ID_SEQ		
2	MERGE JOIN CARTESIAN		260K	4316K
3	MERGE JOIN CARTESIAN		2600	23400
4	INDEX FULL SCAN	A_THRU_Z_PK	26	52
5	BUFFER SORT		100	700
6	INDEX FAST FULL SCAN	TOP_100_LAST_NAME_PK	100	700
7	BUFFER SORT		100	800
8	INDEX FAST FULL SCAN	TOP_100_FIRST_NAME_PK	100	800

Cost (%CPU)	Time
582 (1)	00:00:07
582 (1)	00:00:07
8 (0)	00:00:01
1 (0)	00:00:01
7 (0)	00:00:01
0 (0)	00:00:01
581 (1)	00:00:07
0 (0)	00:00:01

```
15 rows selected.
```

So here's your assignment. Rewrite the preceding SQL INSERT statement, which takes 47 seconds on average to execute on my machine, so the ID values for EMPLOYEE, CONTRACTOR, FEMALE, and MALE come from tables in the SQL INSERT statement's SELECT statement. Figure out if my working assumption about the number of tables in a SQL statement was true for this case, too. So follow these steps in order to find out for yourself:

1. Rewrite the SQL INSERT statement from Listing 5-14, adding two more tables to the SELECT statement, so you can get the ID values for corresponding codes from the database in the SQL statement.

2. Do an EXPLAIN PLAN on your SQL INSERT statement to determine what the Optimizer is planning. Is your plan better than the one for the SQL INSERT statement from Listing 5-14?

3. Look up the ID values for EMPLOYEE, CONTRACTOR, FEMALE, and MALE, and then substitute these values into the SQL INSERT statement from Listing 5-14.

4. Delete the contents of table WORKER_T, and then execute the SQL INSERT statement from Listing 5-14 that you just modified, keeping track of how long it takes to execute. I suggest you do this at least three times, and then calculate the average value for how long it takes for the INSERT statement to execute.

5. Delete the contents of table WORKER_T, and then execute your SQL INSERT statement where you include the GENDER_T and WORKER_TYPE_T tables in its SELECT statement. Once again, I suggest you do this three times, and then calculate the average response time.

6. Compare the results of your timings between the two SQL INSERT statements. Which one was faster? Which SQL INSERT would you choose?

I'll show you my solution to this exercise. First, here's the SQL INSERT statement from Listing 5-14, modified to include tables GENDER_T and WORKER_TYPE_T in its SELECT statement:

```
insert into WORKER_T (
        worker_id,
        worker_type_id,
        external_id,
        first_name,
        middle_name,
        last_name,
        name,
        birth_date,
        gender_id)
select WORKER_ID_SEQ.nextval,
        decode(mod(WORKER_ID_SEQ.currval, 2),
          0, c1.worker_type_id, c2.worker_type_id),
        lpad(to_char(EXTERNAL_ID_SEQ.nextval), 9, '0'),
        first_name,
        letter||'.',
        last_name,
        WORKER_TS.get_formatted_name(
```

```
            first_name, letter||'.', last_name),
        DATES.random(
          to_number(to_char(SYSDATE, 'YYYY')) - 65,
          to_number(to_char(SYSDATE, 'YYYY')) - 18),
        decode(gender_code, 'F', c3.gender_id, c4.gender_id)
from    TOP_100_LAST_NAME,
        TOP_100_FIRST_NAME,
        A_THRU_Z,
        WORKER_TYPE_T c1,
        WORKER_TYPE_T c2,
        GENDER_T c3,
        GENDER_T c4
where   c1.code = 'E'
and     c2.code = 'C'
and     c3.code = 'F'
and     c4.code = 'M';
```

And here's the Optimizer's plan for this SQL INSERT statement:

```
Explained.


Plan hash value: 1896089370


------------------------------------------------------------------------
| Id  | Operation                       | Name                  |
------------------------------------------------------------------------
|   0 | INSERT STATEMENT                |                       |
|   1 |  SEQUENCE                       | WORKER_ID_SEQ         |
|   2 |   MERGE JOIN CARTESIAN          |                       |
|   3 |    MERGE JOIN CARTESIAN         |                       |
|   4 |     NESTED LOOPS               |                       |
|   5 |      NESTED LOOPS              |                       |
|   6 |       NESTED LOOPS            |                       |
|   7 |        NESTED LOOPS          |                       |
|   8 |         TABLE ACCESS BY INDEX ROWID| GENDER_T          |
|*  9 |          INDEX UNIQUE SCAN     | GENDER_UK             |
|  10 |         TABLE ACCESS BY INDEX ROWID| GENDER_T          |
|* 11 |          INDEX UNIQUE SCAN     | GENDER_UK             |
|  12 |        TABLE ACCESS BY INDEX ROWID | WORKER_TYPE_T     |
|* 13 |         INDEX UNIQUE SCAN      | WORKER_TYPE_UK        |
|  14 |       TABLE ACCESS BY INDEX ROWID  | WORKER_TYPE_T     |
|* 15 |        INDEX UNIQUE SCAN       | WORKER_TYPE_UK        |
|  16 |      INDEX FULL SCAN           | A_THRU_Z_PK           |
|  17 |     BUFFER SORT                |                       |
|  18 |      INDEX FAST FULL SCAN      | TOP_100_LAST_NAME_PK  |
|  19 |    BUFFER SORT                 |                       |
|  20 |     INDEX FAST FULL SCAN       | TOP_100_FIRST_NAME_PK |
------------------------------------------------------------------------
```

```
------------------------------------------
Rows  | Bytes | Cost (%CPU)| Time     |
------------------------------------------
 260K|  8378K|   586    (1)| 00:00:08 |
     |       |             |          |
 260K|  8378K|   586    (1)| 00:00:08 |
2600 | 65000 |    12    (0)| 00:00:01 |
  26 |   468 |     5    (0)| 00:00:01 |
   1 |    16 |     4    (0)| 00:00:01 |
   1 |    13 |     3    (0)| 00:00:01 |
   1 |    10 |     2    (0)| 00:00:01 |
   1 |     5 |     1    (0)| 00:00:01 |
   1 |       |     0    (0)| 00:00:01 |
   1 |     5 |     1    (0)| 00:00:01 |
   1 |       |     0    (0)| 00:00:01 |
   1 |     3 |     1    (0)| 00:00:01 |
   1 |       |     0    (0)| 00:00:01 |
   1 |     3 |     1    (0)| 00:00:01 |
   1 |       |     0    (0)| 00:00:01 |
  26 |    52 |     1    (0)| 00:00:01 |
 100 |   700 |    11    (0)| 00:00:01 |
 100 |   700 |     0    (0)| 00:00:01 |
 100 |   800 |   585    (1)| 00:00:08 |
 100 |   800 |     0    (0)| 00:00:01 |
------------------------------------------


Predicate Information (identified by operation id):
---------------------------------------------------

   9 - access("C4"."CODE"='M')
  11 - access("C3"."CODE"='F')
  13 - access("C2"."CODE"='C')
  15 - access("C1"."CODE"='E')
```

35 rows selected.

The SQL INSERT statement with the GENDER_T and WORKER_TYPE_T tables in its SQL SELECT statement is less efficient (cost equal to 586 vs. 582) according to EXPLAIN PLAN. What about how long it actually takes to execute? On my machine, it's actually one second faster than the SQL INSERT statement from Listing 5-14! So much for my experience.

The moral of this story is that you can't assume anything. You must always test the actual performance of your SQL statements before and after you've made modifications to the database, or to your SQL statements, in order to improve performance.

If you want a larger view of SQL statement performance, then perhaps you should use TKPROF.

TKPROF

TKPROF is a tool that's normally available only to your DBA. You're nice to your DBA, aren't you? So asking for his or her help in accessing trace files won't be a problem, right?

TKPROF is a utility that you can use in conjunction with session or system tracing to format the output of tracing into plans similar to those generated by EXPLAIN PLAN. The big difference is that you can gather statistics using package SYS.DBMS_MONITOR, which in turn will create trace files. Then you can use the trcsess utility to format the trace information into a format for TKPROF, and use TKPROF to format the output of the trace files into information you can use to examine the efficiency of an application's SQL statements as they were actually executed in a database.

To use TKPROF, follow these steps:

1. Utilize package DBMS_MONITOR to trace your application's use of SQL.

2. Use the trcsess utility to consolidate trace information into a file that can be analyzed using TKPROF.

3. Examine the consolidated trace file using TKPROF, in order to determine high-cost SQL statements in your application.

Using TKPROF, you'll be able to see the following for each SQL statement executed while you're monitoring the database:

- Resources consumed

- Number of times it was called

- Number of rows processed

- Optimizer's execution plan

Once you're armed with this information, you can use EXPLAIN PLAN to determine if there is a better alternative SQL statement, or if you'll need to come up with an entirely new solution. You may also want to investigate using package SYS.DBMS_SQLTUNE to help you decide how to properly tune a SQL statement.

You can find more information about performance tuning and EXPLAIN PLAN in the *Oracle Database Performance Tuning Guide*. You can find more information about the SYS.DBMS_* PL/SQL packages mentioned in this chapter in the *PL/SQL Packages and Types Reference*.

So what have your learned?

Summary

This chapter was all about troubleshooting. First, we discussed how to reduce the amount of troubleshooting you may have to do by simply preventing trouble in the first place. Second, we talked about adding troubleshooting-enabling code into your PL/SQL program units as you go, in anticipation of and preparation for trouble. Next, we covered four different troubleshooting tools:

- put_line()

- Debug logging

- Remote debugging

- EXPLAIN PLAN

Armed with these tools, you'll be able to handle any PL/SQL problem that comes your way. Now that you know how to fix any defect, how do you go about finding them all? By testing! And that's what we're going to cover next.

CHAPTER 8

■■■

Test, Test, Test, and Test Again

And then test again! By now, you know I like to try to be funny, and most of the time I fail. We all have to fail at something, right? Regardless, the title of this chapter is not a joke on my part. After 20 plus years of enterprise application development, I've found that the actual application development process for programmers consists of three high-level tasks:

- Coding

- Testing

- Documenting

The graph in Figure 8-1 is what I consider the ideal distribution of time for those three tasks. Yes, that's 60% of the development time spent on testing. The first response I get from most developers and project managers is, "Wow, that's an awful lot of time for testing, isn't it?" Not really. All the time you spend testing is time you won't have to spend supporting the application. And it costs a heck of a lot more to fix a defect in production than it does to take care of the problem earlier. It's as simple as that.

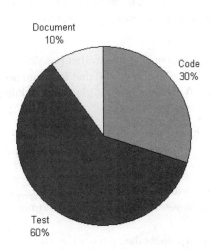

Figure 8-1. *An ideal distribution of development work*

Professional PL/SQL programmers write test units for their PL/SQL program units as they write their program units. I've been having you write them all along, haven't I? These are the only proper ways to reduce the amount of time spent testing:

- Develop with modularity (object orientation), because once a well-encapsulated software component is tested, it's unlikely it will break or need testing if a different unrelated module is modified.

- Automate testing by writing automated test units for every program unit and/or by using a testing application suite.

- Write rerunnable test units. You should be able to run test units over and over again until there are no errors, without having to do any extra work to run them again.

- Update test units with additional tests if a defect not caught by the current test unit rears its ugly head.

- Don't lose your test units.

- Document your test units.

In contrast, nowadays it seems that everyone's favorite way to reduce the amount of time spent testing is to not test at all, which means passing testing on to the end user (not a good idea), which in turn means passing it on to support personnel (even worse). Why is passing testing on to support personnel even worse? At least the end users have a good idea of how things should work. Support personnel usually know even less. It becomes a case of the proverbial "blind leading the blind."

So just whose responsibility is testing?

1. You are primarily responsible for testing your own code. You need to write test plans and test units to execute those test plans.

2. Your peers on your programming team are also responsible if they run into an error when using one of your components. Their responsibility is to inform you that there is a defect in your code, to ask you to update your test plans, update your test units, and then to test your code again.

3. Your supervisor, whether a technical lead, project manager, or in another position, is responsible for verifying that you have executed your test plans and that there are no errors. Your supervisor is also responsible for verifying that your test plans are updated if someone encounters an error.

4. An application's support personnel are responsible for reporting errors to the development team so defects can be fixed, and then test plans and test units can be updated and rerun.

5. An application's end users are responsible for reporting errors to the support team, so defects can be fixed, and then test plans and test units can be updated and rerun.

I used a numbered list for these responsibilities to emphasize that *you are the one most responsible for testing.*

So just what do I mean by "test plan" and "test unit"? A test plan is a document that outlines how an application is to be tested. It should at least answer the following questions:

- How will the persistence layer (database) be tested?

- How will the application layer (middle tier) be tested?

- How will the presentation layer (the various presentation layers: data entry, reporting, interfaces, and so on) be tested?

- What technique will be used to keep track of what needs to be tested?

- What technique will be used to record that something has been tested?

- Who will sign off that the testing has been completed successfully and that there are no errors?

- How many rounds of testing will there be, and who will perform each round of testing?

A test unit is a list of tests to be executed by a tester (a person who tests) or executed by a program, written or scripted, which executes the test steps in an automated fashion. This chapter is about writing test units:

- The commonly executed steps in a PL/SQL test unit for SQL

- The commonly executed steps in a PL/SQL test unit for PL/SQL

- A table to store the tests performed and their results

- A package to aid in writing PL/SQL test units

- A framework for keeping track of what needs to be tested in a persistence layer (database/objectbase)

Let's start by looking at the common tasks involved in testing SQL.

SQL Test Patterns

If you have a PL/SQL method that uses SQL, then you must devise some method to test that the SQL in that program unit works correctly. From an abstract point of view, that boils down to executing some or all of these steps in the following order:

1. DELETE
2. INSERT
3. SELECT
4. UPDATE
5. DELETE

If you're going to test a program unit's ability to INSERT a new entry into a table, you first need to decide on an acceptable set of values to use during the INSERT, and then you must clean up after yourself by removing what you've just added, so the test unit can be run again. Since it's entirely possible that an error may have occurred before your INSERT operation, you need to DELETE first. Otherwise, when you rerun your test on INSERT, you may get an error due to a row that was not properly cleaned up or removed during a prior test. That's why I have DELETE as the number one high-level operation for testing any PL/SQL program unit that automates SQL testing.

Next, if you're going to test a PL/SQL program unit's ability to retrieve values from a table, you first need to INSERT those values so they are available. That means you must INSERT before you SELECT, which, in turn, means you need to DELETE, INSERT, SELECT, and then DELETE in your test unit.

Now if you're going to test a program unit's ability to UPDATE, it follows that you must first SELECT to verify that there is something to UPDATE, which requires you to INSERT before you SELECT and DELETE before you INSERT. Then you need to DELETE in order to clean up after yourself.

Last, if you're going to test a program unit's ability to DELETE, you need to perform a DELETE, then an INSERT, followed by a SELECT, (yes, you can skip UPDATE) and then a DELETE. I like to call this abstract pattern the *SQL Circle of Life*, as illustrated in Figure 8-2.

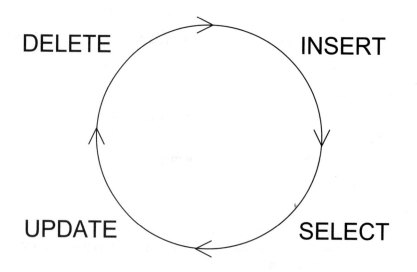

Figure 8-2. *The SQL Circle of Life*

At this moment, this discussion may seem quite silly. Perhaps I'm just adding prose to make my chapter's page-count goal? But you'll see soon enough, when you start writing test units, you will need to keep the SQL Circle of Life in mind when writing rerunnable SQL test units in PL/SQL.

Let's look at patterns found when testing PL/SQL methods next.

PL/SQL Test Patterns

Just as there is an abstract pattern to testing SQL in PL/SQL, there is also a pattern you'll need to follow to test PL/SQL program units themselves. The PL/SQL testing pattern is "blocking" your test code.

You need to wrap each of your PL/SQL tests in a PL/SQL block so you can programmatically maintain control in your test unit. If you can't maintain control in your test unit, it may end abruptly without performing all your tests. Here's an example:

```
...
begin
  -- Perform your test by calling a method with test data here

  -- Then check to ensure test success here
exception
  when OTHERS then
    -- Catch any PL/SQL exception and report the error here
end;
-- Go on to the next test
...
```

You'll end up testing your PL/SQL methods by calling them with test values in your test unit, and then inspecting the results of the operation to verify it worked correctly. In order to maintain control, you'll need to catch any raised exceptions, hence the when OTHERS then clause in the exception-handling section of the PL/SQL block surrounding your code. From the exception-handling section, you'll report any errors that take place, therefore handling the exception, not raising the exception to the outer (enclosing) PL/SQL block. Then you'll go on to perform your next method test.

How will you report and keep track of success or failure in your test units? You'll do that with a testing tool. Let's look at that next.

A Testing Tool

I'm a good primate. I hope you are, too! Primates, especially humans, are very good at creating their own tools. To that end, I've created a "testing tool" that helps me code my PL/SQL test units.

I have two high-level requirements for this testing tool:

- Provide a set of constants that I can use for column values when testing

- Provide a set of methods that I can use to save tests and results for later analysis

Do you recall that in the "SQL Test Patterns" section, I stated that you first need to decide on an acceptable set of values to use during the INSERT? How do you go about that?

Well here's how I do it: I ask the database! Listing 8-1 is a SQL*Plus query I run to determine the varchar2 lengths that are in common use. For the most part, there should only be a few. While in the past, the lengths of character field may have had some meaning, they no longer do. With the advent of globalization, the lengths of character fields only amount to specifying an upper limit on the amount of storage you're willing to use for a given string value.

Listing 8-1. *A Query to Determine Commonly Used Lengths for Varchar2 Columns, data_length_histogram.sql*

```
01  rem data_length_histogram.sql
02  rem by Donald J. Bales on 12/15/2006
03  rem Create a histogram of VARCHAR2 data lengths in use
04
05  column data_type format a13;
06
07  set linesize  1000;
08  set newpage   1;
09  set pagesize  32767;
10  set trimspool on;
11
12  spool data_length_histogram.txt;
13
14  select column_name,
15         min(data_length) min,
16         avg(data_length) avg,
17         max(data_length) max,
18         count(1) occurs
19  from   SYS.ALL_TAB_COLUMNS
20  where  owner = USER
21  and    data_type like 'VARCHAR%'
22  and    table_name not in (
23         'AUTHOR',
24         'AUTHOR_PUBLICATION',
25         'A_THRU_Z',
26         'DEBUG_OT',
27         'DEBUG_T',
28         'PLAN_TABLE',
29         'PLSQL_PROFILER_RUNS',
30         'PLSQL_PROFILER_UNITS',
31         'PLSQL_PROFILER_DATA',
32         'TOP_100_FIRST_NAME',
33         'TOP_100_LAST_NAME' )
34  group by column_name
35  order by max(data_length),
36         column_name
37  /
38
39  spool off;
```

And here's the output from the query in Listing 8-1:

COLUMN_NAME	MIN	AVG	MAX	OCCURS
LOGICAL_INDICATOR	1	1	1	1
PHYSICAL_INDICATOR	1	1	1	1
CAS_NUMBER	30	30	30	1
CODE	30	30	30	10
EXTERNAL_ID	30	30	30	2
FIRST_NAME	30	30	30	2
INSERT_USER	30	30	30	1
LAST_NAME	30	30	30	2
MIDDLE_NAME	30	30	30	2
TEST	30	30	30	1
DESCRIPTION	80	80	80	7
ID_CONTEXT	100	100	100	2
NAME	80	85.7142857	100	7
TITLE	100	100	100	1
NARRATIVE	2000	2000	2000	1

15 rows selected.

Analyzing this output, I have concluded that I will need the following constants for testing:

- A TRUE value for the indicator variables

- A FALSE value for the indicator variables

- A 30-character code value that I can specify anytime I test inserting a new code or partial name value into a code or content table

- An 80-character description value that I can specify anytime I test inserting a new description into a code or content table

- A 100-character value that I can specify anytime I test inserting a new ID context or title into a content or intersection table

- A 2,000-character value that I can specify anytime I test inserting a new comment or narrative into a content table

I'll keep this list of requirements in mind when I code my testing tool's package specification, so the constants will be accessible to all other program units, and therefore available when writing their test units.

WHY ARE WE SPECIFYING CHARACTER COLUMN LENGTHS ANYWAY?

After having internationalized a number of enterprise applications, I began to wonder why we have to specify a maximum column length for character columns at all. In the future, I don't think we'll need to do this; the database will handle the length automatically, and why not?

I've already expressed my disdain at constraining NUMBER data type columns earlier in this book. One programmer I know argued that was important and gave me what he thought was a valid example: "It's important to constrain a number column for money. It should be NUMBER(11,2), because dollars have hundredths values (dimes and pennies)." But that's only valid for dollars; other currencies have thousandths.

Consider that characters used in the English language use one byte of storage. Other languages use characters that require two to four bytes of storage. In addition, sentences, even words, in English are quite compact when compared with other languages. For example, an idea expressed in 30 *characters* in English may take four to fives times as many words and/or *characters* in German.

So just what are we specifying when we constrain a varchar2's length? I think it's just our expectation that nothing entered into the column will ever need to be larger than what we've specified. So until Oracle gets with my line of thinking, we might as well decide on a standard set of character column lengths and stick to it. Here are the lengths I commonly use for character fields in applications.

- *Code:* 30 English only; 60 internationalized

- *Code context:* 500 English only; 1000 internationalized

- *Comments:* 2000 English only; 4000 internationalized

- *Description:* 80 English only; 160

- *ID context:* 100 English only; 200 internationalized

- *Name:* 80 English only; 160 internationalized

- *Name context:* 1000 English only; 2000 internationalized

- *Title:* 80 English only; 160 internationalized

I would like to hear your thoughts: don@donaldbales.com. Now back to our previously scheduled program.

How about some behavior? What will I call the methods that aid me with writing test units? Here's a preliminary set of requirements:

clear(): To erase the results of a previous test run from table TEST_T.

get_id(): To allocate a new primary key value for the table TEST_T .

test(): To test the testing tool.

set_test(): To start a new test.

set_result(): To store the results of a test.

However, before I write a testing tool package, I need to create a table to permanently store the results of my tests.

A TEST Table

Why store my test results in a table? Because then I can use SQL to query the table to analyze the results of my testing. No tool is more powerful at manipulating data than SQL, so a table is the ideal place to save the results of testing.

What do I need to store? Here's my short list of data to store:

- The name of the package or user-defined TYPE (object name) that contains the method being tested

- The name of the method being tested

- An external identifier for the test being performed on a given method so I can identify a given test if it fails

- A short but meaningful description of the test

- The result of the test

In order to store this data, I've written the DDL script in Listing 8-2. It creates a test table named TEST_T. I've also added an ID column for a primary key, and a unique session ID, so testing in one session does not collide with testing going on in another session. I've also included insert user and insert date columns, which are standard columns I add to all tables (to add those bread crumbs I talked about in Chapter 7).

Listing 8-2. *A DDL Script to Create a Testing Results Table, test_t.tab*

```
01   rem test_t.tab
02   rem by Donald Bales on 12/15/2006
03   rem Create test results
04
05   drop   table TEST_T;
06   create table TEST_T (
07   id                      number                     not null,
08   object_name             varchar2(30),
09   method_name             varchar2(30),
10   test_number             number,
11   description             varchar2(80),
12   result                  varchar2(256),
13   unique_session_id       varchar2(24)               not null,
14   insert_user             varchar2(30)  default USER not null,
15   insert_date             date          default SYSDATE not null )
16   tablespace USERS pctfree 0
17   storage (initial 1M next 1M pctincrease 0);
18
19   alter  table TEST_T add
20   constraint   TEST_T_PK
```

```
21   primary key (
22   id )
23   using index
24   tablespace USERS pctfree 0
25   storage (initial 1M next 1M pctincrease 0);
26
27   drop   sequence TEST_ID_SEQ;
28   create sequence TEST_ID_SEQ
29   start with 1 order;
30
31   analyze table TEST_T estimate statistics;
32
33   grant all on TEST_T to PUBLIC;
```

Now that I have a table to store results, let's get to writing a testing tool package.

A TEST Package Specification

In my testing tool's package, I define a set of variables or constants that are suitable as insert values for SQL statements. I can then use these predefined values when writing test units. This approach has several advantages. First, global use of these testing values will create an environment where testing is done with consistency. In turn, because of that consistency, everyone involved in testing will know what these predefined values are, and then know that they are looking at test data if they encounter these values while testing.

Listing 8-3 is the package specification for my testing tool. On the top half of the specification, I've added globally accessible constants to be utilized by all programmers when writing their test units. These are followed by methods designed to aid programmers when writing their test units. By using these methods, the test data is consistently formatted and stored for easy analysis.

Listing 8-3. *A Testing Tool Package Spec, test_ts.pks*

```
001   create or replace package TEST_TS as
002   /*
003   test_ts.pks
004   by Donald J. Bales on 12/15/2006
005   A Testing package
006   */
007
008   -- Result constants
009   v_TEST_ERROR              constant  varchar2(5) := 'ERROR';
010   v_TEST_OK                 constant  varchar2(2) := 'OK';
011   v_TEST_SUCCESS            constant  varchar2(7) := 'SUCCESS';
012
013   -- Testing constants
014   d_TEST_19000101           constant  date        :=
015     to_date('19000101', 'YYYYMMDD');
```

```
016  d_TEST_19991231              constant  date         :=
017     to_date('19000101', 'YYYYMMDD');
018
019  v_TEST_N                     constant  varchar2(1) := 'N';
020
021  v_TEST_Y                     constant  varchar2(1) := 'Y';
022
023  v_TEST_30                    constant  varchar2(30) :=
024     'TEST TEST TEST TEST TEST TESTx';
025
026  v_TEST_30_1                  constant  varchar2(30) :=
027     'TEST1 TEST1 TEST1 TEST1 TEST1x';
028
029  v_TEST_30_2                  constant  varchar2(30) :=
030     'TEST2 TEST2 TEST2 TEST2 TEST2x';
031
032  v_TEST_80                    constant  varchar2(80) :=
033     'Test Test Test Test Test Test Test Test '||
034     'Test Test Test Test Test Test Test Testx';
035
036  v_TEST_100                   constant  varchar2(100) :=
037     'Test Test Test Test Test Test Test Test Test Test '||
038     'Test Test Test Test Test Test Test Test Test Testx';
039
040  v_TEST_2000                  constant  varchar2(2000) :=
041     'Test Test Test Test Test Test Test Test Test Test '||
...
080     'Test Test Test Test Test Test Test Test Test Testx';
081
082  --          1         2         3         4         5
083  -- 12345678901234567890123456789012345678901234567890
084
085  -- Clear the results of the last test
086  PROCEDURE clear(
087  aiv_object_name                    TEST_T.object_name%TYPE);
088
089
090  -- Set the result of the last test to v_TEST_ERROR
091  PROCEDURE error;
092
093
094  -- Set the result of the last test to the passed Oracle error
095  PROCEDURE error(
096  aiv_result                 in    TEST_T.result%TYPE);
097
```

```
098
099   -- Display help text
100   PROCEDURE help;
101
102
103   -- Instantiate the package
104   PROCEDURE initialize;
105
106
107   -- Set the result of the last test to v_TEST_OK
108   PROCEDURE ok;
109
110
111   -- Update the test with its results
112   PROCEDURE set_result(
113   aiv_result                    in      TEST_T.result%TYPE);
114
115
116   -- Add a test
117   PROCEDURE set_test(
118   aiv_object_name               in      TEST_T.object_name%TYPE,
119   aiv_method_name               in      TEST_T.method_name%TYPE,
120   ain_test_number               in      TEST_T.test_number%TYPE,
121   aiv_description               in      TEST_T.description%TYPE);
122
123
124   -- Set the result of the last test to v_TEST_SUCCESS
125   PROCEDURE success;
126
127
128   -- Test unit
129   PROCEDURE test;
130
131
132   end TEST_TS;
133   /
134   @se.sql TEST_TS
```

Let's examine Listing 8-3, line by line:

Lines 9 through 11 add three character constants, ERROR, OK, and SUCCESS, to be used as values for parameter aiv_result, when calling method result(). OK means the test completed successfully, and ERROR means the test did not complete successfully. Constant SUCCESS is called only at the end of a program unit's test unit after recording a test for the package or user-defined TYPE in question, in order to flag that the package or TYPE's test unit completely successfully, without raising any uncaught exceptions. If an uncaught exception does occur, the programmer should pass the value of SQLERRM as the result.

Lines 14 through 80 add constants to be used globally for testing inserts into SQL tables. These "testing" values not only self-document their values as test values, but also exercise the maximum column size constraints on the columns for tables for which they are used to test.

Lines 86 and 87 declare method `clear()`, which a program should call at the beginning of a test unit in order to clear any previous test results before staring a new round of tests.

Line 91 declares method `error()`, which a program should call to record that the test resulted in an error.

Lines 95 and 96 declare an overridden version of method `error()`, which takes one argument. A program should call this method if it needs to record an Oracle exception error message.

Lines 107 and 108 declare method `ok()`, which a program should call to record that an individual test completed without errors.

Lines 112 and 113 declare the method `set_result()`. Methods `error()`, `ok()`, and `success()` call this method to record testing results. This method uses `pragma autonomous_transaction` so entries are not lost if the test fails in the program unit in question because of an uncaught exception.

Lines 117 through 121 declare the method `set_test()`, which a programmer should use to record a test that is about to be executed inside a test unit. This method also uses `pragma autonomous_transaction` so entries are not lost if the test fails in the program unit in question because of an uncaught exception.

Line 125 declares method `success()`, which a program should call at the end of a test unit to flag that the entire test unit completed successfully. That doesn't mean that there weren't errors during the individual tests; it means that the method `test()` itself was completely executed.

Line 129 declares the standard test unit method to be used by every package and user-defined TYPE: `test()`. This is where a programmer codes the test units for every associated PL/SQL program unit. You'll see an example in the testing tool's package body shortly.

The test result constants OK, ERROR, and SUCCESS make it easy to identify errors after tests are run. If you want to know which test unit methods failed, just write a query where you list every object in the table TEST_T that doesn't have a row where the `object_name` can also be found with a result value of SUCCESS. If you want to know which individual tests failed, write a query to list the rows where column `result` starts with ERR or ORA. I'll show you a couple of sample queries like these in the "Automating Testing" section later in this chapter.

Now let's look at the implementation.

A TEST Package Body

Now that you've seen the specification for my testing tool, let's look at its implementation, including an example of its use. Listing 8-4 is the DDL to create the package body for package TEST_TS.

Listing 8-4. *A Testing Tool Package Body, test_ts.pkb*

```
001  create or replace package body TEST_TS as
002  /*
003  test_ts.pkb
004  by Donald J. Bales on 12/15/2006
005  A Testing package
006  */
007
008  -- Hold this value across calls to test() and result()
009  n_id                            TEST_T.id%TYPE;
010
011
012  PROCEDURE clear(
013  aiv_object_name                 TEST_T.object_name%TYPE) is
014
015  pragma autonomous_transaction;
016
017  begin
018    delete TEST_T
019    where  object_name      = aiv_object_name
020    and    unique_session_id = SYS.DBMS_SESSION.unique_session_id;
021
022    commit;
023  end clear;
024
025
026  PROCEDURE error is
027
028  begin
029    set_result(v_TEST_ERROR);
030  end error;
031
032
033  PROCEDURE error(
034  aiv_result                  in     TEST_T.result%TYPE) is
035
036  begin
037    set_result(aiv_result);
038  end error;
039
040
041  FUNCTION get_id
042  return                          TEST_T.id%TYPE is
043
044  n_id                            TEST_T.id%TYPE;
045
046  begin
```

```
047    select TEST_ID_SEQ.nextval
048    into   n_id
049    from   SYS.DUAL;
050
051    return n_id;
052 end get_id;
053
054
055 PROCEDURE help is
056 begin
057    pl('You''re on your own buddy.');
058 end help;
059
060
061 PROCEDURE initialize is
062 begin
063    null;
064 end;
065
066
067 PROCEDURE ok is
068
069 begin
070    set_result(v_TEST_OK);
071 end ok;
072
073
074 PROCEDURE set_result(
075 aiv_result                  in      TEST_T.result%TYPE) is
076
077 pragma autonomous_transaction;
078
079 begin
080    update TEST_T
081    set    result = aiv_result
082    where  id = n_id;
083
084    if nvl(sql%rowcount, 0) = 0 then
085      raise_application_error(-20000, 'Can''t find test'||
086        to_char(n_id)||
087        ' on update TEST'||
088        ' in TEST_TS.test');
089    end if;
090
091    n_id := NULL;
092
093    commit;
```

```
094   end set_result;
095
096
097   PROCEDURE set_test(
098   aiv_object_name                 in      TEST_T.object_name%TYPE,
099   aiv_method_name                 in      TEST_T.method_name%TYPE,
100   ain_test_number                 in      TEST_T.test_number%TYPE,
101   aiv_description                 in      TEST_T.description%TYPE) is
102
103   pragma autonomous_transaction;
104
105   begin
106     n_id := get_id();
107
108     begin
109       insert into TEST_T (
110             id,
111             object_name,
112             method_name,
113             test_number,
114             description,
115             result,
116             unique_session_id,
117             insert_user,
118             insert_date )
119       values (
120             n_id,
121             upper(aiv_object_name),
122             upper(aiv_method_name),
123             ain_test_number,
124             aiv_description,
125             NULL,
126             SYS.DBMS_SESSION.unique_session_id,
127             USER,
128             SYSDATE );
129     exception
130       when OTHERS then
131         raise_application_error(-20000, SQLERRM||
132           ' on insert TEST'||
133           ' in TEST_TS.test');
134     end;
135     commit;
136   end set_test;
137
138
139   PROCEDURE success is
140
```

```
141  begin
142    set_result(v_TEST_SUCCESS);
143  end success;
144
145
146  PROCEDURE test is
147
148  n_number                                number;
149
150  begin
151    pl('TESTS.test()');
152    clear('TEST_TS');
153
154    TEST_TS.set_test('TEST_TS', NULL, 1,
155      'Is v_TEST_N equal to N?');
156    if v_TEST_N = 'N' then
157      TEST_TS.ok();
158    else
159      TEST_TS.error();
160    end if;
161
162    TEST_TS.set_test('TEST_TS', NULL, 2,
163      'Is the length of v_TEST_N equal to 1?');
164    if nvl(length(v_TEST_N), 0) = 1 then
165      TEST_TS.ok();
166    else
167      TEST_TS.error();
168    end if;
169
170    TEST_TS.set_test('TEST_TS', NULL, 3,
171      'Is v_TEST_Y equal to Y?');
172    if v_TEST_Y = 'Y' then
173      TEST_TS.ok();
174    else
175      TEST_TS.error();
176    end if;
177
178    TEST_TS.set_test('TEST_TS', NULL, 4,
179      'Is the length of v_TEST_Y equal to 1?');
180    if nvl(length(v_TEST_Y), 0) = 1 then
181      TEST_TS.ok();
182    else
183      TEST_TS.error();
184    end if;
185
186    TEST_TS.set_test('TEST_TS', NULL, 5,
187      'Is the length of v_TEST_30 equal to 30?');
```

```
188     if nvl(length(v_TEST_30), 0) = 30 then
189       TEST_TS.ok();
190     else
191       TEST_TS.error();
192     end if;
193
194     TEST_TS.set_test('TEST_TS', NULL, 6,
195       'Is the length of v_TEST_30_1 equal to 30?');
196     if nvl(length(v_TEST_30_1), 0) = 30 then
197       TEST_TS.ok();
198     else
199       TEST_TS.error();
200     end if;
201
202     TEST_TS.set_test('TEST_TS', NULL, 7,
203       'Is the length of v_TEST_30_2 equal to 30?');
204     if nvl(length(v_TEST_30_2), 0) = 30 then
205       TEST_TS.ok();
206     else
207       TEST_TS.error();
208     end if;
209
210     TEST_TS.set_test('TEST_TS', NULL, 8,
211       'Is the length of v_TEST_80 equal to 80?');
212     if nvl(length(v_TEST_80), 0) = 80 then
213       TEST_TS.ok();
214     else
215       TEST_TS.error();
216     end if;
217
218     TEST_TS.set_test('TEST_TS', NULL, 9,
219       'Is the length of v_TEST_100 equal to 100?');
220     if nvl(length(v_TEST_100), 0) = 100 then
221       TEST_TS.ok();
222     else
223       TEST_TS.error();
224     end if;
225
226     TEST_TS.set_test('TEST_TS', NULL, 10,
227       'Is the length of v_TEST_2000 equal to 2000?');
228     if nvl(length(v_TEST_2000), 0) = 2000 then
229       TEST_TS.ok();
230     else
231       TEST_TS.error();
232     end if;
233
234     TEST_TS.set_test('TEST_TS', 'get_id', 11,
```

```
235        'Does get_id() work?');
236      begin
237        n_number := get_id();
238        if n_number > 0 then
239          TEST_TS.ok();
240        else
241          TEST_TS.error();
242        end if;
243      exception
244        when OTHERS then
245          TEST_TS.error(SQLERRM);
246      end;
247
248      TEST_TS.set_test('TEST_TS', 'help', 12,
249        'Does help() work?');
250      begin
251        help;
252        TEST_TS.ok();
253      exception
254        when OTHERS then
255          TEST_TS.error(SQLERRM);
256      end;
257
258      TEST_TS.set_test('TEST_TS', NULL, NULL, NULL);
259      TEST_TS.success();
260    end test;
261
262
263    end TEST_TS;
264    /
265    @be.sql TESTS
```

Let's look at Listing 8-4 in detail:

Lines 12 through 23 implement procedure clear(), which is called by method test() to remove any previous test for the same unique session ID.

Lines 26 through 30 implement procedure error(), which is called by method test() to record a generic error.

Lines 33 through 38 implement procedure error(), which is called by method test() inside an exception handler, in order to record an Oracle exception's error message.

■**Note** Do you find the use of the same method names for more than one purpose disturbing? This is called *overriding* the method names. One error() method is used to record a generic error, while the second is used to record an Oracle error message.

Lines 41 through 52 implement function get_id(), which returns the next primary key value to be used when inserting a row into table TEST_T.

Lines 67 through 71 implement procedure ok(), which is called by method test() to record the success of an individual test.

Lines 74 through 94 implement procedure set_result(), which updates the last recorded test with the passed result value. This method uses an instance-level variable, n_id, in coordination with procedure test(). test() saves the last id it allocates to variable n_id in the package's memory, and then set_result() uses that value when saving the result. I do this to reduce the amount of coding required by the test unit writer.

Lines 97 through 136 implement procedure set_test(), which is used by test unit writers to record that a test is about to take place.

Lines 139 through 143 implement procedure success(), which is called by method test() to indicate the successful execution of the test unit itself.

Lines 146 through 260 implement procedure test(), which is the actual test unit for package TEST_TS. Yes, I've used the testing tool to test the testing tool. Neat, huh?

Line 148, inside the test unit method test(), declares a number variable to temporarily hold the result of one of the tests.

Line 151 calls pl() to give feedback to the tester that the test has been started.

Line 152 calls procedure TEST_TS.clear(), passing the name of the object in order to remove any previous test results.

Lines 154 and 155 call procedure TEST_TS.test(), passing it the information about the test I'm about to perform.

Line 156 performs my first test, to see if the constant TEST_TS.v_TEST_N has the correct value. Since I'm certain that this test cannot cause an exception, I have not blocked the code for the test.

Line 157 sets the result for the test to constant TEST_TS.v_TEST_OK by calling procedure ok() if v_TEST_N is indeed the character N; otherwise, on line 159, I set the result to TEST_TS.v_TEST_ERROR by calling procedure error().

Lines 162 through 232 perform tests on the remaining constants in a similar fashion. With all these tests, I'm confident that an exception cannot possibly be raised, so I don't block the test code. This is not so for the next test.

Lines 234 and 235 call procedure TEST_TS.test() in order to record that I'm about to perform a test of function get_id().

Lines 236 through 246 block the call to method get_id() in order to catch any unexpected exception. Next, I execute my actual test, a call to get_id(). If there is no unexpected exception, the next line, 238, tests to see if the ID value was greater than zero. If so, I call method ok(); otherwise, I call error(). If an exception does occur, I call error() passing the value of SQLERRM.

Lines 250 through 256 block a call to help() and then test it in a fashion similar to the previous test.

Line 258 calls test() for the package, therefore passing only the object's name.

Line 259 calls procedure success(). These last two calls will indicate that the test procedure test() itself completed successfully, instead of possibly aborting somewhere in the midst of the test from an unhandled exception.

Now that I've shown you my relational testing tool, it's your turn to create an object-relational version.

It's Your Turn to Create a Testing Tool

Your assignment is to re-create the testing tool I've just shown you as an object-relational TYPE instead of a package. There's one twist, though. You can't declare constants, pseudo-constants, or variables in a TYPE, as I did in the TEST_TS package specification, so you'll need to declare additional parameterless functions that return the constant values.

To create an object-relational testing tool, follow these steps:

1. Write a DDL script to create a TYPE specification named TEST_O. This type should have an attribute for every column name in table TEST_T. It should also have corresponding methods for each method found in package TEST_TS. In addition, you'll add parameterless functions in the place of the constants in package TEST_TS. Include the method signature for, but skip, coding the methods help() and test(). We'll work on coding test() in the next section, and help() in the next chapter.

2. Save your script as test_o.tps.

3. Compile your script: SQL> @test_o.tps.

4. Write a DDL script to create the object table TEST_OT of TEST_O.

5. Save your script as test_ot.tab.

6. Compile your script: SQL> @test_ot.tab.

7. Write a DDL script to create the TYPE BODY for TEST_O.

8. Save your script as test_o.tpb.

9. Compile your script: SQL> @test_o.tpb.

But what about testing your new test tool? I'll devote the entire next section to that task. Do you want to see my solution for this exercise? Listings 8-5, 8-6, and 8-7 are the DDL for the TYPE specification, table, and body, respectively, for my version of TYPE TEST_O.

Listing 8-5. *A DDL Script for TYPE TEST_O's Spec, test_o.tps*

```
01  drop    type TEST_O;
02  create type TEST_O as object (
03  /*
```

```
04  test_o.tps
05  by Donald J. Bales on 12/15/2006
06  A Type for logging test results
07  */
08  -- Type TEST_O's attributes
09  id                                number,
10  object_name                       varchar2(30),
11  method_name                       varchar2(30),
12  test_number                       number,
13  description                       varchar2(80),
14  result                            varchar2(256),
15  unique_session_id                 varchar2(24),
16  insert_user                       varchar2(30),
17  insert_date                       date,
18  -- Allocate the next primary key value for id
19  STATIC FUNCTION get_id
20  return                            number,
21  -- Get the test value for January 1, 1900
22  STATIC FUNCTION get_test_19000101
23  return                            date,
24  -- Get the test value for December 31, 1999
25  STATIC FUNCTION get_test_19991231
26  return                            date,
27  -- Get the test value N for any indicators
28  STATIC FUNCTION get_test_n
29  return                            varchar2,
30  -- Get the test value Y for any indicators
31  STATIC FUNCTION get_test_y
32  return                            varchar2,
33  -- Get the 30 character test value
34  STATIC FUNCTION get_test_30
35  return                            varchar2,
36  -- Get the first 30 character test value duplicate for LIKE
37  STATIC FUNCTION get_test_30_1
38  return                            varchar2,
39  -- Get the second 30 character test value duplicate for LIKE
40  STATIC FUNCTION get_test_30_2
41  return                            varchar2,
42  -- Get the 80 character test value
43  STATIC FUNCTION get_test_80
44  return                            varchar2,
45  -- Get the 100 character test value
46  STATIC FUNCTION get_test_100
47  return                            varchar2,
48  -- Get the 2000 character test value
49  STATIC FUNCTION get_test_2000
50  return                            varchar2,
```

```
51  -- Clear any previous test run for the specified object name
52  STATIC PROCEDURE clear(
53  aiv_object_name                       varchar2),
54  -- Set the result to ERROR
55  MEMBER PROCEDURE error,
56  -- Set the result to Oracle ERROR
57  MEMBER PROCEDURE error(
58  aiv_result                 in     varchar2),
59  -- Set the result to the specified result value
60  MEMBER PROCEDURE set_result(
61  aiv_result                 in     varchar2),
62  -- Show the help text for this object
63  STATIC PROCEDURE help,
64  -- Set the result to OK
65  MEMBER PROCEDURE ok,
66  -- Set the result of the execution of test() to SUCCESS
67  MEMBER PROCEDURE success,
68  -- Test this object
69  STATIC PROCEDURE test,
70  -- Set the test about to be performed
71  MEMBER PROCEDURE set_test(
72  aiv_object_name            in     varchar2,
73  aiv_method_name            in     varchar2,
74  ain_test_number            in     number,
75  aiv_description            in     varchar2),
76  -- Get the map value
77  MAP MEMBER FUNCTION to_map
78  return                            number,
79  -- Parameterless constructor
80  CONSTRUCTOR FUNCTION test_o(
81  self                       in out nocopy test_o)
82  return                     self as result,
83  -- Convenience constructor
84  CONSTRUCTOR FUNCTION test_o(
85  self                       in out nocopy test_o,
86  ain_id                     in     number,
87  aiv_object_name            in     varchar2,
88  aiv_method_name            in     varchar2,
89  ain_test_number            in     number,
90  aiv_description            in     varchar2)
91  return                     self as result
92  );
93  /
94  @se.sql
95
96  grant execute on TEST_O to public;
```

In Listing 8-5, the TYPE specification for TEST_O, I added the static functions get_test_ 19000101() through get_test_2000() to act as and replace the constants d_TEST_19000101 through v_TEST_2000 from the package TEST_TS specification on lines 14 through 80.

Listing 8-6. *The DDL Script for Table TEST_OT, test_ot.tab*

```
01   rem test_ot.tab
02   rem by Donald Bales on 12/15/2006
03   rem Create test results
04
05   drop   table TEST_OT;
06   create table TEST_OT of TEST_O
07   tablespace USERS pctfree 0
08   storage (initial 1M next 1M pctincrease 0);
09
10   alter  table TEST_OT add
11   constraint   TEST_OT_PK
12   primary key (
13   id )
14   using index
15   tablespace USERS pctfree 0
16   storage (initial 1M next 1M pctincrease 0);
17
18   --drop   sequence TEST_ID_SEQ;
19   --create sequence TEST_ID_SEQ
20   --start with 1 order;
21
22   analyze table TEST_OT estimate statistics;
23
24   grant all on TEST_OT to PUBLIC;
```

There's nothing really new in Listing 8-6, the script to create a table based on TYPE TEST_O. I commented out lines 18 through 20, because I've already created the sequence in question when I created the relational table TEST_T.

Listing 8-7. *A DDL Script for TYPE TEST_O's BODY, test_o.tpb*

```
001   create or replace type body TEST_O as
002   /*
003   test_o.tpb
004   by Donald J. Bales on 12/15/2006
005   A Type for logging test results
006   */
007
008   STATIC PROCEDURE clear(
009   aiv_object_name                    varchar2) is
010
011   pragma autonomous_transaction;
```

```
012
013  begin
014    delete TEST_OT
015    where   object_name        = aiv_object_name
016    and     unique_session_id = SYS.DBMS_SESSION.unique_session_id;
017
018    commit;
019  end clear;
020
021
022  STATIC FUNCTION get_id
023  return                             number is
024
025  n_id                               number;
026
027  begin
028    select TEST_ID_SEQ.nextval
029    into   n_id
030    from   SYS.DUAL;
031
032    return n_id;
033  end get_id;
034
035
036  STATIC FUNCTION get_test_19000101
037  return                             date is
038
039  begin
040    return to_date('19000101', 'YYYYMMDD');
041  end get_test_19000101;
042
043
044  STATIC FUNCTION get_test_19991231
045  return                             date is
046
047  begin
048    return to_date('19991231', 'YYYYMMDD');
049  end get_test_19991231;
050
051
052  STATIC FUNCTION get_test_n
053  return                             varchar2 is
054
055  begin
056    return 'N';
057  end get_test_n;
058
```

```
059
060   STATIC FUNCTION get_test_y
061   return                              varchar2 is
062
063   begin
064     return 'Y';
065   end get_test_y;
066
067
068   STATIC FUNCTION get_test_30
069   return                              varchar2 is
070
071   begin
072     return 'TEST TEST TEST TEST TEST TESTx';
073   end get_test_30;
074
075
076   STATIC FUNCTION get_test_30_1
077   return                              varchar2 is
078
079   begin
080     return 'TEST1 TEST1 TEST1 TEST1 TEST1x';
081   end get_test_30_1;
082
083
084   STATIC FUNCTION get_test_30_2
085   return                              varchar2 is
086
087   begin
088     return 'TEST2 TEST2 TEST2 TEST2 TEST2x';
089   end get_test_30_2;
090
091
092   STATIC FUNCTION get_test_80
093   return                              varchar2 is
094
095   begin
096     return 'Test Test Test Test Test Test Test Test '||
097             'Test Test Test Test Test Test Test Testx';
098   end get_test_80;
099
100
101   STATIC FUNCTION get_test_100
102   return                              varchar2 is
103
104   begin
105     return 'Test Test Test Test Test Test Test Test Test Test '||
```

```
106              'Test Test Test Test Test Test Test Test Test Testx';
107  end get_test_100;
108
109
110  STATIC FUNCTION get_test_2000
111  return                             varchar2 is
112  --              1        2        3        4        5
113  --        12345678901234567890123456789012345678901234567890
114  begin
115    return 'Test Test Test Test Test Test Test Test Test Test '||
116           'Test Test Test Test Test Test Test Test Test Test '||
...
154           'Test Test Test Test Test Test Test Test Test Testx';
155  end get_test_2000;
156
157
158  STATIC PROCEDURE help is
159  begin
160    pl('You''re on your own buddy.');
161  end help;
162
163
164  MEMBER PROCEDURE error is
165
166  begin
167    set_result('ERROR');
168  end error;
169
170
171  MEMBER PROCEDURE error(
172  aiv_result                in     varchar2) is
173
174  begin
175    set_result(aiv_result);
176  end error;
177
178
179  MEMBER PROCEDURE ok is
180
181  begin
182    set_result('OK');
183  end ok;
184
185
186  MEMBER PROCEDURE set_result(
187  aiv_result                in     varchar2) is
188
```

```
189   pragma autonomous_transaction;
190
191   begin
192     result := aiv_result;
193
194     update TEST_OT
195     set    result = self.result
196     where  id = self.id;
197
198     if nvl(sql%rowcount, 0) = 0 then
199       raise_application_error(-20000, 'Can''t find test'||
200         to_char(self.id)||
201         ' on update TEST'||
202         ' in TEST_TS.test');
203     end if;
204
205     self := new test_o();
206
207     commit;
208   end set_result;
209
210
211   MEMBER PROCEDURE set_test(
212   aiv_object_name              in      varchar2,
213   aiv_method_name              in      varchar2,
214   ain_test_number              in      number,
215   aiv_description              in      varchar2) is
216
217   pragma autonomous_transaction;
218
219   begin
220     self.id                := TEST_O.get_id();
221     self.object_name       := upper(aiv_object_name);
222     self.method_name       := upper(aiv_method_name);
223     self.test_number       := ain_test_number;
224     self.description       := aiv_description;
225     self.result            := NULL;
226     self.unique_session_id := SYS.DBMS_SESSION.unique_session_id;
227     self.insert_user       := USER;
228     self.insert_date       := SYSDATE;
229
230     begin
231       insert into TEST_OT values (self);
232     exception
233       when OTHERS then
234         raise_application_error(-20000, SQLERRM||
235           ' on insert TEST_OT'||
```

```
236            ' in TEST_O.set_test');
237     end;
238     commit;
239 end set_test;
240
241
242 MEMBER PROCEDURE success is
243
244 begin
245     set_result('SUCCESS');
246 end success;
247
248
249 STATIC PROCEDURE test is
250
251 n_number                        number;
252 o_test                          TEST_O;
253
254 begin
255     pl('TEST_O.test()');
256
257     -- A defect requires the schema owner
258     &_USER..TEST_O.clear('TEST_O');
259
260     o_test := new TEST_O();
261     o_test.set_test('TEST_O', NULL, 1,
262       'Is get_test_N equal to N?');
263     if TEST_O.get_test_N = 'N' then
264       o_test.success();
265     else
266       o_test.error();
267     end if;
268
269     o_test.set_test('TEST_O', NULL, 2,
270       'Is the length of get_test_N equal to 1?');
271     if nvl(length(TEST_O.get_test_N), 0) = 1 then
272       o_test.success();
273     else
274       o_test.error();
275     end if;
276
277     o_test.set_test('TEST_O', NULL, 3,
278       'Is get_test_Y equal to Y?');
279     if TEST_O.get_test_Y = 'Y' then
280       o_test.success();
281     else
282       o_test.error();
```

```
283    end if;
284
285    o_test.set_test('TEST_0', NULL, 4,
286      'Is the length of get_test_Y equal to 1?');
287    if nvl(length(TEST_0.get_test_Y), 0) = 1 then
288      o_test.success();
289    else
290      o_test.error();
291    end if;
292
293    o_test.set_test('TEST_0', NULL, 5,
294      'Is the length of get_test_30 equal to 30?');
295    if nvl(length(TEST_0.get_test_30), 0) = 30 then
296      o_test.success();
297    else
298      o_test.error();
299    end if;
300
301    o_test.set_test('TEST_0', NULL, 6,
302      'Is the length of get_test_30_1 equal to 30?');
303    if nvl(length(TEST_0.get_test_30_1), 0) = 30 then
304      o_test.success();
305    else
306      o_test.error();
307    end if;
308
309    o_test.set_test('TEST_0', NULL, 7,
310      'Is the length of get_test_30_2 equal to 30?');
311    if nvl(length(TEST_0.get_test_30_2), 0) = 30 then
312      o_test.success();
313    else
314      o_test.error();
315    end if;
316
317    o_test.set_test('TEST_0', NULL, 8,
318      'Is the length of get_test_80 equal to 80?');
319    if nvl(length(TEST_0.get_test_80), 0) = 80 then
320      o_test.success();
321    else
322      o_test.error();
323    end if;
324
325    o_test.set_test('TEST_0', NULL, 9,
326      'Is the length of get_test_100 equal to 100?');
327    if nvl(length(TEST_0.get_test_100), 0) = 100 then
328      o_test.success();
329    else
```

```
330      o_test.error();
331    end if;
332
333    o_test.set_test('TEST_O', NULL, 10,
334      'Is the length of get_test_2000 equal to 2000?');
335    if nvl(length(TEST_O.get_test_2000), 0) = 2000 then
336      o_test.success();
337    else
338      o_test.error();
339    end if;
340
341    o_test.set_test('TEST_O', 'get_id', 11,
342      'Does get_id() work?');
343    begin
344      n_number := TEST_O.get_id();
345      if n_number > 0 then
346        o_test.success();
347      else
348        o_test.error();
349      end if;
350    exception
351      when OTHERS then
352        o_test.error(SQLERRM);
353    end;
354
355    o_test.set_test('TEST_O', 'help', 12,
356      'Does help() work?');
357    begin
358      &_USER..TEST_O.help();
359      o_test.success();
360    exception
361      when OTHERS then
362        o_test.error(SQLERRM);
363    end;
364
365    o_test.set_test('TEST_O', NULL, NULL, NULL);
366    o_test.success();
367  end test;
368
369
370  MAP MEMBER FUNCTION to_map
371  return                                number is
372
373  begin
374    return self.id;
375  end to_map;
376
```

```
377
378  CONSTRUCTOR FUNCTION test_o(
379  self                        in out nocopy test_o)
380  return                              self as result is
381
382  begin
383    self.id                 := NULL;
384    self.object_name        := NULL;
385    self.method_name        := NULL;
386    self.test_number        := NULL;
387    self.description        := NULL;
388    self.result             := NULL;
389    self.unique_session_id  := NULL;
390    self.insert_user        := NULL;
391    self.insert_date        := NULL;
392
393    return;
394  end test_o;
395
396
397  CONSTRUCTOR FUNCTION test_o(
398  self                        in out nocopy test_o,
399  ain_id                      in      number,
400  aiv_object_name             in      varchar2,
401  aiv_method_name             in      varchar2,
402  ain_test_number             in      number,
403  aiv_description             in      varchar2)
404  return                              self as result is
405
406  begin
407    self.id                 := ain_id;
408    self.object_name        := aiv_object_name;
409    self.method_name        := aiv_method_name;
410    self.test_number        := ain_test_number;
411    self.description        := aiv_description;
412    self.result             := NULL;
413    self.unique_session_id  := SYS.DBMS_SESSION.unique_session_id;
414    self.insert_user        := USER;
415    self.insert_date        := SYSDATE;
416
417    return;
418  end test_o;
419
420
421  end;
422  /
423  @be.sql TEST_O
```

Did you notice in Listing 8-6 that I used the SQL*Plus defined variable &USER in the source listing? This is a work-around to a defect in the Oracle compiler when trying to resolve the name of a method that is part of the same TYPE BODY.

In the sections that follow, we'll use the relational testing tool to test packages and the object-relational tool you just created to test TYPEs. So let's move on to a discussion of testing with our new testing tools.

Testing

Do you recall our discussion about table types early in Chapter 1, where I said that tables fall into one of three categories: content, codes, or intersections? The types of methods and method names used by each of these three categories will follow a pattern. Content table packages (or TYPEs) will all have a similar set of methods and method names. Code table packages (or TYPEs) will also have a similar set of methods and method names. And so will intersection table packages (or TYPEs).

Accordingly, these three categories will have a pattern of tests that follows the set of methods and method names used by each category. Content table packages will generally have methods to insert, update, delete, and select a specified row from a table. In contrast, a code table will have only a method to get the ID value for a specified code, or code and description for a specified ID. Intersection table packages will have methods like content table packages, and additional methods suitable only for intersections.

So the SQL Circle of Life I talked about earlier in this chapter will be fully employed for content and intersection table packages but not for code table packages. Since content tables are usually dependent on one or more code tables, and intersection tables are dependent on two content tables, let's start with a code table package. I'll cover the testing of the WORKER_TYPE_T table package now, and you'll code and test the GENDER_T table package later in this section.

Testing a Code Table Package

As usual, let's dive right into a code listing. Listings 8-8 and 8-9 are the full-blown, production-ready packages for the WORKER_TYPE_T table.

The package specification lists methods that are specific to a code table:

get_code_descr(): Used to retrieve the code and description values for a specified ID.

get_code_id_descr(): Used to retrieve the code, ID, and description values for a fully or partially specified code. For a partially specified code, the method may return a single matching set of values or raise exception TOO_MANY_ROWS if more than one matching entry exists in the table.

get_id(): Returns the ID that corresponds to the specified code.

The package specification also lists some methods that are universal to all table packages:

get_id(): Returns a newly allocated primary key value for the table.

help(): Displays help text for the package.

test(): Tests the package.

Listing 8-8. *The Specification for Table Package WORKER_TYPE_TS, worker_type_ts.pks*

```
01  create or replace PACKAGE WORKER_TYPE_TS as
02  /*
03  worker_type_ts.pks
04  by Don Bales on 12/15/2006
05  Code Table WORKER_TYPE_T's methods.
06  */
07
08
09  -- Gets the code and description values for the specified work_type_id.
10  PROCEDURE get_code_descr(
11  ain_id                          in    WORKER_TYPE_T.id%TYPE,
12  aov_code                        out WORKER_TYPE_T.code%TYPE,
13  aov_description                 out WORKER_TYPE_T.description%TYPE );
14
15
16  -- Verifies the passed aiov_code value is an exact or like match on
17  -- the date specified.
18  PROCEDURE get_code_id_descr(
19  aiov_code                       in out WORKER_TYPE_T.code%TYPE,
20  aon_id                          out WORKER_TYPE_T.id%TYPE,
21  aov_description                 out WORKER_TYPE_T.description%TYPE,
22  aid_on                          in    WORKER_TYPE_T.active_date%TYPE );
23
24
25  -- Verifies the passed aiov_code value is currently an exact or like
26  -- match.
27  PROCEDURE get_code_id_descr(
28  aiov_code                       in out WORKER_TYPE_T.code%TYPE,
29  aon_id                          out WORKER_TYPE_T.id%TYPE,
30  aov_description                 out WORKER_TYPE_T.description%TYPE );
31
32
33  -- Returns a newly allocated id value.
34  FUNCTION get_id
35  return                          WORKER_TYPE_T.id%TYPE;
36
37
38  -- Returns the id for the specified code value.
39  FUNCTION get_id(
40  aiv_code                        in    WORKER_TYPE_T.code%TYPE )
41  return                          WORKER_TYPE_T.id%TYPE;
42
43
44  -- Text-based help for this package.  "set serveroutput on" in
45  -- SQL*Plus.
```

```
46   PROCEDURE help;
47
48
49   -- Test units for this package.
50   PROCEDURE test;
51
52
53   end WORKER_TYPE_TS;
54   /
55   @se.sql WORKER_TYPE_TS
```

Listing 8-9. *The Body for Table Package WORKER_TYPE_TS, worker_type_ts.pkb*

```
001   create or replace PACKAGE BODY WORKER_TYPE_TS as
002   /*
003   worker_type_ts.pkb
004   by Don Bales on 12/15/2006
005   Table WORKER_TYPE_T's methods
006   */
007
008
009   PROCEDURE get_code_descr(
010   ain_id                      in      WORKER_TYPE_T.id%TYPE,
011   aov_code                       out  WORKER_TYPE_T.code%TYPE,
012   aov_description                out  WORKER_TYPE_T.description%TYPE ) is
013
014   begin
015     select code,
016            description
017     into   aov_code,
018            aov_description
019     from   WORKER_TYPE_T
020     where  id = ain_id;
021   end get_code_descr;
022
023
024   PROCEDURE get_code_id_descr(
025   aiov_code                   in out  WORKER_TYPE_T.code%TYPE,
026   aon_id                         out  WORKER_TYPE_T.id%TYPE,
027   aov_description                out  WORKER_TYPE_T.description%TYPE,
028   aid_on                      in      WORKER_TYPE_T.active_date%TYPE ) is
029
030   v_code                              WORKER_TYPE_T.code%TYPE;
031
032   begin
033     select id,
034            description
```

```
035    into   aon_id,
036           aov_description
037    from   WORKER_TYPE_T
038    where  code = aiov_code
039    and    aid_on between active_date and nvl(inactive_date, DATES.d_MAX);
040  exception
041    when NO_DATA_FOUND then
042      select id,
043             code,
044             description
045      into   aon_id,
046             v_code,
047             aov_description
048      from   WORKER_TYPE_T
049      where  code like aiov_code||'%'
050      and    aid_on between active_date and nvl(inactive_date, DATES.d_MAX);
051
052      aiov_code := v_code;
053  end get_code_id_descr;
054
055
056  PROCEDURE get_code_id_descr(
057  aiov_code                      in out WORKER_TYPE_T.code%TYPE,
058  aon_id                            out WORKER_TYPE_T.id%TYPE,
059  aov_description                   out WORKER_TYPE_T.description%TYPE ) is
060
061  begin
062    get_code_id_descr(
063      aiov_code,
064      aon_id,
065      aov_description,
066      SYSDATE );
067  end get_code_id_descr;
068
069
070  FUNCTION get_id
071  return                         WORKER_TYPE_T.id%TYPE is
072
073  n_id                           WORKER_TYPE_T.id%TYPE;
074
075  begin
076    select WORKER_TYPE_ID_SEQ.nextval
077    into   n_id
078    from   SYS.DUAL;
079
080    return n_id;
081  end get_id;
```

```
082
083
084  FUNCTION get_id(
085  aiv_code                          in       WORKER_TYPE_T.code%TYPE )
086  return                                     WORKER_TYPE_T.id%TYPE is
087
088  n_id                                       WORKER_TYPE_T.id%TYPE;
089
090  begin
091    select id
092    into   n_id
093    from   WORKER_TYPE_T
094    where  code = aiv_code;
095
096    return n_id;
097  end get_id;
098
099
100  PROCEDURE help is
101
102  begin
...
156  end help;
157
158
159  PROCEDURE test is
160
161  n_id                              WORKER_TYPE_T.id%TYPE;
162  v_code                            WORKER_TYPE_T.code%TYPE;
163  v_description                     WORKER_TYPE_T.description%TYPE;
164
165  begin
166    -- Send feedback that the test ran
167    pl('WORKER_TYPE_TS.test()');
168
169    -- Clear the last set of test results
170    TEST_TS.clear('WORKER_TYPE_TS');
171
172    -- First, we need some test values
173
174    -- Let's make sure they don't already exist: DELETE
175    TEST_TS.set_test('WORKER_TYPE_TS', 'DELETE', 0,
176      'Delete test entries');
177    begin
178      delete WORKER_TYPE_T
179      where  code in (
180        TEST_TS.v_TEST_30,
```

```
181          TEST_TS.v_TEST_30_1,
182           TEST_TS.v_TEST_30_2);
183       TEST_TS.ok();
184    exception
185      when OTHERS then
186          TEST_TS.error(SQLERRM);
187    end;
188
189    -- Now let's add three test codes: INSERT
190    TEST_TS.set_test('WORKER_TYPE_TS', 'INSERT', 1,
191      'Insert 3 test entries');
192    begin
193      insert into WORKER_TYPE_T (
194              id,
195              code,
196              description,
197              active_date,
198              inactive_date )
199       values (
200              get_id(),
201              TEST_TS.v_TEST_30,
202              TEST_TS.v_TEST_80,
203              TEST_TS.d_TEST_19000101,
204              NULL );
205
206      insert into WORKER_TYPE_T (
207              id,
208              code,
209              description,
210              active_date,
211              inactive_date )
212       values (
213              get_id(),
214              TEST_TS.v_TEST_30_1,
215              TEST_TS.v_TEST_80,
216              TEST_TS.d_TEST_19000101,
217              TEST_TS.d_TEST_19991231 );
218
219      insert into WORKER_TYPE_T (
220              id,
221              code,
222              description,
223              active_date,
224              inactive_date )
225       values (
226              get_id(),
227              TEST_TS.v_TEST_30_2,
```

```
228              TEST_TS.v_TEST_80,
229              TEST_TS.d_TEST_19000101,
230              TEST_TS.d_TEST_19991231 );
231
232    TEST_TS.ok();
233  exception
234    when OTHERS then
235      TEST_TS.error(SQLERRM);
236  end;
237
238  -- Now that we have test entries,
239  -- let's test the package methods
240  TEST_TS.set_test('WORKER_TYPE_TS', 'get_id()', 2,
241    'Get the ID for the specified code');
242  begin
243    n_id := get_id(TEST_TS.v_TEST_30);
244
245    if n_id > 0 then
246      TEST_TS.ok();
247    else
248      TEST_TS.error();
249    end if;
250  exception
251    when OTHERS then
252      TEST_TS.error(SQLERRM);
253  end;
254
255  TEST_TS.set_test('WORKER_TYPE_TS', 'get_code_descr()', 3,
256    'Get the code and description for the specified ID');
257  begin
258    get_code_descr(
259      n_id,
260      v_code,
261      v_description);
262    if v_code       = TEST_TS.v_TEST_30 and
263      v_description = TEST_TS.v_TEST_80 then
264      TEST_TS.ok();
265    else
266      TEST_TS.error();
267    end if;
268  exception
269    when OTHERS then
270      TEST_TS.error(SQLERRM);
271  end;
272
273  TEST_TS.set_test('WORKER_TYPE_TS', 'get_code_id_descr()', 4,
274    'Get the code, ID, and description for the specified code');
```

```
275    begin
276      v_code := 'TEST';
277      get_code_id_descr(
278        v_code,
279        n_id,
280        v_description);
281      if v_code              = TEST_TS.v_TEST_30 and
282         n_id                > 0                  and
283         v_description       = TEST_TS.v_TEST_80 then
284        TEST_TS.ok();
285      else
286        TEST_TS.error();
287      end if;
288    exception
289      when OTHERS then
290        TEST_TS.error(SQLERRM);
291    end;
292
293    TEST_TS.set_test('WORKER_TYPE_TS', 'get_code_id_descr()', 5,
294      'Get the code, ID, and description for the specified date');
295    begin
296      v_code := 'TEST';
297      -- This test should raise a TOO_MANY_ROWS exception
298      -- because at least three duplicate values will be
299      -- on the date specified
300      get_code_id_descr(
301        v_code,
302        n_id,
303        v_description,
304        TEST_TS.d_TEST_19991231);
305      if v_code              = TEST_TS.v_TEST_30 and
306         n_id                > 0                  and
307         v_description       = TEST_TS.v_TEST_80 then
308        TEST_TS.ok();
309      else
310        TEST_TS.error();
311      end if;
312    exception
313      when TOO_MANY_ROWS then
314        TEST_TS.ok();
315      when OTHERS then
316        TEST_TS.error(SQLERRM);
317    end;
318
319    TEST_TS.set_test('WORKER_TYPE_TS', 'help()', 6,
320      'Display help');
321    begin
```

```
322      help();
323      TEST_TS.ok();
324    exception
325      when OTHERS then
326        TEST_TS.error(SQLERRM);
327    end;
328
329    -- Let's make sure they don't already exist: DELETE
330    TEST_TS.set_test('WORKER_TYPE_TS', 'DELETE', 7,
331      'Delete test entries');
332    begin
333      delete WORKER_TYPE_T
334      where  code in (
335        TEST_TS.v_TEST_30,
336        TEST_TS.v_TEST_30_1,
337        TEST_TS.v_TEST_30_2);
338      TEST_TS.ok();
339    exception
340      when OTHERS then
341        TEST_TS.error(SQLERRM);
342    end;
343
344    TEST_TS.set_test('WORKER_TYPE_TS', NULL, NULL, NULL);
345    TEST_TS.success();
346  end test;
347
348
349  end WORKER_TYPE_TS;
350  /
351  @be.sql WORKER_TYPE_TS
```

I'll explain only the test unit method test() in Listing 8-9 this time around:

Lines 161 through 163 declare a handful of variables that I will need while testing the package's methods.

Line 167 uses pl() to output some feedback to the tester that the test method did indeed execute.

Line 170 clears any previous test results for this package.

Lines 175 through 187 delete any existing "test" entries so they don't cause a problem with the current test. I do this with a SQL DELETE statement, because the code table package pattern of methods has no ongoing use for a routine that deletes code values.

Lines 190 through 236 insert three "test" entries into the code table. The first entry uses the standard 30-character value for the code. I'll try to find an exact match for this value later in testing. The second and third entries exist to cause a TOO_MANY_ROWS exception later in testing. Without explicitly testing the method, get_id(), the method that returns a new primary key value is also tested during the insertion of the three "test" entries.

Lines 240 through 253 test the second get_id() method, the code table package pattern method, which returns a code's ID value.

Lines 255 through 271 test method get_code_descr().

Lines 273 through 291 test the method get_code_id_descr() for an exact match on today's date.

Lines 293 through 317 test the method get_code_id_descr() to verify it will raise exception TOO_MANY_ROWS when there is no exact match.

Lines 319 through 327 test method help().

Lines 330 through 342 delete the "test" entries I added at the beginning of the test. This means I've used DELETE, INSERT, and then DELETE as the SQL Circle of Life for testing this code table package.

Lines 344 and 345 add the entry to the testing table that indicates the test method itself ran successfully.

I can now query the table TEST_T to find the results of the test. Listing 8-10 is a SQL*Plus script to list the results of the last performed test.

Listing 8-10. *A Report to Show the Results of the Last Test, last_test_results.sql*

```
01  rem last_test_results.sql
02  rem by Donald J. Bales on 12/15/2006
03  rem Display the last test results
04
05  set linesize 1000;
06  set newpage  1;
07  set pagesize 32767;
08  set trimspool on;
09
10  column test          format a34;
11  column t#            format 99;
12  column description   format a27;
13  column result        format a7;
14
15  spool last_test_results.txt;
16
17  select object_name||
18         decode(substr(method_name, -1, 1), ')', '.', ' ')||
19         method_name test,
20         test_number t#,
21         description,
22         result
23  from   TEST_T
24  where  unique_session_id = SYS.DBMS_SESSION.unique_session_id
25  and    object_name       = (
```

```
26   select object_name
27   from    TEST_T
28   where   unique_session_id = SYS.DBMS_SESSION.unique_session_id
29   and     id              = (
30   select max(id)
31   from    TEST_T
32   where   unique_session_id = SYS.DBMS_SESSION.unique_session_id))
33   order by id;
34
35   spool off;
```

When I run script last_test_results.sql after testing WORKER_TYPE_TS I get the following output from SQL*Plus:

```
TEST                                T# DESCRIPTION                     RESULT
----------------------------------- --- ----------------------------- -------
WORKER_TYPE_TS DELETE                0 Delete test entries            OK
WORKER_TYPE_TS INSERT                1 Insert 3 test entries          OK
WORKER_TYPE_TS.GET_ID()              2 Get the ID for the specifie OK
                                       d code

WORKER_TYPE_TS.GET_CODE_DESCR()      3 Get the code and descriptio OK
                                       n for the specified ID

WORKER_TYPE_TS.GET_CODE_ID_DESCR()   4 Get the code, ID, and descr OK
                                       iption for the specified co
                                       de

WORKER_TYPE_TS.GET_CODE_ID_DESCR()   5 Get the code, ID, and descr OK
                                       iption for the specified da
                                       te

WORKER_TYPE_TS.HELP()                6 Display help                   OK
WORKER_TYPE_TS DELETE                7 Delete test entries            OK
WORKER_TYPE_TS                                                        SUCCESS

9 rows selected.
```

If any of the tests failed, but the enclosing PL/SQL block caught any raised exception, then the column result would list the word ERROR or the reported Oracle error message from any raised exception. If the enclosing PL/SQL block around a test failed to catch a raised exception, then the test unit itself would not complete, and the last entry in the report, SUCCESS, would not exist. Now that you've seen me do it, it's your turn.

It's Your Turn to Test a Code Table Package

I tested the WORKER_TYPE_T code table package, and you'll test the GENDER_T code table package. The two tests should be very similar. You can find a full-blown, production-ready version of package GENDER_TS in the downloaded code directory for Chapter 8. I suggest you proceed as follows:

1. Copy the method WORKER_TYPE_TS.test() and paste it into package body GENDER_TS.

2. Modify the method for any column name and other changes.

3. Save and compile the package body.

4. Execute the test against GENDER_TS by executing method test().

5. Use report last_test_results.sql to see the results of your test.

No, I'm not going to show you my solution, because it follows the same pattern as any other code table package's test() method. Instead, let's move on to testing a content table's package.

Testing a Content Table Package

This time, for an example of a content table test unit, I'm going to show you only a partial code listing. Listing 8-11 is the test unit from the full-blown, production-ready package for the LOGICAL_WORKPLACE_T table. Its package specification (not shown) lists methods that are specific to a content table package (or TYPE):

get_name() or get_name_context(): Actually, in this case, since table LOGICAL_WORKPLACE_T has a hierarchical relationship with itself, the method is get_name_context(), which shows all the names in the hierarchy separated by periods (.).

get_external_id() or get_code_context(): Once again, since table LOGICAL_WORKPLACE_T has a hierarchical relationship with itself, the method is named get_code_context(), which shows all the external IDs in the hierarchy separated by periods (.).

get_row(): Returns a matching row depending on primary key column or unique key column value(s) set in the record passed to the method.

set_row(): Updates an existing matching row, using the same rules implemented by get_row() to find a matching row, or inserts a new row if a match is not found.

The package specification has one method that is unique to a hierarchical table:

create_id_context(): Creates a hierarchical unique key that represents the hierarchical relationship between rows in the same table as a character value separated by periods (.).

And it also has some methods that are universal to all table packages:

get_id(): Returns a newly allocated primary key value for the table.

help(): Displays help text for the package.

test(): Tests the package.

Listing 8-11. *The test() Method from Table Package Body LOGICAL_WORKPLACE_TS,*
logical_workplace_ts.pkb

```
264  PROCEDURE test is
265
266  /*
267  logical_workplace_t
268  Name                                     Null?     Type
269  ---------------------------------------- --------  -------------
270  ID                                       NOT NULL NUMBER
271  PARENT_ID                                         NUMBER
272  ID_CONTEXT                               NOT NULL VARCHAR2(100)
273  WORKPLACE_TYPE_ID                        NOT NULL NUMBER
274  CODE                                     NOT NULL VARCHAR2(30)
275  NAME                                     NOT NULL VARCHAR2(80)
276  ACTIVE_DATE                              NOT NULL DATE
277  INACTIVE_DATE                                     DATE
278  */
279
280  v_id_context
281    LOGICAL_WORKPLACE_T.id_context%TYPE;
282  r_logical_workplace              LOGICAL_WORKPLACE_T%ROWTYPE;
283
284  begin
285    pl('LOGICAL_WORKPLACE_TS.test()');
286
287    TEST_TS.clear('LOGICAL_WORKPLACE_TS');
288
289    TEST_TS.set_test('LOGICAL_WORKPLACE_TS', 'DELETE', 0,
290      'Delete existing test entries');
291    begin
292      delete LOGICAL_WORKPLACE_T
293      where  code in (
294        TEST_TS.v_TEST_30_1,
295        TEST_TS.v_TEST_30_2);
296
297      delete LOGICAL_WORKPLACE_T
298      where  code = TEST_TS.v_TEST_30;
299
300      TEST_TS.ok();
301    exception
302      when OTHERS then
303        TEST_TS.error(SQLERRM);
304    end;
305
306    TEST_TS.set_test('LOGICAL_WORKPLACE_TS', 'get_id()', 1,
307      'Allocate the next primary key value');
308    begin
```

```
309        r_logical_workplace.id                    := get_id();
310
311        if r_logical_workplace.id > 0 then
312          TEST_TS.ok();
313        else
314          TEST_TS.error();
315        end if;
316      exception
317        when OTHERS then
318          TEST_TS.error(SQLERRM);
319      end;
320
321      TEST_TS.set_test('LOGICAL_WORKPLACE_TS',
322        'create_id_context()', 2, 'Create an ID context value');
323      begin
324        r_logical_workplace.parent_id          := NULL;
325        r_logical_workplace.id_context         :=
326          create_id_context(
327            r_logical_workplace.parent_id,
328            r_logical_workplace.id);
329
330        if r_logical_workplace.id_context =
331          to_char(r_logical_workplace.id) then
332          TEST_TS.ok();
333        else
334          TEST_TS.error();
335        end if;
336      exception
337        when OTHERS then
338          TEST_TS.error(SQLERRM);
339      end;
340
341      TEST_TS.set_test('LOGICAL_WORKPLACE_TS', 'set_row()', 3,
342        'Insert parent test entry');
343      begin
344        r_logical_workplace.workplace_type_id   :=
345          WORKPLACE_TYPE_TS.get_id('C');
346        r_logical_workplace.code                :=
347          TEST_TS.v_TEST_30;
348        r_logical_workplace.name                :=
349          TEST_TS.v_TEST_80;
350        r_logical_workplace.active_date         :=
351          TEST_TS.d_TEST_19000101;
352        r_logical_workplace.inactive_date       := NULL;
353      set_row(r_logical_workplace);
354
```

```
355        TEST_TS.ok();
356     exception
357       when OTHERS then
358          TEST_TS.error(SQLERRM);
359     end;
360
361     TEST_TS.set_test('LOGICAL_WORKPLACE_TS', 'set_row()', 4,
362       'Insert child entries');
363     begin
364       r_logical_workplace.parent_id           :=
365          r_logical_workplace.id;
366       r_logical_workplace.id                   := get_id();
367       r_logical_workplace.id_context          :=
368         create_id_context(
369           r_logical_workplace.parent_id,
370           r_logical_workplace.id);
371       -- save this value for testing get_row()
372       v_id_context                             :=
373          r_logical_workplace.id_context;
374       r_logical_workplace.workplace_type_id    :=
375         WORKPLACE_TYPE_TS.get_id('B');
376       r_logical_workplace.code                 :=
377         TEST_TS.v_TEST_30_1;
378       r_logical_workplace.name                 :=
379         TEST_TS.v_TEST_80;
380       set_row(r_logical_workplace);
381
382
383       r_logical_workplace.id                   := get_id();
384       r_logical_workplace.id_context          :=
385         create_id_context(
386           r_logical_workplace.parent_id,
387           r_logical_workplace.id);
388       r_logical_workplace.code                 :=
389         TEST_TS.v_TEST_30_2;
390       set_row(r_logical_workplace);
391
392       TEST_TS.ok();
393     exception
394       when OTHERS then
395          TEST_TS.error(SQLERRM);
396     end;
397
398     TEST_TS.set_test('LOGICAL_WORKPLACE_TS', 'get_code_context()', 5,
399       'Get the code context for v_TEST_30_2');
```

```
400    begin
401      pl(get_code_context(
402        r_logical_workplace.id));
403
404      TEST_TS.ok();
405    exception
406      when OTHERS then
407        TEST_TS.error(SQLERRM);
408    end;
409
410    TEST_TS.set_test('LOGICAL_WORKPLACE_TS', 'get_name_context()', 6,
411      'Get the name context for v_TEST_30_2');
412    begin
413      pl(get_name_context(
414        r_logical_workplace.id));
415
416      TEST_TS.ok();
417    exception
418      when OTHERS then
419        TEST_TS.error(SQLERRM);
420    end;
421
422    TEST_TS.set_test('LOGICAL_WORKPLACE_TS', 'get_row()', 7,
423      'Get the row using the id for v_TEST_30_2');
424    begin
425 --    r_logical_workplace.id                := NULL;
426      r_logical_workplace.parent_id          := NULL;
427      r_logical_workplace.id_context         := NULL;
428      r_logical_workplace.workplace_type_id  := NULL;
429      r_logical_workplace.code               := NULL;
430      r_logical_workplace.name               := NULL;
431      r_logical_workplace.active_date        := NULL;
432      r_logical_workplace.inactive_date      := NULL;
433
434      r_logical_workplace := get_row(r_logical_workplace);
435
436      if r_logical_workplace.id_context is not NULL then
437        TEST_TS.ok();
438      else
439        TEST_TS.error();
440      end if;
441    exception
442      when OTHERS then
443        TEST_TS.error(SQLERRM);
444    end;
445
446    TEST_TS.set_test('LOGICAL_WORKPLACE_TS', 'get_row()', 8,
```

```
447        'Get the row using the id_context for v_TEST_30_1');
448      begin
449        r_logical_workplace.id                  := NULL;
450        r_logical_workplace.parent_id           := NULL;
451        r_logical_workplace.id_context          :=
452          v_id_context;
453        r_logical_workplace.workplace_type_id   := NULL;
454        r_logical_workplace.code                := NULL;
455        r_logical_workplace.name                := NULL;
456        r_logical_workplace.active_date         := NULL;
457        r_logical_workplace.inactive_date       := NULL;
458
459        r_logical_workplace := get_row(r_logical_workplace);
460
461        if r_logical_workplace.id is not NULL then
462          TEST_TS.ok();
463        else
464          TEST_TS.error();
465        end if;
466      exception
467        when OTHERS then
468          pl('v_id_context="'||v_id_context||'"');
469          TEST_TS.error(SQLERRM);
470      end;
471
472      TEST_TS.set_test('LOGICAL_WORKPLACE_TS', 'get_row()', 9,
473        'Get the row using the code for v_TEST_30');
474      begin
475        r_logical_workplace.id                  := NULL;
476        r_logical_workplace.parent_id           := NULL;
477        r_logical_workplace.id_context          := NULL;
478        r_logical_workplace.workplace_type_id   := NULL;
479        r_logical_workplace.code                :=
480          TEST_TS.v_TEST_30;
481        r_logical_workplace.name                :=
482          TEST_TS.v_TEST_80;
483        r_logical_workplace.active_date         :=
484          TEST_TS.d_TEST_19000101;
485        r_logical_workplace.inactive_date       := NULL;
486
487        r_logical_workplace := get_row(r_logical_workplace);
488
489        if r_logical_workplace.id is not NULL then
490          TEST_TS.ok();
491        else
492          TEST_TS.error();
493        end if;
```

```
494    exception
495      when OTHERS then
496         TEST_TS.error(SQLERRM);
497    end;
498
499    TEST_TS.set_test('LOGICAL_WORKPLACE_TS', 'help()', 10,
500      'Display the help text');
501    begin
502      help();
503
504      TEST_TS.ok();
505    exception
506      when OTHERS then
507         TEST_TS.error(SQLERRM);
508    end;
509
510    TEST_TS.set_test('LOGICAL_WORKPLACE_TS', 'DELETE', 11,
511      'Delete test entries');
512    begin
513      delete LOGICAL_WORKPLACE_T
514      where  code in (
515        TEST_TS.v_TEST_30_1,
516        TEST_TS.v_TEST_30_2);
517
518      delete LOGICAL_WORKPLACE_T
519      where  code = TEST_TS.v_TEST_30;
520
521      TEST_TS.ok();
522    exception
523      when OTHERS then
524         TEST_TS.error(SQLERRM);
525    end;
526
527    commit;
528    TEST_TS.set_test('LOGICAL_WORKPLACE_TS', NULL, NULL, NULL);
529    TEST_TS.success();
530  end test;
```

The test unit for package LOGICAL_WORKPLACE_TS is quite lengthy, so that's why I'm using a partial listing in Listing 8-11. You can find the entire listing in the download directory for Chapter 8.

Let's examine this content table package's test unit line by line:

Lines 280 through 282 declare two variables that I use during the test.

Line 285 outputs some feedback so the tester knows the test has actually executed.

Line 287 clears any previous test data.

Lines 287 through 304 start the SQL Circle of Life for my test entries by pre-deleting any that may still exist.

Lines 306 through 319 test method get_id().

Lines 321 through 339 test method create_id_context().

Lines 341 through 359 test method set_row() by inserting a parent company row based on TEST_TS.v_TEST_30. This begins the INSERT portion of the SQL Circle of Life.

Lines 361 through 396 test method set_row() again, this time inserting two child rows, business units, based on TEST_TS.v_TEST_30_1 and TEST_TS.v_TEST_30_2. This begins the INSERT or UPDATE portion of the SQL Circle of Life.

Lines 398 through 408 test method get_code_context(). This starts the SELECT portion of the SQL Circle of Life.

Lines 410 through 420 test method get_name_context().

Lines 422 through 444 test method get_row() using the primary key column.

Lines 446 through 470 test method get_row() a second time, using the unique id_context column.

Lines 472 through 497 test method get_row() a third time, this time using unique columns: code, name, and active_date.

Lines 499 through 508 test method help().

Lines 510 through 525 delete my test entries from the table. This brings us full circle on our SQL Circle of Life, from DELETE to INSERT to UPDATE to SELECT, and then back to DELETE.

Finally, on lines 528 through 529, I record that the test unit executed successfully.

Did you notice that this example, a content table package's test unit, used the full SQL Circle of Life, whereas the code table package used only a portion of it? And did you see that every test was blocked—executed in its own PL/SQL block in order to catch any raised exceptions, rather than abort the test unit? Now it's your turn.

It's Your Turn to Test a Content Table Package

Now you will create a test unit for content table package PHYSICAL_WORKPLACE_T. In case you haven't noticed yet, table PHYSICAL_WORKPLACE_T is extremely similar to table LOGICAL_WORKPLACE_T, so you should be able to do some "code borrowing" to create a table package for PHYSICAL_WORKPLACE_T, including its test unit method test(). Please follow these steps:

1. Write the DDL scripts to create a table package for table PHYSICAL_WORKPLACE_T by borrowing the code from LOGICAL_WORKPLACE_TS. This means you'll need to do some thinking about the differences between the two tables, and the resulting differences between the two packages, and then make the appropriate changes.

2. Save your specification script as physical_workplace_ts.pks, and your body script as physical_workplace_ts.pkb.

3. Compile your package.

4. Execute the test unit: SQL> execute physical_workplace.test();.

5. Use script last_test_results.sql to view the outcome of your test unit.

6. Add a test to your test unit to change the inactive date for business unit TEST_TS.v_TEST_CODE_30_2 to TEST_TS.d_TEST_19991231.

7. Execute the test unit again: SQL> execute physical_workplace.test();.

8. Use script last_test_results.sql to view the outcome of your test unit.

Once again, I'm not going to show you my solution. But you can find it in the solutions download directory for Chapter 8.

Next, let's test an intersection table package.

Testing an Intersection Table Package

It's time to test the third category of the dynamic trio: an intersection table package. As in the previous example, Listing 8-12 is a partial code listing, showing the test unit from the full-blown, production-ready package for the LOGICAL_ASSIGNMENT_T table. In case you've forgotten, LOGICAL_ASSIGNMENT_T holds a list (a history) of logical assignments for a worker, such as which department the person worked for from one point in time to another. Its package specification lists methods that are specific to an intersection table package (or TYPE):

get_logical_workplace(): Returns the LOGICAL_WORKPLACE_T assigned at the specified point in time.

is_active(): Returns TRUE if the specified worker has a logical assignment at the specified point in time.

The package specification contains several methods in common with a content table package:

get_row(): Returns a matching row depending on primary key column or unique key column value(s) set in the record passed to the method.

set_row(): Updates an existing matching row, using the same rules implemented by get_row() to find a matching row, or inserts a new row if a match is not found.

And the package specification also has some methods that are universal to all table packages:

get_id(): Returns a newly allocated primary key value for the table.

help(): Display help text for the package.

test(): Tests the package.

Listing 8-12. *The test() Method from Table Package Body LOGICAL_ASSIGNMENT_TS,*
logical_assignment_ts.pkb

```
195  PROCEDURE test is
196
197  n_logical_workplace_id
198    LOGICAL_WORKPLACE_T.logical_workplace_id%TYPE;
199  n_logical_workplace_id_1
200    LOGICAL_WORKPLACE_T.logical_workplace_id%TYPE;
201  n_logical_workplace_id_2
202    LOGICAL_WORKPLACE_T.logical_workplace_id%TYPE;
203  n_worker_id                         WORKER_T.worker_id%TYPE;
204  n_worker_id_1                       WORKER_T.worker_id%TYPE;
205  n_worker_id_2                       WORKER_T.worker_id%TYPE;
206  r_worker                            WORKER_T%ROWTYPE;
207  r_logical_workplace                 LOGICAL_WORKPLACE_T%ROWTYPE;
208  r_logical_assignment                LOGICAL_ASSIGNMENT_T%ROWTYPE;
209
210  begin
211    pl('LOGICAL_ASSIGNMENT_TS.test()');
212
213    TEST_TS.clear('LOGICAL_ASSIGNMENT_TS');
214
215    -- In order to make entries into an Intersection table
216    -- you first have to have entries in the two tables
217    -- for which an entry will create an intersection
218    TEST_TS.set_test('LOGICAL_ASSIGNMENT_TS', 'DELETE', 0,
219      'Delete existing test entries from LOGICAL_ASSIGNMENT_T');
220    begin
221      delete LOGICAL_ASSIGNMENT_T
222      where  logical_workplace_id in (
223      select logical_workplace_id
224      from   LOGICAL_WORKPLACE_T
225      where  code in (
226        TEST_TS.v_TEST_30,
227        TEST_TS.v_TEST_30_1,
228        TEST_TS.v_TEST_30_2 ) );
229
230      delete LOGICAL_ASSIGNMENT_T
231      where  worker_id in (
232      select worker_id
233      from   WORKER_T
234      where  external_id in (
235        TEST_TS.v_TEST_30,
236        TEST_TS.v_TEST_30_1,
237        TEST_TS.v_TEST_30_2 ) );
238
```

```
239       TEST_TS.ok();
240    exception
241      when OTHERS then
242         TEST_TS.error(SQLERRM);
243    end;
244
245    TEST_TS.set_test('LOGICAL_ASSIGNMENT_TS', 'DELETE', 1,
246       'Delete existing test entries from LOGICAL_WORKPLACE_T');
247    begin
248      delete LOGICAL_WORKPLACE_T
249      where  code in (
250        TEST_TS.v_TEST_30_1,
251        TEST_TS.v_TEST_30_2 );
252
253      delete LOGICAL_WORKPLACE_T
254      where  code in (
255        TEST_TS.v_TEST_30 );
256
257      TEST_TS.ok;
258    exception
259      when OTHERS then
260         TEST_TS.error(SQLERRM);
261    end;
262
263    TEST_TS.set_test('LOGICAL_ASSIGNMENT_TS', 'DELETE', 2,
264       'Delete existing test entries from WORKER_T');
265    begin
266      delete WORKER_T
267      where  external_id in (
268        TEST_TS.v_TEST_30,
269        TEST_TS.v_TEST_30_1,
270        TEST_TS.v_TEST_30_2 );
271
272      TEST_TS.ok();
273    exception
274      when OTHERS then
275         TEST_TS.error(SQLERRM);
276    end;
277
278    TEST_TS.set_test('LOGICAL_ASSIGNMENT_TS', 'INSERT', 3,
279       'Insert WORKER_T test entries using set_row()');
280    begin
281      r_worker.worker_id      := WORKER_TS.get_id();
282      r_worker.worker_type_id := WORKER_TYPE_TS.get_id('E');
283      r_worker.external_id    := TEST_TS.v_TEST_30;
284      r_worker.first_name     := TEST_TS.v_TEST_30;
285      r_worker.middle_name    := TEST_TS.v_TEST_30;
```

```
286        r_worker.last_name       := TEST_TS.v_TEST_30;
287        r_worker.name            := WORKER_TS.get_formatted_name(
288          r_worker.first_name,
289          r_worker.middle_name,
290          r_worker.last_name);
291        r_worker.birth_date      := to_date('19800101', 'YYYYMMDD');
292        r_worker.gender_id       := GENDER_TS.get_id('M');
293        WORKER_TS.set_row(r_worker);
294        n_worker_id              := r_worker.worker_id;
295
296        r_worker.worker_id       := WORKER_TS.get_id();
297        r_worker.worker_type_id  := WORKER_TYPE_TS.get_id('E');
298        r_worker.external_id     := TEST_TS.v_TEST_30_1;
299        r_worker.first_name      := TEST_TS.v_TEST_30_1;
300        r_worker.middle_name     := TEST_TS.v_TEST_30_1;
301        r_worker.last_name       := TEST_TS.v_TEST_30_1;
302        r_worker.name            := WORKER_TS.get_formatted_name(
303          r_worker.first_name,
304          r_worker.middle_name,
305          r_worker.last_name);
306        r_worker.birth_date      := to_date('19700101', 'YYYYMMDD');
307        r_worker.gender_id       := GENDER_TS.get_id('F');
308        WORKER_TS.set_row(r_worker);
309        n_worker_id_1            := r_worker.worker_id;
310
311        r_worker.worker_id       := WORKER_TS.get_id();
312        r_worker.worker_type_id  := WORKER_TYPE_TS.get_id('C');
313        r_worker.external_id     := TEST_TS.v_TEST_30_2;
314        r_worker.first_name      := TEST_TS.v_TEST_30_2;
315        r_worker.middle_name     := TEST_TS.v_TEST_30_2;
316        r_worker.last_name       := TEST_TS.v_TEST_30_2;
317        r_worker.name            := WORKER_TS.get_formatted_name(
318          r_worker.first_name,
319          r_worker.middle_name,
320          r_worker.last_name);
321        r_worker.birth_date      := to_date('19600101', 'YYYYMMDD');
322        r_worker.gender_id       := GENDER_TS.get_id('M');
323        WORKER_TS.set_row(r_worker);
324        n_worker_id_2            := r_worker.worker_id;
325
326      TEST_TS.ok();
327    exception
328      when OTHERS then
329        TEST_TS.error(SQLERRM);
330    end;
331
332    TEST_TS.set_test('LOGICAL_ASSIGNMENT_TS', 'INSERT', 4,
```

```
333       'Insert LOGICAL_WORKPLACE_T test entries using set_row()');
334     begin
335       r_logical_workplace.logical_workplace_id :=
336         LOGICAL_WORKPLACE_TS.get_id();
337       r_logical_workplace.parent_id              := NULL;
338       r_logical_workplace.id_context             :=
339         LOGICAL_WORKPLACE_TS.create_id_context(
340           r_logical_workplace.parent_id,
341           r_logical_workplace.logical_workplace_id);
342       r_logical_workplace.workplace_type_id      :=
343         WORKPLACE_TYPE_TS.get_id('C');
344       r_logical_workplace.code                   := TEST_TS.v_TEST_30;
345       r_logical_workplace.name                   := TEST_TS.v_TEST_80;
346       r_logical_workplace.active_date            := TEST_TS.d_TEST_19000101;
347       r_logical_workplace.inactive_date          := NULL;
348       LOGICAL_WORKPLACE_TS.set_row(r_logical_workplace);
349       n_logical_workplace_id                     :=
350         r_logical_workplace.logical_workplace_id;
351
352       r_logical_workplace.logical_workplace_id :=
353         LOGICAL_WORKPLACE_TS.get_id();
354       r_logical_workplace.parent_id              :=
355         n_logical_workplace_id;
356       r_logical_workplace.id_context             :=
357         LOGICAL_WORKPLACE_TS.create_id_context(
358           r_logical_workplace.parent_id,
359           r_logical_workplace.logical_workplace_id);
360       r_logical_workplace.workplace_type_id      :=
361         WORKPLACE_TYPE_TS.get_id('B');
362       r_logical_workplace.code                   := TEST_TS.v_TEST_30_1;
363       r_logical_workplace.name                   := TEST_TS.v_TEST_80;
364       r_logical_workplace.active_date            := TEST_TS.d_TEST_19000101;
365       r_logical_workplace.inactive_date          := NULL;
366       LOGICAL_WORKPLACE_TS.set_row(r_logical_workplace);
367       n_logical_workplace_id_1                   :=
368         r_logical_workplace.logical_workplace_id;
369
370       r_logical_workplace.logical_workplace_id :=
371         LOGICAL_WORKPLACE_TS.get_id();
372       r_logical_workplace.parent_id              :=
373         n_logical_workplace_id;
374       r_logical_workplace.id_context             :=
375         LOGICAL_WORKPLACE_TS.create_id_context(
376           r_logical_workplace.parent_id,
377           r_logical_workplace.logical_workplace_id);
378       r_logical_workplace.workplace_type_id      :=
379         WORKPLACE_TYPE_TS.get_id('B');
```

```
380    r_logical_workplace.code                  := TEST_TS.v_TEST_30_2;
381    r_logical_workplace.name                  := TEST_TS.v_TEST_80;
382    r_logical_workplace.active_date           := TEST_TS.d_TEST_19000101;
383    r_logical_workplace.inactive_date       := NULL;
384    LOGICAL_WORKPLACE_TS.set_row(r_logical_workplace);
385    n_logical_workplace_id_2                :=
386      r_logical_workplace.logical_workplace_id;
387
388    TEST_TS.ok();
389  exception
390    when OTHERS then
391      TEST_TS.error(SQLERRM);
392  end;
393
394  -- Now that I have entries in the two tables being intersected
395  -- I can start testing this package...
396  TEST_TS.set_test('LOGICAL_ASSIGNMENT_TS', 'get_id()', 5,
397    'Allocate the next primary key value using get_id()');
398  begin
399    r_logical_assignment.id :=
400      LOGICAL_ASSIGNMENT_TS.get_id();
401
402    if nvl(r_logical_assignment.id, 0) > 0 then
403      TEST_TS.ok();
404    else
405      TEST_TS.error();
406    end if;
407  exception
408    when OTHERS then
409      TEST_TS.error(SQLERRM);
410  end;
411
412  TEST_TS.set_test('LOGICAL_ASSIGNMENT_TS', 'set_row()', 6,
413    'Insert history for v_TEST_30 using set_row()');
414  begin
415    r_logical_assignment.worker_id          := n_worker_id;
416    r_logical_assignment.logical_workplace_id :=
417      n_logical_workplace_id_2;
418    r_logical_assignment.active_date        :=
419      to_date('20000101', 'YYYYMMDD');
420    r_logical_assignment.inactive_date      := NULL;
421    LOGICAL_ASSIGNMENT_TS.set_row(r_logical_assignment);
422
423    TEST_TS.ok;
424  exception
425    when OTHERS then
426      TEST_TS.error(SQLERRM);
```

```
427    end;
...
604    -- Now clean up after the tests by deleting the test entries
605    TEST_TS.set_test('LOGICAL_ASSIGNMENT_TS', 'DELETE', 16,
606      'Delete existing test entries from LOGICAL_ASSIGNMENT_T');
607    begin
608      delete LOGICAL_ASSIGNMENT_T
609      where  logical_workplace_id in (
610      select logical_workplace_id
611      from   LOGICAL_WORKPLACE_T
612      where  code in (
613        TEST_TS.v_TEST_30,
614        TEST_TS.v_TEST_30_1,
615        TEST_TS.v_TEST_30_2 ) );
616
617      delete LOGICAL_ASSIGNMENT_T
618      where  worker_id in (
619      select worker_id
620      from   WORKER_T
621      where  external_id in (
622        TEST_TS.v_TEST_30,
623        TEST_TS.v_TEST_30_1,
624        TEST_TS.v_TEST_30_2 ) );
625
626      TEST_TS.ok();
627    exception
628      when OTHERS then
629        TEST_TS.error(SQLERRM);
630    end;
631
632    TEST_TS.set_test('LOGICAL_ASSIGNMENT_TS', 'DELETE', 17,
633      'Delete existing test entries from LOGICAL_WORKPLACE_T');
634    begin
635      delete LOGICAL_WORKPLACE_T
636      where  code in (
637        TEST_TS.v_TEST_30_1,
638        TEST_TS.v_TEST_30_2 );
639
640      delete LOGICAL_WORKPLACE_T
641      where  code in (
642        TEST_TS.v_TEST_30 );
643
644      TEST_TS.ok;
645    exception
646      when OTHERS then
647        TEST_TS.error(SQLERRM);
648    end;
```

```
649
650    TEST_TS.set_test('LOGICAL_ASSIGNMENT_TS', 'DELETE', 18,
651      'Delete existing test entries from WORKER_T');
652    begin
653      delete WORKER_T
654      where  external_id in (
655        TEST_TS.v_TEST_30,
656        TEST_TS.v_TEST_30_1,
657        TEST_TS.v_TEST_30_2 );
658
659      TEST_TS.ok();
660    exception
661      when OTHERS then
662        TEST_TS.error(SQLERRM);
663    end;
664
665    commit;
666    TEST_TS.set_test('LOGICAL_ASSIGNMENT_TS', NULL, NULL, NULL);
667    TEST_TS.success();
668  end test;
```

The important point about an intersection table package is that it is dependent on test entries in the two tables it intersects. So you'll see that on lines 215 through 392, I must start out by deleting any test entries in the "intersected" tables: WORKER_T and LOGICAL_WORKPLACE_T, and then I must add entries to these tables in order to have entries from which to establish an intersection entry. So every intersection table package must also insert and delete entries from the tables on which it is depends. Now it's your turn to work on an intersection table package.

It's Your Turn to Test an Intersection Table Package

You will now create a test unit for intersection table package PHYSICAL_ASSIGNMENT_T. Just as in the last exercise, the corresponding table for this exercise, PHYSICAL_ASSIGNMENT_T is extremely similar to table LOGICAL_ASSIGNMENT_T, so you should once again be able to do some "code borrowing" to create a table package for PHYSICAL_ASSIGNMENT_T, including its test unit method test(). Follow these steps:

1. Write the DDL scripts to create a table package for table PHYSICAL_ASSIGNMENT_T by borrowing the code from LOGICAL_ASSIGNMENT_TS.

2. Save your specification script as physical_assignment_ts.pks, and your body script as physical_assignment_ts.pkb.

3. Compile your package.

4. Execute the test unit: SQL> execute physical_assignment_ts.test();.

5. Use script last_test_results.sql to view the outcome of your test unit.

Once again, I'm not going to show you my solution. But you can find it in the solutions download directory for Chapter 8.

So just how different can it be to test a TYPE instead of a package? Let's find out.

Testing a Type

Testing a TYPE is not all that different from testing a package. The only significant difference is that when you declare the test() method in a TYPE, it must be declared as a STATIC method. And when you code the method, you must remember that you'll need to work with a variable of that TYPE, and instance, as well as the TYPE when performing your testing. If you don't have an instance of the TYPE, you won't be able to access and test all its methods.

Listing 8-13 is a partial listing of the TYPE TEST_O, an object-relational testing tool. This listing shows only the test unit for the TYPE itself.

Listing 8-13. *The Test Unit from TYPE TEST_O, test_o.tpb*

```
249  STATIC PROCEDURE test is
250
251  n_number                              number;
252  o_test                                TEST_O;
253
254  begin
255    pl('TEST_O.test()');
256
257    -- A defect requires the schema owner
258    &_USER..TEST_O.clear('TEST_O');
259
260    o_test := new TEST_O();
261    o_test.set_test('TEST_O', NULL, 1,
262      'Is get_test_N equal to N?');
263    if TEST_O.get_test_N = 'N' then
264      o_test.success();
265    else
266      o_test.error();
267    end if;
268
269    o_test.set_test('TEST_O', NULL, 2,
270      'Is the length of get_test_N equal to 1?');
271    if nvl(length(TEST_O.get_test_N), 0) = 1 then
272      o_test.success();
273    else
274      o_test.error();
275    end if;
276
277    o_test.set_test('TEST_O', NULL, 3,
278      'Is get_test_Y equal to Y?');
279    if TEST_O.get_test_Y = 'Y' then
280      o_test.success();
```

```
281    else
282      o_test.error();
283    end if;
284
285    o_test.set_test('TEST_O', NULL, 4,
286      'Is the length of get_test_Y equal to 1?');
287    if nvl(length(TEST_O.get_test_Y), 0) = 1 then
288      o_test.success();
289    else
290      o_test.error();
291    end if;
292
293    o_test.set_test('TEST_O', NULL, 5,
294      'Is the length of get_test_30 equal to 30?');
295    if nvl(length(TEST_O.get_test_30), 0) = 30 then
296      o_test.success();
297    else
298      o_test.error();
299    end if;
300
301    o_test.set_test('TEST_O', NULL, 6,
302      'Is the length of get_test_30_1 equal to 30?');
303    if nvl(length(TEST_O.get_test_30_1), 0) = 30 then
304      o_test.success();
305    else
306      o_test.error();
307    end if;
308
309    o_test.set_test('TEST_O', NULL, 7,
310      'Is the length of get_test_30_2 equal to 30?');
311    if nvl(length(TEST_O.get_test_30_2), 0) = 30 then
312      o_test.success();
313    else
314      o_test.error();
315    end if;
316
317    o_test.set_test('TEST_O', NULL, 8,
318      'Is the length of get_test_80 equal to 80?');
319    if nvl(length(TEST_O.get_test_80), 0) = 80 then
320      o_test.success();
321    else
322      o_test.error();
323    end if;
324
325    o_test.set_test('TEST_O', NULL, 9,
326      'Is the length of get_test_100 equal to 100?');
327    if nvl(length(TEST_O.get_test_100), 0) = 100 then
328      o_test.success();
```

```
329    else
330      o_test.error();
331    end if;
332
333    o_test.set_test('TEST_0', NULL, 10,
334      'Is the length of get_test_2000 equal to 2000?');
335    if nvl(length(TEST_0.get_test_2000), 0) = 2000 then
336      o_test.success();
337    else
338      o_test.error();
339    end if;
340
341    o_test.set_test('TEST_0', 'get_id', 11,
342      'Does get_id() work?');
343    begin
344      n_number := TEST_0.get_id();
345      if n_number > 0 then
346        o_test.success();
347      else
348        o_test.error();
349      end if;
350    exception
351      when OTHERS then
352        o_test.error(SQLERRM);
353    end;
354
355    o_test.set_test('TEST_0', 'help', 12,
356      'Does help() work?');
357    begin
358      &_USER..TEST_0.help();
359      o_test.success();
360    exception
361      when OTHERS then
362        o_test.error(SQLERRM);
363    end;
364
365    o_test.set_test('TEST_0', NULL, NULL, NULL);
366    o_test.success();
367  end test;
...
```

First, notice that I've declared the method as a STATIC procedure. This means it will be accessible from the TYPE itself, not through an instance of the type.

Second, on line 252, I declare a variable of the TYPE and then on line 260, I set the variable to a new instance of the TYPE. Then I use this instance when calling MEMBER methods in the test unit. Beyond those two major changes, the differences in methods test() in package TEST_TS and TYPE TEST_0 are only semantic (as in the variations in the programmer-created language).

Now that you have seen an example of testing a TYPE, it's your turn.

It's Your Turn to Test a Type

Now you'll select any TYPE that you've created so far, and code its test unit method test(). However, you'll use your object-relational testing tool. This means you'll also need to modify the SQL*Plus report last_test_results.sql so it queries your testing tool's object table TEST_OT. This time, I'm not even going to give you any steps. You've seen enough examples that you should be able to list the steps you need to complete in order to do this exercise. Good skill! Luck is for losers.

Now, it's time we move on to the automation of testing.

Automating Testing

Do you remember that in the beginning of this chapter I promised you a framework for automating your testing? Well, by utilizing information from Oracle's data dictionary and writing another program unit that calls all your test units, you can execute one PL/SQL method that will in turn execute every test() method you've written, and then report on the test results.

Although there are several data dictionary views that have information about packages, TYPEs, and their methods, the one best suited to our needs of identifying every package and TYPE that does and does not have a test() method is view SYS.ALL_ARGUMENTS. The following is a SQL*Plus description of the view:

```
SYS.ALL_ARGUMENTS
 Name                                      Null?    Type
 ----------------------------------------- -------- -------------
 OWNER                                     NOT NULL VARCHAR2(30)
 OBJECT_NAME                                        VARCHAR2(30)
 PACKAGE_NAME                                       VARCHAR2(30)
 OBJECT_ID                                 NOT NULL NUMBER
 OVERLOAD                                           VARCHAR2(40)
 ARGUMENT_NAME                                      VARCHAR2(30)
 POSITION                                  NOT NULL NUMBER
 SEQUENCE                                  NOT NULL NUMBER
 DATA_LEVEL                                NOT NULL NUMBER
 DATA_TYPE                                          VARCHAR2(30)
 DEFAULT_VALUE                                      LONG
 DEFAULT_LENGTH                                     NUMBER
 IN_OUT                                             VARCHAR2(9)
 DATA_LENGTH                                        NUMBER
 DATA_PRECISION                                     NUMBER
 DATA_SCALE                                         NUMBER
 RADIX                                              NUMBER
 CHARACTER_SET_NAME                                 VARCHAR2(44)
 TYPE_OWNER                                         VARCHAR2(30)
 TYPE_NAME                                          VARCHAR2(30)
 TYPE_SUBNAME                                       VARCHAR2(30)
 TYPE_LINK                                          VARCHAR2(128)
 PLS_TYPE                                           VARCHAR2(30)
```

CHAR_LENGTH	NUMBER
CHAR_USED	VARCHAR2(1)

And here is a sample of the data in the view:

OBJECT_NAME	PACKAGE_NAME	OBJECT_ID	OVERLOAD	ARGUMENT_NAME
TEST	WORKER_TYPE_TS	72692		
HELP	WORKER_TYPE_TS	72692		
GET_ID	WORKER_TYPE_TS	72692	2	AIV_CODE
GET_ID	WORKER_TYPE_TS	72692	2	
GET_ID	WORKER_TYPE_TS	72692	1	
GET_CODE_ID_DESCR	WORKER_TYPE_TS	72692	2	AOV_DESCRIPTION
GET_CODE_ID_DESCR	WORKER_TYPE_TS	72692	2	AON_ID
GET_CODE_ID_DESCR	WORKER_TYPE_TS	72692	2	AIOV_CODE
GET_CODE_ID_DESCR	WORKER_TYPE_TS	72692	1	AID_ON
GET_CODE_ID_DESCR	WORKER_TYPE_TS	72692	1	AOV_DESCRIPTION
GET_CODE_ID_DESCR	WORKER_TYPE_TS	72692	1	AON_ID
GET_CODE_ID_DESCR	WORKER_TYPE_TS	72692	1	AIOV_CODE
GET_CODE_DESCR	WORKER_TYPE_TS	72692		AOV_DESCRIPTION
GET_CODE_DESCR	WORKER_TYPE_TS	72692		AOV_CODE
GET_CODE_DESCR	WORKER_TYPE_TS	72692		AIN_ID

...

Using the information provided by this view, we can write a query that does the following:

- Lists the name of every package and TYPE that has a test() method

- Lists the name of every package and TYPE that does not have a test() method

If we couple that information with the output of our test units that is stored in table TEST_T or TEST_OT, depending on which technology you choose, we can write a query that does the following:

- Lists information about every test that failed

- Lists the name of every package or TYPE where its test method failed

So the information provided by the data dictionary view SYS.ALL_ARGUMENTS and our testing tool's table TEST_T or TEST_OT arms us with all the information we need to automate the testing of our PL/SQL program unit and to report on the test results. Therefore, to automate the testing of our PL/SQL program units, all we need to do is follow these two simple steps:

1. Add a test unit method test() to every PL/SQL package or TYPE definition.

2. Execute a process to execute each test unit method and report the results.

You already know how to do the first step, so let's see an example of how to do the second step.

Automate Test Processing

Listing 8-14 is an example of a PL/SQL program unit that executes all coded test() methods for the current schema, and then reports on the results. It queries view SYS.ALL_ARGUMENTS to get a list of packages and TYPEs that do and do not have test() methods. It executes each test() method, recording the results of execution, as the test method itself records the results of each of its tests. Finally, it reports the results of the tests.

Listing 8-14. *An Example of a Test Unit Processing, test.sql*

```
001  rem test.sql
002  rem by Donald J. Bales on 12/15/2006
003  rem An anonymous PL/SQL procedure to execute all test units
004  rem and to report on the results of each test.
005
006  declare
007
008  -- Get the names of all packages and types that have a test unit
009  cursor c_test is
010  select a.package_name
011  from   SYS.ALL_ARGUMENTS a
012  where  a.owner       = USER
013  and    a.object_name = 'TEST'
014  and    nvl(a.argument_name, 'SELF') = 'SELF'
015  and not exists (
016  select 1
017  from   SYS.ALL_ARGUMENTS x
018  where  x.owner        = a.owner
019  and    x.package_name = a.package_name
020  and    x.object_name  = a.object_name
021  and    nvl(x.overload, 0) = nvl(a.overload, 0)
022  and    x.object_id    = a.object_id
023  and    nvl(a.argument_name, 'SELF') <> 'SELF' )
024  order by 1;
025
026  -- Get the names of all packages and types that don't have a test unit
027  cursor c_missing is
028  select a.package_name
029  from   SYS.ALL_ARGUMENTS a
030  where  a.owner       = USER
031  MINUS
032  select a.package_name
033  from   SYS.ALL_ARGUMENTS a
034  where  a.owner       = USER
035  and    a.object_name = 'TEST'
036  and    nvl(a.argument_name, 'SELF') = 'SELF'
037  and not exists (
038  select 1
```

```
039   from    SYS.ALL_ARGUMENTS x
040   where   x.owner         = a.owner
041   and     x.package_name = a.package_name
042   and     x.object_name  = a.object_name
043   and     nvl(x.overload, 0) = nvl(a.overload, 0)
044   and     x.object_id    = a.object_id
045   and     nvl(a.argument_name, 'SELF') <> 'SELF' )
046   order by 1;
047
048   -- Get the names of all packages and types that have test unit errors
049   cursor c_error is
050   select object_name||
051          decode(substr(method_name, -1, 1), ')', '.', ' ')||
052          method_name object_method,
053          test_number,
054          result
055   from    TEST_T
056   where   result <> 'OK'
057   and     result <> 'SUCCESS'
058   order by 1;
059
060   TYPE error_message_table is table of varchar2(255)
061   index by binary_integer;
062
063   n_error_message                     number := 0;
064   n_object_method_width               number := 39;
065   n_result_width                      number := 29;
066   n_status                            number;
067   n_test_number_width                 number := 5;
068
069   t_error_message                     error_message_table;
070
071   v_line                              varchar2(2000);
072
073   begin
074     -- Execute the test units
075     for r_test in c_test loop
076       begin
077         execute immediate 'begin '||r_test.package_name||'.test(); end;';
078       exception
079         when OTHERS then
080           n_error_message := n_error_message + 1;
081           t_error_message(n_error_message) :=
082             r_test.package_name||'.test() '||SQLERRM;
083       end;
084     end loop;
085     -- Empty the output buffer
```

```
086    loop
087      SYS.DBMS_OUTPUT.get_line(v_line, n_status);
088      if nvl(n_status, 0) < 1 then
089        exit;
090      end if;
091    end loop;
092    -- Show the test units that had errors
093    for r_error in c_error loop
094      if c_error%rowcount = 1 then
095        pl(chr(9));
096        pl('THE FOLLOWING OBJECT''S TEST UNITS HAD ERRORS:');
097        pl(chr(9));
098        pl(
099          rpad(
100            substr('OBJECT/METHOD',
101              1, n_object_method_width),
102            n_object_method_width, ' ')||
103          ' '||
104          lpad(
105            substr('TEST#',
106              1, n_test_number_width),
107            n_test_number_width, ' ')||
108          ' '||
109          rpad(
110            substr('ERROR',
111              1, n_result_width),
112            n_result_width, ' ')
113          );
114        pl(
115          rpad(
116            substr('-------------',
117              1, n_object_method_width),
118            n_object_method_width, '-')||
119          ' '||
120          lpad(
121            substr('-----',
122              1, n_test_number_width),
123            n_test_number_width, '-')||
124          ' '||
125          rpad(
126            substr('-----',
127              1, n_result_width),
128            n_result_width, '-')
129          );
130      end if;
131      pl(
132        rpad(
```

```
133            substr(r_error.object_method,
134              1, n_object_method_width),
135            n_object_method_width, ' ')||
136          ' '||
137          lpad(
138            substr(ltrim(to_char(r_error.test_number)),
139              1, n_test_number_width),
140            n_test_number_width, ' ')||
141          ' '||
142          rpad(
143            substr(r_error.result,
144              1, n_result_width),
145            n_result_width, ' ')
146          );
147      end loop;
148      -- Show the test units that failed to run
149      for i in t_error_message.first..t_error_message.last loop
150        if i = t_error_message.first then
151          pl(chr(9));
152          pl('THE FOLLOWING OBJECT''S TEST UNITS FAILED:');
153        end if;
154        pl(chr(9));
155        pl(t_error_message(i));
156      end loop;
157      -- Show the objects that are missing test units
158      for r_missing in c_missing loop
159        if c_missing%rowcount = 1 then
160          pl(chr(9));
161          pl('THE FOLLOWING OBJECTS ARE MISSING TEST UNITS:');
162          pl(chr(9));
163        end if;
164        pl(r_missing.package_name);
165      end loop;
166    end;
167    /
```

Let's break this listing down line by line:

Lines 9 through 24 declare a cursor, c_test, against data dictionary view SYS.ALL_ARGUMENTS, which gives me a list of packages and TYPEs that have a method test().

Lines 27 through 46 declare second cursor, c_missing, against SYS.ALL_ARGUMENTS, which gives me a list of packages and TYPEs that do not have a test() method.

Lines 49 through 58 declare a cursor, c_error, against table TEST_T that lists all the individual tests that failed during the current test run.

Lines 60 and 61 declare a PL/SQL table TYPE, error_message_table, which I will use to declare an array of exceptions raised during the execution of each test() method.

Lines 75 through 84 execute a cursor for loop, where I call each package and TYPE's test() method. I've blocked the dynamic call to each method, so I can capture and later report on any raised exceptions (test() method failures).

Lines 86 through 91 use a manual for loop to empty the SYS.DBMS_OUTPUT.put_line() buffer after having executed every test unit method. I do this to throw out any put_line() messages generated by each test unit.

Lines 93 through 147 report, using put_line(), about any test failures during the test run.

Lines 149 through 156 report any test() method failures during the test run. I could have created a fourth cursor to show me the test() methods that failed during execution, but I'm already getting this information from the blocked dynamic PL/SQL call to each method on lines 75 through 84.

Lines 158 through 165 list any packages or TYPEs that do not have a test unit method test().

The only thing this procedure cannot do is determine whether or not a programmer has actually taken the time to code the test unit. The following is sample output from this procedure while I was coding in my environment:

```
SQL> @test.sql


THE FOLLOWING OBJECT'S TEST UNITS HAD ERRORS:

OBJECT/METHOD                           TEST# ERROR
--------------------------------------- ----- -----------------------------
TEST_TS HELP                               12 ORA-20999: Testing test unit
TEST_TS HELP                               12 ORA-20999: Testing test unit

THE FOLLOWING OBJECT'S TEST UNITS FAILED:

GENDER_TS.test() ORA-20001: Test Failed

WORKER_O.test() ORA-06550: line 1, column 7:
PLS-00306: wrong number or types of arguments in call to 'TEST'
ORA-06550: line 1, column 7:
PL/SQL: Statement ignored

THE FOLLOWING OBJECTS ARE MISSING TEST UNITS:

DEBUG_O
DEBUG_OTS
DEBUG_TS
NUMBERS
PARAMETERS
SCOPES

PL/SQL procedure successfully completed.
```

The first part of the report, test unit errors, shows that exception ORA-20999 was raised while testing method TEST_TS.help(). This information tells you to go directly to package TEST_TS to examine what might be wrong with the test or the method help().

The second part of the report, test unit failures, shows that exception ORA-20001 was raised during the execution of GENDER_TS.test(). In addition, it shows that exception ORA-06550 was raised while executing WORKER_O.test(). Exception ORA-06550, in this case, is telling me that I declared method test() as a MEMBER method instead of a STATIC method. Oops. With this kind of information, you can go back to the test() method and properly block the test code so a particular test fails and reports why it failed, instead of the entire test method failing.

Finally, the third part of the report, missing test units, lists the packages and TYPEs that are missing a test unit method. With this information, you can add the task of coding test units for these to your to-do list. Don't ignore this list. Anything not tested is something that can and probably will produce errors.

In practice, on an enterprise application, I've seen a test unit process like this take two to three hours to execute. In addition, it always finds one to three errors in each newly coded package. As time goes by, and new defects are detected by end users and others, it's your responsibility to go back and update the test unit method to test for any newly reported defect. Using this kind of automated testing, combined with consistently adding any new test cases, you can make your persistence layer statistically error-free.

I don't think that the "processing" procedure just described should be external (losable) to the database/objectbase. Instead, it should be added to package TEST_TS as method process(). That way, you will be able to test any package or procedure by calling its test() method, and you can test the entire persistence layer by calling TEST_TS.process(). Now that's a powerful testing tool!

It's Your Turn to Automate Test Processing

For your final assignment in this chapter, modify your object-relational testing tool to add STATIC procedure process(), which will execute a program unit similar to test.sql using your testing tool's result table TEST_OT. Then execute TEST_O.process() to see the results of testing you object-relational persistence layer.

Summary

My hope is that you now realize how important, and easy, it is to properly test your PL/SQL program units. A couple of hours of extra coding up front for each program unit can save you hundreds of hours of troubleshooting later on. More important, it will save your end users from hundreds of hours of lost productivity and frustration.

I've shown you the coding patterns involved when coding test units for SQL and PL/SQL. I've shown you how to create a relational and object-relational testing tool that can automatically test every program unit and access to their associated tables in your database by executing one procedure: process().

My final suggestion is that you decide on the use of a relational or an object-relational testing tool and then add the required test units that access that tool to each and every program unit you write. As a developer of enterprise applications, I have had historically low error rates. I've achieved those by incorporating testing into the process of developing. Assume nothing. Test everything.

Just how important is it to test everything? During the coding of the examples for this book, this testing framework found an average of two errors for each package or TYPE. And I've been coding in PL/SQL for more than ten years!

There's one last tactic you can employ to help prevent errors: provide access to good documentation to your developers. And that's what we're going to cover in the next chapter.

■■■

What Does This Thing Do Anyway?

Once, when I was a young executive, I reported to the chief financial officer (CFO). Upon arriving at the new organization, I formulated a strategy to bring the company's computer technology up-to-date. Part of that plan was to provide each computer user in the organization with a computer that best suited that user's needs. This meant that executive administrators got high-powered desktop computers, while executives and consultants were armed with top-of-the-line notebooks. Not only did we make sure everyone was using the latest office automation software and groupware, we also built a state-of-the-art Executive Information System (EIS) that was tightly integrated with the accounting system.

The management team had no issues with authorizing capital expenditures for the computer hardware. Nor did they balk about the investment in software. But when it came to spending money to provide personnel with training so they could take advantage of the new hardware and software, I could not get approval from the CFO. Why? He explained to me that any time you train people, they just move on to a better-paying job, so training was counterproductive.

To say the least, I was amazed and dismayed at the same time. I thought to myself, and further argued with the management team, "Why did you invest in hardware and software if you never had any intention of training people how to use it?" No amount of arguing could move them on this issue. So from my perspective, they attained minimal gains from their investment in hardware and software. Do you find this attitude as strange as I do?

If you do, then you'll logically also have to agree with me that the development of any reusable software component has no value if you don't inform your programming staff members that the reusable component exists, and then educate them on how to use the component. At the very least, you should have some documentation they can refer to in order to find out what is available and how to use it!

Here's a second story. I once worked on a project for a major retailer to package some of its software for distribution to regional offices in the company. As part of that work, I wrote (the missing) technical reference and end-user tutorial documentation so the support staff could figure out how to support the software, and the end users would know how to use the software. A novel idea, don't you think? When it came time to send the software to each regional office, I was told that I first had to remove the documentation from the distribution. Why? Because the documentation held trade secrets that the personnel of the firm could not be trusted with. Argh!

If I ran a tool and die company that made nuts and bolts, created a catalog of available parts, but then never distributed it to perspective customers, I would be out of business in no time at all. If I ran an integrated circuit manufacturing firm, but didn't let anyone know that the firm existed and what electronic components it manufactured, once again, I would be filing for bankruptcy in less than a month.

What's my point? The day and age of the software components has been here for more than 20 years, but reuse depends on the distribution of documentation. Since the first machine language subroutine was written, that subroutine has been available as a reusable component. Since the first procedural programming language library was created, that library has been available as a reusable component. Since object-oriented languages first appeared on the scene, the creation of software components was made simple.

If you've programmed in Windows, you've used the 32-bit API, or better yet, the Microsoft Foundation Classes (MFC). If you've used PowerBuilder, you've had access to the PowerBuilder Foundation Classes (PFC). If you've programmed in Java, you've used the Java Foundation Classes (JFC). If you've programmed in PL/SQL, you've at least used the standard library. I could go on and on. These are all reusable software components.

If you're developing a solution to a business problem, you should have use-case narratives, use-case diagrams, process-flow diagrams, and so on to use a set of requirements for doing your programming work. During the creation of these documents, it should have become obvious what higher-level abstractions and patterns could be discerned from the end user's requirements. Using these abstractions and patterns, you can create components that are reusable through inheritance.

Furthermore, while developing, if you find yourself writing the same SQL statement or PL/SQL routine more than once, it's time to abstract that repeated pattern into a reusable component that can then be used by other components in your solution. If you do this, great! But if you don't document that each and every component exists, what it does, and how to use it, it doesn't exist outside the realm of your own mind. So you must—I mean *must*—document as you go. And second, you must provide other possible users a means to know that reusable (even non-reusable) components exist, what they can do, and how to use them. And that, my friend is what this chapter is all about.

In this chapter, I'll cover the following:

- Documentation that cannot be lost or thrown away

- Documentation that is available on demand

- Distributable documentation

Let's start with documentation that cannot be lost or thrown away.

Indestructible Documentation

What a silly notion—indestructible documentation. Or perhaps not? You know Murphy's Law don't you? "Anything that can go wrong will go wrong." It's easy to lose your documentation if it's stored on a file system that is not part of the ongoing application.

One of those beautiful things about PL/SQL is that the source code is permanently stored in the database. The only way to lose it is to lose the database, and at that point, who needs the source code?

Another beautiful thing about PL/SQL is that most executable code resides in either a package or TYPE specification. And these specifications allow you to comment the code. So the easiest way to document your packages and TYPEs is to put meaningful and properly formatted comments in each object's specification. At the very least, the text of the specification will then be available via the SYS.ALL_SOURCE view.

But before we make up our minds on what to document, how to document it, and where to put any documentation we do create, let's start by looking at what SQL*Plus provides us for package and TYPE documentation.

SQL*Plus Documentation Tools

In SQL*Plus, you can use the describe command to determine the format of a table or the call specifications of a function, procedure, package, or TYPE. Here's an example of using describe on the table WORKER_TYPE_T:

```
SQL> desc WORKER_TYPE_T
```

```
WORKER_TYPE_T
 Name                                      Null?    Type
 ----------------------------------------- -------- ------------
 WORKER_TYPE_ID                            NOT NULL NUMBER
 CODE                                      NOT NULL VARCHAR2(30)
 DESCRIPTION                               NOT NULL VARCHAR2(80)
 ACTIVE_DATE                               NOT NULL DATE
 INACTIVE_DATE                                      DATE
```

And here's an example of using the describe command on the package WORKER_TYPE_TS:

```
SQL> desc WORKER_TYPE_TS
```

```
WORKER_TYPE_TS
PROCEDURE GET_CODE_DESCR
 Argument Name                  Type                    In/Out Default?
 ------------------------------ ----------------------- ------ --------
 AIN_WORKER_TYPE_ID             NUMBER                  IN
 AOV_CODE                       VARCHAR2(30)            OUT
 AOV_DESCRIPTION                VARCHAR2(80)            OUT
PROCEDURE GET_CODE_ID_DESCR
 Argument Name                  Type                    In/Out Default?
 ------------------------------ ----------------------- ------ --------
 AIOV_CODE                      VARCHAR2(30)            IN/OUT
 AON_WORKER_TYPE_ID             NUMBER                  OUT
 AOV_DESCRIPTION                VARCHAR2(80)            OUT
 AID_ON                         DATE                    IN
PROCEDURE GET_CODE_ID_DESCR
 Argument Name                  Type                    In/Out Default?
 ------------------------------ ----------------------- ------ --------
 AIOV_CODE                      VARCHAR2(30)            IN/OUT
 AON_WORKER_TYPE_ID             NUMBER                  OUT
 AOV_DESCRIPTION                VARCHAR2(80)            OUT
FUNCTION GET_ID RETURNS NUMBER
```

```
FUNCTION GET_ID RETURNS NUMBER
Argument Name                     Type                      In/Out Default?
------------------------------    ----------------------    ------ --------
AIV_CODE                          VARCHAR2(30)              IN
PROCEDURE HELP
PROCEDURE TEST
```

The describe command shows the format of the table, or the signature of the methods, but nothing else. It doesn't provide an explanation as to what the column names in the table are supposed to store, nor what the methods may actually do.

Sometimes, you'll already know what a method can do, and you're just looking for its method signature. In that case, describe will suit your purpose. But describe will never be a suitable means of looking up documentation on how something works.

Let's see what GUI development environment tools can provide.

GUI Development Environment Tools

Tools like Oracle SQL Developer and TOAD for Oracle also show table formats and method signatures in much the same manner as SQL*Plus does. In Figures 9-1 and 9-2, you can see how Oracle SQL Developer presents information about a table and package methods. When it comes to help with a package or TYPE definition, Oracle SQL Developer simply displays the source for the package specification.

Figure 9-1. *A table definition as presented in Oracle SQL Developer*

Figure 9-2. *A package definition as presented in Oracle SQL Developer*

So how does TOAD present the same information? Look in Figures 9-3 and 9-4 for the answer. When it comes to package or TYPE information, TOAD also presents the source code of the package specification, just as Oracle SQL Developer does.

From looking at these two IDE program's examples, it occurs to me, once again, that the "best" place for documentation on what methods are for and how they actually work is right there in the specification source code itself, as properly formatted comments.

So if we properly format comments in a package or TYPE specification, we should be able to create a tool to display those comments, along with method call specifications as text or in any format. But first, we'll need to follow some commenting rules.

Figure 9-3. *A table definition as presented in TOAD*

Figure 9-4. *A package specification as presented in TOAD*

Rules for Documentation Comments

In order to be able to do any level of manipulation with the comments placed in the specifications for a package or TYPE, the use of the comments needs to be consistent from one specification to the next. To that end, a minimal set of rules to follow for adding comments to a specification will enable us to later display that information in various formats:

- Place a multiline descriptive comment at the very beginning of each package and TYPE specification. This comment includes the object name, author, date written, and modification history

- Place a single or multiline comment before every:

    - Package constant

    - Package variable

    - List of TYPE attributes

    - Method signature

Given we follow these two simple rules, we can next provide developers with documentation on demand.

Documentation on Demand

We can provide developers with documentation on demand by adding procedure help() to each and every package and TYPE specification. Then anytime they want to know what an executable object is for and what it can do, all they need to is execute its help() method. Here's an example:

```
SQL> WORKER_TYPE_TS.help();
```

But first, we need to code those help() methods so they do something when executed! Now I remember from an earlier chapter that you're a good primate and so am I, so I suggest we build our own tool—a text-based documentation formatting tool for package and TYPE specifications—and then add it as a command in each help() method.

A Text-Based Documentation Formatting Tool

Let's see, what would we like a text-based formatting tool to do for us? How about the following:

- Read a specification and format the output

- Remove any single-line or multiline comment delimiters

- Preserve any hard carriage returns in order to maintain vertical spacing

- Preserve any space or tab indentation in order to maintain horizontal spacing

 Using PL/SQL, we can accomplish these tasks:

- Read through the source code of a specification by accessing view SYS.ALL_SOURCE

- Parse out and replace any single-line or multiline comment delimiters

- Identify a hard carriage return and forward it on to `put_line()`

But the last requirement will be difficult. `put_line()`, our only means of displaying text from PL/SQL, will just truncate any leading spaces, so the best we can do is provide a hack where we send `put_line()` a tab character any time we have a source line that starts with a space character.

Now that we have some requirements, let's build a text-based help tool. Listing 9-1 is the package specification for a text-based documentation formatting tool, or "text-help" tool appropriately named `TEXT_HELP`.

Listing 9-1. *A Package Spec to Create Text-Based Help, text_help.pks*

```
01  create or replace PACKAGE TEXT_HELP as
02  /*
03  text_help.pkb
04  by Donald J. Bales on 12/15/2006
05  A package to produce text-based help
06  */
07
08  /*
09  The help text for this package.
10  */
11  PROCEDURE help;
12
13
14  /*
15  Generate help text for the specified object using its specification.
16  */
17  PROCEDURE process(
18  aiv_object_name            in      varchar2);
19
20
21  /*
22  The test unit for this package.
23  */
24  PROCEDURE test;
25
26
27  end text_help;
28  /
29  @se.sql
```

TEXT_HELP has three methods:

help(): Displays on-demand help for this package by utilizing its second method process().

process(): Retrieves the specified specification from view SYS.ALL_SOURCE, and then displays the specification as nicely formatted text.

test(): The test unit for this package.

Also notice that in Listing 9-1, I followed the commenting rules outlined earlier. Do as I say, *and* as I do!

Listing 9-2 is the implementation for TEXT_HELP. The only "new" method is process(). It's an ugly combination of parsing with substr() and an if-then-elsif-then-else-end if tree that implements the requirements outlined earlier in this section.

Listing 9-2. *A Package Body to Create Text-Based Help, text_help.pkb*

```
001  create or replace PACKAGE BODY TEXT_HELP as
002  /*
003  test_help.pkb
004  by Donald J. Bales on 12/15/2006
005  A package to produce text-based help
006  */
007
008  PROCEDURE help is
009
010  begin
011    TEXT_HELP.process('TEXT_HELP');
012  end help;
013
014
015  /*
016  A procedure to output formatted package or TYPE text
017  */
018  PROCEDURE out(
019  aiv_text                    in     varchar2) is
020
021  v_text                             varchar(255);
022  n_text                             number := 1;
023
024  begin
025    if nvl(length(aiv_text), 0) < 256 then
026      v_text := aiv_text;
027    else
028      v_text := substr(aiv_text, 1, 252)||'...';
029    end if;
```

```
030    if nvl(substr(v_text, 1, 1), chr(32)) = chr(32) then
031      if length(v_text) > 0 then
032        for i in 1..length(v_text) loop
033          if nvl(substr(v_text, i, 1), chr(32)) <> chr(32) then
034            n_text := i;
035            exit;
036          end if;
037        end loop;
038      end if;
039      SYS.DBMS_OUTPUT.put_line(chr(9)||substr(v_text, n_text));
040    else
041      SYS.DBMS_OUTPUT.put_line(v_text);
042    end if;
043  end out;
044
045
046  PROCEDURE process(
047  aiv_object_name              in      varchar2) is
048
049  cursor c1(
050  aiv_object_name              in      varchar2) is
051  select text
052  from    SYS.USER_SOURCE
053  where   name = upper(aiv_object_name)
054  and     type in ('PACKAGE', 'TYPE')
055  order by line;
056
057  b_method                          boolean := FALSE;
058  b_comment                         boolean := FALSE;
059  v_text                            SYS.USER_SOURCE.text%TYPE;
060
061  begin
062    for r1 in c1(aiv_object_name) loop
063      v_text := replace(replace(r1.text, chr(13), NULL), chr(10), NULL);
064      if    substr(ltrim(v_text), 1, 3) = '/* '                  then
065        if nvl(instr(v_text, '*/'), 0) = 0 then
066          b_comment := TRUE;
067        end if;
068        out(substr(ltrim(v_text), 4));
069      elsif substr(ltrim(v_text), 1, 2) = '/*'                   then
070        if nvl(instr(v_text, '*/'), 0) = 0 then
071          b_comment := TRUE;
072        end if;
073        out(substr(ltrim(v_text), 3));
```

```
074    elsif b_comment                                        and
075          substr(rtrim(v_text), -2, 2) = '*/'              then
076       b_comment := FALSE;
077       out(substr(rtrim(v_text), 1, length(rtrim(v_text)) - 2));
078    elsif b_comment                                        then
079       out(v_text);
080    elsif substr(ltrim(v_text), 1, 3) = '-- '              then
081       out(substr(ltrim(v_text), 4));
082    elsif substr(ltrim(v_text), 1, 2) = '--'               then
083       out(substr(ltrim(v_text), 3));
084    elsif upper(substr(ltrim(v_text), 1,  8)) = 'FUNCTION'          or
085          upper(substr(ltrim(v_text), 1,  9)) = 'PROCEDURE'         or
086          upper(substr(ltrim(v_text), 1, 15)) = 'MEMBER FUNCTION'   or
087          upper(substr(ltrim(v_text), 1, 16)) = 'MEMBER PROCEDURE'  or
088          upper(substr(ltrim(v_text), 1, 16)) = 'STATIC FUNCTION'   or
089          upper(substr(ltrim(v_text), 1, 16)) = 'STATIC PROCEDURE' then
090       if nvl(instr(v_text, ';'), 0) = 0 then
091         b_method := TRUE;
092       end if;
093       out(v_text);
094    elsif b_method                                         and
095          substr(rtrim(v_text), -1, 1) = ';'               then
096       b_method := FALSE;
097       out(v_text);
098    elsif b_method                                         then
099       out(v_text);
100    elsif c1%rowcount = 1                                  then
101       out(v_text);
102    elsif upper(substr(ltrim(v_text), 1, 3)) = 'END'       then
103       out(chr(12)); -- form feed
104       exit;
105    else
106       out(v_text);
107    end if;
108  end loop;
109  SYS.DBMS_OUTPUT.new_line();
110 end process;
111
112
113 PROCEDURE test is
114
115 begin
116   pl('TEXT_HELP.test()');
117
118   TEST_TS.clear('TEXT_HELP');
119
```

```
120    TEST_TS.set_test('TEXT_HELP', 'help()', 1,
121      'Test method help()' );
122    begin
123      help();
124
125      TEST_TS.ok();
126    exception
127      when OTHERS then
128         TEST_TS.error(SQLERRM);
129    end;
130
131    TEST_TS.set_test('TEXT_HELP', 'process()', 2,
132      'Test method help()' );
133    begin
134      process('TEXT_HELP');
135
136      TEST_TS.ok();
137    exception
138      when OTHERS then
139         TEST_TS.error(SQLERRM);
140    end;
141
142    TEST_TS.set_test('TEXT_HELP', NULL, NULL, NULL);
143    TEST_TS.success();
144  end test;
145
146
147  end text_help;
148  /
149  @be.sql
```

The code in this package body is not all that impressive, nor important. It's its use that is important, so let's see how to use it.

On lines 8 through 12 in Listing 9-2, I've coded the help() method for TEXT_HELP. In order to produce the text-based help for the package, all you need to do is pass the name of the package or TYPE to method TEXT_HELP.process().

Now, let's see what it produces.

Accessing Documentation on Demand

As I mentioned earlier, now all we need to do to get documentation on demand is to execute a package or TYPE's help() method, assuming that the help() method in turn calls TEXT_HELP. process() to produce the output.

Figure 9-5 is an example of executing the help() method for package WORKER_TYPE_TS. As you can see in Figure 9-5, the output is much more significant than the result from using describe in SQL*Plus or what the IDEs had to offer.

```
Oracle SQL*Plus                                                    [_][□][X]
File  Edit  Search  Options  Help
SQL> execute WORKER_TYPE_TS.help();
PACKAGE WORKER_TYPE_TS as

worker_type_ts.pks
Copyright by Don Bales on 12/15/2006
Code Table WORKER_TYPE_T's methods.



Gets the code and decription values for the specified work_type_id.

PROCEDURE get_code_descr(
ain_worker_type_id            in    WORKER_TYPE_T.worker_type_id%TYPE,
aov_code                            out WORKER_TYPE_T.code%TYPE,
aov_description                     out WORKER_TYPE_T.description%TYPE );


Verifies the passed aiov_code value is an exact or like match on the date specified.

PROCEDURE get_code_id_descr(
aiov_code                     in out WORKER_TYPE_T.code%TYPE,
aon_worker_type_id                  out WORKER_TYPE_T.worker_type_id%TYPE,
aov_description                     out WORKER_TYPE_T.description%TYPE,
aid_on                        in    WORKER_TYPE_T.active_date%TYPE );


Verifies the passed aiov_code value is currently an exact or like match.

PROCEDURE get_code_id_descr(
aiov_code                     in out WORKER_TYPE_T.code%TYPE,
aon_worker_type_id                  out WORKER_TYPE_T.worker_type_id%TYPE,
aov_description                     out WORKER_TYPE_T.description%TYPE );
```

Figure 9-5. *Sample output from TEXT_HELP.process()*

The only limit to the depth of the documentation is the amount of time you're willing to spend writing it as you code each specification. Yes, once again, *you* are responsible for the quality of the outcome of *your* activities. But that's what it means to be a "professional." You're responsible, you know it, and you live up to that responsibility.

Now that you have access to TEXT_HELP, it's your turn to put it to work.

It's Your Turn to Access Documentation on Demand

Here are your tasks for this assignment:

1. Go back to each and every package and TYPE specification you've written, and add properly formatted comments (come on, at least do a couple).

2. Add the specification for procedure help() to each of those specifications, if you haven't already.

3. Access your help text by executing the help() command on each of your PL/SQL executables.

What do you think? Wouldn't you find immediate and easy access to documentation on what an object is for and how to use it invaluable? In practice, I've found that programmers are twice as likely to reuse a component if they have easy access to its documentation. But we can do even better.

Programmers are four times as likely to use a component if they know it exists beforehand and they also know how to use it. That sounds like training, doesn't it? Will your CFO or project manager tell you that you may not provide training; in other words, that you may not reuse your components? If not, then you'll need documentation you can distribute freely. To that end, let's look at the ability to create distributable documentation from a package or TYPE specification next.

Distributable Documentation

All we need to do to create a set of distributable documentation for every specification in the database is to query the database's data dictionary for a list of those specifications, and then save each document to an operating system file. And we could do that by calling the help() method for each executable object. But we can do better than that. Text-based documentation can look quite boring and be quite unfriendly.

I know, let's use HTML instead! Let's create an HTML-based documentation formatting tool, or "HTML-help" tool. We can even go so far as to call it HTML_HELP!

An HTML-Based Documentation Formatting Tool

Listing 9-3 is the package specification for an HTML-based help tool. Working with the capabilities of SQL*Plus, you can use it to produce an HTML help file for each executable object, and then an index to all those documents.

Listing 9-3. *A Package Spec to Create HTML-Based Help, html_help.pks*

```
01  create or replace PACKAGE HTML_HELP as
02  /*
03  html_help.pks
04  by Donald J. Bales on 12/15/2006
05  Package to create HTML-based help files for packages.
06  */
07
08  -- Creates an "object_index" html file for the current USER.
09
10  PROCEDURE create_index;
11
12
13  -- Creates an "<object_name>" html for each package for the current USER.
14
15  PROCEDURE create_help(
16  aiv_object_name              in      varchar2);
17
18
19  -- Text-based help for this package.  "set serveroutput on" in SQL*Plus.
20
21  PROCEDURE help;
22
23
```

```
24   PROCEDURE test;
25
26
27   end HTML_HELP;
28   /
29   @se.sql HTML_HELP
```

HTML_HELP has four methods:

create_index(): Creates an index to all the documents created using the next method, create_help().

create_help(): Creates an HTML-based document from the comments and method signatures in a specification.

help(): Produces on-demand help for this package.

test(): The test unit for this package.

Methods create_index() and create_help() require the use of a SQL*Plus script in order to write the output to operating system files.

Listing 9-4 is the implementation for HTML_HELP. In this case, I'm showing only a partial listing. You will find the full listing in the chapter's download directory. What's important here is the outcome of this package: documentation. And that outcome can be distributable if we save it as individual files on a file system.

Listing 9-4. *A Package Body to Create HTML-Based Help, html_help.pkb*

```
001   create or replace PACKAGE BODY HTML_HELP as
002   /*
003   html_help.pkb
004   by Donald J. Bales on 12/15/2006
005   Package to create HTML-based help files for packages
006   */
007
...
368   PROCEDURE create_index is
369
370   cursor c1 is
371   select distinct name
372   from    SYS.USER_SOURCE
373   where   type in ('PACKAGE', 'TYPE')
374   order by 1;
375
376   cursor c2(
377   aiv_name                        in       varchar2) is
378   select text
379   from    SYS.USER_SOURCE
380   where   type in ('PACKAGE', 'TYPE')
381   and     name = aiv_name
382   order by line;
```

```
383
384  b_comment                        boolean;
385  n_period                         number;
386
387  begin
388    open_html('Package/Type index');
...
414    close_html();
415  end create_index;
416
417
418  PROCEDURE create_help(
419  aiv_object_name              in      varchar2) is
420
421  cursor c1(
422  aiv_object_name              in      varchar2) is
423  select text,
424         type
425  from   SYS.USER_SOURCE
426  where  name = upper(aiv_object_name)
427  and    type in ('PACKAGE', 'TYPE')
428  and    line > 1
429  order by line;
430
431  b_comment                        boolean := FALSE;
432  b_first_sentence                 boolean := FALSE;
433  b_method                         boolean := FALSE;
434  b_method_name                    boolean := FALSE;
435  b_other                          boolean := FALSE;
436  n_backward                       number;
437  n_line_number                    number;
438  n_spec                           number := 0;
439  t_spec                           spec_table;
440  v_comment                        varchar2(2000);
441  v_first_sentence                 varchar2(2000);
442  v_method                         varchar2(2000);
443  v_method_name                    varchar2(2000);
444  v_text                           varchar2(2000);
445  v_type                           varchar2(30);
446
447  begin
448    for r1 in c1(aiv_object_name) loop
...
622    end loop;
623
624    -- Now create the HTML
625    open_html(aiv_object_name);
...
```

```
757    close_html();
758  end create_help;
...
886  end HTML_HELP;
887  /
888  @be.sql HTML_HELP
```

Listing 9-5 is a SQL*Plus script, create_html_help.sql, which in turn writes and executes a SQL*Plus script, html_help.sql, in order to generate distributable HTML-based documentation for the executable objects in a schema, as files in a file system.

Listing 9-5. *A SQL*Plus Script to Create HTML-Based Help, create_html_help.sql*

```
01  rem create_html_help.sql
02  rem by Donald J. Bales on 12/15/2006
03  rem SQL*Plus script to create a SQL*Plus script to create html help for
04  rem the current user.
05
06  set feedback off;
07  set linesize 1000;
08  set newpage  1;
09  set pagesize 0;
10  set trimspool on;
11
12  spool html_help.sql;
13
14  prompt rem html_help.sql
15  prompt rem by Donald J. Bales on 12/15/2006
16  prompt rem Created by SQL*Plus script create_html_help.sql
17  prompt;
18  prompt set feedback off;;
19  prompt set linesize 1000;;
20  prompt set newpage  1;;
21  prompt set pagesize 32767;;
22  prompt set trimspool on;;
23  prompt;
24  select 'spool '||lower(name)||'.html;'||
25    chr(10)||'execute HTML_HELP.create_help('''||name||''');'||
26    chr(10)||'spool off;'||chr(10)
27  from   SYS.USER_SOURCE
28  where  type in ('PACKAGE', 'TYPE')
29  group by name
30  order by name;
31
32  prompt spool object_index.html;;
33  prompt execute HTML_HELP.create_index();;
34  prompt spool off;;
35  prompt;
36  prompt set feedback on;;
```

```
37   prompt set linesize 1000;;
38   prompt set newpage  1;;
39   prompt set pagesize 32767;;
40   prompt set trimspool on;;
41
42   spool off;
43
44   @html_help.sql
```

Now that we have our HTML-help tool built, let's see how easy it is to generate distributable documentation.

Generating Distributable Documentation

All we need to do to generate distributable documentation is compile package HTML_HELP, and then execute SQL*Plus script create_html_help.sql, as in the following example:

```
SQL> @create_html_help.sql
```

Doing so will create an HTML file with the same name as the executable PL/SQL object, but with an .html suffix. It will also create an index named object_index.html, which you can open from your browser. Figure 9-6 is an example of what object_index.html looks like in a browser. The format of this, as well as the rest of the documentation files, is controlled by a CSS style sheet named stylesheet.css, which is placed in the same directory as the HTML files.

Package/Type index - Microsoft Internet Explorer	
Owner BPS	

Packages/Types	
DATES	Additional DATE data type methods.
DEBUG_O	debug_o.
DEBUG_OTS	aiv_text in DEBUG_OT.
DEBUG_TS	return DEBUG_T.
GENDER_O	gender_o.
GENDER_TS	Table GENDER_T's methods.
HTML_HELP	Package to create HTML-based help files for packages.
LOGICAL_ASSIGNMENT_TS	-- Keep track of the number of inserts and updates to made by set_row().
LOGICAL_WORKPLACE_TS	Table LOGICAL_WORKPLACE_T's methods.
TEST_O	test_o.
TEST_TS	aiv_object_name TEST_T.
TEXT_HELP	test_help.
WORKER_TS	Table WORKER_T's methods.
WORKER_TYPE_O	worker_type_o.
WORKER_TYPE_TS	Code Table WORKER_TYPE_T's methods.

Figure 9-6. *Sample output from HTML_HELP.create_index()*

When I select the DATES package from the index in Figure 9-6, my browser opens the generated documentation for the DATES specification as in Figure 9-7. When I select method end_of_day() from the method summary, my browser forwards me to another location in the same document where the detail about the method is listed, as shown in Figure 9-8.

Once again, the depth of the information is bounded only by your imagination and effort. By zipping these HTML files into an archive along with the style sheet, you now have freely distributable, and quite handsome, documentation about your reusable (and non-reusable) components.

Now that you've seen me do it, it's your turn to generate distributable documentation.

Figure 9-7. *Page 1 of sample output from HTML_HELP.create_help()*

Figure 9-8. *Page 2 of sample output from HTML_HELP.create_help()*

It's Your Turn to Generate Distributable Documentation

It's time to generate distributable documentation for your PL/SQL executables. Follow these steps:

1. Find and compile package HTML_HELP, files html_help.pks and html_help.pkb.

2. Create a staging directory where you wish to place the HTML files produced by script create_html_files.sql.

3. Copy script create_html_files.sql and style sheet stylesheet.css to your staging directory.

4. Start a SQL*Plus session from your staging directory.

5. Execute script create_html_files.sql from your staging directory.

You should now have as many .html files as you have PL/SQL executables, plus one for the object_index.html file in your staging directory. Now you need to take the last step, which is to distribute your documentation.

Documentation Distribution

You're almost finished. You're on the home stretch. But the job is not complete until you actually distribute your documentation. Just how do you do that? Here's how I've done it in the past:

1. Create a list of recipients.

2. Send recipients the `create_html_help.sql` script and style sheet so they can generate their own copy.

3. Package it into an archive like a `.zip` file.

4. Publish it on a web site.

Your first step in the distribution process is creating a list of recipients. Just who needs to know about this software? You should maintain this list in a database. Not only can you then keep track of who you sent the documentation to, but you can also keep a categorized list of the recipients' feedback. With this information, you can determine who is actually using the software, what incremental improvements need to be made, and also who is not using the software. If you find you have recipients that should be, but are not, using your software components, then remedial training is in order. You know, "hands-on" training, where you can not only see how they have tried using it in the past, but also find out what they think is wrong with using it in the first place!

Your next step is deciding on how to package it for distribution. Should you let users generate their own? Should you send them an archive? Or should you host the documentation on a web site? I suppose it all depends on how large the audience is, and how often the components are changed.

In a small development group, I like to regenerate the documentation on a daily basis and then have everyone on the team make a copy. In a highly distributed environment and with components that are not modified, it makes more sense to send an archive. If the software changes frequently, it's easier to host the files on a web site.

Regardless of how you distribute the documentation, you should also write some summary documentation about how the components can be used together or about the patterns employed in the use of polymorphic names in the components. We'll talk about the latter in the next chapter.

Keep in mind that just as software development is cyclical and recursive, so is the creation and distribution of any documentation for said software. So you must continually maintain your list of recipients and then redistribute your documentation as needed. Don't stop short of this last step. Otherwise, someone will tell a story about your weird behavior in a book some day.

Summary

I started out this chapter trying to impress on you how important it is to have documentation for your software components. There is no reuse without proper documentation. Second, I showed you how following a small set of commenting rules can turn your package and TYPE specification source into a self-documenting source, which also make losing the documentation impossible.

Next, I showed you how to build and employ a text-based help tool so programmers have access to text-based documentation for any component on demand. Then I followed that up by showing you how to build and employ an HTML-based help tool so you can generate a distributable form of the documentation embedded in your package and TYPE specifications.

Finally, I gave you some pointers on distributing your software. One last suggestion is that you consider actually training your programmers on how to create new software components and use existing components.

Next, I'll tell you some tall tales of success using PL/SQL, and why they were successful. So grab a cup of joe and let's go.

CHAPTER 10

■ ■ ■

Fairy Tales

Polymorphism is the subject of this chapter. No, it's not some kind of New Age religion; it's about using the same message (or command) in order to get the same result, but for different kinds of objects. Let's look at a simple example. Figure 10-1 shows the use of the command draw() for three different geometric shapes: a square, a triangle, and a circle.

square.draw() triangle.draw() circle.draw()

Figure 10-1. *An example of polymorphic command use with different objects*

Although the three geometric shapes in Figure 10-1 are different objects, using the same command, you can communicate what you want each object to do, and the object knows how to do it.

The polymorphic use of commands or messages reduces the use of synonyms in a programming language. If you're a writer, synonyms are wonderful things. They allow you to use words that have similar meanings but sound different, so that your resulting prose can have a somewhat rhythmic cadence. It can sound beautiful.

If you're a programmer, synonyms are awful things. They cause ambiguity because you can't know from "the sound" of the synonym if it means something similar (LIKE) or if it means exactly the same thing (=). And in programming, ambiguity is a really bad thing. Furthermore, synonyms expand the size of a language and make it harder to learn and use. The harder the language is to use, the more defects will be created when using it, and that too is bad.

Let's go back to Figure 10-1 for a second. I could have named the command to draw each geometric shape in the figure draw_square(), draw_triangle(), and draw_circle(). That's the procedural programming paradigm. But by doing so, I would have made the programming language three times larger than when I simply used the same command, draw(), in the context of the object to which it belongs.

Even if you're not using an object-oriented language, you can still use an object-oriented approach by employing modularity and polymorphism. Employing modularity means abstracting large program units into smaller components that can then be reused and assembled to accomplish a larger purpose. Employing polymorphism means abstracting out a set of commands that communicate the same action; however, the action taken will be appropriate for the object executing the command. And that's what I'm going to cover in this chapter, by doing the following:

- Show you a list of polymorphic commands that I have used repeatedly, project after project, always with the same meaning and to take the same action, but an action appropriate to each object.

- Tell you a handful of stories, or fairy tales, in which I use each polymorphic command, so you'll have some real-world examples to draw from when you employ polymorphism in your next project.

- Leave you with some advice about what you should do next.

I'll get you jump-started with a list of time-tempered polymorphic commands.

Polymorphic Commands

Anytime you write or rewrite a program or application, you have an opportunity to abstract out patterns of use that you have experienced beforehand, and employ that experience as the intelligent and wise use of object-orientation. As I've already stated several times, you do not need to be using an object-oriented language in order to employ object-orientation.

Earlier in this book, I introduced you to the idea of creating a "table package" for every table. Each table package contains any executable behavior that "belongs to" the data held in the table in question. Then, in Chapter 6, I showed you how to create an object table, based on a new object TYPE, which contains any executable behavior that "belongs to" its associated object attributes.

Creating a table package is an example of employing object-orientation in a procedural language setting, and creating an object table with a TYPE is an example of employing object-orientation in an object-oriented language setting. Both examples take advantage of polymorphism.

After more than ten years of coding in PL/SQL, I've created a list of 50 polymorphic commands that can be employed to name most, if not all, of the methods you will use while developing components (and applications) with PL/SQL. Table 10-1 is a list of the top 20 polymorphic commands I commonly use for table packages and TYPEs. The first column of the table lists the method name, including whether it is a FUNCTION or PROCEDURE. If a method name is not followed by parentheses, it means that there is a form of the method that takes no parameters. In columns two through four, I indicate whether a method is used for each "kind" of table: a code table, a content table, or an intersection table. Finally, in column five, I indicate whether the method is used in a hierarchical version of one of the three previous table types.

Table 10-1. *Polymorphic Commands for Package Tables and TYPEs*

Method Name	Code	Content	Intersect	Hierarchical
FUNCTION create_id_context()				X
FUNCTION get_code()	X			
FUNCTION get_code_context()				X
FUNCTION get_descr()	X			
FUNCTION get_id	X	X	X	
FUNCTION get_id()	X			
FUNCTION get_id_context()				X
FUNCTION get_name()		X	X	
FUNCTION get_name_context()				X
FUNCTION get_row()		X	X	
FUNCTION is_active()	X	X	X	
FUNCTION is_duplicate()		X	X	
FUNCTION is_history()			X	
PROCEDURE get_code_descr()	X			
PROCEDURE get_code_id_descr()	X			
PROCEDURE get_code_id_name()		X		
PROCEDURE help	X	X	X	
PROCEDURE inactivate()		X	X	
PROCEDURE set_row()		X	X	
PROCEDURE test	X	X	X	

Table 10-2 is a list of polymorphic commands employed by packages and TYPEs that play a particular role in a process, rather than act as merely a persistence entity like a table and table package or object table. The first column of Table 10-2 lists method names along with the type of method. Columns two through six indicate the use of the method name by each of the roles listed in the headings:

Data migration: A "one-time" process where data is moved and/or transformed from one location to another, typically from a "staging table" to an "application table."

On-demand data processing: A process that manipulates data in the database, on demand, for the purpose of completing some ongoing business-related task.

Polling data processing: A process that manipulates data in the database by managing tasks in a queue or simply sleeping between invocations of the process in question, once again for the purpose of completing some ongoing business-related processing.

Data entry: In support of a presentation layer process of entering data into the database for some ongoing business related task.

Reporting: In support of a presentation layer process of viewing data in the database for some ongoing or ad hoc business-related task.

There is some overlap between these five role definitions. For example, a service-oriented interface between two systems will employ data migration, data processing, and table package routines. But that's OK. What I'm trying to do is to get you to think in polymorphic terms.

Table 10-2. *Polymorphic Commands for Roles*

Method Name	Data Migration	Demand Process	Polling Process	Data Entry	Report
FUNCTION calculate()		X	X	X	X
FUNCTION get_next()			X		
FUNCTION get_report					X
FUNCTION get_report()					X
FUNCTION get_status		X	X		
FUNCTION is_authorized()				X	
FUNCTION is_downloaded		X	X		
FUNCTION is_uploaded		X	X		
FUNCTION process	X	X	X		
FUNCTION process()	X	X	X		
PROCEDURE calculate()		X	X	X	X
PROCEDURE disable		X	X		
PROCEDURE download		X	X		
PROCEDURE enable		X	X		
PROCEDURE help	X	X	X	X	X
PROCEDURE initialize	X	X	X	X	X
PROCEDURE load		X	X		
PROCEDURE post_query()				X	
PROCEDURE process	X	X	X		
PROCEDURE process()	X	X	X		
PROCEDURE quit		X	X		
PROCEDURE report					X
PROCEDURE report()					X
PROCEDURE set_downloaded		X	X		

Table 10-2. *Polymorphic Commands for Roles*

Method Name	Data Migration	Demand Process	Polling Process	Data Entry	Report
PROCEDURE set_processed	X	X	X		
PROCEDURE set_report()					X
PROCEDURE set_status()		X	X		
PROCEDURE set_uploaded	X	X	X		
PROCEDURE start_logging()		X	X		X
PROCEDURE status		X	X		
PROCEDURE stop_logging()		X	X		X
PROCEDURE test	X	X	X	X	X
PROCEDURE upload		X			

If you learn to think in polymorphic terms, and then employ polymorphism, once you know what a polymorphic command does on one object, you'll already have a good idea of what it does on the next. And that's quite similar to how we think about the real world. If you tell me you ride a bike, I might respond that I ride a horse. We both know what the other means, even if we've never done the other activity, simply because we apply the word *ride* polymorphically to the context—in your case, a bicycle; in my case, a horse.

In the sections that follow, I'm going to tell you how I've used some (it would take another book to explain them all) of these commands in a particular setting.

Let's start with table packages and TYPEs.

The Unhappy SQL Programmer

I could call this story "The Man Who Hated SQL." The programmer in question was unhappy because he had to break the rhythm of his coding from a procedure language (PL/SQL) to a nonprocedural language (SQL) and back again—back and forth, back and forth, PL/SQL and SQL, PL/SQL and SQL.

While our unhappy programmer was complaining about the nonprocedural nature of SQL and how bad SQL is, he should have been more concerned about reducing the number of different SQL statements used against the database, because reducing the number of SQL statements used against an Oracle database can improve the database's overall performance.

I find it surprising, and at the same time somewhat amusing, how many people hate SQL. You would think its creation was the work of the devil. In contrast, in my opinion, SQL is very effective. You can accomplish a lot of data processing work with very little actual programming effort using SQL. OK, I agree, some things don't work consistently from one implementation to the next, but all in all, no viable alternative has taken its place yet, nor does it appear one will anytime soon.

It's really amazing how easy data processing is with SQL. Regardless, one goal during the development of an application should be to write a particular SQL statement once and only once, just as it should be a goal to write the same code routine once and only once, and then use it as a subroutine. To that end, I create table packages or TYPEs that employ the same set of polymorphic commands to provide a PL/SQL method in place of writing many of the same SQL statements over and over again.

Code Table Methods

As you saw earlier in the book, I use a database architecture where I always store the primary key, which is a sequence-generated ID value that points to a code, into a content or intersection table. I never store the code or description value. Why?

First, modifying the code or description of a given code table entry will require only an UPDATE against the code table. The next time the code and description values are retrieved for a particular ID value, they will then be the "new" values. The primary key, the ID, will always be the same value, but the code and description values can change without impacting the content and intersection tables that have stored the ID value in question.

Second, in an internationalized application, I can transparently switch the code and description values to those with the same meaning in another language, because the only value that is immutable is the ID. With that in mind, think about this. We code programs in English, therefore we should be able to program access to codes in English, and that's why the first method I'm going to talk about exists.

get_id()

Since we code our programs in English, we should be able to specify our code entries as constant values in our programs in English. So anytime you need to get the ID value for a particular code value in English, you call FUNCTION get_id(aiv_code), passing it a code value in English, and it returns the corresponding ID value. If the code you specify does not exist, the underlying singleton SQL SELECT statement raises a NO_DATA_FOUND exception, which you must handle in your calling program unit. Here's an example of the method from code table package WORKER_TYPE_TS:

```
FUNCTION get_id(
aiv_code                        in      WORKER_TYPE_T.code%TYPE )
return                                  WORKER_TYPE_T.worker_type_id%TYPE is

n_worker_type_id                        WORKER_TYPE_T.worker_type_id%TYPE;

begin
  select worker_type_id
  into   n_worker_type_id
  from   WORKER_TYPE_T
  where  code = aiv_code;

  return n_worker_type_id;
end get_id;
```

Once this method is written and in use, one and only one SQL statement need ever be written to retrieve an ID for a specified code value. You will see me use this method quite often in a data migration, data processing, and reporting program units. First, I get the ID values as pseudo-constants in the initialization section of a package whenever there is a small number codes in scope. Next, I reduce the number of tables used in a corresponding cursor's SQL SELECT statement. Instead, I use an IF statement to assign the code entry's code and description values inside the cursor's FOR LOOP. You'll see some examples of this practice later in this chapter, in the "Reporting" section.

get_code_descr()

Once you've decided to use a database architecture where every assigned code value is stored as an ID value, you'll need some way to retrieve the code and description values so they can be displayed in the presentation layer, whether it is for data entry or reporting. And that's the purpose of this method. If you need the code and description values for a specific ID value, you simply call PROCEDURE get_code_descr(ain_id, aov_code, aov_descr), passing it the corresponding ID value. The method returns the code and description values as OUT parameter values. If the ID you specify does not exist, the underlying singleton SQL SELECT statement raises a NO_DATA_FOUND exception, which you must handle in your calling program unit. Here's an example of the method from code table package WORKER_TYPE_TS:

```
PROCEDURE get_code_descr(
ain_worker_type_id            in    WORKER_TYPE_T.worker_type_id%TYPE,
aov_code                            out WORKER_TYPE_T.code%TYPE,
aov_description                     out WORKER_TYPE_T.description%TYPE ) is

begin
  select code,
         description
  into   aov_code,
         aov_description
  from   WORKER_TYPE_T
  where  worker_type_id = ain_worker_type_id;
end get_code_descr;
```

Once again, after this method is written and in use, one and only one SQL statement need ever be written to retrieve a code and description for a specified code ID value. Similar functions can be written to get just the code value or description value, and they would be appropriately named get_code() and get_descr().

get_code_id_descr()

If an application is written for a high volume of data entry, the GUI in question will present a field for the entry of a code value and a second field to display the specified code's description value. The users may also have an icon they can click to see a pop-up list of code values from which to select.

The typical end-user action in this design is for the end user to specify all or part of a code value, and then to tab into the next modifiable field, at which point, the presentation layer validates the user's code value entry. That's what this method is for: validation.

In order to validate a code value, simply pass the code value to PROCEDURE get_code_id_descr(aiov_code, aon_id, aov_description, aid_on). This procedure first tries to find an exact code value match for the specified point in time. If it does not find a match, the procedure tries to find a single LIKE match. If it does not find a single LIKE match, it may return a NO_DATA_FOUND or TOO_MANY_ROWS exception, which the presentation layer will need to handle. Both exceptions mean that the user has specified an invalid code value. Here's an example from code table package WORKER_TYPE_TS:

```
PROCEDURE get_code_id_descr(
aiov_code                      in out WORKER_TYPE_T.code%TYPE,
aon_worker_type_id                out WORKER_TYPE_T.worker_type_id%TYPE,
aov_description                   out WORKER_TYPE_T.description%TYPE,
aid_on                         in     WORKER_TYPE_T.active_date%TYPE ) is

v_code                                WORKER_TYPE_T.code%TYPE;

begin
  select worker_type_id,
         description
    into aon_worker_type_id,
         aov_description
    from WORKER_TYPE_T
   where code = aiov_code
     and aid_on between active_date and nvl(inactive_date, DATES.d_MAX);
exception
  when NO_DATA_FOUND then
    select worker_type_id,
           code,
           description
      into aon_worker_type_id,
           v_code,
           aov_description
      from WORKER_TYPE_T
     where code like aiov_code||'%'
       and aid_on between active_date and nvl(inactive_date, DATES.d_MAX);

    aiov_code := v_code;
end get_code_id_descr;
```

Variable v_code is used in the second half of the method, during the LIKE match, to capture the full-length code value from the database and return it to the presentation layer. You can call this method from the WHEN-VALIDATE-ITEM event in Developer/2000 Forms, from the item_changed() event in PowerBuilder, from JavaScript (through a servlet) in the onChange event of an Ajax-based web page, and so on.

Now let's look at methods used with content tables.

Content Table Methods

What's the difference between a code table and a content table? In most cases, code tables have a very limited number of entries—values agreed upon by the consensus of users or dictation of management. These "agreed-upon" values are used to categorize the input of content and sometimes intersection entries. In contrast, content tables have an unlimited number of entries, where end users select or specify code values, enter numeric values, or enter textual values as part of doing business.

In response to the unlimited number of entries possible in content tables, it's not uncommon to take the effort to code methods to eliminate the repeated coding of the SQL singleton SELECT, INSERT, and UPDATE statements with parametric method calls. Let's start out by looking at one such method.

get_row()

Method get_row() returns a PL/SQL record (a row) from a relational table or an instance of an object TYPE (a row) from an object table, based on the criteria specified in the record or object passed to the method. As the programmer, it's your responsibility to code the method to retrieve by the primary key and any other unique keys defined for the table in question. Then, to use this method, follow these steps:

1. Set column or attribute values in a corresponding PL/SQL record or object instance for only those columns or attributes that are used in a particular primary or unique key constraint.

2. Pass the PL/SQL record or object instance to the method.

get_row() then returns a matching row from the database if a matching row exists; otherwise, it returns a NULL PL/SQL record or object instance.

This method replaces a singleton SQL SELECT statement with a parametric method call based on a set of primary or unique key values. We never need to code that SQL statement ever again. Where's that unhappy SQL programmer now?

The following is an example of the get_row() method from content table package LOGICAL_WORKPLACE_TS:

```
FUNCTION get_row(
air_logical_workplace           in      LOGICAL_WORKPLACE_T%ROWTYPE)
return                                  LOGICAL_WORKPLACE_T%ROWTYPE is

r_logical_workplace                     LOGICAL_WORKPLACE_T%ROWTYPE;

begin
   if    air_logical_workplace.logical_workplace_id is not NULL then
     --pl('retrieve the row by the primary key');
     select *
     into   r_logical_workplace
     from   LOGICAL_WORKPLACE_T
     where  logical_workplace_id =
       air_logical_workplace.logical_workplace_id;
   elsif air_logical_workplace.id_context is not NULL then
     --pl('retrieve the row by the id_context unique key');
     select *
     into   r_logical_workplace
```

```
   from    LOGICAL_WORKPLACE_T
   where   id_context = air_logical_workplace.id_context;
 else
   --pl('retrieve the row by the code, name, and active_date');
   select *
   into    r_logical_workplace
   from    LOGICAL_WORKPLACE_T
   where   code        = air_logical_workplace.code
   and     name        = air_logical_workplace.name
   and     active_date = air_logical_workplace.active_date;
 end if;
 return r_logical_workplace;
exception
 when NO_DATA_FOUND then
   raise;
 when OTHERS then
   raise_application_error(-20001, SQLERRM||
     ' on select LOGICAL_WORKPLACE_T'||
     ' in LOGICAL_WORKPLACE_TS.get_row()');
end get_row;
```

As you will see shortly, get_row() is called by set_row() in order to determine whether to insert or update.

get_code_id_name(), get_code(), and get_name()

The methods get_code_id_name(), get_code(), and get_name() serve the same purpose as their counterparts in code table packages. See the section about get_code_id_descr() earlier in the chapter for an explanation.

is_duplicate()

In a database design where you use sequence-generated ID values for primary keys, every table will have a primary key that is an ID value, and at least one unique key that acts as a "primary key" made up of real-world values. Method is_duplicate() allows the presentation layer to verify that the values specified in fields on a screen are not going to create a row with duplicate values when an entry is saved to the database. Here's an example of FUNCTION is_duplicate(aiv_code, aiv_name, aid_active_date) from content table package LOGICAL_WORKPLACE_TS:

```
FUNCTION is_duplicate(
aiv_code                    in      LOGICAL_WORKPLACE_T.code%TYPE,
aiv_name                    in      LOGICAL_WORKPLACE_T.name%TYPE,
aid_active_date             in      LOGICAL_WORKPLACE_T.active_date%TYPE)
return                              boolean is

n_count                             number;
```

```
begin
  --pl('retrieve the row by the code, name, and active_date');
  select count(1)
  into   n_count
  from   LOGICAL_WORKPLACE_T
  where  code                = aiv_code
  and    name                = aiv_name
  and    trunc(active_date)  = trunc(aid_active_date);

  if nvl(n_count, 0) > 0 then
    return TRUE;
  else
    return FALSE;
  end if;
end is_duplicate;
```

Like its presentation layer counterpart get_code_id_name(), is_duplicate() can be called from any presentation layer. This time, however, in order to provide immediate feedback to users that they are specifying duplicate values, before they try to save an entry to the database. If you're working with a programming language in the presentation layer that does not support a Boolean value from SQL, such as Java, you can simply wrap your call to this function in a stand-alone database function like the following:

```
create or replace FUNCTION to_boolean_number(
aib_boolean                     in      boolean )
return                                  number is
/*
to_boolean_number.fun
by Donald J. Bales on 12/15/2006
A method to return a numeric value for false (0) and true (1).
This is very handy for calling functions that return Boolean
values from JDBC, which can't handle Boolean database values.
*/
begin
  if aib_boolean is not null then
    if aib_boolean then
      return 1;
    else
      return 0;
    end if;
  else
    return NULL;
  end if;
end to_boolean_number;
```

FUNCTION to_boolean_number() takes a Boolean value as a parameter, and then returns a 1 for TRUE or 0 for FALSE. If you call is_duplicate() from a Java program, you'll need to wrap is_duplicate() with to_boolean_number() so you'll get a numeric value 1 for TRUE and 0 for FALSE. For example, you would code your JDBC stored procedure call as follows:

```
...
int                duplicate = 0;
CallableStatement cstmt     = null;

try {
  // Create the callable statement
  cstmt = conn.prepareCall(
    "{ ? = call to_boolean_number(is_duplicate(?, ?, ?)) }");

  // Register the OUT parameter
  cstmt.registerOutParameter(1, Types.INTEGER);

  // Set the IN parameters
  cstmt.setString(2, code);
  cstmt.setString(3, name);
  cstmt.setTimestamp(4, activeDate);

  // Execute the stored procedure
  cstmt.execute();

  duplicate = cstmt.getInt(1);
}
catch (SQLException e) {
  System.err.println("SQL Error: " + e.getMessage());
}
finally {
  if (cstmt != null)
    try {  cstmt.close(); } catch (SQLException ignore) { }
}
...
```

Enough JDBC, let's get back to PL/SQL.

set_row()

Method set_row() is the ultimate parametric method replacement for SQL—that is, as far as our unhappy SQL programmer is concerned! To INSERT or UPDATE the database with the row you desire, you simply pass the row in question, a PL/SQL record or object instance, to PROCEDURE set_row(air_row). When you do, here's what set_row() does:

1. It calls get_row() to determine if a row with the specified primary or unique key values already exists in the database. If it does, get_row() returns the matching row. Otherwise, get_row() returns a NULL row.

2. If the desired row already exists in the database, set_row() will compare the non-primary key columns. If any non-primary key column values are different, set_row() will UPDATE the database with the modified values.

3. If the desired row doesn't exist in the database, set_row() will allocate a primary key value if necessary, and then INSERT the desired row into the database. The row passed to set_row() is an IN OUT parameter, so the value of any allocated primary key will be updated in the passed row if a new row is inserted into the database.

This is a very handy method when you're coding a data migration program. You can call set_row() as many times as you like with the same values, and it will insert a row only once, and update it only if values have changed. This allows you to code data migration programs that can be rerun as needed until you get the "correct" results.

The following is an example of method set_row() from content table package LOGICAL_WORKPLACE_TS:

```
PROCEDURE set_row(
aior_logical_workplace        in out LOGICAL_WORKPLACE_T%ROWTYPE) is

d_null                  constant date        := DATES.d_MIN;
n_null                  constant number      := 0;
v_null                  constant varchar2(1) := ' ';

r_logical_workplace               LOGICAL_WORKPLACE_T%ROWTYPE;

begin
  -- get the existing row
  begin
    r_logical_workplace := get_row(aior_logical_workplace);
  exception
    when NO_DATA_FOUND then
      r_logical_workplace := NULL;
  end;
  -- if a row exists, update it if needed
  if r_logical_workplace.logical_workplace_id is not NULL then
    aior_logical_workplace.logical_workplace_id :=
      r_logical_workplace.logical_workplace_id;
    aior_logical_workplace.parent_id          :=
      r_logical_workplace.parent_id;
    aior_logical_workplace.id_context          :=
      r_logical_workplace.id_context;
    if nvl(r_logical_workplace.workplace_type_id,    n_null) <>
       nvl(aior_logical_workplace.workplace_type_id, n_null) or
       nvl(r_logical_workplace.code,                 v_null) <>
       nvl(aior_logical_workplace.code,              v_null) or
       nvl(r_logical_workplace.name,                 v_null) <>
       nvl(aior_logical_workplace.name,              v_null) or
       nvl(r_logical_workplace.active_date,          d_null) <>
       nvl(aior_logical_workplace.active_date,       d_null) or
       nvl(r_logical_workplace.inactive_date,        d_null) <>
       nvl(aior_logical_workplace.inactive_date,     d_null) then
```

```
        begin
          update LOGICAL_WORKPLACE_T
          set    workplace_type_id    =
                   aior_logical_workplace.workplace_type_id,
                 code                 =
                   aior_logical_workplace.code,
                 name                 =
                   aior_logical_workplace.name,
                 active_date          =
                   aior_logical_workplace.active_date,
                 inactive_date        =
                   aior_logical_workplace.inactive_date
          where  logical_workplace_id =
                   aior_logical_workplace.logical_workplace_id;

          n_updated := nvl(n_updated, 0) + nvl(sql%rowcount, 0);
        exception
          when OTHERS then
            raise_application_error( -20002, SQLERRM||
              ' on update LOGICAL_WORKPLACE_T'||
              ' in LOGICAL_WORKPLACE_TS.set_row()' );
        end;
      end if;
    else
    -- add the row if it does not exist
      begin
        if aior_logical_workplace.logical_workplace_id is NULL then
          aior_logical_workplace.logical_workplace_id := get_id();
        end if;
        aior_logical_workplace.id_context             :=
          create_id_context(
            aior_logical_workplace.parent_id,
            aior_logical_workplace.logical_workplace_id );
        insert into LOGICAL_WORKPLACE_T (
              logical_workplace_id,
              parent_id,
              id_context,
              workplace_type_id,
              code,
              name,
              active_date,
              inactive_date )
        values (
              aior_logical_workplace.logical_workplace_id,
              aior_logical_workplace.parent_id,
              aior_logical_workplace.id_context,
              aior_logical_workplace.workplace_type_id,
```

```
        aior_logical_workplace.code,
        aior_logical_workplace.name,
        aior_logical_workplace.active_date,
        aior_logical_workplace.inactive_date );

    n_inserted := nvl(n_inserted, 0) + nvl(sql%rowcount, 0);
  exception
    when OTHERS then
      raise_application_error( -20003, SQLERRM||
        ' on insert LOGICAL_WORKPLACE_T'||
        ' in LOGICAL_WORKPLACE_TS.set_row()' );
  end;
 end if;
end set_row;
```

You have to admit that that is a pretty cool method—that is, if you hate to code SQL.

WHAT? NO METHODS TO REPLACE CURSORS?

Have you noticed that I have all kinds of table package methods that wrap singleton SQL statements with a method, yet I have none to wrap a cursor with a method call? An esteemed peer of mine, Steven Feuerstein, has written about doing just that: wrapping a cursor with a method that returns a collection. A program is then written to loop through the rows of a collection instead of the rows of a cursor.

Used judiciously—that is, with cursors that return a small number of rows—Steven's method can be quite effective. However, in practice, I don't find much use for this technique. Remember that I advocate the use of PL/SQL methods in order to eliminate "duplicate" code. In contrast, I find that most stored procedures that use cursors use a rather unique cursor. So, because of that, I see very little opportunity for reuse.

At the same time, misuse of wrapping cursors with methods that return collections can lead to inordinately large amounts of shared memory use in an Oracle database. This in turn leads to poor performance. Regardless, at some point in time, I suggest you check out Steven's ideas. Every good idea has its place.

Intersection Table Methods

Tables that act as the intersection between two content tables (commonly called a *many-to-many relationship/entity*) use all the same methods as content tables and a few more. So let's start by listing the methods that an intersection table has in common with a content table:

get_row(): Used to detect and retrieve an existing row based on primary key or unique key data.

is_duplicate(): Used to detect a duplicate entry before a presentation layer program tries to insert the values in question into the database.

set_row(): Used to conditionally insert or update a row in the database, based on use of get_row() to detect an existing entry.

An intersection table has two additional methods that are concerned about the existence of intersection history: is_active() and is_history(). Let's look at is_active() first.

is_active()

Method is_active() returns a Boolean value based on whether or not an "active" entry exists in an intersection table for the specified "primary" content entity at the specified point in time. By "primary" content entity, I mean the content entity that is the subject of the query.

For example, the three intersection entities in our example's ERD from Chapter 1— LOGICAL_ASSIGNMENT, PHYSICAL_ASSIGNMENT, and WORK_ASSIGNMENT—have a primary content entity—WORKER–which is the subject of the relationship. And they have a secondary content entity—LOGICAL_WORKPLACE, PHYSICAL_WORKPLACE, and WORK, respectively—which is the object of the relationship.

By "active," I mean that the specified point in time is between an entry's active date and inactive date. Figure 10-2 illustrates the method's use.

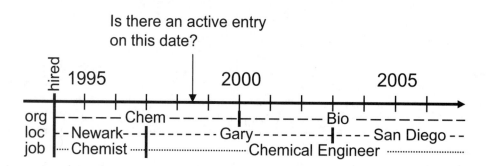

Figure 10-2. *An illustration of method is_active()'s use*

If an active entry exists, FUNCTION is_active(ain_primary_id, aid_on) returns TRUE; otherwise, it returns FALSE. The following is an example of the method from intersection table package LOGICAL_ASSIGNMENT_TS:

```
FUNCTION is_active(
ain_worker_id                in      LOGICAL_ASSIGNMENT_T.worker_id%TYPE,
aid_on                       in      date)
return                               boolean is

n_count                              number;

begin
 select count(1)
 into   n_count
 from   LOGICAL_ASSIGNMENT_T
 where  worker_id      = ain_worker_id
 and    aid_on     between active_date
                   and nvl(inactive_date, DATES.d_MAX);
```

```
 if nvl(n_count, 0) > 0 then
  return TRUE;
 else
  return FALSE;
 end if;
end is_active;
```

is_history()

The second intersection table package method, is_history(), exists for a whole different reason. It determines whether there is any history of an active entry over a specified period of time. FUNCTION is_history(ain_primary_id, aid_active_date, aid_inactive_date) is designed to return TRUE if history does exist; otherwise, it returns FALSE. It also uses pragma autonomous transaction, so it can be used in a before insert for each row (BIR) trigger on an intersection table, to prevent overlapping historical entries. Figure 10-3 illustrates the use of is_history().

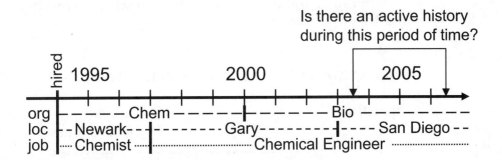

Figure 10-3. *An illustration of method is_history()'s use*

The following is an example of method is_history() from intersection table package LOGICAL_ASSIGNMENT_TS:

```
FUNCTION is_history(
ain_worker_id              in      LOGICAL_ASSIGNMENT_T.worker_id%TYPE,
aid_active_date            in      LOGICAL_ASSIGNMENT_T.active_date%TYPE,
aid_inactive_date          in      LOGICAL_ASSIGNMENT_T.inactive_date%TYPE)
return                             boolean is

pragma autonomous_transaction;

n_count                            number;

begin
  select count(1)
  into   n_count
  from   LOGICAL_ASSIGNMENT_T
```

```
where  worker_id                         = ain_worker_id
and    active_date                       <=
         nvl(aid_inactive_date, DATES.d_MAX)
and    nvl(inactive_date, DATES.d_MAX) >= aid_active_date;
commit;

if nvl(n_count,0) > 0 then
  return TRUE;
else
  return FALSE;
end if;
end is_history;
```

At first glance, most programmers think I've coded the comparisons between the dates in this method incorrectly, but examine Figure 10-4. What I'm asking the database in the query is, "Are there any entries where their active date takes place before the end of the range (inactive date) I'm specifying and at the same time their inactive date takes place after the start of the range (active_date) I'm specifying?" If there are, then these entries are active at some point (or points) in time during the range I've specified.

Is there an active history during this period of time?

Figure 10-4. *An illustration of overlapping historical entries*

The use of an autonomous transaction in this method allows it to be used to verify that no existing entries overlap the history of the new entry, without generating a mutating table error.

Hierarchical Table Methods

Hierarchical entities—those that have a relationship with themselves—have three additional methods, which are centered on the hierarchy. A common example of a hierarchical entity is one that stores organization information, as the LOGICAL_WORKPLACE entity does in our example schema from Chapter 1. From data in this entity, we can build an organization chart, as in Figure 10-5.

Figure 10-5. *An example of a hierarchical relationship*

Determining who reports to an intermediate organization, like Manufacturing in Figure 10-5, can be quite complex and time-consuming. One option is to use Oracle's CONNECT BY clause in a SQL SELECT statement, but the retrieval times can be onerous. So as a performance work-around, I create what I call a "contextual primary key string," which is made up of a list of primary keys in the hierarchy separated by some predetermined separator character. I prefer to use a period (.).

When I want to identify everyone who works for Manufacturing, I look up the ID context for Manufacturing, and then ask for any entry that is LIKE it. Let's investigate this design further by looking at a method to create the ID context.

create_id_context()

Method create_id_context() returns an ID context string for the specified parent entry and new logical workplace ID. An application programmer must make sure that the associated ID context column in the associated table is set to the return value of FUNCTION create_id_ context(ain_parent_id, ain_id) anytime a row is inserted into the database. Here's an example of the method for hierarchical content table package LOGICAL_WORKPLACE_TS:

```
FUNCTION create_id_context(
ain_parent_id                    in      LOGICAL_WORKPLACE_T.parent_id%TYPE,
ain_logical_workplace_id         in
  LOGICAL_WORKPLACE_T.logical_workplace_id%TYPE)
return                                   varchar2 is

v_id_context                             LOGICAL_WORKPLACE_T.id_context%TYPE;

begin
  v_id_context := get_id_context(ain_parent_id);

  if v_id_context is not NULL then
    return substr(v_id_context||'.'||
      to_char(ain_logical_workplace_id), 1, 2000);
  else
    return to_char(ain_logical_workplace_id);
  end if;
end create_id_context;
```

Let's work through an example using the primary key ID values for the organizations represented in Figure 10-5. Table 10-3 lists the primary key values for some of the organizations shown in that figure.

Table 10-3. *Selected LOGICAL WORKPLACE Entries*

Code	Name	logical_workplace_id	id_context
VDMI	Very Dirty Manufacturing, Inc.	1	1
MFG	Manufacturing	5	1.5
CHEM	Chemicals	8	1.5.8
BIO	Biologicals	9	1.5.9
METL	Metals	10	1.5.10
RUSE	Reusables	11	1.5.11
DISP	Disposables	12	1.5.12

The Chemicals department (ID = 8) is part of the Manufacturing business unit (ID = 5). So when FUNCTION create_id_context() is called, its parent's ID value, 5, is passed as ain_parent_id, and its ID value, 8, is passed as ain_logical_workplace_id.

First, the function retrieves the parent's ID context, 1.5. Then the method appends a period and the ID value, 8, to the parent's ID context, to get 1.5.8. This is the value returned by the function.

Once that value is stored in the database, if I want a list of everyone under Manufacturing, all I need to do is add the following SQL to a query:

```
where id_context like aiv_id_context||'%'.
```

get_code_context()

Method get_code_context() returns the hierarchical list of code values as a context string for the specified ID. For example, executing FUNCTION get_code_context(ain_id) will return the string VDMI.MFG.CHEM for the Chemicals department listed in Table 10-3. Here's an example of the method from hierarchical content table package LOGICAL_WORKPLACE_TS:

```
FUNCTION get_code_context(
ain_logical_workplace_id        in
  LOGICAL_WORKPLACE_T.logical_workplace_id%TYPE)
return                          varchar2 is

cursor c_code_context(
ain_logical_workplace_id        in
  LOGICAL_WORKPLACE_T.logical_workplace_id%TYPE) is
select upper(code) code
from   LOGICAL_WORKPLACE_T
connect by prior parent_id              = logical_workplace_id
```

```
start with        logical_workplace_id = ain_logical_workplace_id
order by level desc;

v_code_context                        varchar2(2000);

begin
  for r_code_context in c_code_context(ain_logical_workplace_id) loop
    v_code_context :=
      substr(v_code_context||'.'||r_code_context.code, 1, 2000);
  end loop;
  return v_code_context;
end get_code_context;
```

In this case, I do use the CONNECT BY SQL clause in the method's cursor, c_code_context, to get the list of code values for the context string.

get_id_context()

Method get_id_context() returns the ID context for the specified ID. For example, calling FUNCTION get_id_context(ain_id) for Manufacturing (ID = 5) as in Table 10-3 will return the value 1.5. Here's an example of the method from hierarchical content table package LOGICAL_WORKPLACE_TS:

```
FUNCTION get_id_context(
ain_logical_workplace_id        in
  LOGICAL_WORKPLACE_T.logical_workplace_id%TYPE)
return                          varchar2 is

v_id_context                            LOGICAL_WORKPLACE_T.id_context%TYPE;

begin
  if ain_logical_workplace_id is not NULL then
    select id_context
    into   v_id_context
    from   LOGICAL_WORKPLACE_T
    where  logical_workplace_id = ain_logical_workplace_id;
  end if;

  return v_id_context;
end get_id_context;
```

This method is used by method create_id_context() to get the ID context for a new entry's parent entry.

get_name_context()

Similar to its sibling get_code_context(), get_name_context() returns the hierarchical list of name values as a context string for the specified ID. For example, executing FUNCTION get_name_context(ain_id) will return the string Very Dirty Manufacturing, Inc..Manufacturing. Chemicals for the Chemicals department listed in Table 10-3. Here's an example of the method from hierarchical content table package LOGICAL_WORKPLACE_TS:

```
FUNCTION get_name_context(
ain_logical_workplace_id        in
  LOGICAL_WORKPLACE_T.logical_workplace_id%TYPE)
return                          varchar2 is

cursor c_name_context(
ain_logical_workplace_id        in
  LOGICAL_WORKPLACE_T.logical_workplace_id%TYPE) is
select initcap(name) name
from   LOGICAL_WORKPLACE_T
connect by prior parent_id         = logical_workplace_id
start with        logical_workplace_id = ain_logical_workplace_id
order by level desc;

v_name_context                     varchar2(2000);

begin
  for r_name_context in c_name_context(ain_logical_workplace_id) loop
    v_name_context :=
      substr(v_name_context||'.'||r_name_context.name, 1, 2000);
  end loop;
  return v_name_context;
end get_name_context;
```

As with get_code_context(), I use the CONNECT BY SQL clause in the method's cursor, c_name_context, to get the list of name values for the context string.

That's almost the entire list of table package or object TYPE methods. A few more are also used by most executables, so I will discuss them next.

The Black Box

The notion of a "black box" is something that you use but have no idea how it works. A lot of people drive cars, yet they don't actually know how they work. Even more people use electronic devices, yet they don't know how they work either. To these users, these are black boxes.

These black boxes have an interface. In the case of a car, the interface consists of an ignition switch, steering wheel, gas pedal, brake pedal, and so on. But beyond the use of the interface, users know little about how gasoline put in the tank turns into mechanical energy that takes them from place to place. And why should they?

In this section, I'm going to introduce you to a handful of methods that are used in almost every table package, object TYPE, or role package. Let's start with those that are common to all table packages and object TYPEs.

Table Methods

A couple methods are applicable to almost all, if not all, table packages and object TYPEs. They are get_id and inactivate(). The method get_id is shown without parentheses because it takes no arguments. From my point of view, these "black box" methods should exist in every table package and object TYPE. Let's start with get_id.

get_id

Method get_id allocates and returns a new primary key value from an underlying Oracle sequence. FUNCTION get_id acts as an abstraction layer between the underlying Oracle sequence and PL/SQL. This abstraction layer allows you to later change the means by which you allocate a primary key value without having to recode any PL/SQL program units that call the method.

The following is an example of the get_id method from code table package WORKER_TYPE_TS:

```
FUNCTION get_id
return                          WORKER_TYPE_T.worker_type_id%TYPE is

n_worker_type_id                WORKER_TYPE_T.worker_type_id%TYPE;

begin
  select WORKER_TYPE_ID_SEQ.nextval
  into   n_worker_type_id
  from   SYS.DUAL;

  return n_worker_type_id;
end get_id;
```

inactivate()

Rarely have I encountered an application where I actually delete data from a table. Instead, applications work with the idea of inactivating or invalidating an entry. Method inactivate() handles inactivation.

If you have a code table, you can't delete a code value that's in use (one that has any relationships). Yet, you may want to stop users from using an "outdated" code value. To do so, you write your code value's SELECT statement to utilize the code's inactive date, and then you set a code's inactive date so users can no longer select it from a list of values.

Along the same line of thinking, if you have a content table, and a particular entry has relationships, but you no longer want users to select the content table entry, you can set its inactive date and prevent it from appearing in the presentation layer. Just as with the code, the content entry has historical significance but is no longer to be used.

With an intersection table, the concept is slightly different. With an intersection, the assignment of a relationship between two tables exists for the period of time defined from its active date through its inactive date. So when you inactivate an intersection entry, you're simply defining the end of a historical relationship.

Regardless of the type of table for which an entry is inactivated, inactivate() does the same thing: it sets the inactive date. The following is an example of an inactivate() method from content table package LOGICAL_WORKPLACE_TS:

```
PROCEDURE inactivate(
ain_logical_workplace_id          in
  LOGICAL_WORKPLACE_T.logical_workplace_id%TYPE,
aid_inactive_date                 in
  LOGICAL_WORKPLACE_T.inactive_date%TYPE) is

begin
  update LOGICAL_WORKPLACE_T
  set    inactive_date       = aid_inactive_date
  where  logical_workplace_id = ain_logical_worplace_id;
end inactivate;
```

That's straightforward enough. Now let's look at methods used by all packages and TYPEs.

Universal Methods

I expect some methods to exist in every package or TYPE. You've already been introduced to methods help and test. I have one new one here named initialize. Let's start with help.

help

Method help should display help text for the package or TYPE for which it is executed. PROCEDURE help was covered extensively in Chapter 9. You should code this method to display help text in whatever manner you find suitable. What I showed you in Chapter 9 was just an example. But, whatever you do, you must be consistent; otherwise, programmers won't consider the help as reliable documentation, and then you'll have defeated the purpose of coding the method altogether.

The following is an example of the method from code table package WORKER_TYPE_TS:

```
PROCEDURE help is

begin
  TEXT_HELP.process('WORKER_TYPE_TS');
end help;
```

In this example, PROCEDURE process() in package TEXT_HELP will format and display the contents of the associated specification.

initialize

I know I have not talked about method initialize before, but I feel it's an important part of testing and should exist in any package that uses its initialization section. Just in case you don't know what I mean by "initialization section," let me elaborate.

A package body is a PL/SQL block. Because it is a PL/SQL block, it has a declaration section, which is where you code any instance variables, functions, procedures, and so on, and it has an executable section. Really, it does. If, after all the functions and procedures you coded, you add the keyword BEGIN, any code from the keyword BEGIN to keyword END at the end of the package body is executed once, and only once, any time the package is instantiated. By "instantiated," I mean loaded into memory and initialized. There it is, that word: *initialized.*

So for any package where I use the "initialization section," I add a public PROCEDURE initialize to the package. Why? So I can test the code in the initialization section.

One of the mysterious errors developers, support personnel, and end users encounter is a NO_DATA_FOUND the first time they try to use a particular package, and then the error magically goes away. This is almost always caused by a SQL SELECT statement executed in the initialization section of a package that can't find a matching row in the database. It happens once, and only once, because the package is initialized once, and only once.

A problem like this can be quite elusive. You can go crazy troubleshooting the problem and then testing that your solution works. How do you fix it? Create a PROCEDURE initialize where you put your initialization code, and then execute that procedure in the initialization section of your package. Then, you can execute PROCEDURE initialize as many times as you like during testing, without having to log out and in, in order to get the database to initialize the package.

■Note I used to use an empty initialize() method and kept the initialization code in the initialization section, but a smart young programmer, Nataliya Lopatina, came up with this better idea.

Here's an example of the method:

```
PROCEDURE initialize is

begin
  -- Put your initialization code here!
end initialize;
```

Then add a call to initialize in the initialization section of your package:

```
...
begin
  initialize();
end MY_PACKAGE;
/
```

Once this code is in place, any time you access the package for the first time, the package will execute the code in method initialize. And anytime you need to test the code from the initialization section of a package, all you need do is execute method initialize. Take a look at source file top_100_names.pkb for a complete example.

test

The test procedure should be coded so it performs all necessary tests on its package or TYPE's methods. We covered this method extensively in Chapter 8. Here's a partial example of the method from code table package WORKER_TYPE_TS:

```
PROCEDURE test is

n_worker_type_id                    WORKER_TYPE_T.worker_type_id%TYPE;
v_code                              WORKER_TYPE_T.code%TYPE;
v_description                       WORKER_TYPE_T.description%TYPE;

begin
  -- Send feedback that the test ran
  pl('WORKER_TYPE_TS.test()');

  -- Clear the last set of test results
  TEST_TS.clear('WORKER_TYPE_TS');

  -- First, we need some test values

  -- Let's make sure they don't already exist: DELETE
  TEST_TS.set_test('WORKER_TYPE_TS', 'DELETE', 0,
    'Delete test entries');
  begin
    delete WORKER_TYPE_T
    where  code in (
      TEST_TS.v_TEST_30,
      TEST_TS.v_TEST_30_1,
      TEST_TS.v_TEST_30_2);
    TEST_TS.ok();
  exception
    when OTHERS then
      TEST_TS.error(SQLERRM);
  end;

  -- Now let's add three test codes: INSERT
  TEST_TS.set_test('WORKER_TYPE_TS', 'INSERT', 1,
    'Insert 3 test entries');
  begin
    insert into WORKER_TYPE_T (
          worker_type_id,
          code,
          description,
          active_date,
          inactive_date )
    values (
          get_id(),
          TEST_TS.v_TEST_30,
          TEST_TS.v_TEST_80,
          TEST_TS.d_TEST_19000101,
          NULL );
...
```

```
   TEST_TS.set_test('WORKER_TYPE_TS', NULL, NULL, NULL);
   TEST_TS.success();
end test;
```

If you include and code method `test` in every package, then you can totally automate the testing of your PL/SQL executables.

Divide and Conquer

The traditional concept of "divide and conquer" is a tactic to destroy teamwork. Your actions cause dissention among team members, so they no longer work together toward a mutual goal, but instead each works on his own goals. Hence, they are no longer a team.

So where you had a team of discrete members working together at various tasks to achieve a common goal, you end up with a group of individuals competing with each other to achieve many goals. The latter is what we normally end up with in an application:

- The database tries to optimize its work around the overall use of reads and writes to file system while maintaining a transaction context.

- SQL tries to optimize the overall access to data in the database.

- PL/SQL tries to optimize the overall performance of its executables.

- The communication network tries to optimize the overall consumption of bandwidth.

- The application server tries to optimize the overall performance of its hosted executables.

- The presentation layer tries to optimize the overall end-user experience.

What do these layers of technology all have in common? They are all optimized for a fictitious set of events: "the average." They work as a group of individuals competing with each other to achieve their own goals. So how can you turn them into a team whose members work together for a common goal? You divide and conquer. But this time, divide and conquer means you divide up a larger goal into tasks, and then have the best team member perform each task. I know, it's 180 degrees from the traditional definition of divide and conquer, but it works.

For example, if there is data-intensive work to be accomplished, it should be done in the database. Retrieving data from the database through a network to an application server, or worse, a presentation layer, in order to accomplish data migration or data processing is ludicrous. In addition, you should use SQL and PL/SQL to manipulate data. When you combine the use of these two languages, you have the easiest to code, yet most powerful combination for data processing that has ever existed.

In addition, if there is behavior related to data, like so-called business rules, it should reside in the database. Otherwise, each additional layer may have its own version of "the rules," and you'll end up with business rule anarchy. As I tried to convince you earlier, behavior is just as important to store as the data to which it "belongs."

Overall, I'm suggesting that you use PL/SQL and SQL to create actors—program units to fulfill particular roles—in order to accomplish the following kinds of tasks:

- Data migration

- Data processing

- Reporting

Accordingly, this section will cover each of these roles and the polymorphic commands they typically employ.

Data Migration

As I stated earlier, my concept of data migration (DM), is a one-time task where you move external data into a highly structured schema in a database. The notion of it being a "one-time" task is important here. If you needed to move external data into a database on a regular basis, I would call it *data processing* instead.

Here's the high-level idea: load the external data that is to be moved into an application's data structure into staging tables with whatever method is quickest, and then use a PL/SQL data processing program unit to move the data into the application's data structure.

As illustrated in Figure 10-6, you can use an Oracle database link if you're moving data from one database to another, or you can use C/C++ with the Oracle Call Interface (OCI) API, Java and JDBC, XML, or better yet SQL*Loader, if you're loading the data from a file system into the database. Use whatever method is the most efficient.

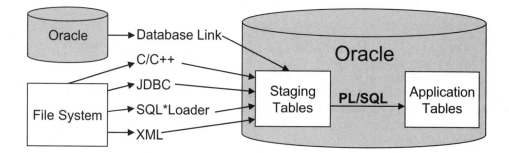

Figure 10-6. *An illustration of data migration*

After the data is loaded into the database, you can then write a PL/SQL package to move the data from the staging tables into a target application's schema. Such a package would have at least one public method: process. When executed, process would do the following:

1. Use the package's initialization section to load code value IDs that can then be used in a cross-reference IF statement to map external code values to ones in the target schema.

2. Initialize the set_row() counters—the public package variables n_inserted and n_updated—to zero for each target table.

3. Use a cursor and cursor FOR LOOP to read through the rows of the staging table.

4. Use the set_row( ) method on the target table(s) to insert the external data.

5. Display the n_insert and n_update counts upon completion in order to confirm that the data migration completed successfully.

After you've coded PROCEDURE process, all you would need to do is execute the method in order to move the data from a staging table to a (or set of) corresponding application table(s).

process

Method process is used to start an on-demand or polling process. The following is an example of the method from data migration package TOP_100_NAMES:

```
PROCEDURE process is

-- This is the cursor for the last names.
cursor c_last is
select last_name
from   TOP_100_LAST_NAME
order by 1;

-- This is the cursor for the first names.
cursor c_first is
select first_name,
       gender_code
from   TOP_100_FIRST_NAME
order by 1;

-- This is the cursor for the middle initials.
cursor c_middle is
select letter
from   A_THRU_Z
order by 1;

-- This is the number of seconds since midnight
-- I'll use it to profile my code's performance.
n_start                        number :=
  to_number(to_char(SYSDATE, 'SSSSS'));

-- I'll use this to keep track of how many rows were selected
n_selected                     number := 0;

-- Here, I declare a record anchored to the table so
-- I can set the column values and then insert using
-- the record.
r_worker                       WORKER_T%ROWTYPE;
```

```
begin
  -- Reset the insert/update counters for set_row()
  WORKER_TS.n_inserted := 0;
  WORKER_TS.n_updated  := 0;

  -- Loop through the last names
  for r_last in c_last loop

    -- While looping through the last names,
    -- loop through the first names
    for r_first in c_first loop

      -- While looping through the last and first names,
      -- loop through the 26 letters in the English
      -- alphabet in order to get middle initials
      for r_middle in c_middle loop
        n_selected              := n_selected + 1;
        -- Initialize the record

        -- Set the PK to NULL so set_row() determines
        -- whether or not the entry already exists
        -- by its unique keys
        r_worker.worker_id      := NULL;

        -- Flip flop from contractor to employee and back again
        if r_worker.worker_type_id = n_WT_CONTRACTOR then
          r_worker.worker_type_id := n_WT_EMPLOYEE;
        else
          r_worker.worker_type_id := n_WT_CONTRACTOR;
        end if;

        -- Set the External ID, UK1, to NULL so set_row() determines
        -- whether or not the entry already exists
        -- by its unique keys
        r_worker.external_id    := NULL;

        -- The first, middle, and last names come from the cursors
        r_worker.first_name     := r_first.first_name;
        r_worker.middle_name    := r_middle.letter||'.';
        r_worker.last_name      := r_last.last_name;

        -- Get the name using the table's package
        r_worker.name           := WORKER_TS.get_formatted_name(
          r_worker.first_name, r_worker.middle_name, r_worker.last_name);

        -- Get the date from determinate function create_birth_date()
        r_worker.birth_date     := create_birth_date(r_worker.name);
```

```
        -- Select the corresponding ID value
        if r_first.gender_code = 'F' then
          r_worker.gender_id       := n_G_FEMALE;
        else
          r_worker.gender_id       := n_G_MALE;
        end if;

        -- Insert the row into the database
        begin
          WORKER_TS.set_row(r_worker);
        exception
          when OTHERS then
            raise_application_error(-20001, SQLERRM||
              ' on call WORKER_TS.set_row()'||
              ' in TOP_100_NAMES.process()');
        end;
      end loop; -- c_middle

      commit;  -- commit every 26 rows

    end loop; -- c_first

  end loop; -- c_last

  -- Display the results
  pl(to_char(n_selected)||' rows selected');
  pl(to_char(WORKER_TS.n_inserted)||' rows inserted');
  pl(to_char(WORKER_TS.n_updated)||' rows updated');
  pl('in '||to_char(to_number(to_char(SYSDATE, 'SSSSS')) - n_start)||
    ' seconds.');
end process;
```

When migrating data, you should be able to take advantage of methods get_row() and set_row() on the target content or intersection tables. Now let's take a look at an on-demand, data processing PL/SQL program unit.

On-Demand Data Processing

If you have a task that needs to be done now, or on an hourly, daily, weekly, or monthly basis, you'll use some kind of an external scheduler like cron in UNIX or Linux, or a Scheduled Tasks in Windows, or perhaps the internal Oracle job queue to execute the process. I call this kind of processing on-demand data processing (ODDP).

Just like its data migration sibling, on-demand data processing is executed through PROCEDURE process. What's different here is the fact that this is not a one-time event. You expect to use this process over and over again. Accordingly, I usually create a table to log when the process runs, along with any performance statistics like how long it took to run, how many rows it inserted, how many rows it updated, and so on.

Since I want to keep track of when a process executes, I now have three common method names used for an on-demand data processing program unit: process, start_logging(), and stop_logging(). Let's look at process first.

process

As before, process is used to start an on-demand or polling process. This time, process incorporates the use of a log so it can record that the process took place, along with some performance statistics. The following is an example of the method from package REPORT_STAGING_TABLES:

```
PROCEDURE process is

-- Get a list of all the tables that start with REPORT_ in BPS' schema
cursor c_table is
select table_name
from    SYS.ALL_TABLES
where   owner         = 'BPS'
and     table_name like 'REPORT\_%' escape '\'
order by 1;

n_selected                          number := 0;
n_deleted                           number := 0;

begin
  -- Start logging
  ON_DEMAND_PROCESS_LOGS.start_logging(
    'REPORT_STAGING_TABLES', 'process');

  -- For each report "staging" table, delete any data over 2 days old
  for r_table in c_table loop
    n_selected := n_selected + 1;

    execute immediate 'delete '||
      r_table.table_name||
      ' where insert_date < SYSDATE - 2';

    n_deleted := n_deleted + nvl(sql%rowcount, 0);
  end loop;

  -- Stop logging
  ON_DEMAND_PROCESS_LOGS.stop_logging(
    n_selected, NULL, NULL, n_deleted, NULL);
exception
  when OTHERS then
    -- Stop logging, but report an error
    ON_DEMAND_PROCESS_LOGS.stop_logging(
      n_selected, NULL, NULL, n_deleted, SQLERRM);
    raise;
end process;
```

If you examine this example, you'll see that the process starts out by calling method start_logging() at the beginning, and then calls method stop_logging() at the end. The underlying log package, ON_DEMAND_PROCESS_LOGS, keeps track of the start and stop time, and then records the statistics to table ON_DEMAND_PROCESS_LOG when method stop_logging() is called.

The process itself deletes any staged reporting data that is over two days old. As with its data migration sibling, if processing data, you should be able to take advantage of methods get_row() and set_row() on any target content or intersection tables.

Now let's take a look at what supporting method start_logging() does.

start_logging()

Method start_logging() stores the time it was called, in memory, allocates and stores a new primary key value, and then inserts a "starting" row in a log table. In this case, it inserts a row into table ON_DEMAND_PROCESS_LOG as defined in the following partial listing from script on_demand_process_log.tab:

```
create table ON_DEMAND_PROCESS_LOG (
on_demand_process_log_id     number                    not null,
object_name                  varchar2(30)              not null,
method_name                  varchar2(30)              not null,
rows_selected                number,
rows_inserted                number,
rows_updated                 number,
rows_deleted                 number,
result                       varchar2(256),
elapsed_time                 number,
insert_user                  varchar2(30) default USER not null,
insert_date                  date         default SYSDATE not null,
update_user                  varchar2(30) default USER not null,
update_date                  date         default SYSDATE not null)
...
```

This log table holds information about how long it took to execute the process, row processing statistics, and the time when the process was started and stopped. The following is an example of the method start_logging() from package ON_DEMAND_PROCESS_LOGS:

```
PROCEDURE start_logging(
aiv_object_name              in
  ON_DEMAND_PROCESS_LOG.object_name%TYPE,
aiv_method_name              in
  ON_DEMAND_PROCESS_LOG.method_name%TYPE) is

pragma autonomous_transaction;

begin
  n_start                    := to_number(to_char(SYSDATE, 'SSSSS'));
  n_on_demand_process_log_id := get_id();
```

```
    insert into ON_DEMAND_PROCESS_LOG (
            on_demand_process_log_id,
            object_name,
            method_name )
    values (
            n_on_demand_process_log_id,
            upper(aiv_object_name),
            upper(aiv_method_name) );
    commit;
end start_logging;
```

Variable n_start in method start_logging() is an instance (package body) variable used to capture the time when the method was called. Similarly, variable n_on_demand_process_log_id is used to capture the new log entry's primary key so the same entry can be updated in method stop_logging(). In addition, this method employs the use of pragma autonomous_transaction so a process that starts but fails will still leave a starting entry in the log.

Now let's look at stop_logging().

stop_logging()

Method stop_logging() takes the row processing information and a result description passed to it, and uses that information along with the stored start time and primary key to update the starting log entry. As part of updating the log entry, the method calculates the elapsed time in seconds between the start and stop of logging. The following is an example of the method from package ON_DEMAND_PROCESS_LOGS:

```
PROCEDURE stop_logging(
ain_rows_selected               in
  ON_DEMAND_PROCESS_LOG.rows_selected%TYPE,
ain_rows_inserted               in
  ON_DEMAND_PROCESS_LOG.rows_inserted%TYPE,
ain_rows_updated                in
  ON_DEMAND_PROCESS_LOG.rows_updated%TYPE,
ain_rows_deleted                in
  ON_DEMAND_PROCESS_LOG.rows_deleted%TYPE,
aiv_result                      in
  ON_DEMAND_PROCESS_LOG.result%TYPE) is

pragma autonomous_transaction;

n_elapsed_time                          number;

begin
  n_elapsed_time := to_number(to_char(SYSDATE, 'SSSSS')) - n_start;
```

```
update ON_DEMAND_PROCESS_LOG
set    rows_selected            = ain_rows_selected,
       rows_inserted            = ain_rows_inserted,
       rows_updated             = ain_rows_updated,
       rows_deleted             = ain_rows_deleted,
       result                   = aiv_result,
       elapsed_time             = n_elapsed_time,
       update_user              = USER,
       update_date              = SYSDATE
where  on_demand_process_log_id = n_on_demand_process_log_id;
commit;

n_on_demand_process_log_id := NULL;

-- Display the results
if ain_rows_selected is not null then
  pl(to_char(ain_rows_selected)||' rows selected.');
end if;
if ain_rows_inserted is not null then
  pl(to_char(ain_rows_inserted)||' rows inserted.');
end if;
if ain_rows_updated is not null then
  pl(to_char(ain_rows_updated)||' rows updated.');
end if;
if ain_rows_deleted is not null then
  pl(to_char(ain_rows_deleted)||' rows deleted.');
end if;
if aiv_result is not null then
  pl(aiv_result);
end if;
pl('Elapsed time: '||to_char(n_elapsed_time)||' seconds.');
end stop_logging;
```

In addition to recording the log statistics, stop_logging() also echoes those statistics to the screen if serveroutput is set to on in SQL*Plus. Like its sibling start_logging(), this method employs the use of pragma autonomous_transaction, so a process that fails can still leave a completed log entry.

Having log information about when on-demand processes execute is an important part of managing their use. Access to statistics about each on-demand process is even more invaluable. Using these statistics, you can determine whether a process is fast and efficient, and make adjustments accordingly.

If you find you're running an on-demand process every few minutes, or if you're interested in offloading a long-running process from the presentation layer, then the process is probably better done as a polling process. Let's look at that next.

Polling Data Processing

Unlike an on-demand process, a polling data process (PDP) just keeps running. It follows three high-level steps:

1. Check a queue for commands.

2. Process the "next" command.

3. Sleep for a predetermined period of time, then go back to step 1.

I'll give you three common examples here of using "divide and conquer" to offload a portion of data processing to the database rather than the presentation or application layer. Doing so makes the presentation or application layer appear to be fast and efficient. And, since the best place to perform data processing is in the database, the offloaded portion of the larger process is fast and efficient. First, let's look at an example with the application layer.

Let's say you have web or message services that, in turn, update your database whenever there is a transaction on an external system. Rather than tie up the services with the entire business process, you can have your services update a set of staging tables in your database, and then have a polling process on your database wake up every so often and finish processing the staged data.

A second example is one where you have a long-running process in the presentation layer. Let's say you have a security system where an administrator can assign access to worker data based on business organization, location, and so on. Rather than tie up the administrator's computer while the mass assignments take place, you can have the presentation layer submit the processing request to your polling process's queue. Then, when your polling process wakes up from its sleep period, it will process your long-running request in the background. What's the result? To the end user using the presentation layer, the application appears easy, fast, and efficient.

A third example is along the same line of thinking. This time, however, you set up your end user's reporting subsystem to submit long-running reports to your polling process's queue, and then have your polling process email the end user with a link (URL) to a completed report when it finishes executing the report in the background. Once again, the end user's experience is one where submitting the report is easy, fast, and efficient.

Using a polling process requires a different design than an on-demand process. Instead of logging each time a process executes (which you can still do), you need to create a queue for process and processing-related commands, and possibly a table to hold the current status of the polling process. I'll start out by showing you an example of the process method, and then follow up with discussions on each of the supporting methods.

process

Once again, process is used to start an on-demand or polling process. In this case, a polling data process. A polling process is one that does its thing, goes to sleep, and then wakes up to do its thing all over again and again. A polling process is dependent on a queue, at the very least, so you can tell the process to quit executing.

The queue can also be used to indicate what needs to be processed. For example, if you have a long-running process that must take place as part of inserting an entry into a particular table, you could have a trigger on that table insert a row into a polling process's queue, like a primary key ID value, and then have the polling process finish the long-running process asynchronously.

The following is an example of a polling process that you can find in package POLLING_PROCESS:

```
PROCEDURE process is

r_polling_process_queue                 POLLING_PROCESS_QUEUE%ROWTYPE;

begin
  DEBUG_TS.set_text('POLLING_PROCESS', 'Starting');

  -- Perform a manual loop until it receives a command to quit
  loop
    DEBUG_TS.set_text('POLLING_PROCESS', 'Getting next command');

    -- Get the next command from the queue
    r_polling_process_queue :=
      POLLING_PROCESS_QUEUES.get_next(r_polling_process_queue);

    -- If it's time to quit, pool the queue once more to delete
    -- the quit command, and then exit
    if r_polling_process_queue.command =
        POLLING_PROCESS_QUEUES.v_QUIT then

      POLLING_PROCESS_STATUSS.set_status('Quiting');

      DEBUG_TS.set_text('POLLING_PROCESS', 'Quiting');

      r_polling_process_queue :=
        POLLING_PROCESS_QUEUES.get_next(r_polling_process_queue);
      exit;
    elsif r_polling_process_queue.command = 'DISABLE' then
      DEBUG_TS.disable('POLLING_PROCESS');
    elsif r_polling_process_queue.command = 'ENABLE'  then
      DEBUG_TS.enable('POLLING_PROCESS');
    end if;

    -- *** Now do all your groovy data processing here! ***

    POLLING_PROCESS_STATUSS.set_status('Processing');

    DEBUG_TS.set_text('POLLING_PROCESS',
      'I''m doing some groovy data processing at '||
      to_char(SYSDATE, 'HH:MI:SS'));

    -- *** End of your groovy data processing section.  ***

    POLLING_PROCESS_STATUSS.set_status('Sleeping');
```

```
    DEBUG_TS.set_text('POLLING_PROCESS', 'Sleeping');

    -- Sleep for 10 seconds
    SYS.DBMS_LOCK.sleep(10);

    DEBUG_TS.set_text('POLLING_PROCESS', 'Awake');
  end loop;
end process;
```

This example currently has many lines that employ the use of DEBUG_TS.set_text() to record what's going on in the process as it runs. The debug logging, as it is called, can be turned on before running the process, or it can be turned on by executing method enable. Conversely, debug logging can be turned off by executing disable. This means you can enable and disable debug logging on this process from any other database session at any point in time while the process is running. That's helpful when it comes to troubleshooting a new polling process.

This example also employs method quit to tell the polling process to stop executing. In addition, it updates a status table POLLING_PROCESS_STATUS with the current status of the process, so you can determine what it's working on at any point in time while it's executing.

In this example, I'm sleeping for only 10 seconds in between processing. I've just coded it that way in order to make it easy to demonstrate. In practice, I normally have a polling process sleep 3 to 5 minutes (180 to 300 seconds).

Let's look at method get_next() next.

get_next()

Method get_next() deletes the last item processed from the queue as specified by the passed parameter, and then retrieves the next command from a queue. In this case, it deletes and selects an entry from table POLLING_PROCESS_QUEUE. The following is an example of a queue table definition from file polling_process_queue.tab:

```
create table POLLING_PROCESS_QUEUE (
polling_process_queue_id      number                          not null,
command                       varchar2(256)                   not null,
insert_user                   varchar2(30)  default USER      not null,
insert_date                   date          default SYSDATE   not null)
...
```

FUNCTION get_next(air_queue_entry) is the "heart and soul" of the polling process. Here's an example of the method from table package POLLING_PROCESS_QUEUES:

```
FUNCTION get_next(
air_polling_process_queue     in      POLLING_PROCESS_QUEUE%ROWTYPE)
return                                POLLING_PROCESS_QUEUE%ROWTYPE is

pragma autonomous_transaction;

r_polling_process_queue               POLLING_PROCESS_QUEUE%ROWTYPE;
```

```
begin
  delete POLLING_PROCESS_QUEUE
  where  polling_process_queue_id =
    air_polling_process_queue.polling_process_queue_id;

  begin
    select q.*
    into   r_polling_process_queue
    from   POLLING_PROCESS_QUEUE q
    where  q.polling_process_queue_id = (
    select min(n.polling_process_queue_id)
    from   POLLING_PROCESS_QUEUE n);
  exception
    when NO_DATA_FOUND then
      r_polling_process_queue := NULL;
  end;

  commit;

  return r_polling_process_queue;
end get_next;
```

The way that this method is written, an entry is removed from the queue only after it has completed successfully.

Let's look at the one method that always uses the queue, quit, next.

quit

Method quit is used to tell a polling or long-running process to quit before its next round of processing. With a polling process, this method stores a quit command in the polling process's queue, so the next time it wakes and starts processing, it quits executing.

PROCEDURE quit inserts a new message into its queue table with a primary key value of –1 so the command jumps to the top of the queue. Here's an example of the method from table package POLLING_PROCESS_QUEUES:

```
PROCEDURE quit is

pragma autonomous_transaction;

begin
  begin
    insert into POLLING_PROCESS_QUEUE (
           polling_process_queue_id,
           command,
           insert_user,
           insert_date )
```

```
      values (
            -1,
            v_QUIT,
            USER,
            SYSDATE );
     pl('Queued to quit.');
  exception
    when DUP_VAL_ON_INDEX then
       pl('Already queued to quit.');
  end;

  commit;
end quit;
```

A convenience method quit also exists in package POLLING_PROCESS, because it's easier to remember to execute POLLING_PROCESS.quit to stop the execution of POLLING_PROCESS.process than it is to remember the name of the queue's table package.

So you can now start and quit the process. Wouldn't it be nice to be able to see what the process is doing whenever you needed to? Well that's what method enable is for. Let's look at it next.

enable

Method enable is used to enable something—in this case, the logging of debug information at any desired point in time. PROCEDURE enable inserts a new command into the queue with a primary key value of -2, so enabling debug logging has an even higher priority than quitting. Here's an example of the method from package POLLING_PROCESS_QUEUES:

```
PROCEDURE enable is

pragma autonomous_transaction;

begin
  begin
    insert into POLLING_PROCESS_QUEUE (
            polling_process_queue_id,
            command,
            insert_user,
            insert_date )
    values (
            -2,
            v_ENABLE,
            USER,
            SYSDATE );
    pl('Queued to enable logging.');
```

```
  exception
    when DUP_VAL_ON_INDEX then
      pl('Already queued enable logging.');
  end;

  commit;
end enable;
```

After executing PROCEDURE enable, and after the polling process's next access to the queue, PROCEDURE process enables debug logging. As with its sibling method quit, a convenience method enable also exists in package POLLING_PROCESS.

And disable?

disable

Method disable is used to disable something—in this case, the logging of debug information at any desired point in time. PROCEDURE disable inserts a new command into the queue with a primary key value of -3, so disabling debug logging has an even higher priority than enabling debug logging and quitting. Here's an example of the method from package POLLING_PROCESS_QUEUES:

```
PROCEDURE disable is

pragma autonomous_transaction;

begin
  begin
    insert into POLLING_PROCESS_QUEUE (
            polling_process_queue_id,
            command,
            insert_user,
            insert_date )
    values (
            -3,
            v_DISABLE,
            USER,
            SYSDATE );
    pl('Queued to disable logging.');
  exception
    when DUP_VAL_ON_INDEX then
      pl('Already queued to disable logging.');
  end;

  commit;
end disable;
```

After executing PROCEDURE disable, and after the polling process's next access to the queue, PROCEDURE process disables debug logging. As with its sibling methods quit and enable, a convenience method disable also exists in package POLLING_PROCESS.

Now let's look at the methods used to record and read the current status of a polling process.

set_status()

Method set_status() is used to record a process's current status in a status table. In this case, set_status() is updating a row in table POLLING_PROCESS_STATUS, as defined from following partial listing of file polling_process_status.tab:

```
create table POLLING_PROCESS_STATUS (
status                          varchar2(256)                  not null,
update_user                     varchar2(30)  default USER     not null,
update_date                     date          default SYSDATE  not null)
...
```

This table is supposed to have one, and only one, row at any point in time. PROCEDURE set_status(aiv_status) updates or inserts an entry in this table as needed. The following is an example of this method from table package POLLING_PROCESS_STATUSS:

```
PROCEDURE set_status(
aiv_status                      in
  POLLING_PROCESS_STATUS.status%TYPE) is

pragma autonomous_transaction;

begin
  update POLLING_PROCESS_STATUS
  set    status      = aiv_status,
         update_user = USER,
         update_date = SYSDATE;

  if nvl(sql%rowcount, 0) = 0 then
    insert into POLLING_PROCESS_STATUS (
           status,
           update_user,
           update_date )
    values (
           aiv_status,
           USER,
           SYSDATE );
  end if;

  commit;
exception
  when OTHERS then
    raise_application_error(-20002, SQLERRM||
      ' on update or insert POLLING_PROCESS_STATUS'||
      ' in POLLING_PROCESS_STATUSS.set_status()');
end set_status;
```

So how do you get the status? Come on now . . .

get_status

Method get_status returns the current status for the associated process from its status table. FUNCTION get_status retrieves the one, and only, row from the table, and then returns the value of column status. Here's an example of the method from table package POLLING_PROCESS_STATUSS:

```
FUNCTION get_status
return
  POLLING_PROCESS_STATUS.status%TYPE is

v_status
  POLLING_PROCESS_STATUS.status%TYPE;

begin
  select status
  into   v_status
  from   POLLING_PROCESS_STATUS;

  return v_status;
exception
  when NO_DATA_FOUND then
    return 'UNKNOWN';
  when OTHERS then
    raise_application_error(-20001, SQLERRM||
      ' on select POLLING_PROCESS_STATUS'||
      ' in POLLING_PROCESS_STATUSS.get_status()');
end get_status;
```

And finally, our last polling process method: status.

status

Since we are in such a "commanding (or demanding) mood" with this section, status is a convenience method that exists in the polling process's package that executes method get_status from the table package for the status table. Once again, it exists in the polling process package because it's simply more intuitive to execute commands for a given process from its own package.

Here's an example from polling process package POLLING_PROCESS:

```
PROCEDURE status is

begin
  pl(POLLING_PROCESS_STATUSS.get_status);
end status;
```

With the queue and status tables and their associated table packages in place, you can now tell the polling process to do the following:

- Quit

- Enable debug logging

- Disable debug logging

- Process a given command

- Display its current status

A common use for on-demand or polling processing is to build interfaces between systems. Let's discuss some common method names used for just that next.

Interfacing

Interfacing, systems integration, or whatever you want to call it, is just data processing. It is commonly a multistep data process (MSDP) that follows a fairly standard set of tasks:

1. Log that you are going to attempt to download data from a source to your target system.

2. Download data from the source to your target system.

3. Log that you downloaded the data successfully.

4. Verify that you have cross-reference values for all mapped fields.

5. Upload data from its staging tables to its target tables.

6. Log that you uploaded the data successfully.

As you can see, interfacing consists of two high-level steps: downloading and uploading (for lack of better terms). Figure 10-7 shows a visual representation of this division of tasks. These steps can be accomplished synchronously or asynchronously. Regardless, I like to separate the major steps by recording their success or failure in a status table. This allows me to rerun the process, as needed, until both steps are completed.

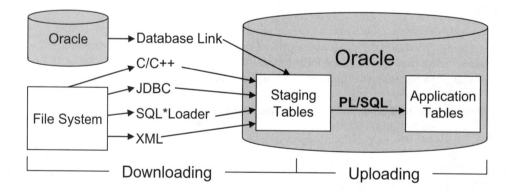

Figure 10-7. *Interfacing with external systems, two steps: downloading and uploading*

Whether or not I use a program external to the database to move data from a source to destination staging tables, the "download" program can record when it starts its processing and when it completes. Then when the upload process starts, it can check to see if the download process has been completed. If the download has been completed, the upload process can log when it starts and when it completes.

Dividing a long-running process into multiple smaller processes like this not only allows you to do asynchronous processing, but also provides you with a framework to build robust processes that can be rerun over and over again until they finish their processing.

For example, if you build an interface with multistep processing that should move data into your database once a week, it can be scheduled to run every day of the week with cron or Scheduled Tasks, and it will just quit if the weekly work has already been completed.

Here, I'll discuss commonly used method names for a multistep interface on-demand process. Let's start with process.

process

Again, process is used to start an on-demand or polling process. In this case, a multistep data process. A multistep process is one that checks which portion of a process needs to be done and (re)starts the process at the required step. A multistep process is dependent on a status table that is used to record when a step is completed successfully.

The following is an example of a multistep process that you can find in package WEEKLY_INTERFACE:

```
PROCEDURE process is

begin
  if not WEEKLY_INTERFACE_STATUSS.is_downloaded() then
    download();
    if not WEEKLY_INTERFACE_STATUSS.is_downloaded() then
      pl('WARNING: download() did not complete successfully.');
    end if;
  end if;

  if WEEKLY_INTERFACE_STATUSS.is_downloaded() then
    if not WEEKLY_INTERFACE_STATUSS.is_uploaded() then
      upload();
      if not WEEKLY_INTERFACE_STATUSS.is_uploaded() then
        pl('WARNING: upload() did not complete successfully.');
      end if;
    end if;
  end if;

  pl('process() completed successfully.');
end process;
```

As you can see from this example, PROCEDURE process is concerned only with the status of the multistep process and calls other procedures to accomplish its required steps.

Let's take a look at the supporting methods. We'll start with is_downloaded.

is_downloaded

Method is_downloaded returns a Boolean value that indicates whether the first step, downloading, has been accomplished. FUNCTION is_downloaded returns TRUE if the download process has been completed; otherwise, it returns FALSE.

The following is an example of the method from supporting table package WEEKLY_INTERFACE_STATUSS:

```
FUNCTION is_downloaded
return                                    boolean is

pragma autonomous_transaction;

d_download_date
  WEEKLY_INTERFACE_STATUS.download_date%TYPE;

begin
  begin
    select download_date
    into   d_download_date
    from   WEEKLY_INTERFACE_STATUS
    where  weekly_interface_status_id =
      WEEKLY_INTERFACE_STATUSS.get_week();
  exception
    when NO_DATA_FOUND then
      d_download_date := NULL;
  end;

  if d_download_date is not NULL then
    return TRUE;
  else
    return FALSE;
  end if;
end is_downloaded;
```

PROCEDURE WEEKLY_INTERFACE.process calls this method directly from package WEEKLY_INTERFACE_STATUSS. In addition, I've added a convenience method, is_downloaded, which returns the number 1 for TRUE and 0 for FALSE to package WEEKLY_INTERFACE, because external programs that might want to know the status of the download process, such as a Java JDBC program, cannot call a stored procedure that returns a Boolean value. Here's an example of the is_downloaded convenience method from package WEEKLY_INTERFACE:

```
FUNCTION is_downloaded
return                                    number is

begin
  -- A function that returns a 1 or 0 from TRUE and FALSE
  -- from WEEKLY_INTERFACE_STATUSS.is_downloaded()
  return to_boolean_number(WEEKLY_INTERFACE_STATUSS.is_downloaded());
end is_downloaded;
```

Next, let's take a look at the download method.

download

Method download is used to start a download process—that is, a process to move data between systems—from a data source to your target staging tables. PROCEDURE download can be utilized in your multistep process if the data can be moved from its source to the destination staging tables from inside the database. You can do this in a variety of ways, using the following:

- A database link between systems

- An embedded JDBC program to access an external database

- Package SYS.UTL_MAIL to access an email server

- Package SYS.UTL_HTTP to access a web server

- Package SYS.UTL_FILE to access the database server's file system

If you need to perform this step externally with another program, you can simply code a put_line() message that reminds the user that this step is accomplished externally. By handling the external process in this fashion, you don't need to modify the code in method process.

The following is an example of the method from package WEEKLY_INTERFACE:

```
PROCEDURE download is

begin
  pl('Executing download()');
  -- You can code this procedure to move data between systems
  -- using an Oracle database link, loaded JDBC driver and class,
  -- etc.  Or, you can change this message to remind the user
  -- that this is an asynchronous process handled by an external
  -- program.

  -- set_downloaded();
end download;
```

If you code this method, then you'll call set_downloaded upon a successful download. If, on the other hand, you code the download process externally, that program will need to call WEEKLY_INTERFACE.set_downloaded in order to let process know that the first step of the multi-step process has been completed asynchronously.

While we're on the topic, let's look at set_downloaded next.

set_downloaded

Method set_downloaded is used to set the status of the download process to complete. Supporting table package's PROCEDURE WEEKLY_INTERFACE_STATUS.set_downloaded is called from inside download, if the download method is actually coded to perform the download process.

The following is an example of the supporting status table WEEKLY_INTERFACE_STATUS from script weekly_interface_status.tab:

```
create table WEEKLY_INTERFACE_STATUS (
weekly_interface_status_id     number                         not null,
download_date                  date,
upload_date                    date,
insert_user                    varchar2(30)  default USER     not null,
insert_date                    date          default SYSDATE  not null,
update_user                    varchar2(30)  default USER     not null,
update_date                    date          default SYSDATE  not null)
...
```

And, here's an example of the method set_downloaded supporting table package WEEKLY_INTERFACE_STATUSS:

```
PROCEDURE set_downloaded is

pragma autonomous_transaction;

begin
  update WEEKLY_INTERFACE_STATUS
  set     download_date          = SYSDATE,
          update_user            = USER,
          update_date            = SYSDATE
  where   weekly_interface_status_id =
    WEEKLY_INTERFACE_STATUSS.get_week();

  if nvl(sql%rowcount, 0) = 0 then
    insert into WEEKLY_INTERFACE_STATUS (
          weekly_interface_status_id,
          download_date )
    values (
          WEEKLY_INTERFACE_STATUSS.get_week(),
          SYSDATE );
  end if;

  commit;
end set_downloaded;
```

I've also created a convenience method set_downloaded in package WEEKLY_INTERFACE, which can be called by an external download program in order to set the download process to complete, as follows:

```
PROCEDURE set_downloaded is

begin
  WEEKLY_INTERFACE_STATUSS.set_downloaded();
end set_downloaded;
```

Enough with the download business. Now let's talk about uploading, starting with method is_uploaded.

is_uploaded

Method is_uploaded returns a Boolean value that indicates whether the second step, uploading, has been accomplished. FUNCTION is_uploaded returns TRUE if the upload process has been completed; otherwise, it returns FALSE.

The following is an example of the method from supporting table package WEEKLY_INTERFACE_STATUSS:

```
FUNCTION is_uploaded
return                                   boolean is

pragma autonomous_transaction;

d_upload_date
  WEEKLY_INTERFACE_STATUS.upload_date%TYPE;

begin
  begin
    select upload_date
    into   d_upload_date
    from   WEEKLY_INTERFACE_STATUS
    where  weekly_interface_status_id =
      WEEKLY_INTERFACE_STATUSS.get_week();
  exception
    when NO_DATA_FOUND then
      d_upload_date := NULL;
  end;

  if d_upload_date is not NULL then
    return TRUE;
  else
    return FALSE;
  end if;
end is_uploaded;
```

PROCEDURE WEEKLY_INTERFACE.process calls this method directly from package WEEKLY_INTERFACE_STATUSS. Unlike its sibling, is_downloaded, there's no need for a convenience method, because the whole point of the multistep process package is to upload the data from staging to application tables. So no external process will ever be used, and hence no convenience method is required.

Now let's look at upload.

upload

Method upload is used to start an upload process—that is, a process to move data from staging tables to an application's tables. This is where you code all your groovy data processing.

Here's an example of the method from package WEEKLY_INTERFACE:

```
PROCEDURE upload is

-- Add cursor(s) used to loop through the staging data here.

begin
  pl('Executing upload()');
  if is_verified() then

    -- Add your data migration code here.

    set_uploaded();
  end if;
end upload;
```

And last, but not least, is set_uploaded.

set_uploaded

Method set_uploaded is used to set the status of the upload process to complete. Supporting table package's PROCEDURE WEEKLY_INTERFACE_STATUS.set_uploaded is called from inside upload, if the upload method completes successfully.

The following is an example of the method from supporting table package WEEKLY_INTERFACE_STATUSS:

```
PROCEDURE set_uploaded is

pragma autonomous_transaction;

begin
  update WEEKLY_INTERFACE_STATUS
  set    upload_date                 = SYSDATE,
         update_user                 = USER,
         update_date                 = SYSDATE
  where  weekly_interface_status_id =
    WEEKLY_INTERFACE_STATUSS.get_week();
```

```
  if nvl(sql%rowcount, 0) = 0 then
    insert into WEEKLY_INTERFACE_STATUS (
           weekly_interface_status_id,
           upload_date )
    values (
           WEEKLY_INTERFACE_STATUSS.get_week(),
           SYSDATE );
  end if;

  commit;
end set_uploaded;
```

Using the WEEKLY_INTERFACE package as a framework for your database destination inter-faces, you can provide a consistent treatment to all interfaces and at the same time have the freedom to perform each high-level step in a manner that is suitable for solving the associated business requirements.

Next, let's look at the polymorphic use of method names in support of the reporting presentation layer.

Reporting

It has become quite fashionable in our industry to develop or implement the data-entry portion of an application and then throw a reporting utility—like Cognos Impromptu, Business Objects, Crystal Reports, and so on—at the application's relational database or data warehouse for reporting needs. Since I'm not selling any of these "solutions," I can share my honest opinion. Throwing a reporting utility at an application for its reporting needs is a poor idea. Suddenly, we've decided to give our customers half of a solution. What's with that? I know that it's all about the money. But I've never seen much large-scale reporting success with end users with this strategy. Here's why that is:

- Most end users know very little about how the information they work with is actually organized and related.

- Most end users know very little about how information is input into their application and how it is consequently stored in the application's database.

- Most end users have no time to spend trying to engineer a set of complex reports to help them run the business.

That's not to say that there aren't exceptions. But for the most part, reporting requirements and deliverables should be a required part of any application's development or implementa-tion (depending on whether you build or buy).

For those exceptional end users who are information and system architects, when they do use reporting utilities, they usually get poor performance from the database. It's not necessarily the database's fault; it's a matter of physics.

A well-designed relational or object-relational database will have tables that are all in their third normal form. Accordingly, any SELECT statements written against a well-designed data-base will have many tables in the FROM clause of a given SELECT statement. The more tables, the more data must be physically read from physical devices, the more physical devices have to work, the longer it takes. It's not a database problem; it's a physics problem.

Now if you recall from previous chapters, I've spent some time showing you the consequences of physics and a database. You can use several tactics to "divide and conquer" in order to improve the speed and efficiency of retrieving data for reporting:

- Use pseudo-constants and PL/SQL IF statements to replace code tables in a FROM clause of a SELECT statement. This reduces the use of physical devices.

- Retrieve data from the smallest table that will produce the smallest set of results, and then do programmatic nested loops with cursors to retrieve the "rest" of the data. This reduces the use of physical devices.

- Create thin (narrow) row extracts of data, and then join them together in a SELECT statement. This reduces the use of memory and physical devices. For example, if the source table has an average row size of 297 bytes, you may extract data from it into a temporary table that has an average row size of 13 bytes. The temporary table is what I call a *narrow row table*.

- Post-sort results. Sort the rows for a report after the report data has already been placed in a staging table(s). This reduces the use of memory and CPU cycles.

However, you can use these tactics only if you write stored procedures to produce the result sets for your reports, placing the results in staging tables, which are then later queried by the presentation layer. What I'm advocating here is heresy to some, and bliss for others. I know many of you may want to send me an email explaining why this is such a bad idea. Do it. I would love to argue with you about it. Here's what I do know:

- In applications with well over one million rows in each content table, I'm able to produce short reports in less than 3 seconds, most in less than 1 second. That's compared to over 3 minutes trying to accomplish the same task with a large, complicated SQL SELECT statement.

- In the same large enterprise applications, I've been able to produce large reports in less than 3 minutes. That's compared to 20 minutes to 28 hours for some of the largest reports. Yes, even reports that took 28 hours to produce using a very large and complicated SQL SELECT statement took less than 3 minutes when these "divide and conquer" principles were applied. And no, there were no accidental Cartesian products in the SELECT statement.

- When this architecture is adopted, the business intelligence on how to produce the report permanently resides in the database where it is easiest and most efficient to process data. This means that any presentation layer can be used to produce the result set for a given report by executing its corresponding stored procedure in the database, and then simply formatting and displaying the data in whatever fashion is desired. Presentation layers come and go. Does the business knowledge that produces your reports have to go with it? No.

Figure 10-8 demonstrates the reporting architecture I'm advocating. In this architecture, producing a report consists of these three high-level steps:

1. The presentation layer calls a function get_report() in the database, passing it any required parameters for producing a report.

2. get_report() produces the result set for the report, placing the results in a staging table specific to the report. Then get_report() returns an ID for the results.

3. The presentation layer executes a SELECT statement against the report's staging table, where the report ID is the one returned from get_report(), and orders the results by the report's sequence.

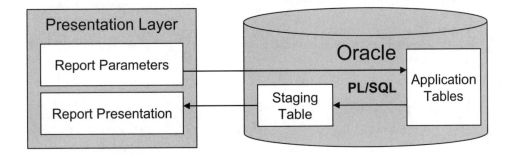

Figure 10-8. *A modular PL/SQL- and SQL-driven reporting architecture*

I call reports produced in this manner "staged data reports." In practice, I've used this architecture to impressively improve the performance and complexity of reports, while also reducing the consumption of server resources. That's a win-win situation. I've called the same report stored procedure from Oracle Reports, PowerBuilder, and a J2EE application on the Web. Here, the same result set is used by three different presentation layers. This means you can consistently produce the results for a report, and present the results in whatever way you see fit.

Accordingly, in this section, I'm going to cover the polymorphic method names I use in this reporting architecture. Let's get started with get_report().

get_report()

Method get_report() produces a report result set by retrieving data from application tables, placing the results in a report specific set of staging tables, and then returning an ID to the result set. FUNCTION get_report() takes runtime parameters passed to it from the presentation layer and uses those to efficiently retrieve and stage the data for a report. Most often, you'll use get_report() to simply improve the performance of a report. However, some reports cannot be created with just SQL statements, and that's where the use of get_report() becomes critically important.

Here's an example of the method from a report stored procedure that produces a work history report for a given worker_id. This method is from package REPORT_WKHSTS:

```
FUNCTION get_report(
ain_worker_id                       in      REPORT_WKHST.worker_id%TYPE)
return                                      REPORT_WKHST.report_wkhst_id%TYPE is

cursor c_date(
ain_worker_id                       in      REPORT_WKHST.worker_id%TYPE) is
select v1.active_date
from ( select active_date
       from   LOGICAL_ASSIGNMENT_T
       where  worker_id = ain_worker_id
       UNION
       select active_date
       from   PHYSICAL_ASSIGNMENT_T
       where  worker_id = ain_worker_id
       UNION
       select active_date
       from   WORK_ASSIGNMENT_T
       where  worker_id = ain_worker_id ) v1
order by 1;

d_logical_inactive_date             REPORT_WKHST.inactive_date%TYPE;
d_physical_inactive_date            REPORT_WKHST.inactive_date%TYPE;
d_work_inactive_date                REPORT_WKHST.inactive_date%TYPE;

r_worker                            WORKER_T%ROWTYPE;

r_report_wkhst                      REPORT_WKHST%ROWTYPE;

begin
  r_report_wkhst.report_wkhst_id  := get_id();
  r_report_wkhst.report_wkhst_seq := 0;

  r_worker.worker_id := ain_worker_id;
  r_worker           := WORKER_TS.get_row(r_worker);

  r_report_wkhst.worker_id   := r_worker.worker_id;
  r_report_wkhst.worker_name :=
    WORKER_TS.get_formatted_name(
      r_worker.first_name,
      r_worker.middle_name,
      r_worker.last_name);

  for r_date in c_date(ain_worker_id) loop
    r_report_wkhst.active_date := r_date.active_date;
```

```
    get_logical_workplace_name(
       r_report_wkhst.worker_id,
       r_report_wkhst.active_date,
       r_report_wkhst.logical_workplace_name,
       d_logical_inactive_date);

    get_physical_workplace_name(
       r_report_wkhst.worker_id,
       r_report_wkhst.active_date,
       r_report_wkhst.physical_workplace_name,
       d_physical_inactive_date);

    get_work_name(
       r_report_wkhst.worker_id,
       r_report_wkhst.active_date,
       r_report_wkhst.work_name,
       d_work_inactive_date);

    r_report_wkhst.inactive_date :=
       least(
          d_logical_inactive_date,
          d_physical_inactive_date,
          d_work_inactive_date);

    set_report(r_report_wkhst);
  end loop;

  commit;

  return r_report_wkhst.report_wkhst_id;
end get_report;
```

If you examine the listing, you'll notice that I call three private methods: get_logical_
workplace_name(), get_physical_workplace_name, and get_work_name, which are used to get
the data in a programmatic nested loop fashion. I suppose if I spent enough time, I could write
a SQL SELECT statement to get these results, but in this case, it's much easier and faster to use
PL/SQL.

The following script, report_wkhsts.get_report.sql, is a test unit I use to run the report
from SQL*Plus during development and troubleshooting:

```
rem report_wkhsts.get_report.sql
rem by Donald J. Bales on 12/15/2006
rem Test Unit for REPORT_WKHST_TS.get_report()

column worker_name              format a21 trunc;
column logical_workplace_name   format a11 trunc;
column physical_workplace_name  format a11 trunc;
column work_name                format a11 trunc;
```

```
column active_date              format a8;
column inactive_date            format a8;

execute pl('report_wkhst_id='||to_char(REPORT_WKHSTS.get_report(11649889)));

select worker_name,
       logical_workplace_name,
       physical_workplace_name,
       work_name,
       to_char(active_date,   'YYYYMMDD') active_date,
       to_char(inactive_date, 'YYYYMMDD') inactive_date
from   REPORT_WKHST
where  report_wkhst_id = &report_wkhst_id
order by report_wkhst_seq;
```

When executed with `worker_id` 11649889, the script produces the following output:

```
WORKER_NAME           LOGICAL_WOR PHYSICAL_WO WORK_NAME   ACTIVE_D INACTIVE
--------------------- ----------- ----------- ----------- -------- --------
PATTERSON, MICHELLE D BIOLOGICALS GRAVITRON 1 ENGINEER1   19740520 19850507
PATTERSON, MICHELLE D BIOLOGICALS GRAVITRON 1 ENGINEER2   19850508 19960425
PATTERSON, MICHELLE D BIOLOGICALS GRAVITRON 1 ENGINEER3   19960426
```

In practice, every report has a different package name that starts with `REPORT_`, whose associated table is the singular form of the package's name. All reports use the same method name, `get_report()`, with the presentation layer passing the method any required parameter values. Since a report package has an associated table, it's only fitting for it to have an associated method name for inserting values into that table, and that name is `set_report()`.

set_report()

Since you're an astute reader, you're probably thinking, "Why doesn't he just use the method name `set_row()`?" It's because `set_report()` does something different than `set_row()`, so I consistently use the name `set_report()` in order to emphasize that difference.

Before I get into an explanation of the difference, let's look at an example of the definition of an associated report staging table. This is the report staging table definition for the work history report. You can find this listing in script `report_wkhst.tab`:

```
create table REPORT_WKHST (
report_wkhst_id              number                          not null,
report_wkhst_seq             number                          not null,
worker_id                    number                          not null,
worker_name                  varchar2(100)                   not null,
active_date                  date,
logical_workplace_name       varchar2(80),
physical_workplace_name      varchar2(80),
work_name                    varchar2(80),
inactive_date                date,
insert_user                  varchar2(30)  default USER      not null,
```

```
insert_date                     date         default SYSDATE  not null)
```

And here is an example of method set_report() that inserts the data into the report staging table:

```
PROCEDURE set_report(
aior_report_wkhst               in out REPORT_WKHST%ROWTYPE) is

begin
  aior_report_wkhst.report_wkhst_seq :=
    aior_report_wkhst.report_wkhst_seq + 1;

  if aior_report_wkhst.inactive_date  = DATES.d_max then
    aior_report_wkhst.inactive_date  := NULL;
  end if;

  aior_report_wkhst.insert_user    := USER;
  aior_report_wkhst.insert_date    := SYSDATE;

  insert into REPORT_WKHST values aior_report_wkhst;
exception
  when OTHERS then
    raise_application_error(-20004, SQLERRM||
      ' on insert REPORT_WKHST'||
      ' in REPORT_WKHSTS.set_report()');
end set_report;
```

In contrast to method set_row(), which selects and then inserts or updates, PROCEDURE set_report(air_row) strictly inserts. In addition, set_report() increments the value of the report's sequence number. The sequence number is the second half of a two-column primary key for the staging table. With this design, get_report() can return a single value, an ID, that will allow the presentation layer to select all the subject rows for a report, and then sort against the sequence value.

This means that the order of the information on the report is driven by a given report's engine in the database, not the presentation layer. This is also what allows you to, as I mentioned earlier, post-sort.

You can code a report stored procedure so that, after it places all of its data in its staging table, you sort the data in the table by opening a cursor against the staging table with an ORDER BY clause, and then update the sequence numbers in the same staging table so the results will have a new sort order.

Now you have a means to get the presentation layer to use a modular and efficient approach to creating reports, but what if you want to email a report from the database? That's the purpose of method report().

report()

Not all reports need human interaction to produce them. Sometimes, an application has a list of reports that should be produced on an hourly, daily, weekly, or monthly basis. Why should you require users to run them? A better design is to provide end users with a set of batch-processed report distribution screens, where they can configure who gets what report, and then have the application produce the reports for them.

If the database produces the reports, it can send the report via email as fixed-length text, HTML, PDF, and so on, or as a link. The following is an example of an HTML emailed report from report procedure REPORT_WKHSTS:

```
PROCEDURE report(
ain_worker_id                     in      REPORT_WKHST.worker_id%TYPE,
aiv_to                            in      varchar2) is

cursor c_report_wkhst(
ain_report_wkhst_id               in      REPORT_WKHST.report_wkhst_id%TYPE) is
select initcap(worker_name) worker_name,
       active_date,
       initcap(logical_workplace_name) logical_workplace_name,
       initcap(physical_workplace_name) physical_workplace_name,
       initcap(work_name) work_name,
       inactive_date
from   REPORT_WKHST
where  report_wkhst_id = ain_report_wkhst_id
order by report_wkhst_seq;

n_line                            number;
t_lines                           EMAILS.LINES;
n_report_wkhst_id                 REPORT_WKHST.report_wkhst_id%TYPE;
v_worker_name                     REPORT_WKHST.worker_name%TYPE;

begin
  n_report_wkhst_id := get_report(ain_worker_id);

  t_lines(incr(n_line)) := '</pre><table>';
  for r_report_wkhst in c_report_wkhst(n_report_wkhst_id) loop
    if c_report_wkhst%rowcount = 1 then
      v_worker_name        := r_report_wkhst.worker_name;
      t_lines(incr(n_line)) := '<tr><td align="center" colspan="5">'||
        '<big>Work History Report</big></td></tr>';
      t_lines(incr(n_line)) := '<tr><td align="center" colspan="5">'||
        'for '||v_worker_name||'</td></tr>';
      t_lines(incr(n_line)) := '<tr><td align="center" colspan="5">'||
        '</td></tr>';
      t_lines(incr(n_line)) := '<tr>'||
        '<th align="left">Logical</th>'||
        '<th align="left">Physical</th>'||
        '<th align="left"></th>'||
        '<th align="left">Active</th>'||
        '<th align="left">Inactive</th>'||
        '</tr>';
```

```
      t_lines(incr(n_line)) := '<tr>'||
        '<th align="left">Workplace</th>'||
        '<th align="left">Workplace</th>'||
        '<th align="left">Work</th>'||
        '<th align="left">Date</th>'||
        '<th align="left">Date</th>'||
        '</tr>';
    end if;
    t_lines(incr(n_line)) := '<tr>'||
      '<td align="left">'||
        r_report_wkhst.logical_workplace_name||'</td>'||
      '<td align="left">'||
        r_report_wkhst.physical_workplace_name||'</td>'||
      '<td align="left">'||
        r_report_wkhst.work_name||'</td>'||
      '<td align="left">'||
        to_char(r_report_wkhst.active_date, 'MM/DD/YYYY')||'</td>'||
      '<td align="left">'||
        to_char(r_report_wkhst.inactive_date, 'MM/DD/YYYY')||'</td>'||
      '</tr>';
  end loop;
  t_lines(incr(n_line)) := '</table><pre>';

  EMAILS.send(
    EMAILS.get_username,
    aiv_to,
    'Work History Report for '||v_worker_name,
    t_lines);
end report;
```

In this case, PROCEDURE report(ain_worker_id, aiv_to), calls get_report() to produce the result set, and then queries the staging table to produce an HTML report. report() then calls supporting package EMAILS.send() to send the report.

The following is an example of a test unit for report(). This is from script report_wkhsts.report.sql:

```
rem report_wkhsts.report.sql
rem by Donald J. Bales on 12/15/2006
rem Test Unit for REPORT_WKHST_TS.report()

execute REPORT_WKHSTS.report(11649889, 'don@donaldbales.com');
```

After I execute this test unit, I get an email report, as shown in Figure 10-9. In practice, I even use this functionality to send an email report to the support personnel anytime a user encounters an error. That way, support personnel can start troubleshooting a given problem before the customer even calls. How's that for customer service?

Figure 10-9. *An example of an emailed report*

Well, that's it for polymorphism. I hope you can appreciate the power and simplicity that the use of polymorphic command names provides when used in the development of software. I also hope you take the time to sit down and think about what method names you should use before you start coding your next program.

Summary

In this chapter, I introduced the concept of organizing the nature of behavior behind a common set of method names. In addition, I demonstrated how I've used each method name in the past. With all the content you've seen in this book, you should be well on your way to solving business and science problems with the use of SQL and PL/SQL in a relational of object-relational setting.

Some have given me the feedback that perhaps the object-relational stuff should be treated as an advanced topic. Phooey! I say it should be treated as the way we should have been doing it for at least the past ten years, but have been distracted by other worldly events from doing so. There's nothing advanced about object-relational content. It's actually the correct and natural way of thinking. So I hope you'll find yourself in a position to use it.

Just how astute are you? Did you notice that I even used polymorphism with table column names? Normally, I even use `id` for the primary key column name, and then the table name concatenated to `_id` for the corresponding foreign key column name. I use the same names in order to make the relationships obvious. By treating column names polymorphically, you can implicitly note what the column is for in every table, just as you do with method names in executable code.

Wow! That was fast, wasn't it? Did I make you work hard? Did you learn anything? I sure hope so. As I stated in the introduction, this was a tutorial—a place to get started. The only way you can learn how to program is to discover the possibilities of a programming language and start mimicking someone else's work by writing programs.

I've been extremely successful in my career when working with Oracle and PL/SQL, so if you mimic my coding behavior, I'm guessing that you will be successful, too. But you've just started. Here's what I suggest you do next:

- Browse the *Oracle Database SQL Reference* or read Lex de Haan's *Mastering Oracle SQL and SQL*Plus* (Apress, 2004), so you can get an idea of what can be accomplished using SQL. You don't have to remember it all; you just need to remember where to look for the information when you realize you can put a possibility to work!

- Read Oracle's *PL/SQL User's Guide and Reference*, or Steven Feuerstein's *Oracle PL/SQL Programming* (O'Reilly). These are both good references. Once again, you don't need to remember everything you read, just the possibilities. You can always refer to the reference later. You have better use for your memory, like remembering your lover's birthday or your anniversary!

- Browse Oracle's *PL/SQL Packages and Types Reference*. Why should you build something that's already been built by experts? Just catalog the possibilities in your gray matter.

- Check out Oracle's *Application Developer's Guides*.

- Share your ideas by writing an article, a white paper, or at least an email about your experience. After you do, go back and write an INSERT statement in order to add yourself to the list of database geniuses from Chapter 1.

As I said before, good skill. Luck is for losers.

How to Download, Install, and Use Oracle

Since knowing Oracle SQL is a prerequisite for learning PL/SQL, I could simply assume that you already have resource-level access to Oracle (you can create objects like tables, views, and so on), already have access to SQL*Plus, and already know SQL. But that might not be the case.

Just in case you don't have access to Oracle, I'm going to give you some advice on these subjects:

- How to download Oracle Database software

- How to install Oracle Database software

- How to use Oracle SQL*Plus

This should get you started in the right direction. Keep in mind that I have no idea how the Apress and Oracle web sites or the Oracle software will look like by the time you read this. Nothing may have changed, but I kind of doubt that. It's more likely that everything will have changed. So my directions will probably no longer be correct, but I think some direction is better than none.

How to Download Oracle Database Software

At the time of this writing, you can download a trial copy of Oracle Database software from Oracle's web site. You can use this trial software for learning purposes only. If you decide to do something commercial with it, like write software that you can then sell, then you'll need to pay for a license. Keep that in mind. Play for free, but earn a fee and you must pay. You should read the license agreement, so you know exactly what you can do.

The URL you use to download trial software at Oracle changes all the time. Try http://www.oracle.com/technology/index.html. When you get to that web page, as in the example in Figure A-1, look for a menu item that says Downloads.

Figure A-1. *An example of an Oracle Technology Network web page*

When you find the Downloads link, click it. When you do, a web page like the one in Figure A-2 may appear. I say "may appear" because who knows how this web site will be organized in the future.

Figure A-2. *An example of an Oracle Software Downloads web page*

On the Oracle Software Downloads page, find the latest version of the database software (currently Oracle Database 10*g*) and click that link. A web page like the one in Figure A-3 may appear.

Figure A-3. *An example of an Oracle Database Downloads web page*

Click the software distribution link for your computer's operating system (OS). I'm choosing Microsoft Windows in the example in Figure A-3. When you click the software distribution link for your OS, a web page like the one in Figure A-4 may appear.

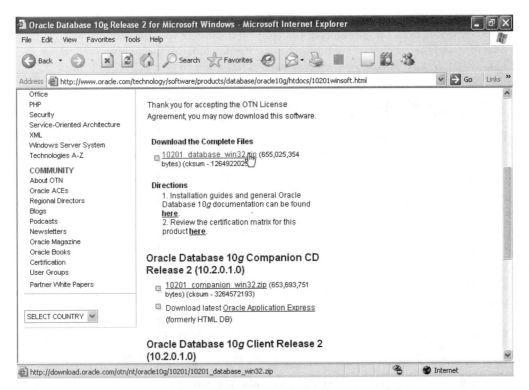

Figure A-4. *An example of the OS-specific Oracle Database distribution web page*

On the OS-specific distribution web page, agree to the license agreement, and then click the download link for the associated archive (zip) file. When you do, a dialog box like the one in Figure A-5 will display.

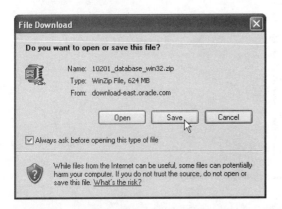

Figure A-5. *An example of a Microsoft Windows File Download dialog box*

Click the Save button in the File Download dialog box. Next, a Save As dialog box will appear, as in Figure A-6. Create a "downloads" directory off the root of your file system, switch to that directory, and then click the Save button to start the download of the archive. *Write down the name of the archive, so you know what its name is when you go to install the software.*

Figure A-6. *An example of a Microsoft Windows Save As dialog box*

When you click the Save button to start the download, a download progress window will appear, as shown in Figure A-7.

Figure A-7. *An example of a Microsoft Windows download progress window*

Once the download is complete, you can move on to the next step, which is to install the Oracle Database software. But first, I suggest you go back to the Downloads link web page and download the installation instructions. Read them before you start the installation.

How to Install Oracle Database Software

OK, for those hackers out there (you know who you are), I'm going to show you an overview of installing the Oracle database software on a Windows machine. On a computer running the Windows OS, here are the steps:

1. Unzip the archive into the "downloads" directory.

2. Navigate to directory \download\database with Windows Explorer, and then run setup.exe.

3. Follow the instructions on the installation screens, answering any prompts as required.

The following screen shots are from an installation I made on my daughter's notebook PC called Kristyn. It's important that you name your machine (in the OS) before you install Oracle, because this is the name that will be used to specify the machine's network address throughout the installation process.

When you execute \downloads\database\setup.exe, the Oracle Universal Installer will start and display the Select Installation Method screen, as shown in Figure A-8. Here, I suggest you specify:

- Basic installation

- An Oracle Home location of \oracle

- The Enterprise Edition

- The creation of a starter database

- orcl as the database name

- welcome1 as the database password

Figure A-8. *An example of the first Oracle Universal Installer screen*

You can specify whatever you want when filling in the form in Figure A-8, but write everything down, because you'll need the information later. When you click the Next button, the Product-Specific Prerequisite Checks screen may appear, as shown in Figure A-9. Assuming there are no missing prerequisites, you should click the Next button. When you do, the Summary screen may appear, as shown in Figure A-10.

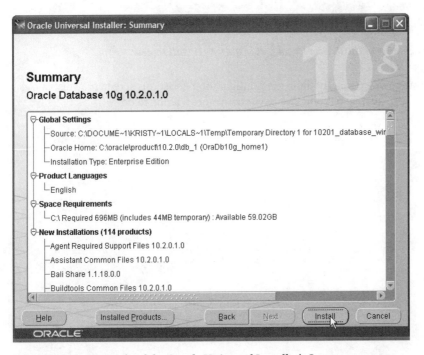

Figure A-9. *An example of the Oracle Univeral Installer's Prerequisites screen*

Figure A-10. *An example of the Oracle Universal Installer's Summary screen*

Once again, assuming that the summary is correct, you should click the Install button. Clicking the Install button may display the Install screen, as shown in Figure A-11. This is where you can get up and get a cup of coffee.

Figure A-11. *An example of the Oracle Universal Installer's Install screen*

After some annoying period of time, the Configuration Assistants screen may display, as shown in Figure A-12. Just be patient. You have some more waiting to do.

Figure A-12. *An example of the Oracle Universal Installer's Configuration Assistants screen*

Next, the Database Configuration Assistant screen may appear, as shown in Figure A-13. This is the step where the installation process creates your starter database. Wait, wait . . .

Figure A-13. *An example of the Database Configuration Assistant screen*

Just when you're about to bang your head against your monitor, the Database Configuration Assistant summary screen may display, as shown in Figure A-14. This screen simply confirms that the starter database has been created.

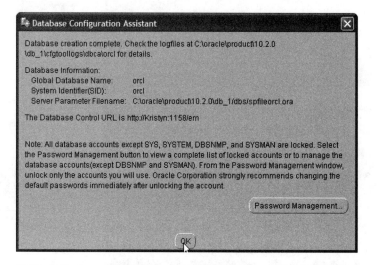

Figure A-14. *An example of the Database Configuration Assistant summary screen*

You're on the home stretch now! After you click the OK button to dismiss the summary screen, the End of Installation screen may appear, as shown in Figure A-15. *Write down the URLs on this screen. You will need them!*

After you write down the URLs, click the Exit button to complete the installation. At this point, Oracle should be installed, and up and running on your computer. Congratulations!

Now you need to open SQL*Plus to create a resource-enabled account.

Figure A-15. *An example of the Oracle Universal Installer's End of Installation screen*

How to Use SQL*Plus

You are going to be using SQL*Plus as your primary user interface to the Oracle database. With it, you will do the following:

- Create a username to use when doing the assignments in this book: bps.

- Execute Data Definition Language (DDL) in order to create tables, indexes, views, types, and stored procedures.

- Execute Data Manipulation Language (DML) in order to insert into, update, delete from, and select data from tables in the database.

To get started, create a directory named \bps on your file system. You'll download this book's source code and solutions to that directory.

How to Download This Book's Source Code

To download the source code for this book, go to the Apress web site at http://www.apress.com, which may look something like Figure A-16. Click the Quick Links menu item, and then click the Source Code/Download menu item. When you do, the Source Code/Download page may appear.

Figure A-16. *An example of the Apress web site's home page*

This is where you'll search for the source code by the name of the book. When you find the source code download link for this book, click it and the save this book's source code archive in your newly created \bps directory on your file system.

Next, decompress the archive (unzip it) into your \bps directory. This should create a directory structure that looks like Figure A-17.

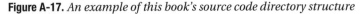

Figure A-17. *An example of this book's source code directory structure*

Now that you have the book's source code in place, you can create a shortcut to SQL*Plus in directory \bps\Appendix.

1. Navigate to directory Appendix using Windows Explorer.

2. Right-click any empty part of the directory's listing window.

3. Select New ➤ Shortcut.

4. Specify the location of the SQL*Plus executable, sqlplusw.exe, and then click the Next button. The SQL*Plus executable should be in the "Oracle Home" BIN directory, such as c:\oracle\product\10.2.0\db_1\BIN\sqlplusw.exe.

5. Specify the name for the shortcut. I name the shortcut after the database, so I suggest orcl. Click the Finish button.

6. Right-click your new shortcut and select Properties.

7. Delete the entry for the Start-in directory, as in Figure A-18, and then click the OK button. This will make SQL*Plus use the directory where the shortcut exists as the default source directory when running a script, and that will make your life a lot easier.

Figure A-18. *An example of a shortcut's Properties dialog box*

At this point, you should have a SQL*Plus shortcut icon in directory \bps\Appendix. Double-click the icon to start SQL*Plus. When you do, SQL*Plus will display a Login dialog box, where you specify the following:

- The username SYSTEM

- Password welcome1, or whatever you decided to use for a password

- Host string orcl, or whatever you decided to name the database

After you specify the login information, SQL*Plus should log you in to the database as user SYSTEM. If you see a screen like the one shown in Figure A-19, you have successfully logged in to your Oracle database.

The reason you create the shortcut in the same directory that contains the example source code files is to give yourself easy access to those files. When you invoke SQL*Plus using the shortcut that you've just created, the source code directory becomes the default directory that SQL*Plus will search when you invoke a SQL script.

Figure A-19. *An example of a SQL*Plus screen*

How to Create a New Username

I suggest you create a username, bps, just for working with the examples and doing the exercises in this book. To do that, type the following at the SQL*Plus prompt (SQL>), and then press the Enter key.

```
SQL> @create_user.sql
```

This will execute SQL*Plus script create_user.sql in directory \bps\Appendix, which will create a new username, bps, with password, bps, that you can then use while learning from this book. Now, the next time you log in to your database, use username bps.

How to Write a SQL*Plus Script

You may type a command directly into SQL*Plus. However, I don't recommend that if you're programming. I think you should write a SQL*Plus script so you can make corrections to your code, as needed, and then execute the code again without needing to retype it. Having your code in a script file will allow you to do just that.

You may use any text editor you like—Notepad, WordPad, TextPad, and so on, but you can't use Word. (I actually prefer to use TextPad when I edit my SQL or PL/SQL scripts. You can search for TextPad on the Internet, and download a trial copy.)

To create a SQL*Plus script, follow these steps:

1. Open a new text file.

2. Type one of more SQL or PL/SQL commands using the correct syntax.

3. Save the script to a directory that is accessible by SQL*Plus.

Once you've created a script, you can run it whenever you like, and your commands will not be lost. They will forever reside in your script file. So how do you execute a SQL*Plus script?

How to Execute a SQL*Plus Script

I've already had you execute a SQL*Plus script earlier, in order to create username bps for this book. To execute a SQL*Plus script, you type an at sign character (@) followed by the name of the script to execute. SQL*Plus expects this script to exist in the SQL*Plus startup directory.

If the script isn't in the startup directory, you must specify the entire path and filename. If the path or filename has space characters in it, you need to enclose the path and filename in double quote characters ("). Here's an example:

```
SQL> @"c:\Program Files\Not a convenient location\my script.sql"
```

So I suggest you be lazy, and create a shortcut with a blank "start in" directory in every directory where you have scripts. That way, you can start a SQL*Plus session with the default directory set to where your script files exist.

How to Describe Your Tables and Stored Procedures

While you're in SQL*Plus, you can use the describe command to display the definition of a table or stored procedure. For example, you can type the following to get a definition for view SYS.USER_OBJECTS:

```
SQL> desc SYS.USER_OBJECTS
```

Then SQL*Plus will respond:

Name	Null?	Type
OBJECT_NAME		VARCHAR2(128)
SUBOBJECT_NAME		VARCHAR2(30)
OBJECT_ID		NUMBER
DATA_OBJECT_ID		NUMBER
OBJECT_TYPE		VARCHAR2(19)
CREATED		DATE
LAST_DDL_TIME		DATE
TIMESTAMP		VARCHAR2(19)
STATUS		VARCHAR2(7)
TEMPORARY		VARCHAR2(1)
GENERATED		VARCHAR2(1)
SECONDARY		VARCHAR2(1)

However, SQL*Plus has this annoying defect: it aligns the right portion of a table description to the right side of the line width, and that usually prevents you from seeing the Type, so I use a script, desc.sql, to describe a table or stored procedure instead. For example, to describe utility package SYS.DBMS_OUTPUT, I would type the following at the SQL*Plus prompt (SQL>):

```
SQL> @desc SYS.DBMS_OUTPUT
```

Then SQL*Plus will respond:

```
SYS.DBMS_OUTPUT
PROCEDURE DISABLE
PROCEDURE ENABLE
Argument Name                    Type                     In/Out Default?
------------------------------   ----------------------   ------ --------
BUFFER_SIZE                      NUMBER(38)               IN     DEFAULT
PROCEDURE GET_LINE
Argument Name                    Type                     In/Out Default?
------------------------------   ----------------------   ------ --------
LINE                            VARCHAR2                  OUT
STATUS                          NUMBER(38)                OUT
PROCEDURE GET_LINES
Argument Name                    Type                     In/Out Default?
------------------------------   ----------------------   ------ --------
LINES                           TABLE OF VARCHAR2(255)    OUT
NUMLINES                        NUMBER(38)                IN/OUT
PROCEDURE NEW_LINE
PROCEDURE PUT
Argument Name                    Type                     In/Out Default?
------------------------------   ----------------------   ------ --------
A                               VARCHAR2                  IN
PROCEDURE PUT_LINE
Argument Name                    Type                     In/Out Default?
------------------------------   ----------------------   ------ --------
A                               VARCHAR2                  IN
```

This description looks different from the first one, not because I used @desc.sql, but because the described object is a stored procedure, not a view. All that @desc.sql does for you is set the SQL*Plus linesize property to 80, uses the describe command, and then returns the linesize to its prior length.

At this point, you should know how to do the following:

- Download Oracle

- Install Oracle

- Create username bps

- Write a SQL*Plus script

- Execute a SQL*Plus script

- Describe a table or stored procedure

So it's time for you to get started with Chapter 1. I wish you good skill on your journey.

Index

You Need the Companion eBook

Your purchase of this book entitles you to buy the companion PDF-version eBook for only $10. Take the weightless companion with you anywhere.

We believe this Apress title will prove so indispensable that you'll want to carry it with you everywhere, which is why we are offering the companion eBook (in PDF format) for $10 to customers who purchase this book now. Convenient and fully searchable, the PDF version of any content-rich, page-heavy Apress book makes a valuable addition to your programming library. You can easily find and copy code—or perform examples by quickly toggling between instructions and the application. Even simultaneously tackling a donut, diet soda, and complex code becomes simplified with hands-free eBooks!

Once you purchase your book, getting the $10 companion eBook is simple:

❶ Visit **www.apress.com/promo/tendollars/**.

❷ Complete a basic registration form to receive a randomly generated question about this title.

❸ Answer the question correctly in 60 seconds, and you will receive a promotional code to redeem for the $10.00 eBook.

THE EXPERT'S VOICE™

2855 TELEGRAPH AVENUE | SUITE 600 | BERKELEY, CA 94705

Offer valid through 2/27/08.